Introduction to Tensor Computing in Python

From First Principles to Deep Learning

Manal Helal

Dedication

I dedicate this book to my family, particularly my parents and my nieces.

About the Author

Manal Helal is a Computer Science Lecturer at the University of Hertfordshire, Hatfield, UK. She had her PhD at the University of New South Wales, Sydney, Australia, and MSc and BSc from the American University in Cairo, Egypt.

Contents

Acknowledgements

I would like to acknowledge and give my warmest thanks to my educators and supervisors all through my education years. I am in debt to Professor Lenore Mullin, who introduced me to the topic and invited me to the NSF workshop on Future Directions in Tensor-Based Computation and Modelling, organised by Professor Charles Van Loan, held in Arlington, Virginia, at the National Science Foundation, February 20-21, 2009. This workshop introduced me to various topics that formed the foundations of this book. The public domain and open publishing communities have made available valuable resources that are very difficult to list in full. The most notable public domain reference is the Linear Algebra for Frontiers course on the edX platform. I am also grateful for the various teaching and research experiences that added more insights into some foundations presented in this book. I participated in teaching the Foundations of Data Science Postgraduate module at the University of Hertfordshire, UK, to which many academics participated in its contents and references. The module links mathematical foundations to machine learning algorithms. This module gave me the needed iterations through Linear Algebra topics that might be difficult to link with related Algorithms from the first reading. This foundation is essential to build further multi-linear and non-linear models and their requirements.

Introduction to the Book

Being a computer science graduate interested in research and further applying my skills where needed, I came across topics in computational science for my master's and PhD experimentations that required more fundamental mathematical understanding than what I was taught. Any typical computer science degree includes a minimum of five Mathematics courses, and two Physics courses, leaving many concepts (including tensors and their applications) utterly foreign to computing graduates, who will self-study if their work needs them. Since I suffered in selfstudying these concepts with very little guidance and math books targetting mathematicians only, I thought about writing this book. I would not consider myself an authority on tensor computing and all its fundamental math requirements; I simply want to communicate my self-learning quest, which hopefully will be helpful for some readers from a similar educational background. I aim to summarise my experience and shed some light on the missing concepts that could have made the material easier if studied in sequence and from a computer scientist to computer scientists. The book idea started in 2013, with an outline and aims only defined. The actual writing started in 2021 because of teaching loads and incomplete research positions. All along, the aim remained to enable vivid understanding and visualisation of these concepts through practicals and tutorials and to discuss conceptual aspects from first principles rather than just listing the definitions, notations, applications, libraries, and algorithms. The python code provided aims to link the high-level code that builds on a massive stack of building blocks to the required theoretical understanding that is often hard to find in one book. Other books or surveys would either fall into the theoretical side (building intuition using text explanation), mathematical side (using equations and deep dive into proofs and properties), or programming higher-level code examples without much explanation of the theory behind it. I aimed to combine the three levels of explanations to draw a big picture that does not lack details of implementation and theory.

The big picture of the current advances in tensor computing is published in papers; surveys are the most educational. The underlying building blocks are assembled from many books, mainly written for mathematicians, that would detail all proofs, properties, and circular definitions. This book summarises introductory/fundamental material from different topics needed to understand the current applications of tensor methods, and each has its many books written at various levels of abstraction and targeting different audiences. A computer scientist would find it hard to pull the threads together coherently to link the statistical machine learning algorithms with the kernel methods in Hilbert space, to the tensor methods in the Riemannian space, and then to learning representation theory with the abstract algebra potentials, and finally to deep learning and its complex generalisation potential.

It will be astonishing after this learning journey to find out that it all comes down to matrix multiplication to achieve coordinate basis change/projections in the different algorithms. The change of basis aims to achieve a better representation of a dataset. This better representation might be a dimensionality reduction, such as the methods in chapter two. The aim might be to disentangle sources or map to a higher dimensional space in which a non-linearly separable dataset, in its current dimension, will be linearly separable in the higher dimension. Mapping to higher dimensions includes the Kernel method introduced in chapter two and further explained in chapter five. This is the first attempt the author is aware of to align the tensor decomposition methods from first principles in linear algebra generalised to multilinear Algebra. Then, compare their applications and performance evaluations as a generalisation to the matrix decomposition methods and their applications and performance evaluation. This alignment and succession of presentations should enable a vivid understanding of the topic. The prerequisite knowledge to benefit from this book is mainly some problem-solving skills, exposure to algorithms, and programming experience in any language. Python code can quickly be learned from online tutorials. Using Python as a popular data mining and machine learning language and providing sample source code, or referring to where a good tutorial is found, for every topic covered and application example should serve as building blocks ready for reuse in various applications. Most published papers and their open-source code use high-level calls to functions that build on a stack of mathematical functions that are sometimes parameterised on the high-level call. This book aims to close the gap between the high-level application of these concepts and the mathematical understanding of the operations performed under the hood.

Chapter One introduces linear algebra concepts in relation to machine learning requirements. Chapter two focuses on linear algebra algorithms that address learning the latent structure of a given matrix dataset. Those with a Linear algebra and dimensionality reduction algorithms
background can skip chapters one and two, but the remaining chapters are sequential in order. Chapter three focuses on the multilinear algebra concepts and introduces fundamental tensor decomposition methods. Chapter four expands the tensor decomposition methods to tensor networks' notation and decomposition, starts the applications with tensor completion and tensor regression and finally introduces neural networks and how to tensorise them. Those with previous tensor decomposition backgrounds or who wish to skip the mathematical foundation can skip chapter three. Chapter Four understanding enables the sequential reading of chapters six and seven.

Chapter five is an additional topic usually omitted when discussing tensor methods. Tensors provide better representation, expressiveness and interpretability that is usually assumed to be understood. The chapter discusses representation learning aligned with methods from abstract algebra and traditional methods to identify how representation is usually performed traditionally in hand-tailored coordinate change and by using deep learning and regularisation. It then considers how tensor methods enriched the representation further and how deep learning enables identifying the most suitable representation for a given dataset and task. The applications in chapter six should widen the horizon for graduation/MSc thesis project topics rather than the black box approach to machine learning tasks. Many dataset sources discussed with their applications are not as popular as the known Kaggle and UCI datasets. Projects can aim to reproduce existing work or compare the performance of several approaches and identify shortcomings and possible enhancements. Chapter Seven discusses implementation optimisation using parallel programming models and available hardware architectures. Future trends and challenges are also discussed as material for research level that PhD and researchers might need to build on to enhance the methods explained in the book or address the discussed challenges and literature gaps. Although the book covers statistical analysis methods, machine learning and deep learning methods, it can
not be considered a reference on these topics. These topics are considered application domains for tensor computing approaches only, omitting many important details found in other references. Similarly, the linear algebra and multi-linear algebra concepts discussed are
introductory to build for how they are used in the applications presented.

Tensor computing is difficult to be included in a data structures course and can only be an elective in an advanced year of an undergraduate computer science degree or equivalent. The course is preferably taught at a postgraduate level as well or used as a reference for practitioners and researchers working with high-dimensional data structures. Topics covered will include introduction & definition, notation, libraries and packages, applications, and parallel programming models. Machine Learning and Deep Learning algorithms are explained when used in the applications. The equations might be daunting, but they concisely explain a concept or algorithm better than Pseudocode and text. Getting used to reading equations in connection to the intuition explanation in the text and the source code examples enables deeper understanding and closes the gap between theoreticians, computer scientists, and practitioners in the field. If not clear, skip the equation and focus on the intuition and the source code examples. An errata web link is at http://book.manalhelal.com/tensor/book-review-errata/. Please use it to correct any mistake, request a citation that I might have missed by mistake, further clarification, the inclusion of an algorithm or package review, or anything that can make this book clearer and complete. I did my best to cite all original contributors to the material I covered, but there is always a possibility of forgetting or using a newer citation where an older one is required. The aim is to make this book self-contained as much as possible. All accompanying source code is published at https://github.com/mhelal/TensorsPyBook.

The book aims at unifying the notation used in all chapters, with some inevitable violations that are explained when needed. The general notation rules are as follows:

- Mathematicians start indexing from 1, while computer scientists start indexing from 0.
- Scalars and vectors are represented in small letters such that vectors are indexed, while matrices are represented with capital letters. Tensors are represented with calligraphy letters, but sometimes with capital letters for simplicity or for generalising all tensor shapes. Running indices are in small letters such as i, j, and capital letters I, J denote the upper bound of an index in a mode. Indices are sometimes indicated as subscripts and sometimes between round brackets if more convenient.
- Pseudocode and source code is presented in a boxed outline.

Chapter 1: Introduction

This chapter introduces the reader to linear algebra basics required in machine learning and deep learning algorithms and their operations from the mathematical representation to the Python data structures. Starting from vectors, the presentation progresses to matrices using Linear Algebra concepts that get generalised to Tensors that will be introduced in chapter three. Several references provide examples and applications of these concepts in their entirety. The primary operations that will be discussed in subsequent chapters are explained with some preliminary examples and applications. Every chance to visualise these concepts vividly is presented, and references to more details and discussions are included.

1.1 History

Structured data is used in computer algorithms in many different ways. The primary data structures for most algorithms are scalars, linear arrays, matrices, and multidimensional arrays. Multidimensional arrays are not tensor structures but share some of their properties. Tensors can be defined as functions of any point in space coordinates, which transform linearly between coordinate systems. The three-dimensional space has 3r components, where r is the rank. The tensors of rank zero are scalars, the tensors of rank one are vectors, and the tensors of rank two are matrices.
Since tensors transform linearly between coordinates, they are commonly used in differential non-Ecludiean geometry to study curves and surfaces in three-dimensional space by using calculus techniques applicable in higher-dimensional spaces (Pressley, 2010; Fortney, 2018). A tensor may refer to different objects in different domains, for instance, a stress tensor, moment of inertia tensor, field tensor, metric tensor, and tensor product, which are defined in physics and are not what we aim to explain in this book, however, chapter three will introduce these for the curious. Tensors are rarely defined carefully, and the definition usually has to do with transformation properties and domain-specific definitions, making it difficult to visualise what these objects are. We focus on tensor definitions related to data mining and machine learning, including deep learning. Data conversion into information is aided by differential and integral calculus. Differential calculus is used for studying the rates of change, while integral calculus is used to study areas and volumes. The definitions, properties, and applications of these two related concepts enable studying multivariate function dynamics. In chapter three, we will explain more.
Motivation: What are the benefits of studying tensors in computer science disciplines? To answer this question, we need to discuss how tensor applications are implemented and how many algorithms have been developed to process data in tensor spaces. This book attempts to answer this question with various applications' essential mathematical backgrounds, algorithms, and code examples. A motivational example problem appears in section 1.3. In each chapter, more applications are discussed, with chapter six devoted entirely to applications.
Absolute differential calculus is the earliest foundation of tensor theory. It was developed by Gregorio Ricci-Curbastro in 1887–96 and subsequently popularised in a paper (Ricci and Levi-Civita, 1900) written with his student Tullio Levi-Civita. The general relativity theory described the geometry of gravitation in space-time curvature with respect to the energy and momentum of the matter and radiation in a system of partial differential equations. The following is a detailed timeline for developing tensor computing techniques. More theoretical concepts are mentioned in the timeline that this book will not cover but are referenced for the readers interested in a deeper dive.
1846: "Tensor" was first introduced by William Ron Hamilton and later became known to scientists through the publication of Levi-Civita's book "The Absolute Differential Calculus".

1853: Matrix, Matrix Theory, and the principles of Universal Algebra are developed by Joseph Sylvester and Arthur Cayley.
1874: Set theory is developed by George Cantor; it represents collections of abstract objects, including notions like Venn diagrams and set memberships.
1908: Axiomatic Set Theory is developed by Ernst Zermelo, reformulating the now "naive set theory" in first-order logic to resolve its paradoxes, for example, Russell's paradox, the Burali-Forti paradox, and Cantor's paradox. This theory does not allow the construction of ordinal numbers, while most ordinary mathematics can be developed without using ordinals. The latter is an essential tool in most set-theoretic investigations.
1922: Abraham Fraenkel and Thoralf Skolem propose operationalising a definite property as one is formulated in first-order logic, with all atomic formulae involving set membership or identity. This adds the axioms of replacement and regularity, yielding the theory of ZF. Then adding the axiom of choice becomes the ZFC theory. This cannot be axiomatised by a finite set of axioms because of the replacement axiom.
1925: Werner Heisenberg, Max Born, and Pascual Jordan formulate matrix mechanics, a formulation of quantum mechanics.
1922-1940: Von Neumann-Bernays-Godel (NBG) set theory can be finitely axiomatised. The ontology of NBG includes classes as well as sets; a set is a class that is a member of another class. NBG and ZFC are equivalent set theories such that any theorem about sets is provable in NBG if and only if it is in ZFC.
1942-1945: Samuel Eilenberg and Saunders Mac Lane first introduced the category theory in connection with the algebraic topology. It has several aspects, such as "general abstract nonsense". The latter refers to the high abstraction level compared to more classical branches of mathematics. Homological algebra is a category theory in organising and suggesting calculations in abstract algebra. Diagram chasing is a visual method of arguing with abstract "arrows". The topos theory is a form of abstract sheaf theory with geometric origins; it leads to ideas such as the pointless topology.
1964: Iverson uses the Array Programming Language (APL) APL notation to describe IBM's system 360. (FALKOFF, AD, Iverson, KE, Sussenguth, EH, 1964)
1957 to 1965: APL is the first homogenous simple array programming language designed by Kenneth E. Iverson. The language works on entire arrays simultaneously, like the SIMD architecture's vector instruction set. It yields smaller and more concise programs though no iteration is involved.
1973: Based on APL, Trenched More proposes an array theory that offers a robust set of operators and operations on nested, heterogeneous rectangular arrays (MORE, T, 1973).
1979: Programming Language/Systems PL/S II or AT/370 languages is developed to implement More's array theory operations, using an APL interface. NIAL2 (Nested Interactive Array Language) is developed as a programming language based on array theory and its applications to make it easy to rapidly develop loop-free data-driven algorithms (JENKINS, MA, Franksen, OI, 1992). APL2 was another implementation of More's nested Array theory. For a while, it was IBM's strategic language for HPC.
1988: Mathematics of Arrays and the Ψ-Calculus were first introduced in the PhD thesis of Dr Lenore Mullin in Computer and Information Science at Syracuse University, Syracuse, NY. The thesis introduces an algebraic formulation representing all data structures invariant of dimensionality and shape. An MoA structure describes scalars as rank 0, linear arrays (vectors) as rank one, 2-D arrays (matrices) as rank two, and similar higher rank structures. The representation is stored in memory in a linear structure with elements stored in a row or column-major order in a linear array, a dimensionality scalar, and a shape vector. A list of constructs is provided. The Ψ-Calculus is a way to combine expressions in the MoA algebra by composing indices; it uses the Ψ-Function as its foundation. Mullin's dissertation put closure on work started by Phil Abrams ("An APL Machine", Stanford '72, Harold Stone advisor), who believed there was formalism for array reasoning based on shapes and indexing. His work was augmented by Hassett and Lyon, Guibas and Wyatt, Perlis, Miller, Minter, Tu, Gerhart, Berkling, and Budd, to name a few.
1990: A Comparison of Array Theory with Mathematics of Arrays is presented by L. Mullin and M. Jenkins. (JENKINS, MA, Mullin, LR, 1991).

1993: L. Mullin and G. Hains show how to use the Bird-Meertens Formalism to define MoA. (HAINS, G, Mullin, LR, 1993).
2000: MoA library was built as a dynamic link library (dll); it is then used in basic image and video processing applications in an MSc. thesis (Helal, 2001).
2001: Faster Fast Fourier Transform (FFT) and generalised Radix n FFT using MoA are presented by L. Mullin and S. Small (MULLIN, LR, Small, S, 2002).
2004: "Multi-Way Analysis with Applications in the Chemical Sciences" book detailed how multi-way PCA and Multi-way Factor analysis and other methods are applied to various computational chemistry problems. (Smilde, Bro and Geladi, 2004)
2005: L. Mullin used MoA and the Ψ-Calculus to map Digital Signal Processing (DSP) algorithms to multiple processor/memory hierarchies. "A Uniform way of reasoning about array-based computation in radar: Algebraically connecting the hardware/software boundary" presented by Mullin (MULLIN, LR, 2005). Mullin and Raynolds applied the Conformal Computing Techniques by using MoA and Ψ-Calculus to solve problems in Computational Physics (MULLIN, LR, Raynolds, J, 2005).
2009: A comprehensive survey of multi-way analysis and their applications was presented (Kolda and Bader, 2009).
2009: The NSF held a workshop to decide future trends in tensor computation. In this workshop, researchers from mathematics, physics and computing presented state-of-the-art in the field (Charles Van Loan *et al.*, 2009).
2010: A PhD thesis applied the MoA methods in the high-dimensional scientific computation problem "Multiple Sequence Alignment in Bioinformatics" in the MSA dynamic programming algorithm to score a tensor of alignments. Partitioning is processed in parallel providing automatic load balancing (Helal, 2009).
2014: "Multilinear subspace Learning" detailed the advances from linear subspace learning applying dimensionality reduction algorithms based on linear algebra and how it scales to multilinear subspace learning through tensor projections and decompositions (Lu, Plataniotis and Venetsanopoulos, 2014).
2006 - onwards: various neural networks and data mining applications applied tensor decomposition proving advances in accuracy and efficient computation, using less memory and time. This led to being coined "Compressive Neural Networks" due to the performance benefits of employing tensor decomposition techniques.

1.2 Linear Algebra

Linear algebra can be better reviewed or studied for the first time with complete books such as (Chahal, 2018), (Carter, 1995) and (Dym, 2007). The Online edX platform course Linear Algebra for Frontiers by The University of Texas at Austin is a valuable resource for learning efficient computation of linear algebra concepts (Geijn and Quintana-Ort´, 2008). The AI algorithms' mathematical foundations and their Python packages are covered in (Farrell, 2020). The intuition that this book is trying to build is to vividly understand the notion of projections from lower to higher spaces or from higher to lower spaces using linear algebra tools, then expanding to other types of Algebra in later chapters. Vector and matrix operations, including linear transformations and independence, must be understood to understand higher-order tensor operations and properties. Vector addition, subtraction, normalisation, dot product, cross product, outer product, and derivatives (rate of change) are the basic operations on vectors required for machine learning. The next section will focus on the main matrix operations and properties that will be necessary for the following chapters. The accompanying python notebook ch1.ipynb has a helpful review of the operations discussed in these two sections with some preliminary operations and visualisations.

Motivation: Machine learning (ML) algorithms aim to explain the dynamics of a given dataset of any sample. A training dataset is often represented as a matrix, with rows as m entities and columns as n features. Each entity is a row vector of all features describing the entity. Each feature is a column vector, representing the domain and distribution of values that any entity can take. When data is linear, it is easy to describe it with a linear equation in the form y=f(x) =w.x + b that satisfies all rows equations (samples in the dataset). This is also described as inferring a relationship between (x,y) pairs that reflect a hypothesis to which an accuracy measure is required from a testing dataset. The weights/ coefficients/parameters w measures the correlation and is estimated by the ML algorithm, which is the slope in a line equation or gradients in higher dimensions. The independent features/predictors x is read from the dataset along with the dependent/outcome/target value y. b is the y-intercept in the line equation and is the bias in higher dimensions, and is usually represented as an extra weight element in the weights vector rather than a variable of its own. Solving for w using a set of equations from the samples x, as shown below, is a deterministic approach to identifying the parameters or the weights w (the unknowns) with the given values in the dataset (the knowns or observations) using different algorithms. If a solution is found, this defines a static relationship between x and y. Solving equations with approximations might not converge in a reasonable time, even for a small dataset, because of the redundancy or very close samples and redundant and proportional columns.

Otherwise, a deterministic approach would create a lookup table for identifying a y given x by applying use cases and if conditions for ranges of values that fall in each given class or a distance measure between the samples in x for unsupervised (unlabelled) data. Machine learning enables algorithms to learn this mapping from the training dataset using a representation that can generalise to unseen examples without hard coding any rules. Failing to generalise to unseen data is called overfitting. In classification models, y is the dependent discrete variable/feature in the prelabelled dataset extracted from the x vector. In binary classification, y can be the set {1, -1}, or more codes for more classes. In regression models, $y \in \mathbb{R}$ is the predicted continuous value. The last section in this chapter will explain both models in more detail, and explains clustering (unsupervised) cases.

This equation mapping $x \in \mathbb{R}^n$ to $y \in \mathbb{R}$ is called functionals $F: \mathbb{R}^n \rightarrow \mathbb{R}$, which will be further explained in chapter three. For now, these different spaces of y and x are vector spaces, domains and the range of the function that maps between them. These linear mapping functions have the linearity property:

$f(w_1x_1 + w_2x_2) = w_1f(x_1) + w_2f(x_2)$, in the higher dimension $f(WX) = \sum_{i=1}^{n} w_i x_i$, which is equivalent to:

1. $f(x_1 + x_2) = f(x_1) + f(x_2)$: Addition
2. $f(wx) = wf(x)$: Scaling

Intuition: Linear equations draw a line for one-dimensional space when x is a scalar value, a plane for 2-dimensional space when x is a vector of 2 values, and a hyper-plane for higher dimensions. An animation can be found at https://youtu.be/slBI5YuVUTM to visualise regression in the higher-dimensional space.

1.2.1 Vector Operations

Let us define vectors and their calculus. A vector $v \in \mathbb{R}^N$ is not just a one-dimensional array of N scalars; it is a trajectory with the given magnitude (elements values) along N coordinates corresponding to each element. It represents displacement and velocities compared to scalar values such as temperature and mass.

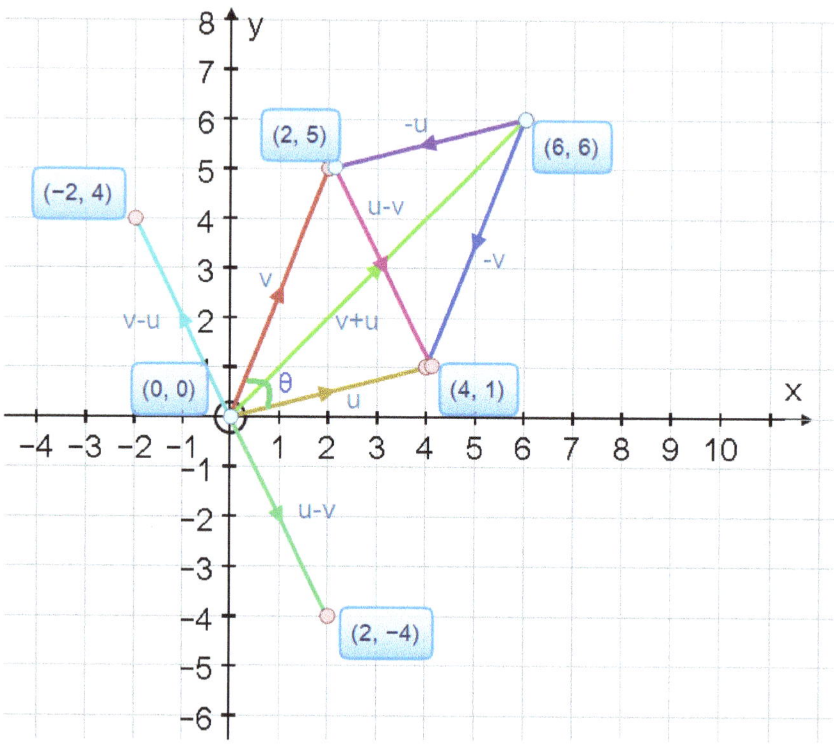

Figure 1: Geometric interpretations of vector addition, subtraction, and dot products. Angle ϑ is meant to represent the angle between vectors v and u. A green arc highlights this angle.

1.2.1.1 Vector Addition, Subtraction and Normalisation, and Transposition

Vector operations have geometric interpretations. The addition of two vectors measures the length of the longer diagonal of the parallelogram formed by these two vectors, as shown in Figure 1.

The p-norm of a vector is a positive-definite scalar function defined as $\|v\|_p = \left(\sum_{i=1}^{N} |v_i|^p\right)^{\frac{1}{p}} \geq 0, \forall p \geq 1$, where $|v_i|$ is the absolute value of each element v_i .
This means that 1-norm is the sum of the absolute values of the elements. The 2-norm is the magnitude of the vector v ∈ $\mathbb{R}^N$, which is its length (Frobenius norm) and is denoted $\|v\|_2$ or $\|v\|_F$. It is the Euclidean distance from the origin to the point reached by the vector and calculated as follows = $\sqrt{\sum_{i=1}^{N} v_i^2}$. The infinity-norm is defined as the case where $p \to \infty$, as $\|v\|_\infty = \lim_{p\to\infty} \left(\sum_{i=1}^{N} |v_i|^p\right)^{\frac{1}{p}} = \max(|v_i|)$. For example, given v = $\begin{bmatrix}2\\5\end{bmatrix}$, then $\|v\|_1 = 7$, $\|v\|_2 = 5.38$, $\|v\|_\infty = 5$.

A vector is normalised such that adding all its elements equals one. Dividing all its elements by the vector's length normalises the vector, such that normalised $v = \frac{v}{\|v\|_2}$. The normalised above vector v is = $\begin{bmatrix} \frac{2}{5.38} & \frac{5}{5.38} \end{bmatrix}$. The transposition of a vector does not change the order of its elements but changes its representation as a row or column vector.

1.2.1.2 Vector Dot (Inner) Product

Vectors are generally represented as column vectors. A dot product between vectors v and u $\in \mathbb{R}^N$ is denoted $\langle v, u \rangle$ or $v^T t$ and measures the similarity between similar dimensions. For Example, given:

$v = \begin{bmatrix} 2 \\ 5 \end{bmatrix}, u = \begin{bmatrix} 4 \\ 1 \end{bmatrix}$, then $v^T u = \begin{bmatrix} 2 & 5 \end{bmatrix} . \begin{bmatrix} 4 \\ 1 \end{bmatrix} = (2 \times 4) + (5 \times 1) = 13.$

The general rule of the dot product is, for any two given vectors v and u $\in \mathbb{R}^n$: $\sum_{i=1}^{N} v_i u_i$. Another formula for the cross product is $\langle v, u \rangle = \|u\| \|v\| \cos \theta$, where θ is the angle between vectors v and u. For the above example, $\cos \theta = \frac{\langle v,u \rangle}{\|u\| \|v\|} = \frac{13}{\sqrt{29}\sqrt{17}} = 0.58, \theta = 54.16$. The result of a dot product is a scalar that denotes the projection of one vector over the other. It gives a measure of similarity between two vectors. When θ is 90° between any given two vectors, i.e. they are perpendicular to each other, their dot product will be 0. This means that these vectors are orthogonal/perpendicular.

1.2.1.3 Vector Cross Product

The cross product is denoted $\times$, and it measures the similarity between the different dimensions. It is performed as follows for v = $\begin{bmatrix} 10 \\ 2 \\ -6 \end{bmatrix}$ and u = $\begin{bmatrix} -3 \\ 0 \\ -2 \end{bmatrix}$ $\in \mathbb{R}^3$ (2 (-2) – -6(0), -6(-3) – 10(-2), 10(0) – -2(-3)) = (-4, 38, 6).

The general rule for the cross-product in $\mathbb{R}^3$ is: $(v_1, v_2, v_3) \times (u_1, u_2, u_3) = (v_2 u_3 - v_3 u_2,\ v_3 u_1 - v_1 u_3, v_1 u_2 - v_2 u_1)$. The output is a third vector in $\mathbb{R}^3$ that is perpendicular to both input vectors. The length of the output vector is equal to the area of the parallelogram formed by the input vectors. The general rule in $\mathbb{R}^n$, it is $v \times u = \|u\| \|v\| \sin \theta\, n$, where θ is the angle between vectors v and u, and n is the unit vector perpendicular to the plane containing vectors v and u and given by the right-hand rule.

1.2.1.4 Vector Outer and Hadamard Products

The Hadamard product $\odot$ measures the interactions between elements in the same order and position between two vectors and is defined as follows:

$$v \odot u = [v_1 u_1 \quad \cdots \quad v_n u_n] = [10 \times -3 \quad 2 \times 0 \quad -6 \times -2] = [-30 \quad 0 \quad 12]$$

The outer product (also called the dyadic/external) product) is denoted $\otimes$ and is performed as follows for the same v $\in \mathbb{R}^n$ and u $\in \mathbb{R}^m$ produces a Matrix $M \in \mathbb{R}^{n \times m}$. For example, given v and u above:

$$v \otimes u = \begin{bmatrix} v_1 u_1 & \cdots & v_1 u_n \\ \vdots & \ddots & \vdots \\ v_n u_1 & \cdots & v_n u_n \end{bmatrix} = \begin{bmatrix} 10 \times -3 & 10 \times 0 & 10 \times -2 \\ 2 \times -3 & 2 \times 0 & 2 \times -2 \\ -6 \times -3 & -6 \times 0 & -6 \times -2 \end{bmatrix} = \begin{bmatrix} -30 & 0 & -20 \\ -6 & 0 & -4 \\ 18 & 0 & 12 \end{bmatrix} \in \mathbb{R}^{3 \times 3}$$

The general rule for the outer product for $\mathbb{R}^n$ is shown above with the $\mathbb{R}^3$ example. The output is a matrix, called a dyad, with rows and columns equal to the number of elements in the input vectors, which is generalised to tensor of order two and rank one, as will be explained in chapter three. The outer product is generalised as the tensor product. The multiplications of every element in the first vector with every element in the second vector measure the interaction between all elements in the first vector with all elements in the second vector. The Dirac notation or bra-kit notation uses this dyadic algebra in quantum mechanics, such that a ket denoted $|v\rangle$ is a vector in an abstract (complex) vector space V (will be explained below), and a bra denoted $\langle f|$ is a linear mapping $f: V \rightarrow \mathbb{C}$, to each vector v in V to complex plane $\mathbb{C}$.

1.2.1.5 Vector Calculus: Derivatives and Gradients

Calculus measures the rate of change of a function, such as the rate of change of x as a ratio to the rate of change of y in a linear equation. This measures the slope of the line tangent to the curve at the point x_0. Differentiation measures the rate of change as the delta change goes to zero is:

$$f'(x) = \lim_{h \to 0} \frac{f(x_0+h)-f(x_0)}{f}$$

$f'(x)$is called the first derivative of function $f(x)$. If the derivative can be formed at each point of a subdomain of the domain of f, then f is said to be differentiable on that subdomain. dy=$f'(x)\ dx$ is called the differential of y or $f(x)$. Therefore, $f'(x) = \frac{dy}{dx}$. Many calculus books such as (Banner, 2007) and online cheat sheets and calculators can give the rules of differentiation for different functions, and various exercises on the chain rule are applied when many functions are composed together.

The second (order) derivative $f''(x)$ of a function is the derivative of the derivative of the function. On the graph of a function, the second derivative corresponds to the curvature of the graph.
For functions of two or more variables, the partial derivative is the derivate with respect to one of those variables, keeping all other variables constant. For example $f(x, y) = 3x^2y^3$, we can differentiate with respect to x, $\frac{df}{dx}(x, y) = 6xy^3$ or with respect to y, $\frac{df}{dy}(x, y) = 9x^2y^2$.
The gradient of a function, for example, $f(x,y,z)$, is a vector function of all first partial derivatives of all its variables. $\nabla f = [\frac{\delta f}{\delta x}(x, y, z), \frac{\delta f}{\delta y}(x, y, z), \frac{\delta f}{\delta z}(x, y, z)]$. More on this will be explained in chapter three.

1.2.1.6 Vector Field, Spaces and Independence

A field is a set $\mathbb{F}$ with at least two elements, 0 and 1 and two functions: addition and multiplication. We can define $\mathbb{F}: \mathbb{F}^n \rightarrow \mathbb{F}^m\{0, 1, x, v|x + y \in \mathbb{F}\ and\ xy\ \in \mathbb{F}\}$. For example, the field $\mathbb{Q}$ of rationals, that is, fractions of the form $\frac{m}{n}$, where m, n are integers and n > 0, the field $\mathbb{R}$ of real numbers, and the field $\mathbb{C}$ = {x + iy | x, y $\in \mathbb{R}$ } of complex numbers. Vector was defined earlier as a magnitude and direction. This makes adding any two vectors or scaling any of them, or both by a factor create new vectors that are linearly dependent on the input vectors and belong to the same vector space defined over a field $\mathbb{F}$ = $\mathbb{R}$, $\mathbb{Q}$, $\mathbb{C}$, ..., and so forth, or in the span of the input vectors. For a complete definition of vector space properties, spans and linear dependence and independence, please review complete books like (Carter, 1995) and (Deisenroth, Faisal and Ong, 2019). You can also follow the link to "the Jupyter Guide to Linear Algebra" from the ch1.ipynb notebook. We will summarise this critical concept as vector space is a subset, S, of $\mathbb{R}^n$ with the following properties:

- 0 ∈ S (the zero vector of size n is in the set S); and
- If v;w ∈ S then (v+w) ∈ S; and — addition
- If $\alpha \in \mathbb{R}$ and $v\ \in$ S, then $\alpha v \in$ S. — scalar multiplication

Any linear combinations can be defined on the unit base vectors describing the vector span of all members of the vector space. The Vector span is the set containing all linearly dependent vectors on a given vector.

The vector span is explained as:

$$\left\{\alpha_1 \begin{pmatrix}1\\0\end{pmatrix} + \alpha_2 \begin{pmatrix}0\\1\end{pmatrix} \mid \alpha_1, \alpha_2 \in \mathbb{R}\right\}$$

is the set of all linear combinations of the unit basis vectors $e_1;e_2 \in \mathbb{R}^2$. The basis vectors have two fundamental properties: completeness, such that every vector can be written as a linear combination of basis vectors, and uniqueness, such that the coefficients in the expansion of vectors are unique. For example, all vectors in $\mathbb{R}^n$ (an uncountable infinite set) can be described with just these n basis vectors. For example, given $v = \begin{bmatrix}10\\2\\-6\end{bmatrix}$ in $\mathbb{R}^3$, it is expressed as:

$$v = 10\begin{bmatrix}1\\0\\0\end{bmatrix} + 2\begin{bmatrix}0\\1\\0\end{bmatrix} - 6\begin{bmatrix}0\\0\\1\end{bmatrix}$$

This is generalised to $\mathbb{R}^n$ by: $x_1e_1 + x_2e_2 + \ldots + x_ne_n$. Let $\{v_1,v_2, \ldots,v_n\} \in \mathbb{R}^n$. $e_i \in \mathbb{R}^n$ is defined as the unit basis for dimension i=1, 2, … n such that only the ith position is equal to 1, and all other values = 0, for $1 \le i \le n$, $e_i = \begin{bmatrix}0\\\vdots\\1\\\vdots\\0\end{bmatrix}$.

Then the span of these vectors,($\{v_1,v_2, \ldots,v_n\}$), is said to be the set of all vectors that are formed by a linear combination of the given set of vectors.

Given two vectors, v above, and u = $\begin{bmatrix}20\\4\\-12\end{bmatrix}$, both are said to be linearly dependent as u = 2v, under scalar multiplication, such that the scalar is 2.

Let $\{v_1,v_2, \ldots,v_n\} \in \mathbb{R}^n$. Then this set of vectors is said to be linearly independent if $x_1v_1 + \cdots + x_nv_n = 0$. This implies that $x_1 = \cdots = x_n = 0$. A set of linearly dependent vectors is defined as such when at least one of the vectors can be expressed as a linear combination of another.

Example of a vector space that satisfies a plane of vectors = $\begin{bmatrix}0\\x_1\\x_2\end{bmatrix}$, is it a subspace of $\mathbb{R}^3$? we need to test the three conditions. 1) the zero vector is included in the set since variables x_1 and $x_2$are meant to accept any values, including zero. 2) if u and v and two vectors are in this set, will u+v be in the set? Yes because $\begin{bmatrix}0+0\\u_1+v_1\\u_2+v_2\end{bmatrix}$, and all elements satisfy the set definition. 3) if $\alpha \in \mathbb{R}$ and v are in the set, will αv be in the set? Yes because $\begin{bmatrix}\alpha 0 = 0\\\alpha v_1\\\alpha v_2\end{bmatrix}$, and all elements satisfy the set definition. Then this set is a subspace of $\mathbb{R}^3$.

Another example of a vector space that satisfies a plane of vectors = $\begin{bmatrix}1\\x_1\\x_2\end{bmatrix}$, will not be a subspace of $\mathbb{R}^3$ the zero vector is not in the set.

Intuition: Dot products are functionals that reduce the dimensionality of any two vectors to 1 scalar, measuring similarity between them. Cross products keep the dimensionality as is measuring the area of the parallelogram formed by the two vectors. Outer products increase the dimensionality by 1 to show the correspondence of each element of the first vector by each element of the second vector. Independent vectors are vectors that can not be linearly composed of each other. Being perpendicular to each other indicates that the two vectors are uncorrelated and independent. The first derivative of one dimension variable is the slope of the line formed by the vector equation. At the same time, the first derivative of the multivariate vector is comprised of a partial derivative of each variable, forming the gradient vector. Second derivatives are defined to check for minimum or maximum or saddle points of the first derivatives.

1.2.2: Matrix Operations

As introduced in the motivation section earlier, matrices are linear mapping between the rows and the columns. In data science, this would be a map between the entities and their features. A matrix M ∈ $\mathbb{R}^{m \times n}$ is composed of m rows forming the entities as m vectors v, each containing N elements v_i ∈ $\mathbb{R}^n$ for $1 \le i \le N$. The n elements or features describe the rows and form the columns. Vectors are special kinds of matrices containing one row or column, such that either the m or n is equal to one, and the other is the number of elements it contains. Element-wise operations, such as addition and subtraction, require matrices if equal dimensions. Scalar multiplication and division require a matrix and a scalar. The transposition of a matrix turns its rows into columns and vice versa. For a given matrix $M \in \mathbb{R}^{m \times n}$, the transpose is defined as: $M^T \in \mathbb{R}^{n \times m}$. We will explain matrix multiplication, orthonormal matrices, determinants, inverse matrices, and Hessian and Jacobian Matrices.

1.2.2.1: Matrix Multiplication

As the motivation section illustrates, linear algebra studies linear maps or function dynamics. For example, if given three breakfast recipes (R), Pancakes (P), Biscuits (B), and Waffles (W) that feed 3 people. Pancake ingredients are 2 cups of baking mix (BM), 2 eggs (E), and 1 cup of Milk (M). Biscuits' ingredients are 2.25 cups of baking mix and 0.75 cups of milk. Waffles ingredients are 2 cups of baking mix, 1 egg, 1.3 cups of milk, and 2 tablespoons of oil (O). We can represent this data using the three vectors: [2, 2, 1, 0], [2.25, 0, 0.75, 0] and [2, 1, 1.3, 2]. To unify the representation, we form a matrix $M \in \mathbb{R}^{3 \times 4}$ in which the three recipes are the entity of the rows, the ingredient quantities needed per recipe are in the columns, and each has its weight metric defined in the dataset metadata. This will produce the following dataset matrix (labels in the bold first row are usually omitted):

$$M = \begin{bmatrix} \boldsymbol{BM} & \boldsymbol{E} & \boldsymbol{M} & \boldsymbol{O} \\ 2 & 2 & 1 & 0 \\ 2.25 & 0 & 0.75 & 0 \\ 2 & 1 & 1.3 & 2 \end{bmatrix} \begin{cases} \boldsymbol{R} \\ P \\ B \\ W \end{cases}$$

Element a_{ij} denotes the value in the ith row and j^{th} column starting indexing from 0 for both rows and columns. For example, $a_{1,1}$ in M = 0, which is the number of eggs required for making 1 serve of Biscuits. Matrix addition can be defined as having more data about the same entities in the same order of features, and it is safe to do element-wise addition. For example, to double the ingredients to feed six people, M+M, which is also equal to 2M, calculates the ingredients:

$$2M = \begin{bmatrix} 4 & 4 & 2 & 0 \\ 4.5 & 0 & 1.5 & 0 \\ 4 & 2 & 2.6 & 4 \end{bmatrix}$$

If we want to feed 1 person a pancake, 12 people biscuits, and 9 people waffles, we need to make one batch of pancakes, 4 batches of biscuits, and 3 batches of waffles. To find out the total ingredients needed for this, we can use a vector v = [1, 4, 3] and multiply it by M to produce:

$$v \times \mathrm{M} = [1, 4, 3] \times \begin{bmatrix} 2 & 2 & 1 & 0 \\ 2.25 & 0 & 0.75 & 0 \\ 2 & 1 & 1.3 & 2 \end{bmatrix} =$$

$$[1\times2+4\times2.25+3\times2 \quad 1\times2+4\times0+3\times1 \quad 1\times1+4\times0.75+3\times1.3 \quad 1\times0+4\times0+3\times2]$$
$$= [17, 5, 8, 6]$$

We need 17 cups of baking mix, 5 eggs, 8 cups of milk, and 6 tablespoons of oil.

This is a matrix multiplication between a vector v, which is a special matrix ∈ $\mathbb{R}^{1 \times 3}$ and a matrix M ∈ $\mathbb{R}^{3 \times 4}$. We did a dot product (inner product) between each row of the first matrix (here was only one) and each column of the second matrix. Matrix multiplication requires that the number of elements of the rows in the first matrix matches the number of elements of the columns in the second matrix. This means the dimension of the columns of the first matrix should be equal to the dimension of the rows of the second matrix. For example, the matrix multiplication $M_1 \in \mathbb{R}^{1\times3} \times M_2 \in \mathbb{R}^{3\times4} = M_{out} \in \mathbb{R}^{1\times4}$. The inner dimensions of the input matrices should match to produce an output matrix with the outer dimension of both matrices. Using the labels and the meaning of the multiplication, as illustrated in Figure 2, we can see that matrix multiplication combines information from two matrices to calculate the contribution of the rows entities of the first matrix to the features columns of the second matrix.

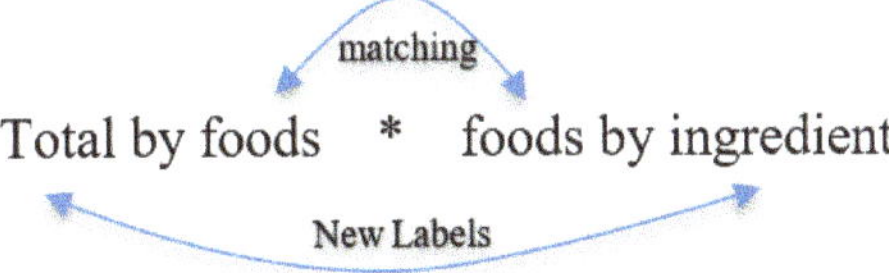

Figure 2: Matrix Multiplication Label Matching and meaning

Another linear mapping example credited to Nichola Schulze, is when given two gas producers (A and B) that send different proportions of the gas they produce to three suppliers (1, 2 and 3), with proportions defined in matrix P $\in \mathbb{R}^{2\times3}$. Each supplier then forwards gas in different proportions to four gas stations (X, Y, Z and W) as defined in matrix S $\in \mathbb{R}^{3\times4}$. To find out the proportion of each producer output that goes to each gas station, matrix multiplication computes this as follows:

$$P \times S = \begin{bmatrix} 0.5 & 0.2 & 0.3 \\ 0.0 & 0.4 & 0.6 \end{bmatrix} \times \begin{bmatrix} 0.4 & 0.6 & 0.0 & 0.0 \\ 0.0 & 0.7 & 0.3 & 0.0 \\ 0.0 & 0.5 & 0.0 & 0.5 \end{bmatrix} = \begin{bmatrix} 0.20 & 0.59 & 0.06 & 0.15 \\ 0.00 & 0.58 & 0.12 & 0.30 \end{bmatrix} \in \mathbb{R}^{2\times4}$$

The general rule of matrix multiplication is:
$C = A \times B$ such that Matrix C contains elements c indexed by i and j $c_{ij} = \sum_{k=1}^{n} a_{ik}\, b_{kj}$. For example, the above $v \in \mathbb{R}^{1\times3}$ multiplied by M $\in \mathbb{R}^{3\times4}$ $c_{12} = a_{11}b_{12} + a_{12}b_{22} + +a_{13}b_{32}$ = $1 \times 2 + 4 \times 2.25 + 3 \times 2 = 5$, then repeat for all c_{ij} $1 \le i \le 1$ and $1 \le j \le 4$.
Lie Product is a square matrix produced by the difference of the simple product order of two square matrices of the same order ($(A, B) \in \mathbb{F}^{n\times n}$), using the following rule:

$$[[A, B]]_{i,j} = \sum_{k=1}^{n} \{a_{ik}b_{kj} - b_{ik}a_{kj}\} \Rightarrow [A, B] = AB - BA \in \mathbb{F}^{n\times n}$$

1.2.2.2 Systems of Equations Solving

The most straightforward way to solve a system of equations is by substitution. Substitution requires moving all variables on the right-hand side of the equal sign and leaving only one variable on the left-hand side. Then to find a variable solution, simplifying the equation and substituting backwards in other equations assigns a specific value to the variable on the left-hand side. This process is repeated for the remaining variables using the solved variables' values until all are solved. Solving a system of equations can be represented in matrix form. For example:
Given two equations:

$$5x_1 + 3x_2 = 93$$
$$-4x_1 - 2x_2 = -66$$

can be written as Matrix A and vector x and outputs vector b, Ax=b.

$$A = \begin{bmatrix} 5 & 3 \\ -4 & -2 \end{bmatrix}, x = \begin{bmatrix} x_1 \\ x_2 \end{bmatrix}, b = \begin{bmatrix} 93 \\ -66 \end{bmatrix},$$

This is represented as an augmented matrix combining A and b:

$$\left[\begin{array}{cc|c} 5 & 3 & 93 \\ -4 & -2 & -66 \end{array}\right]$$

1.2.2.2.1 Elementary Row Operations

Using Elementry Row Operations (ERO) such as: interchanging any rows, multiplying any row by a non-zero scalar, and replacing any row by the sum of that row and any other row. Any ERO can be chosen in any order until matrix A is converted into an identity matrix I, such that only ones are on the diagonal and all other elements are zeros. The diagonal elements represent the unknowns per column that become equal to the output in the rows of b after the vertical bar. The procedure relies on the fact that its solution does not change if:

1. An equation in the system is modified by subtracting a multiple of another equation in the system from it; and/or
2. Both sides of an equation in the system are scaled by a non-zero.
3. Equations (rows) can be reordered to maintain the strictly lower triangle equal to zero.

These three basic rules are an effort to reduce the system to an upper triangular system, which is easier to solve. An upper triangular matrix is defined as having every entry below the diagonal be zero, i.e. $a_{ij} = 0$ if $i > j$. It is lower triangular $a_{ij} = 0$ for $i < j$. When there are no zeros in the diagonal, the columns are linearly independent. This is formalised algorithmically using Gauss Jordan Elimination as illustrated in the ch1.ipynb python notebook. Additional Rules of the Gauss-Jordan Elimination to get to **reduced row echelon** form are:

4. make each row starts its non-zero coefficients with 1. This is the pivot of the row.
5. move all rows consisting of only zeroes to the bottom of the matrix.

Intuitively, the row that contains 1 in the first column should be moved to be the first row. If none is available, divide the first row by the value of the first column to get 1 in the first diagonal element. To turn a non-diagonal element into a zero, find another row that, when scaled by a value, will produce a negative value to the element to zero out and add them together. The following steps solve the previous example:

1. Form the Augmented Matrix:

$$\left[\begin{array}{cc|c} 5 & 3 & 93 \\ -4 & -2 & -66 \end{array}\right]$$

2. Divide Row 1 by 5: r1 ÷ 5

$$\left[\begin{array}{cc|c} 1 & 0.6 & 18.6 \\ -4 & -2 & -66 \end{array}\right]$$

3. We now have a 1 as the first entry in row 1, column 1. Now let us obtain a 0 in row 2, column 1. This can be accomplished by multiplying row 1 by 4 and then adding the result to row 2, leaving row 1 unaffected: 4 * r1 +r2.

$$\left[\begin{array}{cc|c} 1 & 0.6 & 18.6 \\ 0 & 0.4 & 8.4 \end{array}\right]$$

4. To have 1 in the second diagonal element, we divide row 2 by 0.4: r2 ÷ 0.4

$$\left[\begin{array}{cc|c} 1 & 0.6 & 18.6 \\ 0 & 1 & 21 \end{array}\right]$$

5. To have zero in the non-diagonal elements in row 1, we multiply row 2 by -6 and then add the result to row 1, leaving row 2 unaffected: -6 * r2 +r1.

$$\left[\begin{array}{cc|c} 1 & 0 & 6 \\ 0 & 1 & 21 \end{array}\right]$$

This forms the equations:

$$1x_1 + 0x_2 = 6$$
$$0x_1 + 1x_2 = 21$$

Making $x_1 = 6$ and $x_2 = 21$. We can stop at step four since we can continue by backword substitution forming the Gaussian Elimination only to reduce the computational steps, which is helpful for larger matrices.

1.2.2.2.2 Matrix Inverse

A matrix inverse is defined A^{-1} such that A A^{-1}=I, where I is the identity matrix as defined above. For solving equations of the form Ax=b, then x = A^{-1}b is an equivalent representation to solve for x. This makes a system of equations solved by multiplication rather than by Gauss Jordan Elimination. To find A^{-1} for matrix A defined above, we can follow the same steps as above to solve $A^{-1}A = I$:

1. Form the Augmented Matrix:

$$\left[\begin{array}{cc|cc} 5 & 3 & 1 & 0 \\ -4 & -2 & 0 & 1 \end{array}\right]$$

2. r1 ÷ 5

$$\left[\begin{array}{cc|cc} 1 & 0.6 & 0.2 & 0 \\ -4 & -2 & 0 & 1 \end{array}\right]$$

3. 4 * r1 +r2.

$$\left[\begin{array}{cc|cc} 1 & 0.6 & 0.2 & 0 \\ 0 & 0.4 & 0.8 & 1 \end{array}\right]$$

4. r2 ÷ 0.4

$$\left[\begin{array}{cc|cc} 1 & 0.6 & 0.2 & 0 \\ 0 & 1 & 2 & 2.5 \end{array}\right]$$

5. -6 * r2 +r1.

$$\left[\begin{array}{cc|cc} 1 & 0 & -1 & -1.5 \\ 0 & 1 & 2 & 2.5 \end{array}\right]$$

Therefore $A^{-1} = \begin{bmatrix} -1 & -1.5 \\ 2 & 2.5 \end{bmatrix}$

Finding the inverse of a matrix computationally for large matrices is inefficient. Matrix factorisation/decomposition algorithms are used instead, as explained in chapter two. A matrix inverse is not always defined for all given matrices, just as much as scalar zero has no inverse. This happens when the columns of the matrix are not linearly independent, as defined in the previous section. The parallelogram formed by these vectors has an area that equals zero and is labelled a degenerate matrix.

The general formula to find an inverse of a matrix A ∈ $\mathbb{R}^{2\times 2} = \begin{bmatrix} a & b \\ c & d \end{bmatrix}$ can be found by following the same steps above:

1. Form the Augmented Matrix:

$$\left[\begin{array}{cc|cc} a & b & 1 & 0 \\ c & d & 0 & 1 \end{array}\right]$$

2. r1 ÷ a

$$\left[\begin{array}{cc|cc} 1 & \frac{b}{a} & \frac{1}{a} & 0 \\ c & d & 0 & 1 \end{array}\right]$$

3. -c * r1 +r2.

$$\left[\begin{array}{cc|cc} 1 & \frac{b}{a} & \frac{1}{a} & 0 \\ 0 & \frac{ad-bc}{a} & \frac{-c}{a} & 1 \end{array}\right]$$

4. r2 ÷ $\frac{ad-bc}{a}$

$$\left[\begin{array}{cc|cc} 1 & \frac{b}{a} & \frac{1}{a} & 0 \\ 0 & 1 & \frac{-c}{ad-bc} & \frac{a}{ad-bc} \end{array}\right]$$

5. $-\frac{b}{a}$ * r2 +r1.

$$\left[\begin{array}{cc|cc} 1 & 0 & \frac{d}{ad-bc} & \frac{-b}{ad-bc} \\ 0 & 1 & \frac{-c}{ad-bc} & \frac{a}{ad-bc} \end{array}\right]$$

Therefore $A^{-1} = \frac{1}{ad-bc}\begin{bmatrix} d & -b \\ -c & a \end{bmatrix}$

1.2.2.2.3 Orthonormal Matrix

Orthogonal matrix A of order n is defined such that the inner product of all its column or row = 0 if different or a value if the same index.

$\langle \mathrm{a}_i, \mathrm{a}_j \rangle = \begin{cases} 0, \ if \ i \neq j \\ \alpha_i = \|\mathrm{a}_i\|^2 > 0, \ if \ i = j \end{cases}$, where $\mathrm{a}_i, \mathrm{a}_j$ are any two rows in the matrix, or any two columns, and α_i is the square of the euclidian norms of the given row or column.

An orthogonal matrix, or orthonormal matrix, is a real square matrix whose columns and rows are orthonormal vectors that are orthogonal and normalised such that $\alpha_i = 1$. A matrix A $\in \mathbb{R}^{m \times n}$ orthonormal with respect to the rows if $A \cdot A^T = I \in \mathbb{R}^{m \times m}$, and orthonormal with respect to the columns if $A \cdot A^T = I \in \mathbb{R}^{n \times n}$.
Knowing that a matrix is orthonormal means its determinant is equal to one and it has an inverse, $A^{-1} = A^T$. This makes solving a system of equations $Ax = b$→ $A^{-1}Ax = A^{-1}b$→ $A^TAx = A^Tb$→ $x = A^Tb$→ $Ix = A^Tb$.

1.2.2.3 Matrix Determinant

The square matrix determinant measures the area of the parallelogram formed by the column vectors of the matrix and gives valuable information about the matrix. A determinant of a 1×1 matrix that contains only one element is just the value of this element, which is interpreted as the length of one dimension. A determinant of a 2×2 matrix = $\begin{bmatrix} a & b \\ c & d \end{bmatrix}$ is defined as $ad - bc$. This is visually defined as: $\begin{bmatrix} a & b \\ c & d \end{bmatrix}$. This formula is used as a divisor of the inverse formula above. This means that if the determinant is equal to zero, the matrix has no inverse. To generalise, we subtract the products of the diagonals from each other, beginning from the main diagonal that goes from the top left to the bottom right. In the 2×2 matrix, this covered all elements of the matrix and did triangularisation of the matrix by replacing the second row by the result of itself minus the first row weighted with factor c/a, yielding: $\begin{bmatrix} a & b \\ c - \frac{c}{a}a & d - \frac{c}{a}b \end{bmatrix} = \begin{bmatrix} a & b \\ 0 & d - \frac{c}{a}b \end{bmatrix}$.

A determinant of a 3×3 matrix can not be produced using the subtraction of the diagonal products method that will cover only 4 out of the 9 elements of the matrix. We can augment the first two columns to the right of the matrix such that all elements fall on diagonals, as illustrated visually below:

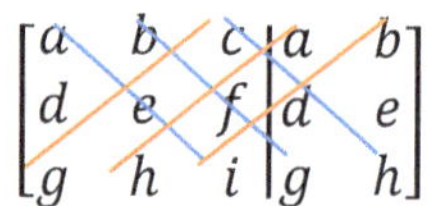

Using the diagonals that have 3 numbers only, we can deduce the 3×3 matrix determinant formula to be: $(a \times e \times i + b \times f \times g + c \times d \times h) - (c \times e \times g + a \times f \times h + b \times d \times i)$.

This procedure does not generalise well to the $n \times n$ matrices when n > 3. The expansion by minor method works for all values of n. It works by computing a determinant for the "minor" which is a submatrix $A_{ij} \in \mathbb{R}^{n-1 \times n-1}$ that does not include row i and column j from the original matrix, using alternating sign and cofactors C_{ij}. We either take each element of a column by making j spans the columns while i is fixed to the column we are expanding on, or take all rows and make j fixed to the row we are expanding on. It uses the formula:

$$C_{ij} = s_{ij} M_{ij}$$

$s_{11} = 1$, then as we increment i along with the columns and j along with the rows, it keeps changing the sign.

For a 3×3 matrix, $S = \begin{bmatrix} 1 & -1 & 1 \\ -1 & 1 & -1 \\ 1 & -1 & 1 \end{bmatrix}$

For $A \in \mathbb{R}^{3\times 3} = \begin{bmatrix} 4 & 2 & 3 \\ 0 & 2 & 4 \\ 1 & 3 & 6 \end{bmatrix}$, if we expand on column 1, we can calculate the determinant as:

$\det(A) = |A| = a_{11}s_{11}M_{11} + a_{21}s_{21}M_{21} + a_{31}s_{31}M_{31}$

$= 4(+1)\begin{vmatrix} 2 & 4 \\ 3 & 6 \end{vmatrix} + 0(-1)\begin{vmatrix} 2 & 3 \\ 3 & 6 \end{vmatrix} + 1(+1)\begin{vmatrix} 2 & 3 \\ 2 & 4 \end{vmatrix}$

$= 4(12 - 12) - 0(12 - 9) + 1(8 - 6)$

$= 4 \times 0 - 0 \times 3 + 1 \times 2 = 2$

For $A \in \mathbb{R}^{4\times 4} = \begin{bmatrix} 5 & 4 & 6 & 3 \\ 0 & 2 & 1 & 0 \\ 9 & 7 & 4 & 6 \\ 2 & 8 & 1 & 3 \end{bmatrix}$, Then, for $M_{1,1} = \begin{bmatrix} \cancel{5} & \cancel{4} & \cancel{6} & \cancel{3} \\ \cancel{0} & 2 & 1 & 0 \\ \cancel{9} & 7 & 4 & 6 \\ \cancel{2} & 8 & 1 & 3 \end{bmatrix} = \begin{bmatrix} 2 & 1 & 0 \\ 7 & 4 & 6 \\ 8 & 1 & 3 \end{bmatrix}$. The complete determinant is calculated as:

$\det(A) = |A| = 0(-1)\begin{vmatrix} 4 & 6 & 3 \\ 7 & 4 & 6 \\ 8 & 1 & 3 \end{vmatrix} + 2(+1)\begin{vmatrix} 5 & 6 & 3 \\ 9 & 4 & 6 \\ 2 & 1 & 3 \end{vmatrix} + 1(-1)\begin{vmatrix} 5 & 4 & 3 \\ 9 & 7 & 6 \\ 2 & 8 & 3 \end{vmatrix} + 0(+1)\begin{vmatrix} 5 & 4 & 6 \\ 9 & 7 & 4 \\ 2 & 8 & 1 \end{vmatrix}$

For a 4×4 matrix,

$$S = \begin{bmatrix} 1 & -1 & 1 & -1 \\ -1 & 1 & -1 & 1 \\ 1 & -1 & 1 & -1 \\ -1 & 1 & -1 & 1 \end{bmatrix}$$

For $A = \begin{bmatrix} 5 & 4 & 6 & 3 \\ 0 & 2 & 1 & 0 \\ 9 & 7 & 4 & 6 \\ 2 & 8 & 1 & 3 \end{bmatrix}$, Then, for $M_{2,1} = \begin{bmatrix} \cancel{5} & 4 & 6 & 3 \\ \cancel{0} & \cancel{2} & \cancel{1} & \cancel{0} \\ \cancel{9} & 7 & 4 & 6 \\ \cancel{2} & 8 & 1 & 3 \end{bmatrix} = \begin{bmatrix} 4 & 6 & 3 \\ 7 & 4 & 6 \\ 8 & 1 & 3 \end{bmatrix}$. If we expand on row 2 since it contains two zeros, the complete determinant is calculated as:

$\det(A) = |A| = a_{21}s_{21}M_{21} + a_{22}s_{22}M_{22} + a_{23}s_{23}M_{23} + a_{24}s_{24}M_{24}$

$= 0(-1)\begin{vmatrix} 4 & 6 & 3 \\ 7 & 4 & 6 \\ 8 & 1 & 3 \end{vmatrix} + 2(+1)\begin{vmatrix} 5 & 6 & 3 \\ 9 & 4 & 6 \\ 2 & 1 & 3 \end{vmatrix} + 1(-1)\begin{vmatrix} 5 & 4 & 3 \\ 9 & 7 & 6 \\ 2 & 8 & 3 \end{vmatrix} + 0(+1)\begin{vmatrix} 5 & 4 & 6 \\ 9 & 7 & 4 \\ 2 & 8 & 1 \end{vmatrix}$

Then further reduce until we find the $\det(A) = |A| = -93$.

The general formula for the determinant of any square matrix $A \in \mathbb{R}^{n\times n}$ is,

$\det(A) = |A| = a_{i1}s_{i1}M_{i1} + a_{i2}s_{i2}M_{i2} + \cdots + a_{in}s_{in}M_{in} = a_{1j}s_{1j}M_{1j} + a_{2j}s_{2j}M_{2j} + \ldots + a_{nj}s_{nj}M_{nj}$

$\det(A) = |A| = \sum_{j=1}^{n} a_{ij}s_{ij}M_{ij}$ *for the chosen* $i = \sum_{i=1}^{n} a_{ij}s_{ij}M_{ij}$ for the chosen j. Choosing the row or column with the most zeros saves much work.

Placing all cofactors in matrix C, the formula for the inverse $A^{-1} = \frac{C^T}{\det(A)}$, such that $(A^{-1})_{ij} = \frac{c_{ji}}{\det(A)}$.
This process is still computationally inefficient since it requires n! operations $(n \times (n-1) \times (n-1) \ldots \times 2 \times 1)$. It is tractable only for small values of n.

Another method to compute the determinant is by using ERO knowing the following properties:

1. Interchanging any two adjacent rows changes the sign of the determinant. Non-adjacent rows interchanges require counting the number of adjacent rows swappings; an even number of swaps will result in a positive determinant, and an odd number of swaps will result in a negative determinant.
2. Multiplying a row by a scalar multiplies the determinant by the same scalar.
3. Replacing any row by the sum of that row and any other row does not change the determinant.
4. The determinant of a triangular matrix (upper or lower) is the product of the diagonal elements.

For a 2×2 matrix,

$A = \begin{bmatrix} 5 & 3 \\ -4 & -2 \end{bmatrix}$ → det(A) = D_1

1. r1 ÷ 5

$\begin{bmatrix} 1 & 0.6 \\ -4 & -2 \end{bmatrix}$ → det(A) = D2 ÷ 5

2. 4 * r1 +r2.

$\begin{bmatrix} 1 & 0.6 \\ 0 & 0.4 \end{bmatrix}$ → det(A) = D3 ÷ 5

D_3 = 0.4 ➔ det(A) =0.4 ÷ 5 = 2
The original determinant formula is det(A) = 5(-2)-3(-4) = -10+12 = 2
For a 3×3 matrix,

$A = \begin{bmatrix} 0 & 2 & 4 \\ 4 & 2 & 3 \\ 1 & 3 & 6 \end{bmatrix}$ → det(A) = D_1

1. Swap r1 and r3, two adjacent row exchanges, with no change to the determinant sign.

$\begin{bmatrix} 1 & 3 & 6 \\ 4 & 2 & 3 \\ 0 & 2 & 4 \end{bmatrix}$ → det(A) = D2

2. -4 * r1 +r2.

$\begin{bmatrix} 1 & 3 & 6 \\ 0 & -10 & -21 \\ 0 & 2 & 4 \end{bmatrix}$ → det(A) = D3

3. r2 ÷ (-10).

$\begin{bmatrix} 1 & 3 & 6 \\ 0 & 1 & 2.1 \\ 0 & 2 & 4 \end{bmatrix}$ → det(A) = D4÷ (-10)

4. -2 * r2 +r3.

$\begin{bmatrix} 1 & 3 & 6 \\ 0 & 1 & 2.1 \\ 0 & 0 & -0.2 \end{bmatrix}$ → det(A) = D5÷ (-10)

D_5 = -0.2 ➔ det(A) =-0.2 ÷ (-10) = -2

The ERO is computationally more efficient for large n and is used more often. There is also modular triangularisation of any square matrix, such that determinants or 2x2 matrices is used in the equations of the 3x3 and so on. This recursive calculation is defined from blocks of triangulated matrices. The determinant of an nxn matrix becomes the product of the diagonal elements of the triangulated matrix: $det(A) = \prod_{i_1}^{n} \det(A_{ii})$.
A singular matrix is a square matrix order n, such that its determinant is equal to zero; otherwise, it is non-singular.

1.2.2.4 Consistent and Inconsistent Systems of Equations

The system of equations example that was given previously is a **consistent system** since it has only one valid solution. This solution is found at the point of intersection of the two lines formed by the two given equations. For three unknowns and three equations, the solution is at the point of intersection of the three planes formed by each equation. The same concept applies to the higher dimensions. Systems Ax = b with one unique solution are defined as when b is in the column space of A. For practising Gaussian Elimination, these online calculators show all intermediate steps:

- http://ulaff.s3.amazonaws.com/GaussianEliminationPractice/index.html
- https://onlinemschool.com/math/assistance/equation/gaus/

Sometimes there is more than one point of intersection, such that the system is defined to be a **consistent dependent system**. This case happens when the system Ax = b has Ax_s = b and Ax_n = 0, then x_s+x_n is a solution for $A(x_s+x_n)$ = b (we have many solutions), which signifies that there are linear combinations between the column vectors of A. For example:
A = $\begin{bmatrix} 1 & 1 \\ 2 & 2 \end{bmatrix}$, x = $\begin{bmatrix} x_1 \\ x_2 \end{bmatrix}$, and b= $\begin{bmatrix} 4 \\ 8 \end{bmatrix}$,

We need to find x such that Ax = 2x. To solve, we subtract 2x from both sides Ax-2x = 0 and have this matrix to apply Gaussian Elimination on:

x_1+x_2 = 4
$2x_1$+$2x_2$ = 8

1. Form the augmented form $\left[\begin{array}{cc|c} 1 & 1 & 4 \\ 2 & 2 & 8 \end{array}\right]$
2. R2 - 2 R1 → R2 (multiply 1 row by 2 and subtract it from 2 row)

$\left[\begin{array}{cc|c} 1 & 1 & 4 \\ 0 & 0 & 0 \end{array}\right]$

If we have a zero on the diagonal, then we have fewer equations than variables, i.e. we have more than one solution, but we have the upper equation that describes the possible solutions as the solution set: x_1+x_2 = 4, which means x_1 = 4-x_2, which gives a bound on the values of x_1 and x_2. x can be
$\begin{bmatrix} 1 \\ 3 \end{bmatrix}$ or $\begin{bmatrix} 2 \\ 2 \end{bmatrix}$ or $\begin{bmatrix} 3 \\ 1 \end{bmatrix}$ and so forth.

To formalise this process for any variables, we say we are going to make the last variable a "free variable", meaning that it can take on any value in $\mathbb{R}$, and we will see how to describe the "bound variables" using the free variable. In the exercise above, we say x_2 = b and x_1 = 4-b. Therefore x = $\begin{bmatrix} 4-b \\ b \end{bmatrix}$.

We now claim that this captures all solutions of the system of linear equations. We will call this the **general solution**. Try different values of b and substitute in the original matrices to find that they always produce the same results. i.e. this is the vector space of the solution.

Because there is a non-trivial solution to Ax = 0, the null space of A has more than just the zero vector, and A's columns are linearly dependent.

Sometimes there is no point of intersection, such that the system is defined to be inconsistent. When system Ax = b, b is not in the column span of A, there will be no solution. For example, solve Ax = b, for the following:

A = $\begin{bmatrix} 1 & 0 \\ 0 & 1 \\ 1 & 1 \end{bmatrix}$, and b = $\begin{bmatrix} 1 \\ 1 \\ 0 \end{bmatrix}$

Reduce it to row echelon form by hand or use the online calculators to find out that the last row contains all zeros, while the last element in b is -2 since zero is not equal to -2, then b is not in the columns space of A, and there is no solution to this system of equation. The appended form of final output after Gaussian Elimination will be:

$$\left[\begin{array}{cc|c} 1 & 0 & 1 \\ 0 & 1 & 1 \\ 0 & 0 & -2 \end{array}\right]$$

Other ways to solve a system of equations are to reduce column echelon form.

1.2.2.5 Linear Combinations and Linear Transformations

Revisiting vector spaces and generalising to linear matrix transformation, as explained in (Geijn and Quintana-Ort´, 2008), a linear transformation L takes a vector in R^n space and transform it to R^m can be expressed as a matrix of size m rows and n columns. A transformation L is linear if the following properties hold for α, β as scalars, and u and v as vectors:

1. L(αu) = αL(u)
2. L(u+v) = L(u) + L(v) The transformation is distributive with respect to vector addition.
3. L(αu + βv) = L(αv) + L(βv)
4. $L(\alpha_1 v_1 + \alpha_2 v_2 + \ldots + \alpha_n v_n) = L(\alpha_1 v_1) + L(\alpha_2 v_2) + \ldots + L(\alpha_n v_n)$

The unit vectors e_j as defined earlier, when multiplied by linear transformation matrix L, produces the required output vector. A linear transformation is defined as $L(\sum_{j=0}^{n-1} x_j e_j)$ for input vector x of n elements. The following matrix describes this transformation:

$y \in \mathbb{R}^m = L(x) \in \mathbb{R}^{mxn} = L(x_0 e_0 + x_1 e_1 + \cdots + x_{n-1} e_{n-1}) = x_0 L(e_0) + x_1 L(e1) + \cdots + x_{n-1} L(e_{n-1})$
$= x_0 a_0 + x_1 a_1 + \cdots + x_{n-1} a_{n-1},$

Such that a_j is the output of the transformation L at the jth unit vector e_j and size m each, which is the size of the output vector y. This linear transformation can be expressed as a matrix A as follows;

$$y = L(x) = Ax = \begin{bmatrix} a_{0,0} & \cdots & a_{0,n-1} \\ \vdots & \ddots & \vdots \\ a_{m-1,0} & \cdots & a_{m-1,n-1} \end{bmatrix} x = \begin{bmatrix} a_{0,0}x_0 & + \ldots + & a_{0,n-1}x_{n-1} \\ \vdots & \ddots & \vdots \\ a_{m-1,0}x_0 & + \ldots + & a_{m-1,n-1}x_{n-1} \end{bmatrix}$$

Example: Rotation Linear Transformation matrix:

To define the Linear transformation $R_{\emptyset}$ that performs the rotation of a vector on the 2D plane by Ø angle, we need to define the output of the transformation on all unit basis vectors. For the first unit vector, $e_0 = \begin{bmatrix} 1 \\ 0 \end{bmatrix}$ visualised as illustrated in Figure 3 a, a point with coordinates (1, 0) is transformed to the $R_{\emptyset}(1, 0)$ using trigonometry rules.

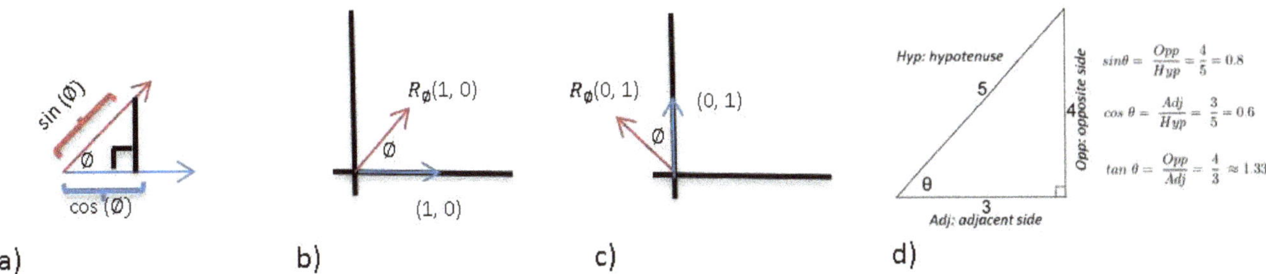

Figure 3: a) trigonometry rules to calculate the length of a side of the right angle triangle b) Rotation of first Unit basis using trigonometry, c) rotation of second basis vector (Geijn, 2012), d) an example

$R_{\emptyset}(1, 0) = a_0 = \begin{bmatrix} \cos\emptyset \\ \sin\emptyset \end{bmatrix}$

$R_{\emptyset}(0, 1) = a_1 = \begin{bmatrix} -\sin\emptyset \\ \cos\emptyset \end{bmatrix}$

Using the matrix notation defined previously to express the linear rotation transformation, the following Matrix A is composed of the a_i output produced from the transformation of the unit basis:

$R_{\emptyset} = \begin{bmatrix} \cos\emptyset & -\sin\emptyset \\ \sin\emptyset & \cos\emptyset \end{bmatrix}$

For rotating a vector x = (3, 5) for angle Ø = 45, the following matrix-vector multiplication is performed to produce the new output vector

$$R_{\emptyset}(x) = \begin{bmatrix} \cos 45 & -\sin 45 \\ \sin 45 & \cos 45 \end{bmatrix} \begin{bmatrix} 3 \\ 5 \end{bmatrix} = \begin{bmatrix} 3\cos(45) - 5\sin(45) \\ 3\sin(45) + 5\cos(45) \end{bmatrix} = \begin{bmatrix} 5.6568 \\ 1.4142 \end{bmatrix}$$

In computer graphics, objects are defined by their vertices coordinates in matrix form. Various transformation matrices are used to apply rotation, reflection on an axis, translation by shifting points along a coordinate, skewing, and sheering are applied by matrix multiplication. More examples of forming linear transformation matrices for spatial images are found in (Ashburner and Friston, 1997), or generally, to do ERO in solving systems of equations are found in (Chahal, 2018). These concepts are visualised in https://youtu.be/IrggOvOSZr4.

1.2.2.6 Matrix Calculus

The Jacobian Matrix is defined to be a matrix of partial derivatives of n functions, d variables, such as n functions and d variables as follows:

$$J = \begin{bmatrix} \frac{\delta f_1}{\delta x_1} & \frac{\delta f_1}{\delta x_2} & \cdots & \frac{\delta f_1}{\delta x_d} \\ \frac{\delta f_2}{\delta x_1} & \frac{\delta f_2}{\delta x_2} & \cdots & \frac{\delta f_2}{\delta x_d} \\ \vdots & \vdots & \ddots & \vdots \\ \frac{\delta f_n}{\delta x_1} & \frac{\delta f_n}{\delta x_2} & \cdots & \frac{\delta f_n}{\delta x_d} \end{bmatrix} = \begin{bmatrix} \nabla f_1 \\ \nabla f_2 \\ \vdots \\ \nabla f_n \end{bmatrix}$$

The following link has more examples to practice: http://mathonline.wikidot.com/the-jacobian-matrix-of-differentiable-functions-examples-1. This link contains more advanced topics using the Jacobian matrix in artificial neural networks computations "Jacobian Matrix –the Joys of the Jacobian": http://chalkdustmagazine.com/features/the-joys-of-the-jacobian/.

Intuitively, the Jacobian matrix applies the first-order derivative analysis of a mapping function from n input variables to m output classes, each explained by its function. The m functions on the rows have their 1st-order partial derivative with respect to each variable on the columns. This is used in gradient descent algorithms in neural networks to estimate the error sensitivity with respect to each weight or parameter.

The Hessian matrix of f is a square $n \times n$ symmetric matrix of second-partial derivatives of f that is defined as follows:

$$\mathcal{H}f(x_1, x_2, \dots, x_n) = \begin{bmatrix} \frac{\delta^2 f}{\delta x_1^2} & \frac{\delta^2 f}{\delta x_1 x_2} & \cdots & \frac{\delta^2 f}{\delta x_1 x_n} \\ \frac{\delta^2 f}{\delta x_2 x_1} & \frac{\delta^2 f}{\delta x_2^2} & \cdots & \frac{\delta^2 f}{\delta x_2 x_n} \\ \vdots & \vdots & \ddots & \vdots \\ \frac{\delta^2 f}{\delta x_n x_1} & \frac{\delta^2 f}{\delta x_n x_2} & \cdots & \frac{\delta^2 f}{\delta x_n^2} \end{bmatrix}$$

The symmetry of $\frac{\delta^2 f}{\delta x_i x_j} = \frac{\delta^2 f}{\delta x_j x_i}$ simplifies the computation. Hessian Matrices are helpful in finding extreme values of multivariate functions using the matrix eigenvalues. The extreme values of a function are the local minima, local maxima, and saddle points, which define the function curvature. These values are useful in optimisation algorithms such as Newton's method, Quasi-Newton, Gauss-Newton, BFGS, and (L)BFGS. These methods apply a 2nd-order derivative optimisation approach. The determinant of the hessian matrix (D-test) provides a function discriminant. The inverse of this matrix identifies the least relevant components of a function to use in pruning and reducing model complexity (Singh and Alistarh, 2020). More details can be viewed at: http://mathonline.wikidot.com/hessian-matrices.

Intuition: A matrix represents entities' labels in rows and features values in columns. Matrix addition and subtraction are defined as element-wise increasing or decreasing values by known augmenting datasets. A scalar product scales the values element-wise by a given magnitude. A vector and matrix multiplication is a special case of matrix-matrix multiplication, in which the inner dimensions (with their corresponding labels) should match, and the outer dimensions are the output dimension. A matrix multiplication by a vector represents a linear transformation on the vector, such as projection to a higher or lower dimension, rotation, reflection, scaling, or any linear combination. This transformation is defined in terms of the basis vectors of the corresponding coordinates. To solve a linear system of equations in matrix form, we apply elementary row operations to decompose a matrix representing the equations to a diagonal matrix.

1.3 Motivational Problem

Motivation: Any given dataset in a matrix form is said to be high dimensional as the number of columns increases. Because the degree of freedom increases with the number of columns, for example, the Matrix-High-DImensional-DF.ipynb shows the Kaggle Cardiovascular Disease dataset's degree of freedom increases as we add a new column in the analysis. The concept is emphasised by the pair-wise plots and how different they are for any pair of columns. This illustrates that matricising a high-dimensional dataset loses important structure. The importance of having various indices in tensor forms rather than the two indices in the matrix form lies in capturing this multi-way structure or variance between each pair or more dimensions in the higher dimensional space. However, this easily creates the curse of dimensionality problem as N grows for an Nth-order tensor of size $(I_1, I_2, \dots, I_N)$, as the number of elements exponentially grows. As will be discussed in chapters two and three, this will be handled by learning subspaces that approximate the high-dimensional space with reasonable accuracy deterioration. Chapter four discusses other approaches to dividing the large-scale tensors into several lower-rank tensors that only capture the relevant information.

In python notebook, tensorisation.ipynb, the Kaggle Heart disease factors dataset is tensorised using both the direct columns from the dataset and the PCA as a 2-way dimensionality reduction approach from which the first three principal components created a three-way tensor. Several tensorisation examples are demonstrated, with many more used in the literature mentioned. Then, various regression and compression approaches are demonstrated. For a small dataset, it was easy to create the full-format tensor space. Other examples attempted to allocate space that was not available in the testing machine. Two approaches can solve this dimensionality curse: 1) Sparse tensor structures are required, and 2) creating the decomposed tensor components and working on them directly without creating the complete tensor. These methods are embedded in the tensorisation step by various approaches.

1.3.1 Regression/Classification

Regression is a supervised learning algorithm that estimates the decision line equation parameters (weights) w from a prelabelled dataset X with y label. Either analytically or using the gradient descent algorithm, the aim is to minimise the error ε by adjusting the weights using matrix form. $Xw + \varepsilon = y$, where y is the target/response/dependent variable in the dataset such that $y \in \mathbb{R}^N$, and N is the number of samples (data points or rows), X is the remaining columns in the dataset that represent the features/predictors/independent variables such that $X \in \mathbb{R}^{N \times d+1}$ and w is the coefficients or weights of each feature such that $w \in \mathbb{R}^{d+1}$, and d is the number of features (columns) or the dimensionality. We add one extra dimensionality for the bias weight(0) to be multiplied by x[0] = 1. Since N is usually much more than d, we have more equations than variables and can not use Gaussian Elimination to solve this system of equations. The Normal Equation can be used to find the least error squares solutions (best fit) to systems with more equations than unknowns: $X^T X w = X^T y$, solving for $w = (X^T X)^{-1} X^T y$.

The normal equation solution is computationally expensive for larger matrices. Other solutions include minimising the error by partial derivatives with respect to each weight being set to zero or maximising the likelihood function

by using the gradient descent algorithm and its variants. The performance evaluation of the regression is estimated by mean squared error: $\hat{\sigma}^2 = \frac{\sum_{i=1}^{N}(y_i - \hat{y_i})}{N} = \frac{\sum_{i=1}^{N}(y_i - (w_i x_i))}{N}$.
The same algorithm can be used for classification when Y is a categorical value (the class labels). Then the performance evaluation becomes the accuracy rate or the confusion matrix. Most machine learning algorithms and neural networks start from the regression and further specify the equation to add more objectives or constraints. The tensorisation.ipynb Python notebook shows more details.

1.3.2 Clustering

Clustering is an unsupervised machine learning approach such that given an unlabelled data matrix X, it can be represented as $X \approx AB^T$, such that each row in A (the canonical basis vector) selects a row in B, which contains the clustering vectors. Estimating A and B from X enables multi-way clustering. Dictionary Learning Algorithms, Source Seperation Algorithms such as Independent Component Analysis, attempt to estimate two matrices for the given data matrix. Chapter two will explain more details.

1.3.3 Data Distributions and Mixtures

Data distribution guides the statistical analysis and the generative methods in machine learning. A Gaussian distributed feature has its expected value calculated using an equation completely different from Poisson, Bernoulli, Binomial or any known distribution. Predefining the distribution of the dataset is used in estimating the parameters in parametric machine learning methods. When the distribution is not known, non-parametric or kernel methods are used. Bayesian methods are probabilistic methods that rely on understanding the data distribution. These methods are generative because they know how samples are generated in each class, rather than the discriminative machine learning methods that can only identify the sample's class without creating a complete generative model. The assumption of Gaussian distributions because of the central limit theorem has failed in many situations. Some analysts justify the 2008 financial crises to be caused by this assumption in banking and financial modelling and prediction software (Watts, 2016).

Data often come from various distributions and mixtures of Gaussians. Studying the data distribution properly leads to appropriate analysis. Often there are latent variables that are not directly observed in the dataset that methods like factor analysis reveal. Chapter two will explain these methods and more as we proceed. There is a lot to learn about the various data distribution shapes, expected variable, standard deviation calculations, and their effects on building a model. Books such as (Sun and Kim, 2020), (Downey, 2013) cover topics required to understand parametric Bayes, and a deep dive into the non-parametric Bayes will make it even clearer, such as in (Ghosal and Vaart, 2017).

1.3.4 Graph Structures

Graphs are made up of vertices and edges, where edges are defined as ordered pairs of vertices, like (i,j). A graph with n vertices and m edges can be represented as an $n \times n$ matrix M, where M[i,j] denotes the number (or weight) of edges from vertex i to vertex j. There are surprising connections between combinatorial properties and linear algebra, such as the relationship between paths in graphs and matrix multiplication and how vertex clusters relate to the eigenvalues/vectors of appropriate matrices.

Tensors elements can be sparse, and the coordinate connecting them is not steadily growing to contain data points in every unit increment across all coordinates. A Manifold of points in a dataset can be connected (mapped) to a lower dimension embedding forming a network or a graph structure that does not need to follow a Euclidean coordinate system. The graph structure of the gas distribution example earlier is illustrated in Figure 4. Various schematic higher dimension graph representations are shown in Figure 5, such as a graph is just the data structure representing the entity, such as a real value or class in a. A one-dimensional tensor (vector) is represented with one arrow connecting two points and can be extended to more points on the same single dimension. A two-dimension tensor (matrix) is represented with a graph with two arrows at every node, representing every change of coordinate value. Similarly, in the d to f illustrations in Figure 5, you will find that each node has arrows in each dimension to connect to the previous or following index value on that coordinate.

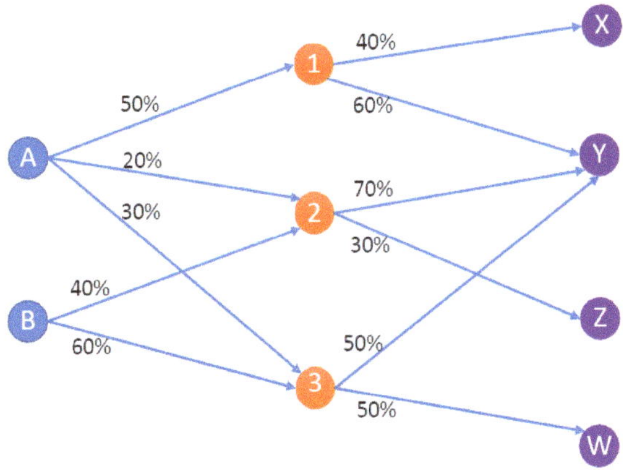

Figure 4: Gas Distribution Example Graph structure

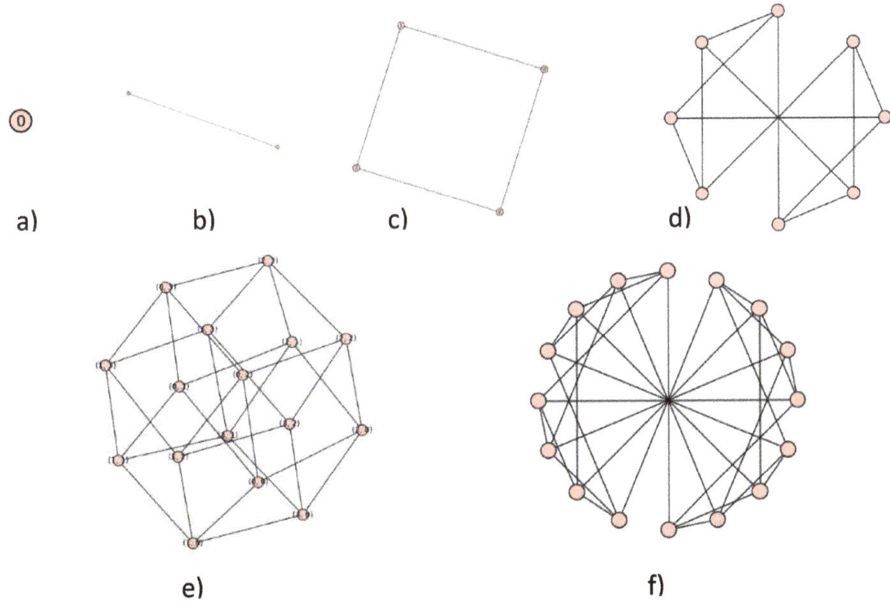

Figure 5: Tensors Graph Structures: a) scalar, b) 2D, c) 3D, d) 4D, e) 5D, and f) 6D

Python has several stable packages implementing graph/network data structures with various analysis tools and efficient parallel implementation. Python-igraph is the set of Python bindings for igraph, a collection of network analysis tools emphasising efficiency, portability and ease of use. NetworkX is another package for the creation, manipulation, and study of the structure, dynamics, and functions of complex networks. It is implemented based on NumPy and SciPy and therefore supports all common platforms. Graph-tool is yet another efficient package for manipulation and statistical analysis of graphs, based on the C++ Boost Graph Library and parallelised using OpenMP.

Chapter 2: Subspace Learning

This chapter provides a tour through matrix-based (two-dimensional) methods to analyse a dataset. As mentioned in chapter one, datasets are present in matrix forms, in which a row is a sample or separate entity described by values (elements of a vector or tuple) given in the columns representing the different features. Each feature is a dimension of this dataset with a random variable in an acceptable domain of values with a minimum, maximum, mean, median, standard deviation, variance and covariance with other dimensions. These measures explain the dynamics or the structure of the dataset of the sample being studied. Various methods explain the different levels of analysis, such as:

- Descriptive statistics of the sample. These will be described in section 2.1.
    - Analysing the variance and covariance of the features observed or measured.
- Inferential statistics methods infer new knowledge based on the dataset sample provided. This can be a causal analysis or prediction of future values.
- Linear subspace learning (LSL) reduces the data dimensionality using various methods. These methods are divided into projective methods and manifold modelling methods.
    - The projective methods identify latent variables, factors or indicators that are unobserved in the dataset but explain the correlations between the observed variables. This is useful for feature extraction and reducing the dimensionality of a dataset. These methods use linear projections such as principal component analysis (PCA), Singular Value Decomposition (SVD), independent component analysis (ICA), linear discriminant analysis (LDA), canonical correlation analysis (CCA), and partial least squares (PLS), Factor Analysis (FA), Non-Negative Matrix Factorisation (NMF), and the generalised Nyström method. These will be described in section 2.2.
    - The manifold modelling methods learn a lower-dimensional manifold containing that data points that are embedded in the original high-dimensional space preserving the non-linear structures ignored in the projective methods. Multidimensional scaling (MDS) maps the original dataset to a lower-dimensional manifold without modelling the manifold. Methods that model the lower-dimensional manifolds include Isometric Feature map (Isomap), locally linear embedding, and spectral clustering. These will be described in section 2.3.
- Sometimes the data are not separable in the lower dimension, and mapping to a higher dimension makes it linearly separable there. The SVM and the Kernel trick will be described in section 2.4, and the Kernel trick will be further explained using representation theory in chapter five.
- Multimodal and heterogenous datasets analysis (multiway). This process is called multilinear subspace learning (MSL), which **directly** extracts features from their multidimensional space to lower-dimensional space. These will be discussed in chapters three and onward.

2.1 Descriptive statistics and analytic statistics

Descriptive statistics explain the values of features captured in 2-dimensional arrays. A complete review of statistical analysis with python is found in books such as (Farrell, 2020). This book will review only the statistical concepts that we will need in the remaining discussions in this or the following chapters. The simplest understanding of a dataset's (column x out of d dimensional columns containing N values in rows), numerical values domains is performed by identifying the minimum, the maximum, the mean $\bar{x} = \frac{1}{N}\sum_{i=o}^{N-1} x_i$, the median =

$\begin{cases} x\left[\frac{N+1}{2}\right] & if\ N\ is\ odd \\ \frac{x\left[\frac{N}{2}\right]+x\left[\frac{N}{2}+1\right]}{2} & if\ N\ is\ even \end{cases}$, which is the value at the middle index, the mode (the most occurring value), and the first, second, and third quartile. To identify how the values are distributed around the mean and towards the extreme values, a standard deviation is calculated as the square root of the average of the squared difference of each value of x and the mean $\overline{x}$, $std\ dev\ (x) = \sqrt{\frac{\sum_{i=0}^{n-1}(x_i - \bar{x})^2}{n-1}}$. The variance is the standard deviation squared, which is a more stable metric. The mean and the standard deviation are the main metrics of the central limit theorem illustrated in the normal (Gaussian) distribution. This is considered first-order statistics.

On the other side, an analysis of the observed features' variance can explain the dataset's structure and how the observed features change together and affect each other. The variance of a variable is defined as the squared standard deviation. The covariance between two features in the dataset explains how a change in one value can or can not affect the other. A covariance between two features, x and y vectors, is measured as $\sum = cov\ (x, y) = \frac{\sum_{i=0}^{n-1}(x_i - \bar{x})(y_i - \bar{y})}{n-1}$. A covariance square matrix is measured for all covariances between all features and each other, in which the diagonal values are the variance of one feature with its mean, and it is calculated as follows:

$$\begin{bmatrix} var(x_0) & \cdots & cov\ (x_{n-1}, x_0) \\ \vdots & \ddots & \vdots \\ cov\ (x_0, x_{n-1}) & \cdots & var(x_{n-1}) \end{bmatrix}$$

A correlation coefficient r between two features x and y is measured as $r = \frac{cov(x,y)}{\sqrt{var(x)var(y)}}$

The correlation coefficient r ranges from -1, indicating negative correlation (inverse proportional features, an increase in one causes a decrease in the other), going through 0, indicating uncorrelated features, to 1, indicating positive correlation (proportional features, an increase in one causes an increase in the other). The outcome is identifying redundant features that do not add much information by being highly correlated with another feature in the dataset. This information is captured by linear Algebra as second-order statistics. The remaining chapters in the book will handle the cases of multilinear algebra, which is considered higher-order statistics.

The above-explained statistical methods handle the observed features as measured without the required extra preprocessing steps of handling missing values, sample size, unbalanced datasets, power analysis, standardisation and others to complete an efficient statistical analysis of a dataset. Books such as (Farrell, 2020) can be checked for complete statistical analysis reference. The following methods of dimensionality reductions are applied to reduce the number of features/variables to include only the features that contribute more to the variance using well-preprocessed datasets.

2.2 Projective Methods - Linear Subspace Learning (LSL)

We have learned in chapter one that vectors usually are members of a vector space under linear transformations of addition and scalar multiplication. Learning a low-dimensional subspace representing a dataset is the primary method in dimensionality reduction that does not lose much information. When we multiply a vector v in a higher dimension m by a linear transformation matrix M of rows equals the high dimensions of the input vector m, and the required lower dimension in columns as n, this process projects the input vector v to the lower dimension vector u specified by the projection matrix M. $vM = u$, where $v \in \mathbb{R}^m, M \in \mathbb{R}^{m \times n}, u \in \mathbb{R}^n$. Various algorithms learn matrix M that is most suitable for various assumptions and objectives.

For example, the principal component analysis method reduces the dimensionality while capturing the most variance, using transformation matrix M of the eigenvectors of the dataset, which will be further explained below. Also, Dictionary Learning algorithms aim to estimate from the known observations X, the sparse dictionary vectors, and the Mixing Matrix of these vectors constructing the observations. The estimated dictionary vectors should be as sparse as possible, so combinations of these dictionary vectors can represent a high dimensional large dataset. Similarly, Factor Analysis algorithms estimate hidden/latent factors and their effects on the observations. Example Application is extracting sources in Blind Source Separation (BSS) problem; BSS aims to learn separate data components representing an entangled dataset. Each algorithm adds additional constraints to be suitable for different problems. Estimating two unknowns from one known is an underdetermined system of equations on which various iterative algorithms are proposed.

Linear Subspace Learning (LSL) methods identify various structures in matrices using various approaches, including projections and mixing from shared dictionary elements or latent factors and also decomposition. Matrix decomposition help identify the dynamics of a dataset such that the complexity can be reduced by identifying lower-rank components interacting together to form the higher-rank dataset. The simplest matrix decomposition is the rank-1 decomposition of a given matrix X of linearly dependent columns, such that $X=ab^T$, where a and b are two vectors that can construct matrix X as follows:

$$X = \begin{bmatrix} 1 & 2 & 3 \\ 2 & 4 & 6 \\ 3 & 6 & 9 \end{bmatrix} = \begin{bmatrix} 1 & 2 & 3 \end{bmatrix} \begin{bmatrix} 1 \\ 2 \\ 3 \end{bmatrix}$$

This is generalised as rank-R factorisation, such that X is composed of R rank-1 components: $X = a_1 b_1^T + \cdots + a_R b_R^T = AB^T$. This will be further explained in the Singular Value Decomposition (SVD) later as the foundation for matrix compression and completion algorithms.

These two-way analysis methods apply covariance analysis between the features' pairs or other pair-wise statistical analyses. We can repeat the data collection in different time slots adding a third dimension to the time series. We can also divide a column into groups such as age groups 1-3, 3-5, and so forth. We can correlate different entities/objects (like students and subjects) using different variables (exam scores, teachers, sessions, ... etc), in which different modes will describe either an object or a variable based on the analysis requirements. This needs a three-way analysis or higher that will gradually be described in this book starting from chapter three.

Among various LSL algorithms, principal component analysis (PCA) and linear discriminant analysis (LDA) are the two most widely used in many applications. PCA is an unsupervised algorithm that does not require labels for the training samples, while LDA is a supervised method that makes use of class-specific information (Lu, Plataniotis and Venetsanopoulos, 2011).

2.2.1 Motivational Problem

A motivational problem will illustrate how to model a real-life problem into a matrix and what the eigenpairs represent to help understand eigenvalues and eigenvectors. The following example is from (Carter, 1995) and formulated using methods from (Geijn, 2012). The following table shows how three pizza kitchens on campus, labelled by their locations as A, B, and C, historically deliver pizza to all locations. Figure 6 illustrates the transition matrix of drivers' locations on the left and the graph representing the transitions on the right.

	A	B	C
A	0.3	0.3	0.4
B	0.4	0.4	0.2
C	0.5	0.3	0.2

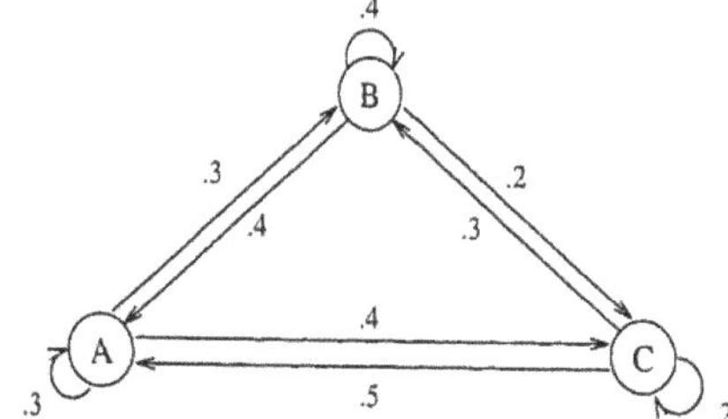

Figure 6: Pizza delivery drivers' location distribution transition matrix and graph.

The first row in this table is interpreted as follows: Kitchen in location A delivers 30% of the calls it receives to location A, 30% to location B, and 40% to location C. The other two rows read the same. Delivery drivers start from the row location and end at the column location after one delivery based on the given probability distribution. The rows are the probability distribution of all possibilities and sum to 1. A driver must be at one of the three locations.

Let $p_{BB}^{(K)}$denote the probability that a driver starts at location B and ends at location B after k deliveries

Let $p_{Ac}^{(k)}$ denote the probability that a driver starts at location A and ends at location C after k deliveries.

Same for $p_{AA}^{(k)}, p_{AB}^{(k)}, p_{Ac}^{(k)}, p_{BA}^{(k)}, p_{BB}^{(k)}, p_{Bc}^{(k)}, p_{CA}^{(k)}, p_{CB}^{(k)}$, and $p_{CC}^{(k)}$

Then predicting if a driver starts at C, what is the probability it will be at B after 2 deliveries? Based on probabilities in the first move:

$p_{CB}^{(2)} = p_{CA}^{(1)}p_{AB}^{(2)} + p_{CB}^{(1)}p_{BB}^{(2)} + p_{CC}^{(1)}p_{CB}^{(2)}$=0.33

Notice that this is the dot product between row 3 (C) and column 2 (B).

Another example is if a driver starts at B, the probability of being at B after two deliveries are:

$p_{BB}^{(2)} = p_{BA}^{(1)}p_{AB}^{(2)} + p_{BB}^{(1)}p_{BB}^{(2)} + p_{BC}^{(1)}p_{CB}^{(2)}$=0.34

This is the dot product between row B and column B:

$p_{CC}^{(2)} = 0.2\ p_s^{(k)} + 0.4\ p_c^{(k)} + 0.3\ p_r^{(k)}$

$p_l^{(k)}$ is the probability vector denoting a driver's probability after k deliveries starting from location l, using the probabilities represented as a (transition) matrix S:

$$p_l^{(k)} = \begin{bmatrix} p_{lA}^{(k)} \\ p_{lB}^{(k)} \\ p_{lC}^{(k)} \end{bmatrix}, \ S = \begin{bmatrix} 0.3 & 0.3 & 0.4 \\ 0.4 & 0.4 & 0.2 \\ 0.5 & 0.3 & 0.2 \end{bmatrix}$$

The transition from delivery number k to delivery k+1 is then written as the matrix-vector product (multiplication).

$$\begin{bmatrix} p_l^{(k+1)} \\ p_l^{(k+1)} \\ p_l^{(k+1)} \end{bmatrix} = \begin{bmatrix} 0.3 & 0.3 & 0.4 \\ 0.4 & 0.4 & 0.2 \\ 0.5 & 0.3 & 0.2 \end{bmatrix} \begin{bmatrix} p_l^{(k)} \\ p_l^{(k)} \\ p_l^{(k)} \end{bmatrix}$$

To know all probabilities from all locations to all locations after two deliveries, we can do matrix-matrix multiplication two times: S^2.

$$S^2 = \begin{bmatrix} 0.42 & 0.32 & 0.26 \\ 0.38 & 0.34 & 0.28 \\ 0.37 & 0.33 & 0.30 \end{bmatrix}$$

We can easily now calculate where all drivers will be after three deliveries by another matrix multiplication, tracing where they start at the rows and where they end on the columns:

$$S^2S = S^3 = \begin{bmatrix} 0.42 & 0.32 & 0.26 \\ 0.38 & 0.34 & 0.28 \\ 0.37 & 0.33 & 0.30 \end{bmatrix} \begin{bmatrix} 0.3 & 0.3 & 0.4 \\ 0.4 & 0.4 & 0.2 \\ 0.5 & 0.3 & 0.2 \end{bmatrix} = \begin{bmatrix} 0.385 & 0.333 & 0.282 \\ 0.390 & 0.334 & 0.276 \\ 0.393 & 0.333 & 0.274 \end{bmatrix}$$

Repeating this process using Python rather than by hand, we can find the probabilities for the drivers' location distribution for the next eight days:

```
import   numpy   as   np
S = np.array(
    [[0.3, 0.3, 0.4],
    [0.4, 0.4, 0.2],
    [0.5,0.3,0.2]])
p = S
for k in range(8):
    print(p)
    p =  p.dot(S)
```

$S^{(k)}$	$S^{(1)}$	$S^{(2)}$
	$\begin{bmatrix} 0.3 & 0.3 & 0.4 \\ 0.4 & 0.4 & 0.2 \\ 0.5 & 0.3 & 0.2 \end{bmatrix}$	$\begin{bmatrix} 0.41 & 0.33 & 0.26 \\ 0.38 & 0.34 & 0.28 \\ 0.37 & 0.33 & 0.30 \end{bmatrix}$
$S^{(k)}$	$S^{(3)}$	$S^{(4)}$
	$\begin{bmatrix} 0.385 & 0.333 & 0.282 \\ 0.390 & 0.334 & 0.276 \\ 0.393 & 0.333 & 0.274 \end{bmatrix}$	$\begin{bmatrix} 0.3897 & 0.3333 & 0.2770 \\ 0.3886 & 0.3334 & 0.2780 \\ 0.3881 & 0.3333 & 0.2786 \end{bmatrix}$
$S^{(k)}$	$S^{(5)}$	$S^{(6)}$
	$\begin{bmatrix} 0.38873 & 0.33333 & 0.27794 \\ 0.38894 & 0.33334 & 0.27772 \\ 0.38905 & 0.33333 & 0.27762 \end{bmatrix}$	$\begin{bmatrix} 0.388921 & 0.333333 & 0.277746 \\ 0.388878 & 0.333334 & 0.277788 \\ 0.388857 & 0.333333 & 0.277810 \end{bmatrix}$
$S^{(k)}$	$S^{(7)}$	$S^{(8)}$
	$\begin{bmatrix} 0.3888825 & 0.3333333 & 0.2777842 \\ 0.3888910 & 0.3333334 & 0.2777756 \\ 0.3888953 & 0.3333333 & 0.2777714 \end{bmatrix}$	$\begin{bmatrix} 0.38889017 & 0.33333333 & 0.2777765 \\ 0.38888846 & 0.33333334 & 0.2777782 \\ 0.38888761 & 0.33333333 & 0.27777906 \end{bmatrix}$

Observe that the prediction starts to change less and less as we go from one delivery to the next in the future. As columns change less and less below a specified threshold, we say that the system converges.

If a vector of the initial distribution of drivers per location, such as [0.3, 0.3, 0.3], is multiplied by S, it will show the distribution of drivers after one delivery:

$$p^{(1)} = [0.3 \quad 0.3 \quad 0.3] \begin{bmatrix} 0.3 & 0.3 & 0.4 \\ 0.4 & 0.4 & 0.2 \\ 0.5 & 0.3 & 0.2 \end{bmatrix} = [0.36 \quad 0.3 \quad 0.24]$$

After two deliveries throughout the day, S^2, the right-hand side, will converge to the same number no matter what we started from.

$$p^{(2)} = [0.3 \quad 0.3 \quad 0.3] \begin{bmatrix} 0.42 & 0.32 & 0.26 \\ 0.38 & 0.34 & 0.28 \\ 0.37 & 0.33 & 0.30 \end{bmatrix} = [0.3504 \quad 0.3 \quad 0.2496]$$

After nine deliveries throughout the day, S^9, the right-hand side, will converge to the same number no matter what we started from.

$$p^{(9)} = [0.3 \quad 0.3 \quad 0.3] \begin{bmatrix} 0.38888894 & 0.33333333 & 0.27777773 \\ 0.38888887 & 0.33333333 & 0.27777779 \\ 0.38888884 & 0.33333333 & 0.27777783 \end{bmatrix} = [0.35 \quad 0.3 \quad 0.25]$$

From the 10th delivery onward, it converges to this driver's location vector and does not change any future: $[0.35 \quad 0.33 \quad 0.25]$

If we continue to predict the drivers' locations after many deliveries from now by executing the previous python loop for 64 iterations for the same probability distributions of calls and deliveries, we will observe that the prediction does not change very much. The resulting drivers' location vectors will predict the typical location probability distribution they might be at after any number of deliveries.

If we change the initial drivers' locations vector to reflect any initial distributions, we will also end up with the same typical drivers' locations prediction. At any given time step, 35% of the drivers will be at location A, 33% at location B, and 25% at location C. The drivers' initial distribution should not change the typical distribution after several deliveries.

These are called **Markov Processes**. These kinds of techniques apply to many problems. For example, the Google page rank algorithm determines which website is the most important (highest rank) based on the probability that the user will select the page link from several incoming links to other pages. Another example is predicting the next day's weather based on today's weather using probabilities collected over several days in a given location.

We predicted the next drivers' location distribution after one delivery by multiplying the probabilities of calls' location distribution and transitions in matrix S by the current drivers' location distribution: $\mathbf{d}^{(k+1)} = \mathbf{Sd}^{(k)}$, which can be extended to any number of deliveries prediction by $\mathbf{d}^{(k)} = \mathbf{S}^k\mathbf{d}^{(0)}$, to observe that eventually $\mathbf{d}^{(k+1)} \approx \mathbf{Sd}^{(k)}$. This diminished change means that $\mathbf{d}^{(k+1)}$ came arbitrarily close to an eigenvector, x, associated with the eigenvalue $\lambda = 1$ of matrix S: $\mathbf{Sx} = \lambda\mathbf{x}$. For stochastic transition matrices, the dominant Eigenvalue λ is 1 according to Perron–Frobenius theorem (Cairns, 2016).

The dominant Eigenvector represents the typical drivers' location distribution in the previous example. This is known as the **(algebraic) eigenvalue problem**. Scalars λ that satisfy $Ax = \lambda x$ for non-zero vector x are known as Eigenvalues, while the corresponding non-zero vector x to each λ Eigenvalue is known as Eigenvectors. From the previous calculations, we can answer questions like "what is the typical drivers' location distribution for this Pizza kitchen calls' distribution?" (Answer: 35% at A, 33% at B, and 25% at C). A similar approach can be used to answer questions like "what is the most requested pizza topping in a given order?"

The **power method** finds an eigenvector associated with the largest Eigenvalue (in magnitude). It starts by guessing an initial value for x, then loops multiplying Ax to get new x, optionally dividing the new x by the last element of the previous value (or any normalisation step) until the new value does not change (much) anymore. The dominant Eigenvalue is the Rayleigh quotient of eigenvector x, which is $\frac{x^T A x}{x^T x}$.

```
import numpy as np
rand=np.random.RandomState(235)
A = np.array(rand.random(size=(3, 3)))
x = np.array(rand.random(size=3))
x_Old = np.array(rand.random(size=3))
i=0
while np.isclose(x, x_Old).all() == False:
    i=i+1
    x_Old = x
    x =  A.dot(x)
    if x[-1] != 0:
        x = np.true_divide(x, x[-1])
    print("i: ", i, " x = ", x)
```

Matrices, Markov chains, Eigenvalues, and Eigenvectors have many real-world applications. There are many, many examples of the use of Markov chains. A brief look at some significant applications can be found in (VON HILGERS and LANGVILLE†, no date) (Geijn, 2012) (Carter, 1995).

2.2.2 Eigendecomposition

The algebraic eigenvalue problem is a matrix decomposition method that reveals various algebraic properties that make working with matrices easier. Scalars $\boldsymbol{\lambda}$ are the eigenvalues of matrix A that satisfy Ax = $\boldsymbol{\lambda}$x for non-zero eigenvectors x. The pizza delivery drivers' location distribution examples in the previous section illustrate how a Markov Process uses a transition Matrix, such that the power method converges to the most dominant Eigenvector corresponding to the largest Eigenvalue, which was 1 for transition matrices. Then we saw how to generalise the power method to identify the most dominant eigenpair for any given non-transition matrices using the Rayleigh quotient for the dominant Eigenvalue. We need another method to find all eigenvalues and corresponding eigenvectors (eigenpairs). Eigenvalues and eigenvectors often explain the bases that are invariant to linear transformations. All eigenvalues are non-negative, real numbers because covariance matrices are symmetric and positive semi-definite. Eigenvalues can be found as the roots of the characteristic polynomial (Margalit and Rabinoff, 2019).
In Python:

```
# eigen decomposition of a matrix A
from numpy import linalg as LA
eignVal, eignVec = LA.eig(A)
```

2x2 Matrix Example:

To find the Eigenvalues and Eigenvectors of a matrix A ∈ $\mathbb{R}^{2\times 2}$ = $\begin{bmatrix} 7 & 3 \\ 3 & -1 \end{bmatrix}$, we need to perform the following steps:

Step 1: Find the characteristic polynomial of $\boldsymbol{A}$. Since $Ix = x$ for any given vector x and the identity matrix I, then Ax= $\lambda\boldsymbol{I}$x, therefore Ax- $\lambda\boldsymbol{I}$x = 0 → (A- $\lambda\boldsymbol{I}$)x = 0, for Eigenvector x and Eigenvalue λ. Since x should be a non-zero vector, solving for (A- $\lambda\boldsymbol{I}$) = 0 by calculating the determinant is called the characteristic equation. This will find the non-zero solution.

$\boldsymbol{M}$=$\boldsymbol{A}$-$\lambda\boldsymbol{I}$ = $\begin{bmatrix} 7-\lambda & 3 \\ 3 & -1-\lambda \end{bmatrix}$

Det(M) = |$\boldsymbol{M}$|=|$\boldsymbol{A}$-$\lambda\boldsymbol{I}$| , using the 2x2 determinant rule:

$= \begin{bmatrix} 7-\lambda & 3 \\ 3 & -1-\lambda \end{bmatrix}$

$= (7-\lambda)(-1-\lambda) - 9 = \lambda^2 - 6\lambda - 16 = (\lambda - 8)(\lambda + 2)$

The characteristic polynomial of a 2×2 matrix is generalised for matrix $A = \begin{bmatrix} a & b \\ c & d \end{bmatrix}$, as = $\lambda^2 - (a+d)\lambda + (ad - bc) = \lambda 2 - Tr(A)\lambda + det(A)$.

Step 2: Find the roots of the characteristic polynomial of $\boldsymbol{A}$ to obtain the Eigenvalues of $\boldsymbol{A}$.

$(\lambda - 8)(\lambda + 2) = 0$ **Then the roots are** $\lambda_1 = 8, \lambda_2 = -2$

Step 3: Repeat the following (i) and (ii) steps for each Eigenvalue λ of $\boldsymbol{A}$

For Eigenvalue $\lambda_1 = 8$:	For Eigenvalue $\lambda_2 = -2$:
(i)Form the matrix $\boldsymbol{M}$=$\boldsymbol{A}$−8$\boldsymbol{I}$	(i)Form the matrix $\boldsymbol{M}$=$\boldsymbol{A}$+2$\boldsymbol{I}$
$\begin{bmatrix} 7-8 & 3 \\ 3 & -1-8 \end{bmatrix} = \begin{bmatrix} -1 & 3 \\ 3 & -9 \end{bmatrix}$	$\begin{bmatrix} 7+2 & 3 \\ 3 & -1+2 \end{bmatrix} = \begin{bmatrix} 9 & 3 \\ 3 & 1 \end{bmatrix}$
(ii)Find the solution of $\boldsymbol{Mx}$=(These non-zero vectors are linearly independent Eigenvectors of $\boldsymbol{A}$ belonging to λ.)	(ii)Find the solution of $\boldsymbol{Mx}$=(These non-zero vectors are linearly independent Eigenvectors of $\boldsymbol{A}$ belonging to λ.)
$\begin{bmatrix} -1 & 3 \\ 3 & -9 \end{bmatrix}\begin{bmatrix} x_1 \\ x_2 \end{bmatrix} = 0$	$\begin{bmatrix} 9 & 3 \\ 3 & 1 \end{bmatrix}\begin{bmatrix} x_1 \\ x_2 \end{bmatrix} = 0$
$-x_1 + 3x_2 = 0$, and $3x_1 - 9x_2 = 0$	$9x_1 + 3x_2 = 0$, and $3x_1 + x_2 = 0$
Then $x_1 = 3x_2$	Then $3x_1 = -x_2$

The Eigenvector x= $\begin{bmatrix}3x_1\\x_1\end{bmatrix}$, or $x_1\begin{bmatrix}3\\1\end{bmatrix}$, for $x_1 \neq 0$ such that $\begin{bmatrix}3\\1\end{bmatrix}$, $\begin{bmatrix}9\\3\end{bmatrix}$ are possible Eigenvectors.	The Eigenvector x= $\begin{bmatrix}x_1\\-3x_1\end{bmatrix}$ or $x_1\begin{bmatrix}1\\-3\end{bmatrix}$ for $x_1 \neq 0$ such that $\begin{bmatrix}1\\-3\end{bmatrix}$, $\begin{bmatrix}3\\-9\end{bmatrix}$ are possible Eigenvectors.

3x3 Matrix Example:

To find the Eigenvalues and Eigenvectors of a matrix A ∈ $\mathbb{R}^{3\times 3}$ = $\begin{bmatrix}4 & 1 & -1\\2 & 5 & -2\\1 & 1 & 2\end{bmatrix}$, we follow the same steps as above:

Step 1: Find the characteristic polynomial of $\boldsymbol{A}$.

$$\boldsymbol{M}=\boldsymbol{A}-\lambda\boldsymbol{I} = \begin{bmatrix}4-\lambda & 1 & -1\\2 & 5-\lambda & -2\\1 & 1 & 2-\lambda\end{bmatrix}$$

Det(M) = $|\boldsymbol{M}|=|\boldsymbol{A}-\lambda\boldsymbol{I}|$, using the 3x3 determinant rule:

$$=\begin{bmatrix}4-\lambda & 1 & -1\\2 & 5-\lambda & -2\\1 & 1 & 2-\lambda\end{bmatrix}\begin{matrix}4-\lambda & 1\\2 & 5-\lambda\\1 & 1\end{matrix}$$

$$= (4-\lambda)(5-\lambda)(2-\lambda) - 2 - 2 + (5-\lambda) + 2(4-\lambda) - 2(2-\lambda)$$

$$= -\lambda^3 + 11\lambda^2 - 39\lambda + 45 = -(\lambda-5)(\lambda-3)^2$$

Step 2: Find the roots of the characteristic polynomial of $\boldsymbol{A}$ to obtain the eigenvalues of $\boldsymbol{A}$.

$-(\lambda-5)(\lambda-3)^2 = 0$ **The roots are** $\lambda_1 = 5, \lambda_2 = 3$

Step 3: Repeat (i) and (ii) for each eigenvalue λ of $\boldsymbol{A}$

For Eigenvalue $\lambda_1 = 5$: (i)Form the matrix $\boldsymbol{M}$=$\boldsymbol{A}$−5$\boldsymbol{I}$ $\begin{bmatrix}4-5 & 1 & -1\\2 & 5-5 & -2\\1 & 1 & 2-5\end{bmatrix} = \begin{bmatrix}-1 & 1 & -1\\2 & 0 & -2\\1 & 1 & -3\end{bmatrix}$ (ii)Find the solution of $\boldsymbol{Mx}$=(These non-zero vectors are linearly independent Eigenvectors of $\boldsymbol{A}$ belonging to λ.) $\begin{bmatrix}-1 & 1 & -1\\2 & 0 & -2\\1 & 1 & -3\end{bmatrix}\begin{bmatrix}x_1\\x_2\\x_3\end{bmatrix} = 0$ Then $x_1 = x_3, x_2 = 2x_1$ The Eigenvector x= $\begin{bmatrix}x_1\\2x_1\\x_1\end{bmatrix}$, or $x_1\begin{bmatrix}1\\2\\1\end{bmatrix}$, for $x_1 \neq 0$ such that $\begin{bmatrix}1\\2\\1\end{bmatrix}$ is one possible Eigenvector.	For Eigenvalue $\lambda_2 = 3$: (i)Form the matrix $\boldsymbol{M}$=$\boldsymbol{A}$−3$\boldsymbol{I}$ $\begin{bmatrix}4-3 & 1 & -1\\2 & 5-3 & -2\\1 & 1 & 2-3\end{bmatrix} = \begin{bmatrix}1 & 1 & -1\\2 & 2 & -2\\1 & 1 & -1\end{bmatrix}$ (ii)Find the solution of $\boldsymbol{Mx}$=(These non-zero vectors are linearly independent Eigenvectors of $\boldsymbol{A}$ belonging to λ.) $\begin{bmatrix}1 & 1 & -1\\2 & 2 & -2\\1 & 1 & -1\end{bmatrix}\begin{bmatrix}x_1\\x_2\\x_3\end{bmatrix} = 0$ Then $x_1 + x_2 = x_3$ The Eigenvector x= $\begin{bmatrix}x_1\\x_2\\x_1+x_2\end{bmatrix}$, or $x_1\begin{bmatrix}1\\0\\1\end{bmatrix}$ + $x_2\begin{bmatrix}0\\1\\1\end{bmatrix}$, for $x_1 \neq 0, x_2 \neq 0$, such that $\begin{bmatrix}1\\1\\2\end{bmatrix}$ is one possible Eigenvector.

PS the Product of Eigenvalues is equal to the determinant of the matrix. For the First example, det(A) = det $\begin{pmatrix}7 & 3\\3 & -1\end{pmatrix}$ = −16 and the product of the eigenvalues = 8 x -2 = -16. For the second example, det(A) = 4 . det $\begin{pmatrix}5 & -2\\1 & 2\end{pmatrix}$-1 . det $\begin{pmatrix}2 & -2\\1 & 2\end{pmatrix}$-1 . det $\begin{pmatrix}2 & 5\\1 & 1\end{pmatrix}$ = 45, and the product of the eigenvalues = $5 \times 3 \times 3 = 45$.

Eigenvalues and Eigenvectors of a square matrix have many applications in Communication systems, engineering disciplines such as in designing bridges, art applications such as music composition, and signal processing such as designing car stereo systems and concert halls, among many more. An online calculator can be found at https://www.symbolab.com/solver/matrix-eigenvalues-calculator.

This simple method is not computationally efficient for larger matrices, as it might attempt to create memory a typical computer might not have. An algorithm based on the QR factorisation is used, and various iterative methods are similar to the power method and its convergence criteria. Calling any of these functions, such as numpy.linalg.eig, usually achieve speed-ups by employing the available hardware in the machine to process the computation in parallel.

Another computational consideration is the Roundoff errors. These affect small and large matrices equally. $\frac{1}{3}$ is stored as a rounded decimal point figure using normal notation. In normal notation, a number is written as m x 10^a where $0.1 \leq |m| < 1$. (In scientific notation, $1 \leq |m| < 10$), where m is mantissa and a is abscissa. The number 1234 is represented as 0.1234 x 10^4, mantissa = 0.1234 and abscissa = 4. This representation affects the accuracy of any numerical calculations, particularly multiplication. This is why the log of any value is often used to turn multiplication into an addition operation.

2.2.3 Principal Component Analysis (PCA)

The principal components analysis is defined as linear feature projection on new **orthogonal** coordinates such that it captures the most variance in the first coordinate (principal component) and lesser remaining variance in decreasing order in the following coordinates. Adding the orthogonality objective makes the computation of approximate solutions to systems of equations Ax = b easier, as explained in chapter six of (Margalit and Rabinoff, 2019), published at https://textbooks.math.gatech.edu/ila/chap-orthogonality.html. These principal components are the eigenvectors of the dataset and are orthogonal to each other to be considered uncorrelated latent factors, and found using constraint optimisation procedure by adding the constraints as Lagrange multipliers. For more information about optimisation and Lagrange multipliers, refer to Appendix E in (Bishop, 2006) and the documentation in scipy.optimize Python package. Finding the projection of the original dataset onto the most significant initial principal components (typically 2 or 3) will produce an uncorrelated model that captures the most variance of the original dataset in which the signal-to-noise ratio is highest. The steps to calculate the PCA are simply calculating the eigenvectors of the covariance matrix of a dataset.
PCA can be calculated using a direct projection matrix such that $y = U^T x$, where $y \in \mathbb{R}^p$ is the projected data, $U \in \mathbb{R}^{m \times p}$ is the projection matrix containing the p Eigenvectors, and $x \in \mathbb{R}^m = (x_m - \bar{x})$ is the centred m-dimensional dataset standardised to zero-mean. This standardisation is achieved in Python by:

```
x = x-np.mean(x)
# or the following for normalisation as well
x = (x-np.mean(x))/np.std(x)
# equivalantly
from scipy import stats
x = stats.zscore(x)
```

The projected dataset on each principal component u_i will produce a new lower dimension dataset, on which a component C_j for $0 \leq j \leq p-1$ (p being the lower dimension number of components capturing the most variance) will be a weighted sum of the original dataset features:
$C_j = w_1(x_1) + w_2(x_2) + \ldots + w_n(x_n)$.
One possible constrained optimisation steps to calculate the principal components maximising the variance from the covariance matrix are as follows:
Step 1: Center the dataset around zero means.

$$1.\ X = \forall m\ (x_m - \bar{x})$$

Step 2: Calculate the scatter matrix S_T of the dataset as the covariance matrix multiplied by (m-1)

$$2.\ S_T = \sum_{m=1}^{M} x_m x_m^T = XX^T$$

Step 3: Solve for the first component as the unit vector $||u_1|| = 1$ maximising the variance:

3. $\widehat{u_1} = \underset{u_1}{\text{argmax}}\, u_1^T S_T u_1$ subject to $u_1^T u_1 = 1$ as a normalisation constraint.
4. This can be solved by Lagrange multiplier λ to include the constraint in the equation: $\psi = u_1^T S_T u_1 - \lambda(u_1^T u_1 - 1)$
    1. Then we minimise by differentiating with respect to u_1: and set to 0,

$$\frac{\delta\psi}{\delta u_1} = \mathrm{S}_T u_1 - \lambda u_1 = (\mathrm{S}_T - \lambda\mathrm{I})u_1 = 0$$

Therefore, λ and u_1 are an Eigenvalue, and its corresponding Eigenvector of S_T and the quantity to be maximised is: $u_1^T S_T u_1 = u_1^T \lambda u_1 = \lambda u_1^T u_1 = \lambda I = \lambda$. This will be the largest Eigenvalue λ_1, and the corresponding Eigenvector u_1 as the first principal component.

Step 4: Solve for remaining p components by adding the orthogonality constraints by repeating steps 5:7 for each Eigenvector. For example, solving for u_2 require the following steps:

5. $\widehat{u_2} = \underset{u_2}{\text{argmax}}\, u_2^T S_T u_2$ subject to $u_2^T u_2 = 1$ as a normalisation constraint and $u_2^T u_1 = 0$ as the orthogonality constraint with the previous Eigenvector.
6. Again use the Lagrange multiplier μ to include the second constraint in the equation: $\psi = u_2^T S_T u_2 - \lambda(u_2^T u_2 - 1) - \mu(u_2^T u_1)$
7. Differentiate with respect to u_2 and set = 0,

$$\frac{\delta\psi}{\delta u_2} = \mathrm{S}_T u_2 - \lambda u_2 - \mu u_1$$

8. Multiply on the left by $u_1^T = u_1^T S_T u_2 - \lambda u_1^T u_2 - \mu u_1^T u_1 = 0 \rightarrow \mu = 0$
9. The first two terms are zero, and $u_1^T u_1 = 1$, leaving it $= (\mathrm{S}_T - \lambda\mathrm{I})u_2 = 0$ as for u_1.

Step 5: Assemble the projection Matrix U from the columns, $\boldsymbol{u}_1, \boldsymbol{u}_2, \dots, \boldsymbol{u}_p$.
Step 6: Project the dataset y = Ux
PCA can be expressed in a more succinct matrix form if U is the (orthonormal) matrix of column Eigenvectors of the covariance matrix C, and Λ the diagonal matrix of (non-negative) Eigenvalues of C, then CU = UΛ. The order of the columns of U needs to be such that the $\lambda_i \equiv \Lambda_{ii}$ is in descending order: $\lambda_i \leq \lambda_{i-1}\ \forall\ i = 1, \dots, d-1$. Now for some unit vector $n_1 \in R^d$ consider the quantity: $n_1' U^T C U n_1 = n_1' \Lambda n_1$. The left-hand side is the variance of the projections of the (centred) data along the unit vector principal component Un_1. The right-hand side is $\sum_i n_{1_i}^2 \lambda_i$.
The variance of the data projected along the direction of this principal component is just λ_i. This can be repeated until the required variance is captured by searching for the unit vector n_2 that is orthogonal to n_1 (i.e., for which $n_{21} = 0$) and which maximises the right-hand side, which is given by $n_{2i} = \delta_{i,2}$ (Burges, 2009).
Other methods optimise the loadings of each column on each principal component to estimate the principal components. The above and other formulations are explained in detail in (Jolliffe, 2010). A choice of the simplest method to explain each algorithm in this book is made, while the implemented methods in Python libraries usually employ the most advanced recently published method. Starting from the referenced educational books and tracing the papers cited in the documentation of the libraries used in the accomanying code provides a deeper dive into each algorithm for those interested.

Many PCA-based algorithms exist, including Kernel PCA, Probabilistic PCA, and oriented PCA. In summary, PCA projects the existing data on fewer linearly independent components capturing as much variance of the data as possible. When the remaining variance along all directions orthogonal to the p principal components chosen is zero or very negligible, then the dataset lies along a lower-dimensional manifold $\in \mathbb{R}^p$ embedded in R^m. (Lu, Plataniotis and Venetsanopoulos, 2014).

PCA Matrix example:

Find the PCA of a matrix $X \in \mathbb{R}^{4\times3} = \begin{bmatrix} 2 & 3 & 1 \\ 3 & 1 & 0 \\ 2 & 0 & 1 \\ 5 & 0 & 2 \end{bmatrix}$

Step 1: Data preprocessing: remove mean values from each feature

```
# First Step by Step calculations, but using implemented functions for mean,
covariance, and Eigendecomposition.
import numpy as np
X = np.array([[2,3, 1], [3, 1, 0], [2, 0, 1], [5, 0, 2]])
X
array([[2, 3, 1],
       [3, 1, 0],
       [2, 0, 1],
       [5, 0, 2]])

# Calculate the mean of each column
M = np.mean(X.T, axis=1)
M
array([3., 1., 1.])

#center columns by subtracting column means
C = X - M
C
array([[-1.,  2.,  0.],
       [ 0.,  0., -1.],
       [-1., -1.,  0.],
       [ 2., -1.,  1.]])
```

Step 2: Calculate the covariance matrix.

```
#calculate covariance matrix
sigma = np.cov(C.T)
sigma
array([[ 2.        , -1.        ,  0.66666667],
       [-1.        ,  2.        , -0.33333333],
       [ 0.66666667, -0.33333333,  0.66666667]])
```

Step 3: Calculate the eigenvectors and eigenvalues.

```
# eigen decomposition of covariance matrix
from numpy import linalg as LA
eignVal, eignVec = LA.eig(sigma)
eignVal, eignVec
(array([3.19940358, 1.0821583 , 0.38510479]),
 array([[-0.70083477,  0.57765664, -0.41850141],
        [ 0.65971771,  0.74802961, -0.07227894],
```

```
        [-0.27129904,   0.32674839,   0.90533548]]))
```

Step 4: Select Principal components. This small example did not reduce the dimensionality and selected all principal components. Sometimes you need to reduce the dimensionality to 2 or 3 PCs out of 10 or more features by capturing the highest variance by checking the "elbow" in the curve of a scree plot.

```
# Print principal components
PC1 = eignVec[:,0].T.dot(C.T) # u0.x
PC2 = eignVec[:,1].T.dot(C.T) # u1.x
PC3 = eignVec[:,2].T.dot(C.T) # u2.x
print("PC1: ", PC1)
print("PC2: ", PC2)
print("PC3: ", PC3)
PC1:  [ 2.02027019  0.27129904  0.04111706 -2.33268629]
PC2:  [ 0.91840258 -0.32674839 -1.32568625  0.73403206]
PC3:  [ 0.27394352 -0.90533548  0.49078035  0.1406116 ]
```

Step 5: Derive the new projected dataset: Projected_data = normalised_data x selected_principal_components.

```
# project data
P = eignVec.T.dot(C.T)
P.T

array([[ 2.02027019,  0.91840258,  0.27394352],
       [ 0.27129904, -0.32674839, -0.90533548],
       [ 0.04111706, -1.32568625,  0.49078035],
       [-2.33268629,  0.73403206,  0.1406116 ]])

# Using Sklearn PCA implementation
#Second numpy Calculations
from sklearn.decomposition import PCA

#create PCA instance
pca = PCA(3)
#fit on Data
pca.fit(X)
#access values and vectors
print("PCA Components = ", pca.components_)
print("PCA Explained variance ", pca.explained_variance_)
print("PCA Explained variance ratio ", pca.explained_variance_ratio_)
B = pca.transform(X)
print("Transformed Data  ", B)
PCA Components =  [[ 0.70083477 -0.65971771  0.27129904]
 [-0.57765664 -0.74802961 -0.32674839]
 [ 0.41850141  0.07227894 -0.90533548]]
PCA Explained variance  [3.19940358 1.0821583  0.38510479]
PCA Explained variance ratio  [0.68558648 0.23189106 0.08252245]
Transformed Data   [[-2.02027019 -0.91840258 -0.27394352]
 [-0.27129904  0.32674839  0.90533548]
 [-0.04111706  1.32568625 -0.49078035]
 [ 2.33268629 -0.73403206 -0.1406116 ]]
```

2.2.4 Singular Value Decomposition (SVD)

SVD decomposes a matrix X into three constituent matrices to remove the redundancy in the original features by choosing the highest singular values and their corresponding features resulting in dimensionality reduction. The Gauss-Jordan Elimination in chapter one showed that the diagonalisation of a matrix reduces it to an easy-to-analyse matrix. The Eigendecomposition takes the form $Au_i = \lambda_i u_i$ where u_i is the eigenvector corresponding to the λ_i eigenvalue. This can be expressed in diagonalised form as: $AU = \Lambda U$ or $A = U\Lambda U^{-1}$ such that Λ is a diagonal matrix containing the eigenvalues on the diagonal elements, and U contains the eigenvectors as its columns (Deisenroth, Faisal and Ong, 2019).

$$A = \begin{bmatrix} u_{0,0} & \cdots & u_{o,n-1} \\ \vdots & \ddots & \vdots \\ u_{n-1,0} & \cdots & u_{n-1,n-1} \end{bmatrix} \begin{bmatrix} \lambda_0 & \cdots & 0 \\ \vdots & \ddots & \vdots \\ 0 & \cdots & \lambda_{n-1} \end{bmatrix} \begin{bmatrix} u_{0,0} & \cdots & u_{o,n-1} \\ \vdots & \ddots & \vdots \\ u_{n-1,0} & \cdots & u_{n-1,n-1} \end{bmatrix}^{-1}$$

Where $u_i = [u_{o,i}, u_{1,i}, \dots, u_{n-1,i}]$

The inverse Eigenvectors matrix exists only if the Eigenvectors are linearly independent. This is possible only if A is a square matrix. To develop a similar decomposition for non-square matrices, SVD starts by converting the input matrix to a special square matrix by multiplying it by its transpose. A^TA matrix has the following properties:

- Symmetrical. Therefore, we can choose its eigenvectors to be orthogonal with unit length (orthonormal) to each other.
- Square, i.e., invertible
- At least positive semi-definite (Eigenvalues are zero or positive),
- Both matrices (A and A^TA) have the same positive Eigenvalues, and
- Both have the same rank r as A.

The equation to decompose a matrix X is given by: $X_{mxn} = U_{mxn} S_{nxn} V_{nxn}^T$
Where

- **S** is an nxn diagonal matrix, and the diagonal values in the **S** matrix are known **as the singular values** of the original matrix **X**.
    - The singular values are the square root of the Eigenvalues. The singular values are arranged in descending order along the main diagonal in **S**.
    - It is a diagonal matrix that can be reduced to only ***r*** important values, the rest of the matrix being zero. The choice of the rank is based on eliminating linear dependant rows, which is the default matrix rank definition and can be any smaller value than n to achieve lossy compression (leaving out some non-zero but small Eigenvalues).
- **V** is an orthonormal column matrix; the columns of **V** are called **the right singular vectors** of **X**
    - Note that we always use V in its transposed form, so the rows of V^T are orthonormal.
    - It is a matrix that holds important information about the columns of **X**, and the most important information about $\mathbf{V^T}$ is stored in the first row, the dominating values.
    - V is the corresponding unit Eigenvectors to the Eigenvalues squared and placed in S.
- **U** is an orthonormal column matrix; the columns of the **U** matrix are called **the left singular vectors** of **X**;
    - Each of its columns is a unit vector, and the dot product of any two columns is 0 (orthogonal).
    - It is a matrix that holds important information about the rows of **X**, and the most important information about ***U*** is stored in the first column.
    - It is calculated by using the property US(:,i) = XV(:,i)

For compression, we define the rank for the middle projection:

$$X_{mxn} = U_{mxr} S_{rxr} V_{rxn}^T$$

Where $\boldsymbol{r}$ is rank $r \leq$ m and $r \leq$ n, the rank of a matrix is the largest number of columns we can choose for which no selected column is a linear combination of another selected column. This is to say that such columns are linearly independent. This can also be expressed in vectors form as linear combinations of orthonormal basis directions weighted by the singular value σ in descending order: $X = USV^T = \sigma_1 u_1 v_1^T + \sigma_2 u_2 v_2^T + \cdots + \sigma_r u_r v_r^T$. This is illustrated in Figure 7.

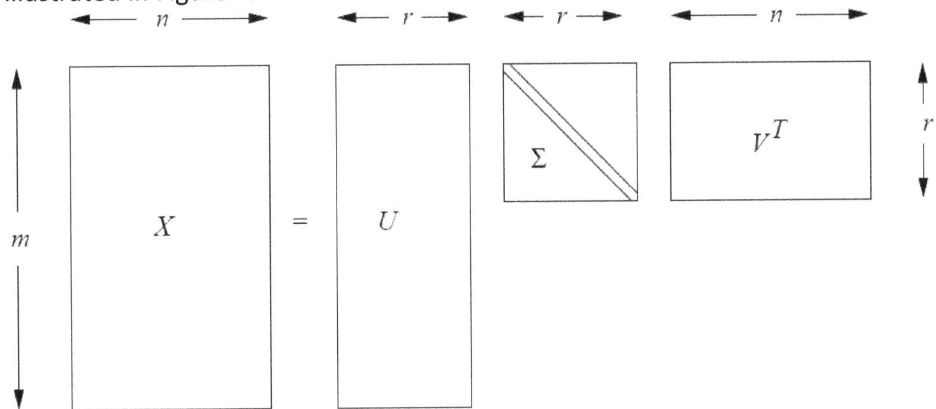

Figure 7: SVD matrix decomposition illustration

Steps to calculate SVD:

Given a matrix X:

Step 1: Compute A=X^{T}X

Step 2: Do Eigendecomposition of A

Step 3: Calculate the singular values, which are the square root of the Eigenvalues

1. Sort the singular values in decreasing order, and arrange them in S or Σ matrix along the diagonal.

Step 4: Calculate the right singular vectors (columns of V)

1. the corresponding unit Eigenvectors are the right singular vectors of X, stored in V

Step 5: Find the left singular vectors U by using the property US(:, i) = MV(:, i)

Example 1:

Find Singular Value Decomposition (SVD) of a Matrix M ∈ $\mathbb{R}^{mxr}$ = $\begin{bmatrix} -1 & 0 \\ 0 & 3 \end{bmatrix}$

SVD(M) = U Σ V^T

Step 1: Calculate A = M^{T}M = $\begin{bmatrix} -1 & 0 \\ 0 & 3 \end{bmatrix} \begin{bmatrix} -1 & 0 \\ 0 & 3 \end{bmatrix} = \begin{bmatrix} 1 & 0 \\ 0 & 9 \end{bmatrix}$

Step 2: Find Eigenvalues and Eigenvectors of A = M^{T}M

$|A - \lambda I| = 0$

$\begin{bmatrix} 1-\lambda & 0 \\ 0 & 9-\lambda \end{bmatrix} = 0$

Then arranging by highest Eigenvalue, we have $\lambda_0 = 9,\ \lambda_1 = 1$

For $\lambda_0 = 9$, the corresponding Eigenvector is computed as follows:

$$\begin{bmatrix} 1-9 & 0 \\ 0 & 9-9 \end{bmatrix} \begin{bmatrix} x_0 \\ x_1 \end{bmatrix} = 0$$

$$\begin{bmatrix} -8 & 0 \\ 0 & 0 \end{bmatrix} \begin{bmatrix} x_0 \\ x_1 \end{bmatrix} = 0$$

Now, reduce this matrix as follows: (check the Gaussian Elimination in chapter one)

R1←R1÷-8

$$\begin{bmatrix} 1 & 0 \\ 0 & 0 \end{bmatrix} \begin{bmatrix} x_0 \\ x_1 \end{bmatrix} = 0$$

Then $x_0 = 0 \; and \; x_1 = 1$

Then $\boldsymbol{v_0} = \begin{bmatrix} \mathbf{0} \\ \mathbf{1} \end{bmatrix}$ is the Eigenvector corresponding to the Eigenvalue $\lambda_0 = 9$

For $\lambda_1 = 1$, the corresponding Eigenvector is computed as follows:

$$\begin{bmatrix} 1-1 & 0 \\ 0 & 9-1 \end{bmatrix} \begin{bmatrix} x_0 \\ x_1 \end{bmatrix} = 0$$

$$\begin{bmatrix} 0 & 0 \\ 0 & 8 \end{bmatrix} \begin{bmatrix} x_0 \\ x_1 \end{bmatrix} = 0$$

Now, reduce this matrix by swapping the rows

$$\begin{bmatrix} 0 & 8 \\ 0 & 0 \end{bmatrix} \begin{bmatrix} x_1 \\ x_0 \end{bmatrix} = 0$$

Then, reduce this matrix as follows:

R1←R1÷-8

$$\begin{bmatrix} 0 & 1 \\ 0 & 0 \end{bmatrix} \begin{bmatrix} x_1 \\ x_0 \end{bmatrix} = 0$$

Then $x_0 = 1 \; and \; x_1 = 0$

Then $\boldsymbol{v_1} = \begin{bmatrix} \mathbf{1} \\ \mathbf{0} \end{bmatrix}$ is the Eigenvector corresponding to the Eigenvalue $\lambda_1 = 1$

Step 3: Calculate the singular values, which are the square root of the eigenvalues

$$\sigma_0 = \sqrt{\lambda_0} = \sqrt{9} = 3$$

$$\sigma_1 = \sqrt{\lambda_1} = \sqrt{1} = 1$$

This forms your singular values diagonal matrix $\Sigma \in \mathbb{R}^{r \times r} = \begin{bmatrix} \sigma_0 & 0 \\ 0 & \sigma_1 \end{bmatrix} = \begin{bmatrix} 3 & 0 \\ 0 & 1 \end{bmatrix}$

Step 4: Calculate the right singular vectors (columns of V)

V is the corresponding unit eigenvectors, now called the right singular vectors of M $\; V \in \mathbb{R}^{r \times n} = [v_0 \;\; v_1] = \begin{bmatrix} 0 & 1 \\ 1 & 0 \end{bmatrix}$

PS V^TV = I (V has orthonormal columns: orthogonal and unit bases – of length 1).

Step 5: Find the left singular vectors U by using the property US(:,i) = MV(:,i)

Which is $u_0 = \frac{1}{\sigma_0} M^T . v_0 = \frac{1}{3}\begin{bmatrix} -1 & 0 \\ 0 & 3 \end{bmatrix} . \begin{bmatrix} 0 \\ 1 \end{bmatrix} = \begin{bmatrix} \frac{-1}{3} & 0 \\ 0 & 1 \end{bmatrix} . \begin{bmatrix} 0 \\ 1 \end{bmatrix} = \begin{bmatrix} 0 \\ 1 \end{bmatrix}$

And $u_1 = \frac{1}{\sigma_1} M^T . v_1 = \frac{1}{1}\begin{bmatrix} -1 & 0 \\ 0 & 3 \end{bmatrix} . \begin{bmatrix} 1 \\ 0 \end{bmatrix} = \begin{bmatrix} -1 & 0 \\ 0 & 3 \end{bmatrix} . \begin{bmatrix} 1 \\ 0 \end{bmatrix} = \begin{bmatrix} -1 \\ 0 \end{bmatrix}$

$U \in \mathbb{R}^{m \times r} = [u_0 \;\; u_1] = \begin{bmatrix} 0 & -1 \\ 1 & 0 \end{bmatrix}$

PS U^TU = I (U has orthonormal columns: orthogonal and unit bases – of length 1).

The complete solution is: SVD(M) = U Σ V^T = $\begin{bmatrix} 0 & -1 \\ 1 & 0 \end{bmatrix} \begin{bmatrix} 3 & 0 \\ 0 & 1 \end{bmatrix} \begin{bmatrix} 0 & 1 \\ 1 & 0 \end{bmatrix} = \begin{bmatrix} -1 & 0 \\ 0 & 3 \end{bmatrix}$

Example 2:

Given $X = \begin{bmatrix} -2 & 2 \\ -4 & -4 \\ 4 & 4 \\ 2 & -2 \\ 0 & 0 \end{bmatrix}$

To compute SVD:

Step 1: Compute M=XX^T= $\begin{bmatrix} 8 & -16 & 16 & 0 & 0 \\ -16 & 32 & -32 & 0 & 0 \\ 16 & -32 & 32 & 0 & 0 \\ 0 & 0 & 0 & 8 & 0 \\ 0 & 0 & 0 & 0 & 0 \end{bmatrix}$

Step 2: do Eigendecomposition of M, to find the characteristic polynomial as $-\lambda^5 + 80\lambda^4 - 576\lambda^3 = 0$, which is equivalent to $-\lambda^3(\lambda - 8)(\lambda - 72) = 0$:

Eigenvalues: $\lambda_1 = 72, \lambda_2 = 8$, and $\lambda_3 = \lambda_4 = \lambda_5 = 0$, with corresponding Eigenvectors:

$$u_1^T \begin{bmatrix} 0.5 \\ -1 \\ 1 \\ 0 \\ 0 \end{bmatrix}, u_2^T \begin{bmatrix} 0 \\ 0 \\ 0 \\ 1 \\ 0 \end{bmatrix}, u_3^T \begin{bmatrix} 2 \\ 1 \\ 0 \\ 0 \\ 0 \end{bmatrix}, u_4^T \begin{bmatrix} -0.4 \\ 0.8 \\ 1 \\ 0 \\ 0 \end{bmatrix}, u_5^T \begin{bmatrix} 0 \\ 0 \\ 0 \\ 0 \\ 1 \end{bmatrix}$$

Step 3: Find Σ. From the square roots of the eigenvalues on the diagonal

$s_1=\sqrt{72}$, $s_2=\sqrt{8}$, then all the rest zeros

$$\Sigma = \begin{bmatrix} \sqrt{72} & 0 \\ 0 & \sqrt{8} \end{bmatrix}$$

Step 4: Find V. From the eigenvectors, using only rank-2

$$V=\begin{bmatrix} \frac{1}{\sqrt{2}} & -\frac{1}{\sqrt{2}} \\ \frac{1}{\sqrt{2}} & \frac{1}{\sqrt{2}} \end{bmatrix}$$

Step 5: Find U. For example:

$$u_1 = \frac{1}{s_1} \times M^T . v_1 = \frac{1}{8}\begin{bmatrix} 40 & 24 \\ 24 & 40 \end{bmatrix}\begin{bmatrix} -\frac{1}{\sqrt{2}} \\ -\frac{1}{\sqrt{2}} \end{bmatrix} = \begin{bmatrix} \frac{1}{\sqrt{2}} \\ -\frac{1}{\sqrt{2}} \end{bmatrix},$$

$$u_2 = \frac{1}{s_2} \times M^T . v_2 = \frac{1}{4}\begin{bmatrix} 40 & 24 \\ 24 & 40 \end{bmatrix}\begin{bmatrix} -\frac{1}{\sqrt{2}} \\ \frac{1}{\sqrt{2}} \end{bmatrix} = \begin{bmatrix} \frac{1}{\sqrt{2}} \\ \frac{1}{\sqrt{2}} \end{bmatrix}$$

$$U = \begin{bmatrix} \frac{1}{\sqrt{2}} & \frac{1}{\sqrt{2}} \\ -\frac{1}{\sqrt{2}} & \frac{1}{\sqrt{2}} \end{bmatrix}$$

Starting from reversing the first step multiplication as M=X^TX =$\begin{bmatrix} 40 & 24 \\ 24 & 40 \end{bmatrix}$, will lead to the same results with Eigenvalues: $\lambda_1 = 64$ and $\lambda_2 = 16$ and corresponding Eigenvectors in V=$\begin{bmatrix} \frac{1}{\sqrt{2}} & -\frac{1}{\sqrt{2}} \\ \frac{1}{\sqrt{2}} & \frac{1}{\sqrt{2}} \end{bmatrix}$, hence singular values $s_1=\sqrt{64}$=8, $s_2=\sqrt{16}$=4, $\Sigma = \begin{bmatrix} 8 & 0 \\ 0 & 4 \end{bmatrix}$, and $U = \begin{bmatrix} \frac{1}{\sqrt{2}} & \frac{1}{\sqrt{2}} \\ -\frac{1}{\sqrt{2}} & \frac{1}{\sqrt{2}} \end{bmatrix}$.

Python example:

```
from numpy import array
from scipy.linalg import svd, diagsvd

X = array([[1, 2], [3, 4], [5, 6]])
print (X)
U, S, VT = svd(X)
# to reconstruct  the matrix:
Sigma = diagsvd(S, X.shape[0], X.shape[1])
X_reconstructed = np.dot(U, np.dot(Sigma, VT))
print(X_reconstructed)
```

```
np.allclose(X, X_reconstructed)
X =  [[1 2]
 [3 4]
 [5 6]]

U =  [[-0.2298477   0.88346102  0.40824829]
 [-0.52474482  0.24078249 -0.81649658]
 [-0.81964194 -0.40189603  0.40824829]]

S =  [9.52551809 0.51430058]

VT =  [[-0.61962948 -0.78489445]
 [-0.78489445  0.61962948]]

X Reconstructed =  [[1. 2.]
 [3. 4.]
 [5. 6.]]
Allclose: True
```

2.2.4.1 Data Science with SVD

This example is credited to (Leskovec, Rajaraman and Ullman, 2014). Given Ratings of five movies by seven users. The movies belong to a category or concept, and this information is hidden in the observed data. We know that the movies belong to 2 categories: science fiction and romance, so we choose r equals 2 to reveal these hidden (latent) features. We can do SVD to identify the users' interest in the concept in general and evaluate the weights of ratings by the concept, such that:

$\boldsymbol{M}^{n\times d}=\boldsymbol{U}^{n\times r}\boldsymbol{\Sigma}^{r\times r}\,(\boldsymbol{V}^{r\times d})^{\boldsymbol{T}}$

$\boldsymbol{M}$: number of users (n) x number of movies (d)

$\boldsymbol{U}$: n users x r concepts: connects people to concepts.

$\boldsymbol{\Sigma}$: the strength of each concept

$\boldsymbol{V}$: d movies x r concepts: relates movies to concepts

	Matrix	Alien	Star Wars	Casablanca	Titanic
Joe	1	1	1	0	0
Jim	3	3	3	0	0
John	4	4	4	0	0
Jack	5	5	5	0	0
Jill	0	0	0	4	4
Jenny	0	0	0	5	5
Jane	0	0	0	2	2

Doing SVD on this matrix:

$$\underset{X}{\begin{bmatrix} 1 & 1 & 1 & 0 & 0 \\ 3 & 3 & 3 & 0 & 0 \\ 4 & 4 & 4 & 0 & 0 \\ 5 & 5 & 5 & 0 & 0 \\ 0 & 0 & 0 & 4 & 4 \\ 0 & 0 & 0 & 5 & 5 \\ 0 & 0 & 0 & 2 & 2 \end{bmatrix}} = \underset{U}{\begin{bmatrix} 0.14 & 0 \\ 0.42 & 0 \\ 0.56 & 0 \\ 0.70 & 0 \\ 0 & 0.60 \\ 0 & 0.75 \\ 0 & 0.30 \end{bmatrix}} \underset{\boldsymbol{\Sigma}}{\begin{bmatrix} 12.4 & 0 \\ 0 & 9.5 \end{bmatrix}} \underset{V^T}{\begin{bmatrix} 0.58 & 0.58 & 0.58 & 0 & 0 \\ 0 & 0 & 0 & 0.71 & 0.71 \end{bmatrix}}$$

Note: Generally, the concepts will not be as clearly delineated as in this hand-crafted example. There will be fewer zeros in $\boldsymbol{U}$and $\boldsymbol{V}$. Check the source code examples in ch2.ipynb to see actual values generated from the sklearn Python package implementation of "TruncatedSVD".
We can read various information from the SVD decomposition:

- **V^T:** the first row of V^T says that the first three movies belong to science fiction, while the second row of V^T tells us that the last two movies belong to the romance genre.
- **U:** We can tell that Joe, Jim, John, and Jack are interested in science fiction only, while Jill, Jenny, and Jane are interested in romance only and do not rate science fiction movies at all.
- $\boldsymbol{S_1}$: the strength of the first concept: sci-fic;
- $\boldsymbol{XV_1}$: each user's rating is an average of all five movies, weighted by the first concept;
- $||\boldsymbol{XV_1}||$: a score by the overall seven users, weighted by the first concept.
- $S_i = ||\boldsymbol{X}V_i||$, where $\boldsymbol{S_i}$ is the ith value along the main diagonal line of $\boldsymbol{S}$, and $\boldsymbol{V_i}$ is the ith column of $\boldsymbol{V}$.

Online SVD Calculators:
https://atozmath.com/MatrixEv.aspx?q=svd
https://keisan.casio.com/exec/system/15076953160460

2.2.4.2 Compression with SVD

Other applications of SVD ($X_{nxd} = U_{nxr}S_{rxr}V_{rxd}^T$) is to choose the highest rank-r approximation to a given matrix X that is given by $X_{nxd} = AW^T$, such that A $=U_{nxr}$and W = $S_{rxr}V_{rxd}^T$. The choice of small rank can be useful for compression. This happens by setting the s=n-r smallest singular values to 0; then, we can also eliminate the corresponding s columns of U and V. Choosing the lowest singular values to drop minimises the root-mean-square error between the original matrix X and its reconstructed approximation. The choice of r can be made by studying the decay of the singular values. Python notebook ch2.ipynb shows an image compression SVD example and how the choice of rank affects the quality of the image.

2.2.5 Linear Discriminant Analysis (LDA)

LDA is a supervised dimensionality reduction algorithm that works on labelled data to discriminate between classes, unlike unsupervised PCA, which diagonalises the covariance matrix to make data points independent of each other. The most straightforward Binary (2 classes) Linear Discriminant is based on the mean of both classes $\mu_{c_i}^k$ and their variance $s_{c_i}^k$, creating a metric $J_k = \frac{(\mu_{c_1}^k - \mu_{c_2}^k)^2}{(s_{c_1}^k)^2 + (s_{c_2}^k)^2}$, where k spans the features/columns assuming only two features, i spans the classes (assuming two classes), and the discriminate becomes identifying the value of k at which the highest value of J_k is found. Then, taking the classes' means as the threshold draws the line that separates both classes $c = \frac{\mu_{c_1}^k + \mu_{c_2}^k}{2}$. To generalise for multiple features to draw a discriminant line equation, y=wx, we need to solve for w, through the following steps:

1. Calculate a middle point of all n features from the means of both classes as a vector, $M = \left(\frac{\mu_{c_1}^{f_1} + \mu_{c_2}^{f_1}}{2}, \dots \frac{\mu_{c_1}^{f_n} + \mu_{c_2}^{f_n}}{2}\right)$,
2. Calculate the covariance matrices of both classes, S_1, S_2 and compute their average $S_{avg} = \frac{1}{2}[S_1 + S_2]$

3. Solve for weights vector from the inverse of the average, $w = S_{avg}^{-1}(\mu_{c_1} + \mu_{c_2})$
4. Identify the threshold c using the middle point, c=wm
5. For every new test sample x, solve for y=wx, if y > c, then x belongs to c_1, and when y < c, the sample belongs to c_2.

Another method to divide the data into separate classes is to maintain two scatter matrices for the input space: the within-class scatter S_w to maximise, and the between-class scatter S_b to minimise for a dataset X with M instances and C classes. The scatter matrices are covariance matrices multiplied by the number of entities (Lu, Plataniotis and Venetsanopoulos, 2014).
The steps to perform LDA using scatter matrices are as follows:
Step 1: Calculate the scatter matrices for the input space:

1. $S_w = \sum_{i=1}^{M}(x_i - \bar{x}_{c_i})(x_i - \bar{x}_{c_i})^T$ and $S_b = \sum_{i=1}^{C} M_c(x_i - \bar{x})(x_i - \bar{x})^T$, where $\bar{x}_{c_i} = \frac{1}{M_c}\sum_{i\ in\ M_c}^{M_c} x_i$, is the class mean for entities belonging to the class Mc, and $\bar{x}$ is the feature column mean across all classes. The sum of these two scatter matrices is the total scatter S_t for the dataset.

Step 2: Estimate the projection matrix into the output space:

2. The input space scatter-matrices are projected into the output space using projection matrix U as follows:

$S_{wY} = U^T S_w U$, and $S_{bY} = U^T S_b U$ and the Total scatter in the output space: $S_{tY} = U^T S_t U$

3. LDA aims to maximise the between-class scatter in the output space S_{bY}, while minimising the within-class scatter in the output space S_{wY} by solving for U. This can be done by using the trace of the scatter matrices and the inverse if it is singular:

$$\hat{U} = \underset{U}{\text{argmax}}\ tr(S_{wY}^{-1} S_{bY}) = \underset{U}{\text{argmax}}\ tr((U^T S_w U)^{-1} U^T S_b U)$$

- It can also be done using any substitutions of S_{tY}, or by using the determinants:

$$\hat{U} = \underset{U}{\text{argmax}} \frac{|S_{bY}|}{|S_{wY}|} = \underset{U}{\text{argmax}} \frac{|U^T S_b U|}{|U^T S_w U|}$$

$\hat{U} = \underset{U}{\text{argmax}}\, U^T S_b U$, subject to $U^T S_w U = 1$.

4. This can be solved by the Lagrange multiplier: $\psi = U^T S_b U - \lambda(U^T S_w U - 1)$, then differentiate with respect to u, and set = 0,

$$\frac{\delta\psi}{\delta u} = S_b U - \lambda S_w U = 0 \rightarrow S_b U = \lambda S_w U$$

which is the generalised eigenvalue problem.
Step 3: Get the highest C-1 eigenvectors to form U:

5. The eigenvectors corresponding to the largest C-1 eigenvalues λ form the columns of U.

Step 4: Project the test data into the new LDA output space:

6. Then data are projected like in PCA as y = U^Tx.

The above approaches build discriminative classifiers by learning to discriminate the classes from a training dataset, not how the data points are generated. A generative classifier uses probabilistic methods to learn how points are generated in each class, applying Bayes Theorem. LDA is implemented in Scikit learn Python packages using its generative model. The LDA generative model assumes the class-conditional densities, $f_k(x)$ for class k, are Gaussian with a common covariance matrix so that $f_k(x) = \frac{1}{(2\pi)^{M/2}|\Sigma|^{1/2}} e^{\frac{1}{2}(x-\mu_k)^T\Sigma^{-1}(x-\mu_k)}$, where the Gaussian is described using its mean and standard deviation, or covariance matrix Σ. The function includes the exponent constant e, M is the number of features, and μ_k is means for class k. Given $N_k$as the number of entities in class k, such that the LDA classifier assumes that $\hat{\pi}_k = \frac{N_k}{N}$ is the maximum likelihood estimates (MLE) of $f_k(.)$, across all classes, i.e. π_k is the probability of class Y being k, P(Y = k). The $f_k(x)$ predictors (for k=1,...,K) all share the same covariance matrix $\hat{\Sigma} = \frac{\sum_{k=1}^{K}\sum_{y_i=k}(x-\hat{\mu}_k)(x-\hat{\mu}_k)^T}{N-k}$ but may have different means $\hat{\mu}_k = \sum_{yi=k}\frac{x_i}{N_k}$. The Bayes Theorem: $\hat{Y} = \underset{Y}{\operatorname{argmax}}\,\hat{P}\,(Y|X) = \underset{Y}{\operatorname{argmax}}\,\hat{P}(X|Y)\hat{P}(Y)$, predicts the class $\hat{Y}$ of test sample X. The generative LDA classifier satisfies the following: $\hat{Y}(x) = \underset{k}{\operatorname{argmax}}\frac{\hat{f}_k(x)\hat{\pi}_k}{\sum_{j=1}^{k}\hat{f}_j(x)\hat{\pi}_j}$.
LDA can separate multiple classes by training multiple classifiers to separate each pair of classes and use voting between the classifiers to identify the class of a test sample, which can be considered a basic multilinear model. Instead of using a linear equation, a quadratic equation is used in QDA. The Bayesian Probabilistic models of LDA and QDA are implemented in the Scitkit-learn library, assuming Gaussian densities for $\hat{P}(X|Y)$, while the other generative model, such as Naive Bayes, assumes $P(X|Y) = \prod_j P(X_j|Y)$, such that the features are independent conditional on Y. For more about Bayesian generative models, read books such as (Sivia and Skilling, 2006), (Downey, 2013). Check the Python code in LDA.ipynb for an LDA example compared to PCA.

2.2.6 Independent Component Analysis (ICA)

Independent Component Analysis (ICA) is a generative model that assumes a dataset to be a linear mixture of some latent factors such that x = As, where A∈ $\mathbb{R}^{p \times p}$ is the mixing matrix, and s is the source or the independent components. ICA uses information theory to capture mutually independent factors in a dataset, unlike PCA, which captures uncorrelated factors. ICA estimates p unordered sources that should not be more than the observed mixtures x (Lu, Plataniotis and Venetsanopoulos, 2014).
ICA attempts to find the unmixing matrix by employing non-Gaussianity from the central tendency theorem to retrieve the independent components from the mixture: s = A^{-1}x. One possible computational set of steps to estimate ICs is as follows:
Step1: Normalise and Whitening:

1. Subtract the mean: x_{norm}=x $-\bar{x}$

2. Remove the correlations by Eigendecomposition to end up with zero covariance and 1 variance: x_w=($ED^{-\frac{1}{2}}E^T$)x, Where D is a diagonal matrix of eigenvalues, every diagonal element is an eigenvalue of the covariance matrix, and E is an orthogonal matrix of eigenvectors.

Step 2: Maximise Non-Gaussainty by Negative Entropy

3. A=($VD^{-\frac{1}{2}}E^T$), where V is an unknown rotation matrix that we need to solve for it and A using the eigenvalues and eigenvectors. Solving for two unknown iteratively by Lagrange multiplier for the constraints that the dot product of transpose of A and itself is approximately equal to 1: $A^T A \approx 1$, and the Newton iterations by randomly initialising A with any values, and iterate using an objective function objFunc that aims to non-Gaussian maximisation such as tanh and its derivative dObjFunc as follows:
4. A_new = $\frac{1}{n}\sum_{i=1}^{n} \mathrm{X} \times \mathrm{objFunc}(\mathrm{A}^T.\mathrm{X}) - \frac{1}{n}\sum_{i=1}^{n} \mathrm{dObjFunc}(\mathrm{A}^T.\mathrm{X}) \times \mathrm{A}$

Step 3: Define the convergence scheme:

1. A is initialised to a random variable
2. $A^T A \approx 1$ is the basis of orthogonality and indicates the convergence
3. Once the resulting matrix A is calculated, the dot product of it and the whitened x_w signal gives the sources s.

There are other algorithms to perform ICA, such as infomax, FastICA, and JADE.
Real-World Example:
ICA is important for Blind Source Separation (BSS) problems. A classical BSS problem is the cocktail party problem (CPP), defined as having two microphones in a room in different locations while two people are talking simultaneously. The mixed-time-signals received at both microphones are $x_1(t) = a_{11}s_1(t) + a_{12}s_2(t)$ *and* $x_2(t) = a_{21}s_1(t) + a_{22}s_2(t)$, such that a_{ij} are the weight parameters dependent on the distances between microphone i and speaker j collected in matrix A. In this case, it is a 2x2 matrix but could be expanded to n microphone and m sources problem. The aim is to estimate s_1 and s_2 from both equations, with only x_1(t) and x_2(t) are known. Check the Python code ICA_FOBI.ipynb for an audio BSS example, followed by an image mixture separation example.

2.2.7 Canonical Correlation Analysis (CCA)

The CCA and the PLS (in the following section) algorithms consider mapping from two paired datasets, x ∈ $\mathbb{R}^{I\times M}$ and y∈ $\mathbb{R}^{J\times M}$. Learning the symmetric relationship between them is performed by learning the Linear projections for both by maximising the correlations. Symmetric relationships mean both datasets are different views or representations of the same entities. A classic example is audio and video datasets from the same individuals (Lu, Plataniotis and Venetsanopoulos, 2014).
The steps to perform CCA are as follows:
Step 1: Define the covariance matrix of each dataset and the cross-covariance matrices:

1. $\Sigma_{xx} = \frac{1}{M-1}\sum_{i=1}^{M}(x_i - \bar{x})(x_i - \bar{x})^T$, $\Sigma_{yy} = \frac{1}{M-1}\sum_{i=1}^{M}(y_i - \bar{y})(y_i - \bar{y})^T$

$\Sigma_{xy} = \frac{1}{M-1}\sum_{i=1}^{M}(x_i - \bar{x})(y_i - \bar{y})^T$, $\Sigma_{yx} = \frac{1}{M-1}\sum_{i=1}^{M}(y_i - \bar{y})(x_i - \bar{x})^T$, note that $\Sigma_{xy} = \Sigma_{yx}^T$

Step 2: Find The correlations between the projections:

2. The pth pair of projections $(u_{x_p}^T, u_{y_p}^T)$, $r_{m_p} = u_{x_p}^T x_m$, and $s_{m_p} = u_{y_p}^T y_m$ such that coordinate vectors w_p = $u_{x_p}^T(x_i - \bar{x}) = r_{m_p}$, and $z_p = u_{y_p}^T(y_i - \bar{y}) = s_{m_p}$ has the correlation $\rho_p = \frac{u_{xp}^T \Sigma_{xy} u_{yp}}{\sqrt{(u_{xp}^T \Sigma_{xx} u_{xp})(u_{yp}^T \Sigma_{yy} u_{yp})}}$

Step 3: Find the first projection pair $\{\boldsymbol{u_{x1}}, \boldsymbol{u_{y1}}\}$ such that $\boldsymbol{\rho_1}$ is maximised similar to the algorithm presented in the PCA section,

3. $(u_{x1}, u_{y1}) = \underset{(u_{x1}, u_{y1})}{\operatorname{argmax}}\, u_{x_1}^T \Sigma_{xy} u_{y_1}$, subject to $u_{x_1}^T \Sigma_{xx} u_{x_1} = 1$, and $u_{y_1}^T \Sigma_{yy} u_{y_1} = 1$.
4. Using Lagrange Multipliers: $\psi_1 = u_{x_1}^T \Sigma_{xy} u_{y_1} - \frac{1}{2}\lambda(u_{x_1}^T \Sigma_{xx} u_{x_1} - 1) - \frac{1}{2}\mu\,(u_{y_1}^T \Sigma_{yy} u_{y_1} - 1)$
5. Differentiate with respect to u_{x1} and u_{y1}, and set to 0:
   $\frac{\delta\psi}{\delta u_{x1}} = \Sigma_{xy} u_{y_1} - \lambda\Sigma_{xx} u_{x_1} = 0$, then multiply $u_{x_1}^T$ on the left
   $\frac{\delta\psi}{\delta u_{y1}} = \Sigma_{yx} u_{x_1} - \mu\Sigma_{yy} u_{y_1} = 0$, then multiply $u_{y_1}^T$ on the left
6. We have $u_{x_1}^T \Sigma_{xy} u_{y_1} - \lambda u_{x_1}^T \Sigma_{xx} u_{x_1} = 0$, and $u_{y_1}^T \Sigma_{yx} u_{x_1} - \mu u_{y_1}^T \Sigma_{yy} u_{y_1}$
7. Since we have $u_{x_1}^T \Sigma_{xx} u_{x_1} = 1$, and $u_{y_1}^T \Sigma_{yy} u_{y_1} = 1$, then we have $\lambda = \mu = u_{x_1}^T \Sigma_{xy} u_{y_1}$ to maximise.
8. If Σ_{xx} is non-singular, $u_{x_1} = \frac{\Sigma_{xx}^{-1}\Sigma_{xy}}{\lambda} u_{y_1}$, then we have: $\Sigma_{yx}\Sigma_{xx}^{-1}\Sigma_{xy} u_{y_1} = \lambda^2 \Sigma_{yy} u_{y_1}$, which is the generalised eigenvalue problem such that $\hat{u}_{y_1}$ is the Eigenvector corresponding to the largest Eigenvalue.
9. If Σ_{yy} is non-singular, then we have: $\Sigma_{yy}^{-1}\Sigma_{yx}\Sigma_{xx}^{-1}\Sigma_{xy} u_{y_1} = \lambda^2 u_{y_1}$, and $\Sigma_{xx}^{-1}\Sigma_{xy}\Sigma_{yy}^{-1}\Sigma_{yx} u_{x_1} = \lambda^2 u_{x_1}$.

Step 4: Find the following projections

10. Each projection p should maximise the correlation ρ_p by adding the zero correlation constraints such as for p=2, w_2 and z_2 are uncorrelated with w_1 and z_1, and for later steps p, w_p and z_p are uncorrelated with w_q and z_q, for 1<= q <= p-1

Step 5: Assemble the Projection Matrices

11. Projections matrices $U_x \in \mathbb{R}^{I \times p}$ and $U_y \in \mathbb{R}^{J \times p}$ columns are the calculated projection pairs, respectively.
12. Make the projections to the dataset as $x_{projected} = U_x^T x$, and $y_{projected} = U_y^T y$.

Check the Python code in CCA_PLS.ipynb for a CCA example compared to PLS.

2.2.8 Partial Least Squares Analysis (PLS)

It is like CCA in mapping the symmetric relationship between two paired datasets, but by maximising the covariance, not the correlation, and is useful when Σ_{xx} and Σ_{yy} are not singular. When the inconsistent system of equations Ax = b, has no solution, the best approximate solution is the least squares solution. PLS is implemented

in the scikit-learn Python package, in the cross-decomposition module as PLSCanonical. Maximising the covariance between datasets is suitable when modelling X as one dataset and Y as another dataset, such that the target is not a single value but a vector of several targets as multilabel. PLS is also an acronym for "Projection to Latent Structures" since it uses latent variables to identify the association between blocks of observed variables.
The pth pair of projections (u_{x_p} , u_{y_p}) are the weight vectors that are estimated such that coordinate vectors w_p = $u_{x_p}^T(x_i - \bar{x})$ = r_{m_p}, and z_p = $u_{y_p}^T(y_i - \bar{y})$ =s_{m_p} maximise the sample covariance between $\{w_p, z_p\}$, which are the score vectors, forming the **score Matrices** W and Z. This is calculated by: $\left(\hat{u}_{x_p}, \hat{u}_{y_p}\right) = \underset{u_{xp}, u_{yp}}{\text{argmax}} \frac{u_{xp}^T \Sigma_{xy} u_{yp}}{\sqrt{(u_{xp}^T u_{xp})(u_{yp}^T u_{yp})}}$. The non-linear iterative partial least squares (NIPALS) algorithm iteratively finds the dominant Eigenvector similar to the power method. By deflating the X, and Y matrices, the algorithm finds the subsequent dominant Eigenvector (Lu, Plataniotis and Venetsanopoulos, 2014).
The steps to perform PLS are as follows:
Step 1: Repeat Until Convergence:

1. Initialise Y-score vector z_p^T with the first row of Y
2. Calculate the X-weight vectors: u_{x_p}=$\frac{X_{z_p}}{\|X_{z_p}\|}$,
3. Calculate the X-score vector: $\mathrm{w}_p = \mathrm{X}^T u_{x_p}$
4. Calculate the Y-weight vector: u_{y_p}=$\frac{Y_{\mathrm{w}_p}}{\|Y_{\mathrm{w}_p}\|}$
5. Update Y-score vector $\mathrm{z}_p = \mathrm{Y}^T u_{y_p}$
6. Repeat steps 1:5 until $\frac{\|\text{old } \mathrm{w}_p - \text{new } \mathrm{w}_p\|}{\|\text{new } \mathrm{w}_p\|}$< stopping criteria η, $u_{x_p}$and $u_{y_p}$are the dominant eigenvectors of this round.
7. Calculate the X loading vector $v_{x_p} = \frac{X_{\mathrm{w}_p}}{\mathrm{w}_p^T \mathrm{w}_p}$, coefficients of regressing X on w_p forming matrix V_x
8. Calculate the Y-loading vector $v_{y_p} = \frac{Y_{z_p}}{z_p^T z_p}$, coefficients of regressing Y on z_p forming matrix V_y
9. Rank-one deflate both X and Y: $X \leftarrow X - v_{x_p}\mathrm{w}_p^T$ and $Y \leftarrow Y - v_{y_p}\mathrm{z}_p^T$
10. Repeat steps 1:9 until $\|X\|$< stopping criteria η.

Step 2: Assemble the weight Matrices

11. Weight matrices $U_x \in \mathbb{R}^{I \times p}$ and $U_y \in \mathbb{R}^{J \times p}$columns are the calculated projections pairs, respectively.
12. Make the projections to the dataset as $x_{projected} = U_x^T x$, and $y_{projected} = U_y^T y$.

PLS can be used for regression when the relationship between X and Y is asymmetric, and considering Y the response (outcome or dependent) on X (the predictor or the independent dataset), such that the score vectors $\{w_p\}$ are good predictors of Y. The residual matrices (**the error terms**) are E_x, E_y, such that $X = V_x W^T + E_x$, and $Y = V_y Z^T + E_y$, assembled in matrix E, can be used to linearly approximate the relationship between W and Z, such that Z = WD + E, and D are the regression coefficients calculated below. PLS for regression performs the following steps:
Step 1: Repeat for p latent factors:

1. Calculate the X-weight vectors: $\hat{u}_{x_p}$=$\frac{X_y}{\|X_y\|}$,

2. Calculate the X-score vector: $w_p = X^T \hat{u}_{x_p}$

3. Calculate the regression coefficient $d_p = \frac{w_p^T y}{(w_p^T w_p)}$

4. Calculate the X loading vector $v_{x_p} = \frac{X w_p}{w_p^T w_p}$, coefficients of regressing X on w_p forming matrix V_x

5. Rank-one deflate both X and Y: $X \leftarrow X - v_{x_p} w_p^T$ and $Y \leftarrow Y - d_p w_p$

Step 2: Assemble the weight Matrix, loadings, and regression coefficients

6. Weight matrices $U_x \in \mathbb{R}^{I \times p}$ columns are the calculated weights $\hat{u}_{x_p}$, the d_p are the diagonal elements of Matrix D$\in \mathbb{R}^{p \times p}$, and the loading Matrix V columns v_{x_p}.

PLS can also be applied as a supervised method by encoding Y as the class memberships. This will be closely related to Fisher Discriminant Analysis (Binary LDA).

2.2.9 Factor Analysis

The latent factors are latent variables that are not measured, but they are sometimes planned in the design of the measured dataset or reconstructed from the dataset after collection by grouping variables by their correlations. A group of observed variables will have a high correlation among themselves and a low correlation with other observed variables in other groups, such that each group will imply a different latent factor. The principal components capture the highest variance in the dataset in the first component and decreasing-order of variance in the following components. The main objective is to project a high-dimensional dataset into a smaller-dimension model for visualisation or compression reasons. The PCA components are not interpretable as data objects themselves. The factors are interpretable data that cannot be measured directly in one variable, and several observed variables together represent one or more latent factor(s) (Brown, 2006).
Each measured indicator x_i contributes to the factors being measured η_j with loading or weight λ_{ij}, forming the general equation:
$x_i = \lambda_{i1}\eta_1 + \lambda_{i2}\eta_2 + \ldots + \lambda_{im}\eta_m + \varepsilon_i$
$x_i = \varepsilon_i + \sum_{j=0}^{m-1} \lambda_{ij}\eta_j$
A single equation that relates the observed variables x to the latent variables/factors η and the unique variance ε is: $x = W x\eta + \varepsilon$ That can be captured in matrix form as $\Sigma = W_x \Psi W_x^T + \Theta_\varepsilon$, where $\Sigma \in \mathbb{R}^{d \times d}$ is the symmetric correlation matrix of d indicators X$\in \mathbb{R}^d$, $W_x \in \mathbb{R}^{d \times m}$ is the factor loadings matrix containing m $\lambda \in \mathbb{R}^d$, $\Psi \in \mathbb{R}^{m \times m}$ is the symmetric correlation matrix of the factor correlations, and $\Theta_\varepsilon \in \mathbb{R}^{d \times d}$ is the diagonal matrix of unique variances ε.
Various algorithms can estimate the factors and their loading. The most predominantly used are maximum likelihood (ML is most suitable to normally distributed datasets) and principal factors (PF makes no data distribution assumptions). Other methods include but are not limited to: weighted least squares, unweights least squares, generalised least squares, imaging analysis, minimum residual analysis, and alpha factoring (Brown, 2006).
The diagonalisation of the covariance or correlation matrix always calculates all the components at once. Also, the NIPALS method (Non-linear Iterative Partial Least Squares), explained in the previous section, calculates the components stepwise and is much faster than the diagonalisation of the covariance matrix if only the first few eigenvalues are desired. Also, Probabilistic PCA (PPCA) also estimates W and Ψ iteratively, using the Expectation. Maximisation (EM) algorithm (Burges, 2009).

Finding common factors in a dataset is often conducted in the exploratory model, in which the Exploratory Factor Analysis (EFA) method estimate both the number of factors and the loadings. EFA is like PCA, which is simpler to compute, accounting for the dataset's variance. EFA differs in considering the unique variance ε_i and explains the correlations among the observed variables while accounting for measurement errors. EFA can also be used to reconstruct the intercorrelations between the measured variables and a small set of latent factors.
Real-Life Application: a single factor of depression cannot be measured directly. Observed indicators, for example, can be scores for hopelessness, feelings of worthlessness/guilt, psychomotor retardation, and sleep disturbance. This four-dimensional dataset X can measure how they contribute to the depression latent factor η_1 as follows:
$x_1 = \lambda_{11}*\eta_1 + \varepsilon_1$
$x_2 = \lambda_{21}*\eta_1 + \varepsilon_2$
$x_3 = \lambda_{31}*\eta_1 + \varepsilon_3$
$x_4 = \lambda_{41}*\eta_1 + \varepsilon_4$
Check the Python code FA.ipynb for another psychometric dataset FA example.

2.2.10 Non-negative matrix factorisation (NMF)

NMF extracts a set of sparse meaningful factors from dataset X of non-negative values. It is a probabilistic model suitable for high-dimensional data. $X \in \mathbb{R}^{n \times d}$ is decomposed into $W \in \mathbb{R}^{n \times r}$, and $H \in \mathbb{R}^{r \times d}$ matrices with reduced dimensionality to rank r approximation. Matrix W columns contain the basis features; basis features are persistent features in all the n data points. Matrix H columns explain wherein X (coordinates) these bases are found and how important they are to help reconstruct the dataset. In facial images X dataset of n images and d pixels, the basis might be noses, eyes, hair, moustache, and other facial features. In text dataset X of n document and d words, the basis W can be topics that are defined to contain specific words, and H can be the importance of a word in the document. The rank r optimisation works by: $\underset{W \in \mathbb{R}^{n \times r}, H \in \mathbb{R}^{r \times d}}{\operatorname{argmin}} \|X - WH\|_f^2$ subject to $W \geq 0$ and $H \geq 0$. The partial derivatives are:
$\Delta_W F = WHH^T - XH^T \geq 0$, such that $W \circ \Delta_W F = 0$, and $W \geq 0$
$\Delta_H F = W^T WH - W^T X \geq 0$, such that $H \circ \Delta_H F = 0$, and $H \geq 0$
where $\circ$ is the component-wise product of two matrices.
The following generally are the steps performed to estimate W and H alternatively, such as the Hierarchical alternating least squares (HALS) algorithm:
Step 1: Initialize W and H randomly
Step 2: Repeat For $\ell = 1, 2, \ldots, r$:

1. Update W(:, ℓ) such that the objective function decreases: $W(:,\ell) \leftarrow \underset{W(:,\ell) \geq 0}{\operatorname{argmin}} \|X - \sum_{k \neq \ell} W(:,k)H(k,:) - W(:,\ell)H(\ell,:)\|_f$,
2. Update H accordingly to continue decreasing the objective function while maintaining the constraints:
3. Convergence is checked by: $C(W,H) = C_w(W) + C_H(H)$, where $C_w(W) = \|\min(W,0)\|_f + \|\min(\Delta_W F, 0)\|_f + \|W \circ \Delta_W F\|_f$ for all constraints, and $C_H(H) = \|\min(H,0)\|_f + \|\min(\Delta_H F, 0)\|_f + \|H \circ \Delta_H F\|_f$

Some regularisation is required to guarantee convergence. Detailed problems and research outcomes on how to avoid them can be found in (Suykens *et al.*, 2014).
Check the Python code NMF.ipynb for text mining NMF example compared with MiniBatchNMF and Latent Dirichlet Allocation (LDA) as implemented by scikit-learn.

2.2.11 Other Factorisations

The literature presents a plethora of algorithms that serve different objectives and constraints, and researchers will keep advancing the performance by addressing existing problems. Some of the factorisation techniques that we did not discuss are as follows:

- LU factorization: A = LU;
  - where L is the lower triangle and U is the upper triangle of matrix A. In the Gaussian Elimination algorithm used in chapter one to solve a system of equations Ax = b, we applied elementary row operations (ERO) to reduce a matrix to an upper triangular matrix. This is composed of a forward substitution Lz = b, and backward substitution, Ux = b.
- LU factorization with row pivoting: PA = LU;
- The Cholesky factorisation, $A \approx LL^T$
- The QR factorisation, $A \in \mathbb{R}^{m \times n} \approx QR$;

where $Q \in \mathbb{R}^{m \times m}$ has the special property of being an orthonormal matrix with respect to its columns, such that QTQ = I and $R \in \mathbb{R}^{m \times n}$ is an upper triangular matrix. If m > n, a reduced QR decomposition – or thin QR factorisation – can be computed, i.e. $Q \in \mathbb{R}^{m \times n}$ and $R \in \mathbb{R}^{n \times n}$.

- When a matrix is indefinite symmetric, there is a factorisation called the LDL^T (pronounced as L D L transpose) factorisation: $A \approx LDL^T$;
  - where L is a unit lower triangular matrix and D is a diagonal matrix. The Cholesky factorisation can derive an algorithm for the LDL^T factorisation (Geijn and Quintana-Ort´, 2008).
- Dictionary Learning A ≈ DC, such that D is a dictionary of all entities (signals or called atoms), and C contains sparse coefficients or codes (the different signal representations and their frequency or importance). The Dictionary Learning approach has many algorithms and applications in compressive sensing and signal recovery and implemented in sklearn.decomposition.DictionaryLearning.

2.2.12 Comparing Methods

You can notice that eigendecomposition Av = λBv is the fundamental decomposition technique that the most discussed algorithm reduces to after considering the problem objectives and constraints. Table 1 is adopted from (Lu, Plataniotis and Venetsanopoulos, 2014) with the extra methods added and a summary of objectives and limitations of methods.

Table 1: Comparison of Linear Subspace Learning Methods

Method	Maximise	A	B	v	Objective	Limitations
PCA	Total scatter (variation)	S_T	I	u_1	only for the Gaussian data representation method. Closed Formula Exists.	First and second-order statistics: mean and std, ignoring correlations of higher statistics. Assumes linear dataset. Hard to interpret the PCs' relation to data – not suitable for feature extraction.
SVD	Covariance matrix	A^TA	U	V	Relates to data well. Singular values are stable for all matrices. Useful for compression.	
LDA	Between-class to within-class scatter ratio	S_B	S_W	u_1	Supervised Data Disciminitive method.	Suffer from high variance in SSS (small sample size).
CCA	Correlation	$\begin{bmatrix} 0 & \Sigma_{xy} \\ \Sigma_{yx} & 0 \end{bmatrix}$	$\begin{bmatrix} \Sigma_{xx} & 0 \\ 0 & \Sigma_{yy} \end{bmatrix}$	$\begin{bmatrix} u_{x1} \\ u_{y1} \end{bmatrix}$	Correlation between two symmetric datasets	Require the inverse of Σ_{xx}, Σ_{yy}, which can be solved by regularisation or Cholesky decomposition. Suffer from high variance in SSS.
PLS	Covariance	$\begin{bmatrix} 0 & \Sigma_{xy} \\ \Sigma_{yx} & 0 \end{bmatrix}$	$\begin{bmatrix} I & 0 \\ 0 & I \end{bmatrix}$	$\begin{bmatrix} u_{x1} \\ u_{y1} \end{bmatrix}$	Covariance between asymmetric Datasets Work well when Σ_{xx}, Σ_{yy} are singular.	Work well for a small number of latent variables.
FA	PLS and other variations can perform FA	$\begin{bmatrix} 0 & \Sigma_{xy} \\ \Sigma_{yx} & 0 \end{bmatrix}$	$\begin{bmatrix} I & 0 \\ 0 & I \end{bmatrix}$	$\begin{bmatrix} u_{x1} \\ u_{y1} \end{bmatrix}$	Map Directly to meaningful unobserved data	

ICA	Iterative Algorithm to estimate both the mixing matrix A and the sources/ICs s subject to constraints	x	A	s	Works for non-Gaussian data. Higher-order statistics: kurtosis or negentropy. Iterative methods.	ICs are not ordered, and the actual number can not be estimated.
NMF	Iterative Algorithm, to estimate both the bases matrix W and the sources/ICs s subject to constraints	X	W	H	Sparse Meaningful features in high-dimensional datasets	Probabilistic model.

Since the Eigendecomposition is at the heart of dimensionality reduction methods, approximating this decomposition for a submatrix of the given dataset can speed up the training. The generalised Nyström method does this by a quadrature method that solves an integral equation by replacing the integral with a representative weighted sum. For a dataset X ∈ $\mathbb{R}^d$, the density p(x), is represented by the integral form, which reduces to a quadrature rule as follows:

$$\int k(x,y)u(y)p(y)dy = \lambda u(x) \approx \frac{1}{m}\sum_{i=1}^{m} k(x,x_i)u(x_i)$$

When the approximate equation on the right-hand side is applied to the sample points, it becomes a matrix equation $k_{mm}u_m = m\lambda u_m$, where u is ($u_i \equiv u(x_i)$) is the eigenfunction for some chosen m points such that the rank r of X (number of linearly independent columns) is $\gg m$, and k_{mm} means indices mm and that $K \in M_m$ is a submatrix of X, (with components $K_{ij} \equiv k(x_i,x_j)$). When m=r, then the approximation is exact. The eigenvalues λ_i approximately scale with the number of points chosen m. The full steps of solving the Nyström method exact and approximate variant (dropping the requirement that eigenvectors be orthogonal to each other) are explained in (Burges, 2009). The point to emphasise is that the projections of a mapped test point along principal components in a kernel feature space (the submatrix K) are equal to the expression for the approximate eigenfunctions evaluated at the new point, computed according to the approximate quadrature rule equation mentioned above. This mapping to a submatrix approximates the full eigenfunctions at all points. The main objective of the following section is to find Manifolds of lower dimensions that approximate the points in a dataset in the higher dimension.

2.3 Manifolds

Data in high dimensional spaces tend to be sparse, with most vectors containing zeros. This makes most vectors orthogonal to each other and equidistant, which means there is no structure to learn. These properties disable distance-measure-based dimensionality reduction algorithms to identify the linear subspace efficiently. Consequently, any regression or classification algorithm estimating the decision line or hyperplane in a higher dimension will fail to draw a line between equidistant points. Learning a Manifold M that contains the data points of the given dataset represented in a lower dimension than the input higher dimension space is a non-linear unsupervised dimensionality reduction approach that reduces the computation cost and increases the accuracy of the ML algorithm. In Natural Language Processing (NLP), words must be numerically encoded. If we encode all

words in a dictionary, this might be sparse, and not all words will be used in a specific document or dataset. The word embeddings (manifold) from a given corpus can be learned using deep learning layers and can be constructed by statistical methods, maintaining closer codes for semantically close words.
This learning of the points' relationships to their neighbours in the manifold does not need to be using a similar relationship, equation, or geometric shape. This would create a grid of some sort of basis along each dimension, creating a dimensionality curse. On the contrary, the manifold can be learned using several relationships in different neighbourhoods embedded in the manifold. For example, instead of learning the same unified principal components of a dataset and projecting the dataset onto the initial principal components for reduction, a manifold learning algorithm would partition the data into closer neighbourhoods. Then, the algorithm would learn the principal components for each neighbourhood independently and project the relevant points onto their initial PCs that are different from the other neighbourhood, then form a manifold of all projections. Similar to the power method in estimating the Eigenvector, starting from random embedding and optimising it is a popular manifold learning approach. Check Python notebook Manifolds.ipynb for a comprehensive example using MNIST dataset comparing manifolds created by linear unsupervised PCA, supervised LDA and QDA, and manifold learning algorithms, MDS, Isomap, LLE, t-SNE, and Spectral Embedding.

2.3.1 Multidimensional Scaling (MDS)

MDS searches for a measure of dissimilarity between each pair of data points in X ∈ $\mathbb{R}^{m \times d}$ to map them to a low-dimensional Euclidean Space, forming a squared distances matrix to be used for visualisation or dimensionality reduction and feature extraction. This can be performed using similar steps to the following as adapted from (Glen., 2015):
Step 1: Assign some points to coordinates in n-dimensional space.

1. Choose N points in 2D or 3D to be able to visualise and easily modelled. The coordinates' orientation is arbitrary and depends on the features' nature. For example, two coordinate axes representing north/south and east/west are suitable for modelling a dataset containing map locations.

Step 2: Calculate the symmetric similarity matrix A using a suitable distance measure for all pairs of points.

2. The Euclidean distance is the Euclidean norm ||. || that is based on the Pythagorean theorem becomes more complicated for n-dimensional space (see https://hlab.stanford.edu/brian/euclidean_distance_in.html). For two pairs of data points x, y ∈ $\mathbb{R}$: dist(x, y) = x-y, for x, y ∈ $\mathbb{R}^2$, dist(x, y) = $\sqrt{x^2 - y^2}$, and for x, y ∈ $\mathbb{R}^d$, dist(x, y)= $\sqrt{\sum_{i=1}^{d}(x_i^d + y_i^d)}$. This results in the similarity matrix A whose ij-th element is $\|x_i - x_j\|^2$ for some x_i, x_j ∈ $\mathbb{R}^d$. Other distance metrics can be used. Also, non-metric scaling in ordinal MDS can be performed by using a given rank ordering of the original data points in this matrix that is minimised using a suitable cost function of the difference between the embedded squared distances and some monotonic function of the dissimilarities.

Step 3: Find the lower-dimensional embedding:

3. The Schoenberg theorem states that the class of symmetric matrices A ∈ $\mathbb{R}^{n \times n}$ such that $A_{ij} \geq 0$ and $A_{ii} = 0$ ∀i, j. Then $\bar{A} \equiv$ −PAP is positive semi-definite if and only if A is a distance matrix (with embedding space $\mathbb{R}^d$ for some d). Given that A is a distance matrix, the minimal embedding dimension d is the rank of $\bar{A}$,

and the embedding vectors are any set of Gram vectors of $\bar{A}$, scaled by a factor of $\frac{1}{\sqrt{2}}$. Further discussions on positivity and geometric metrics in the dimension-free settings when the size of matrices is unconstrained can be found in (Belton *et al.*, 2019).

a. Defining the projection matrix $P^c \equiv (1 - ec')$, for any $c \in R^m$ such that $e'c = 1$, then for any conditionally negative definite (CND) matrix A, the matrix $-P^cAP'^c$ is positive semi-definite (and hence a dot product matrix). We can map a distance matrix A to a dot product matrix K by using P^c in the above manner for any set of numbers c_i that sum to unity. Again, this reduces to Eigendecomposition $\bar{A}E = E\Lambda$, where $\bar{A}$ is the positive semi-definite matrix that we need to solve for, E be the matrix of column eigenvectors $e^{(\alpha)}$ (labelled by α), ordered by eigenvalue λ_α, so that the first column is the principal Eigenvector and Λ is the diagonal matrix of eigenvalues. Defining the matrix $\tilde{E} \equiv E\sqrt{\Lambda}$, we see that the Gram vectors are just the rows of $\tilde{E}$. The Gram matrix for column matrix X is X*X for complex numbers and A^TA for real numbers. Gram matrices, when invertible, indicate that columns of A are linearly independent. Gram Matrices have broad applications in Riemannian geometry, kernels functions as explained later, SVD calculates instead of a covariance matrix, and other domains.
b. If $\bar{A} \in \mathbb{R}^{n \times n}$ has rank r ≤ n, then the final n − r columns of $\tilde{E}$ will be zero, and we have directly found the r-dimensional embedding vectors that we are looking for. If $\bar{A} \in \mathbb{R}^{n \times n}$ is full rank, but the last n − p eigenvalues are much smaller than the first p, then it's reasonable to approximate the ith Gram vector by its first p components $\sqrt{\lambda_\alpha}\tilde{e}_\alpha^{(i)}$, α = 1, ..., p, and we have found a low dimensional approximation. MDS, Laplacian eigenmaps, and spectral clustering perform this latter approach of removing the last few components. The unexplained squared residuals measure the quality of the approximation. Thus the fraction of the "unexplained residuals" is $\sum_{a=p+1}^{r} \frac{\lambda_a}{\sum_{a=1}^{r} \lambda_a}$, in analogy to the fraction of "unexplained variance" in PCA.

Step 4: Compare the similarity matrix with the original input matrix by evaluating the stress function.

4. Stress is a goodness-of-fit measure based on differences between predicted and actual distances. In the original MDS paper (Kruskal, 1964), it was mentioned that fits close to zero are excellent, while anything over 0.2 should be considered "poor". More recent authors suggest evaluating stress based on the quality of the distance matrix and how many objects are in that matrix.

Step 5: Adjust coordinates, if necessary, to minimise stress by repeating the above steps.
The complexity of MDS is reduced by using a Landmark MDS algorithm (Borg, Groenen and Mair, 2013).

2.3.2 Isometric Feature Map (Isomap)

MDS maps the dataset to a lower-dimensional embedding such that the data points are isotropically represented in the lower space (maintaining equivalent distances) without modelling the underlying manifold. Isomap and Locally Linear Embedding are methods to model the lower dimensional manifold without keeping the equivalent distances constraint. To preserve the non-linear structures in the dataset, Isomap assumes that the data points lie on a curve and not a straight line, and instead of measuring the dissimilarity matrix between data points, it measures the distance along the curve between the two points. It accounts only for large distances along this curve, even if the two points are close in $\mathbb{R}^d$. The basic idea is to construct a graph whose nodes are the data points, where a pair of nodes are adjacent only if the two points are close in $\mathbb{R}^d$, and then to approximate the geodesic distance along the manifold between any two points as the shortest path in the graph, computed using the Floyd algorithm or the faster Dijkstra's algorithm with Fibonacci heap (Qu and Cai, 2017); and finally to use MDS to extract the low dimensional representation (as vectors in $\mathbb{R}^{d'}, d' \ll d$) from the resulting matrix of squared distances. Isomap does not provide a direct mapping function: $\mathrm{I}: \mathbb{R}^{d} \rightarrow \mathbb{R}^{d'}$.

2.3.3 Locally Linear Embedding (LLE)

LLE models the manifold by treating it as a union of linear patches, in analogy to using coordinate charts to parameterise a manifold in differential geometry. Suppose $X \in \mathbb{R}^{m \times d}$ with each point $x_i \in \mathbb{R}^{d}$ has a small number of close neighbours indexed by the set $\mathcal{N}(i)$ up to n neighbours, and let $y_i \in \mathbb{R}^{d'}$ be the low-dimensional representation of x_i. The idea is to express each x_i as a linear combination of its neighbours and then construct the y_i so that they can be expressed as the same linear combination of their corresponding neighbours (Ghojogh *et al.*, 2020). Similar steps to the following can achieve this as adapted from (Burges, 2009):
Step 1: Find the W's $\in \mathbb{R}^{m \times n}$ that minimises the sum of the reconstruction errors

1. The reconstruction error: $E_i \equiv \left\| x_i - \sum_{j \in \mathrm{N(i)}} W_{i,j}\, x_j \right\|^2$ that is invariant of global translation, which creates the constraint: $\sum_{j \in \mathrm{N(i)}} W_{i,j} = 1\, \forall i$, should also be invariant of data scaling, rotation, and/or reflection. i, j, k $\in \mathcal{N}(i)$, k will be used later.
2. This is achieved by minimising the following objective function:
$$F \equiv \sum_i F_i \equiv \sum_i \left(\frac{1}{2} \left\| x_i - \sum_{j \in \mathcal{N}(i)} W_{i,j}\, x_j \right\|^2 - \lambda_i \Big(\sum_{j \in \mathcal{N}(i)} W_{i,j} - 1 \Big) \right)$$
3. Differentiate each F_i with respect to $W_{i,j}$, and require that $W_{i,j}$vanishes and set to zero.

Step 2: Find a set of eigenvectors $y_i \in \mathbb{R}^{d'}$

4. Perform Eigendecomposition of the product of two sparse matrices $(1 - W)'(1 - W) \in \mathbb{R}^{m}$ with the smallest eigenvalues. This step guarantees that the y is zero mean (since they are orthogonal to e.
5. This is achieved by minimising the following objective function:
$$F = \sum_i \left(\frac{1}{2} \left\| y_i - \sum_j W_{i,j}\, y_j \right\|^2 - \frac{1}{2} \sum_{\alpha\beta} \lambda_{\alpha\beta} \Big(\sum_i \frac{1}{m} Y_{i\alpha} Y_{i\beta} - \delta_{\alpha\beta} \Big) \right)$$
6. Differentiate each F with respect to $Y_{k\delta}$ and choosing $\lambda_{\alpha\beta} = \lambda_\alpha \delta_{\alpha\beta} \equiv \Lambda_{\alpha\beta}$ gives the matrix equation: $(1 - W)'(1 - W)Y = \frac{1}{m} Y\Lambda$

LLE tends to create a dense manifold in the centre, with various emerging rays. This is justified by the LLEs approach to learning the multilinear function from a set of simpler linear functions, making it suitable for simple structures in smaller datasets.

2.3.4 t-distributed Stochastic Neighbor Embeddings (t-SNE)

t-SNE represents a dataset as a t-distribution or normal distribution of smaller sizes. It is almost like a neural network being trained using a stochastic gradient descent algorithm to minimise the entropy metric. It is an unsupervised approach that clusters the data points into local groups of neighbourhoods and focuses on learning about their local structures than unfolding them. It is an efficient manifold learning algorithm for multi-scale datasets with complex structures and multiple manifolds. However, it is computationally expensive compared to the other manifold learning algorithms.

2.3.5 Spectral Graph decomposition: Spectral Clustering

A simple mapping from each data point in a dataset to a node in an undirected graph G, and apply minimum spanning tree or nearest neighbour algorithm to fill the adjacency matrix W_{ij}, with a similarity measure between node i and node j. The normalised Laplacian matrix for any weighted, undirected graph is defined by $L \equiv D^{-\frac{1}{2}}LD^{-\frac{1}{2}}$, where $L_{ij} \equiv D_{ij} - W_{ij}$ and $D_{ij} \equiv \delta_{ij}(\sum_k W_{ik})$. L is positive semi-definite, and so is the normalised Laplacian. The spectral Graph theory states that the graph spectrum properties defined by the eigenvalues of its Laplacian, characterise the global graph properties as follows:

- A complete graph (that is, one for which every node is adjacent to every other node) has a single zero eigenvalue, and all other eigenvalues are equal to $\frac{m}{m-1}$.
- If G is connected but not complete, its smallest non-zero Eigenvalue is bounded above by unity.
- The number of zero Eigenvalues is equal to the number of connected components in the graph, and in fact, the spectrum of a graph is the union of the spectra of its connected components.
- The sum of the eigenvalues is bounded above by m, with equality if G has no isolated nodes.

In light of these results, it seems reasonable to expect that global properties of the data — how it clusters or what dimension manifold it lies on — might be captured by properties of the Laplacian. Laplacian Eigenmaps and Spectral Clustering manifold learning methods apply spectral graph theory to model a dataset's lower-dimensional manifold. Clustering generally reduces the dimensionality of the number of data points to the number of clusters of similar structural features at its largest scale. Partitioning a graph into two disjoint clusters of nodes requires removing arcs such that the cut is defined as the sum of removed arcs weights. The minimum cut implies the maximum dissimilarity between the clusters. Each node is labelled by $z_i = 1$ for nodes in one cluster and $z_i = -1$ for nodes in the other cluster. The solution to the normalised min-cut problem is given by: $\min_y \frac{y'Ly}{y'Dy}$ such that $y_i \in \{1, -b\}$ and $y'De = 0$, where $y \equiv (e + z) + b(e - z)$, and b is a constant that depends on the partition. The following steps are generally followed:

Step 1: Weighted Graph Construction.

1. Transform the raw input data points into graph representation using affinity (adjacency) matrix representation A such that two points x_i and x_j has W_{ij} weight/similarity measure on the arc/link connecting them. The weights can be calculated using a minimum spanning tree algorithm or N-Nearest Neighbours

Step 2: Graph Laplacian Construction.

2. Unnormalised Graph Laplacian is constructed as L = D - A for and normalised one as $L \equiv D^{-\frac{1}{2}}(D-A)D^{-\frac{1}{2}}$

Step 3: Partial Eigenvalue Decomposition.

3. Eigenvalue decomposition is done on graph Laplacian: $Ly = \lambda Dy$
4. The clustering is achieved by thresholding a single eigenvector y_i so that the nodes are split into two disjoint sets. The dimension reduction is achieved by treating the element y_i as the first component of a reduced dimension representation of sample x_i. Otherwise, a simple clustering algorithm such as K-means can be applied to the reduced dimensionality dataset and is observed to perform much better than on the full dataset.

2.4 Mapping to the Higher Dimensions

The estimated decision line/hyperplane function needs to shatter the dataset's N points, i.e., the dataset is separable by the classifier. Figure 8a) illustrates the classifications of N=3 points $\in \mathbb{R}^2$ classified into blue (1) and white (-1) classes. All possible assignments of labels (all random datasets that can be obtained) are 2^3=8 different possible datasets. The figure shows the estimated decision line for all possible datasets as a set of functions such as f(x, w) to separate the classes. In $\mathbb{R}^2$ it is possible to find three points that this set of functions can shatter, but it is not possible to find four. This is measured by the Vapnik Chervonenkis (VC) dimension as defined below. The set of oriented lines in $\mathbb{R}^2$ is three. Figure 8b) shows how a given set of N=4 points $\in \mathbb{R}^1$ are not shattered by the function f(w, x) = sine (wx), which generally has an infinite VC dimension for being able to shatter a subset of the set $\{2^{-m} \mid m \in \mathbb{N}\}$. This is because these points are equally spaced and labelled in this order.

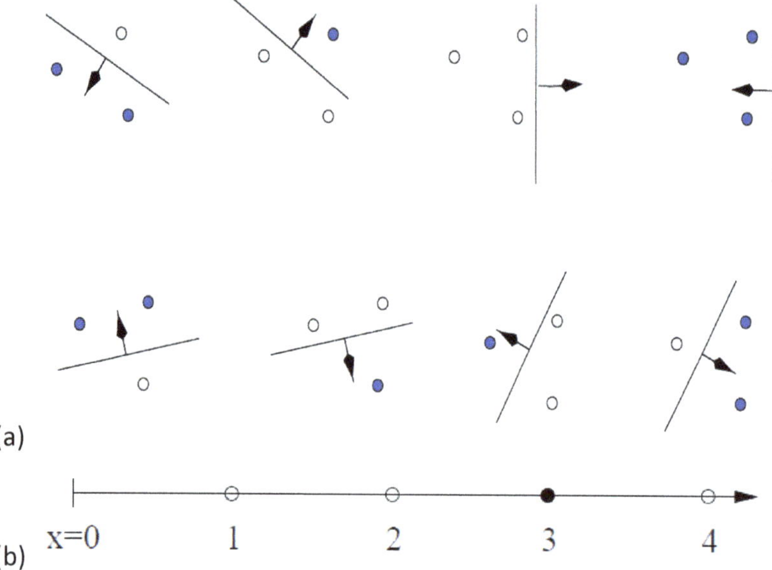

Figure 8a) Three points in $\mathbb{R}^2$that shattered by decision lines function.b) Four points that cannot be shattered by {sin(wx)}, despite infinite VC dimension by the function set.

2.4.1 Support Vector Machine (SVM)

SVM estimates the decision line using a convex quadratic programming algorithm. Linear programming minimises or maximises a linear function subject to defined constraints, such as solving for minimum weights to satisfy the classification or regression of a given dataset, given regularisation constraints, and others. A quadratic programming optimisation problem is a form of non-linear programming involving a quadratic convex objective function, and the points that satisfy the required constraints also form a convex set. Any linear constraint defines a convex set, and a set of N simultaneous linear constraints defines the intersection of N convex sets, which is also a convex set. For a labelled dataset $\{x_i, y_i\}$ i from 1 to N, $y \in \{1, -1\}$, and $x_i \in \mathbb{R}^d$, the optimisation aims to find the weights/parameters for the separating hyperplane that separates the positive classes from the negative classes. For the linearly separable dataset, a possible set of steps are as follows:

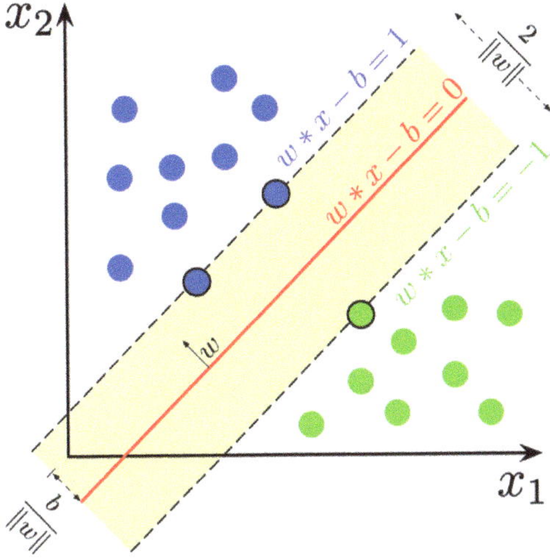

Figure 9: Maximum-margin hyperplane and margin for an SVM trained on two classes with $x \in \mathbb{R}^2$. Samples on margins are called support vectors.(Larhmam, 2018)

Step 1: the geometric preliminaries of the algorithm to identify the optimisation requirements:

1. Generally, any data point x which lies on the hyperplane satisfies wx + b = 0, where w is normal to the hyperplane, $\frac{|b|}{\|w\|}$ is the perpendicular distance from the hyperplane to the origin, and $\|w\|$ is the Euclidean norm of w. But in SVM, we need to find the hyperplane that maximises the margin between the closest points from both classes. Therefore, no x points should fall on the separating hyperplane.
2. To achieve this, we need to identify two hyperplanes, each one passes through the support vectors (points x closest to the hyperplane from both directions). Therefore, all data points support the following constraints:
    a. $wx_i + b \geq +1$ for $y_i = +1$, these points lie on the hyperplane H_1: $wx_i + b = 1$ with normal w, and perpendicular distance from the origin = $\frac{|1-b|}{\|w\|}$
    b. $wx_i + b \leq -1$ for $y_i = -1$, these points lie on the hyperplane H_2: $wx_i + b = -1$ with normal w, and perpendicular distance from the origin = $\frac{|-1-b|}{\|w\|}$
3. Let d_+ (d_-) be the shortest distance from the separating hyperplane to the closest positive (negative) example, such that the margin of the separating hyperplane is equal to $d_+ + d_-$. No data points fall between H_1 and H_2.

4. To maximise the margin between H_1 and H_2 hyperplanes, we need to minimise $\|w\|^2$ subject to the combined constraints above as: $y_i\ (wx_i + b) - 1 \geq 0\ \forall i$, such that d+ = d- = $\frac{1}{\|w\|}$, and the margin between H_1 and H_2 = $\frac{2}{\|w\|}$.

Step 2: Apply the Lagrangian optimisation formulation

5. The Primal Lagrangian equation adds a Lagrange constant for every data point, checking if it is a support vector $\alpha_i > 0$, or not $\alpha_i = 0$ if it lies on one of the hyperplanes. The equation becomes: $L_P = \frac{1}{2}\|w\|^2 - \sum_{i=1}^{N} \alpha_i y_i\ (x_i . w + b) + \sum_{i=1}^{N} \alpha_i$
6. We have two sets of constraints forming a Wolfe dual problem:
   a. Minimise L_P with respect to w and b, subject to the constraint that the derivatives of L_P with respect to all the α_i vanish, all subject to the constraints $\alpha_i \geq 0$.:
   b. Maximise L_P with respect to α_i, subject to the constraints that the gradient of L_P with respect to w and b vanish, and subject also to the constraints that the $\alpha_i \geq 0$: $w = \sum_{i=1}^{N} \alpha_i y_i\ x_i$
   c. A mild constraint to make b=0, will make all hyperplanes pass through the origin and reduce the degree of freedom by one: $\sum_{i=1}^{N} \alpha_i y_i = 0$
   d. Now the Dual Lagrangian equation is: $L_D = \sum_i \alpha_i - \frac{1}{2}\sum_{i,j} \alpha_i \alpha_j y_i y_j\ x_i . x_j$ subject to the mild constraint in 6.c. by adding an extra Lagrange constant λ.
   e. We can use the Hessian $H_{ij} = y_i y_j x_i\ .\ x_j$, to formulate the Dual Lagrangian equation is: $L_D = \sum_{i=1}^{N+1} \alpha_i - \frac{1}{2}\sum_{i,j=1}^{N+1} \alpha_i H_{ij} \alpha_j - \lambda \sum_{i=1}^{N+1} \alpha_i y_i$
7. Differentiate with respect to w and b:
   a. $\frac{\delta L_D}{\delta \alpha_i} = (H\alpha)_i + \lambda y_i = 1\ \forall i = 1, \ldots l$, one for each Lagrangian constraint.
   b. $\frac{\delta L_P}{\delta w_v} = w_v - \sum_i \alpha_i y_i x_{iv} = 0$ for v=1, ...d
   c. $\frac{\delta L_P}{\delta b} = -\sum_i \alpha_i y_i = 0$

Toy examples of the linearly separable data are "AND", and "OR" are shown in Figure 10. The "XOR" dataset is not linearly separable. One solution requires two separation 1-D lines processed in 2 layers, and one class spans two areas. Another solution presented in Figure 11 is to map the dataset to a higher dimension, in which it will be separable linearly.

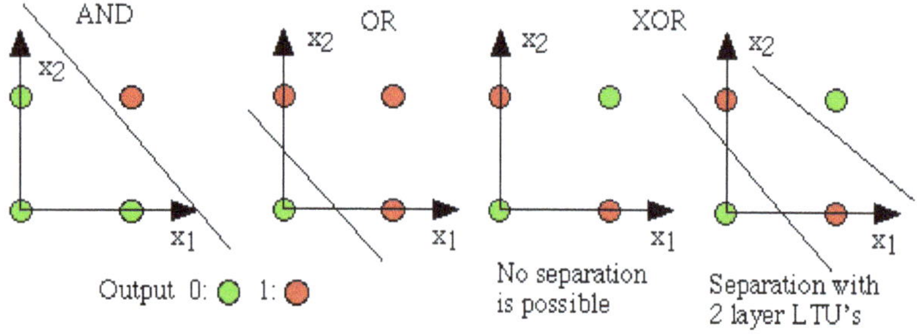

Figure 10: Linearly Separable toy examples in the AND and OR functions. The XOR function is not linearly separable and requires 2 1-D lines processed in 2 Layers

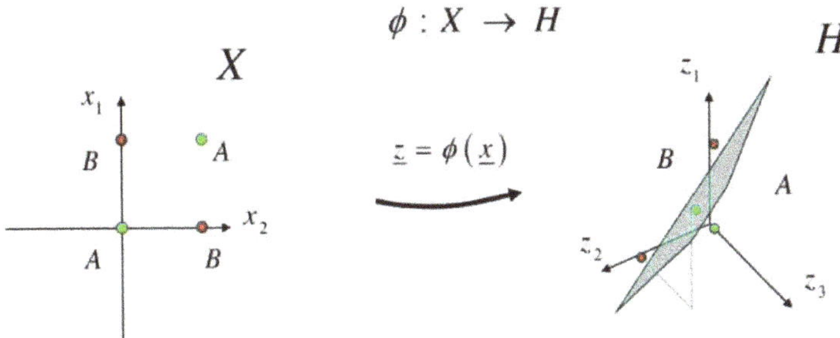

Figure 11: Mapping the XOR dataset to a higher dimension here $\mathbb{R}^3$, enable it to be linearly separable by 2-D plane, as shown

For example, a 2-D plane separates the "XOR" dataset after mapping it to $\mathbb{R}^3$ using the following mapping function:

$\Phi(\begin{bmatrix} x_1 \\ x_2 \end{bmatrix}) = \begin{bmatrix} x_1 \\ x_2 \\ x_1 x_2 \end{bmatrix}$, such that:

$\Phi(0, 0) = (0, 0, 0)$
$\Phi(0, 1) = (0, 1, 0)$
$\Phi(1, 0) = (1, 0, 0)$
$\Phi(1, 1) = (1, 1, 1)$

2.4.2 Kernel Trick

First, the following concepts need to be understood about the measure of data separability given classifier functions to understand the non-linearly separable dataset: VC Dimension and Hilbert Spaces, in which a non-linear dataset in the low dimension can be separable in the higher dimension.

The Vapnik Chervonenkis (VC) dimension is a non-negative integer property that measures the ML algorithm flexibility to learn a decision line for a large set of points of any possible labelling. The ML algorithm produces a set of functions H= {f(w)} (w is the estimated vector of weights/parameters for different datasets and not a specific value for w that makes a function a particular function for a particular dataset). It can be defined for various classes of function f (different algorithms such as different complexity, higher polynomial, or radial basis functions). Here we will only consider functions that correspond to the two-class pattern recognition case so that f(x, w) ∈ {1, -1} $\forall x, w$. A given set C of N points labelled in all possible 2^N ways are said to be shattered by the ML algorithm when for each labelling, a member of the set {f(w)} can be found that correctly assigns those labels. The intersection of sets H and C is defined as the following set family: $H \cap C = \{h \cap C: h \cap H\}$. C is shattered by H, if $H \cap C$ contains all subsets of C: $|H \cap C| = 2^{|C|}$. The VC dimension for the set of functions H is defined as the largest cardinality of sets (training points) that can be shattered by it (correctly classified without errors). VC dimension is ∞ if it is too large. Note that if the VC dimension is h, then there exists at least one set of h points that can be shattered, but in general, it will not be true that every set of h points can be shattered (Burges, 1998). The VC dimension of a finite classification model, which can return at most 2^d different classifiers, is at most d, depending on the structure of the model (chosen class of the function). Generally, some bounds are proven on the different dimensionalities and classifiers:

- A constant classifier (with no parameters), its VC dimension is 0 since it cannot shatter even a single point.
- A single-parametric threshold classifier on real numbers; i.e., for a certain threshold w, the classifier f(w) returns one if the input number is larger than w and 0; otherwise, the VC dimension of f(w) is one because: it can shatter a single point, but it cannot shatter any set of two points.

- A single-parametric interval classifier on real numbers; i.e., for a certain threshold w, the classifier f(w) returns one if the input number is within the interval w and 0; otherwise, then the VC dimension of f(w) is two because it can shatter some sets of two points, but it cannot shatter any set of three points.
- In a line classifier model (such as regression and perceptron), for each pair of distinct points, there is one line that contains both of them, lines that contain only one of them, and lines that contain none of them, so every set of size two is shattered. The line should separate positive data points from negative data points. There exist sets of 3 points that can indeed be shattered using this model (any 3 points that are not collinear can be shattered). However, no set of 4 points can be shattered because they can be partitioned into two subsets with intersecting convex hulls, so it is impossible to separate one of these subsets from the other. Thus, the VC dimension of this particular classifier is 3. This is the example shown in Figure 8a).
- A k-nearest neighbour with a k=1 classifier has infinite VC dimension and zero prediction error as, eventually, all points will be learned.
- A single-parametric sine classifier on real numbers; i.e., for a certain threshold w, the classifier f(w) returns one if the input number x has sine (wx) > 0 and 0 otherwise, then the VC dimension of f(w) is infinite because: it can shatter a finite subset of the set $\{2^{-m} \mid m \in \mathbb{N}\}$. Figure 8b) shows an example of a set of points that are not shattered by this function to emphasise that not every set of cardinality equal to the VC dimension of a classifier will be shattered.

Hilbert Space $\mathcal{H}$ is a generalisation of Euclidian space in the infinite dimension. More details will be explained in chapter five. In the infinite dimension, the inner product in step 6.d in the SVM linear solution steps above $(x_i . x_j)$ can be performed after mapping both vectors to the higher dimensions using a mapping function: $\Phi: \mathbb{R}^d \to \mathcal{H}$, where $\mathcal{H}$ is an infinite dimension and $\mathbb{R}^d$ is considered in the $\mathcal{L}$ as a lower dimension. The algorithm would do the dot products as $(\Phi(x_i) . \Phi(x_j))$ everywhere a lower-dimensional dot product $(x_i . x_j)$ is applied. Possible mappings to $\mathbb{R}^3$ are as follows:

$$\Phi(\begin{bmatrix} x_1 \\ x_2 \end{bmatrix}) = \begin{bmatrix} x_1^2 \\ \sqrt{2}x_1x_2 \\ x_2^2 \end{bmatrix}, \text{ or } \Phi(\begin{bmatrix} x_1 \\ x_2 \end{bmatrix}) = \frac{1}{\sqrt{2}} \begin{bmatrix} (x_1^2 - x_2^2) \\ 2x_1x_2 \\ (x_1^2 + x_2^2) \end{bmatrix}$$

Or a possible mapping to $\mathbb{R}^4$:

$$\Phi\left(\begin{bmatrix} x_1 \\ x_2 \end{bmatrix}\right) = \begin{bmatrix} x_1^2 \\ x_1x_2 \\ x_1x_2 \\ x_2^2 \end{bmatrix}$$

We can replace the mapping with a Kernel function $K(x_i, x_j) = (\Phi(x_i) . \Phi(x_j))$ that produces the same result without explicitly mapping every vector in the dataset or even defining a specific mapping. This will be further explained in chapter five while discussing the representer theorem and how it reduces searching the large space $\mathcal{H}$ to just finding the optimal values of the m coefficients $\alpha_1, \dots, \alpha_m$ of $x_1, \dots, x_m$ with each x_i vector of the features. Example Kernel functions are:

- $K(x_i, x_j) = (x_i . x_j + 1)^p$, results in a classifier polynomial equation of degree = p.
- $K(x_i, x_j) = e^{\frac{-\|x_i - x_j\|^2}{2\sigma^2}}$, results in a classifier Gaussian radial basis function (RBF) equation.
- $K(x_i, x_j) = \tanh(\kappa x_i . x_j - \delta)$, results in a particular kind of two-layer sigmoidal neural network.

This requires that the Hilbert Space Higher dimension $\mathcal{H}$ defines an inner product (not just the scalar dot product) such that any Cauchy sequence of points (that grows very close as the sequence progresses less than a given small positive distance) converges to a point in the space.

Mercer's condition: The kind of Kernel functions that define a dot product in some infinite space should conform with Mercer's condition, which states that there exists a mapping Φ and an expansion such that: $\mathrm{K}(x, \mathrm{y}) = \sum_i \Phi(\mathrm{x})_i \Phi(\mathrm{y})_i$ if and only if, for any g(x) such that $\int g(x)^2\, dx$ is finite. Then, $\int \mathrm{K}(x, \mathrm{y}) g(x) g(y)\, dxdy \geq 0$. Therefore, any kernel satisfies Mercer's condition if it is of the form $\mathrm{K}(x, y) = \sum_{p=0}^{\infty} c_p\, (x.y)^p$, where the c_p are positive real coefficients, and the series is uniformly convergent. Using such kernel produces a Hilbert Space Higher dimension $\mathcal{H}$of the dimensionality equals the combination $C(d + p - 1, p) = C\binom{d + p - 1}{p} = \frac{(d+p-1)!}{(p!(d+p-1)!)}$. For example, for a degree p = 4 polynomial, and for images data consisting of 16 by 16 pixels (d=256), dim($\mathcal{H}$) is 183,181,376.

The kernel trick can now be defined as a technique to implicitly map data into a higher-dimensional feature space without explicitly calculating the transformed feature vectors. This allows linear algorithms to operate effectively in a nonlinear feature space, enabling them to learn complex decision boundaries. It also avoids the computational and memory-intensive operations required to map the data into the higher-dimensional space explicitly. The kernel trick is closely tied to the dual formulation of SVMs. In the dual formulation, the decision function is expressed as a linear combination of the support vectors, which are the data points closest to the decision boundary.

Python notebook Classification_Linear_NonLinear.ipynb compares a number of classification algorithms on different types of datasets. It shows clearly the linearly separable datasets and the non-linearly separable ones classified by different SVM kernel functions and other linear and non-linear algorithms.

Chapter 3: Geometry & Algebra of Tensors

Chapter two discussed linear subspace learning using projective and manifold learning methods using mapping functions. The main emphasis was to use linear algebra to project to a lower-dimensional space. The mapping function is mainly dependent on the eigendecomposition of the dataset applied with different assumptions and constraints. Other approaches learn a manifold that belongs to a lower dimension using a submatrix by defining neighbourhood or adjacency between data points. Projecting the data points to a higher dimensional space in which they will be linearly separable is another method to apply when data are not linearly separable in their current dimension. The Kernel trick enables the dot product to be performed in Hilbert space without doing the actual mapping.
This chapter starts with the intuition of data analysis in higher dimensional spaces and their applications, then introduces the prelimanry mathematical concepts required to understand the following chapters. Section one will introduce multilinear algebra, such as tensor operations. Multilinear algebra will be explained in two subsections of section two. The first subsection introduces non-linear algebra as expressed in non-Euclidean spaces using hyperbolic and elliptic geometry, defining curves as conic sections, such as circles, ellipses, parabolas, and hyperbolas. The section continues to solve a system of equations employing these non-linear shapes. The second subsection will introduce Differential geometry on Manifolds using coordinate-free approaches. This subsection mainly focuses on the preliminaries to understand exterior derivatives using differential forms and their projections in many subspaces of any higher space $\mathbb{R}^n$. This section explains a definition of a subset of tensors: differential forms as skew-symmetric (or anti-symmetric) covariant tensors. This leads to the third subsection, in which tensors on Manifolds are explained. Then an introduction to Multi-linear subspace learning (MSL) algorithms as a generalisation of the LSL in chapter two will be presented in the third section.
The chapter might look full of equations. However, the proofs, derivation, and properties of each equation and consequent identities are omitted, although they are usually used in simplifying equations and computations. The aim is to familiarise the reader with the logical flow of these topics and how they build together and are used in machine learning algorithms. Visualisations from interesting books have been used, and python libraries in which these mathematical operators are implemented are provided. These are usually used at the bottom of the stack of a machine learning algorithm. Understanding what is happening under the hood gives the reader a better opportunity to choose the suitable algorithms with the suitable parameters, and the ambitious reader might start developing these algorithms further or apply them better in new domains.

Motivation and Intuition

In the previous two chapters, we have seen examples of data that is usually collected in a 2-dimensional array as rows being samples or entities and features being columns. However, multiple datasets are usually interacting or correlated in latent variables; hence, multiple datasets need to be studied together in multi-way analysis. The following are examples of generalisations of all ranks of tensors that data can appear in:

- A single temperature value as a scalar can be a rank-zero tensor.
- 1-way data for temperatures can be a vector as a rank-one tensor of a set of values for a given set of cities or the same city over date/time. Cities are the labels of the columns or the date/time.
- 2-way data describing temperatures for different map locations can be a matrix as a rank-two tensor, where the first coordinate is latitude, the second is the longitude coordinate, and the value of the tensor is the temperature. We do not usually have labels for rows and columns in data science, but in tensors, we can. This is achieved by Pivot tables that can be created of two columns in a Pandas data frame in Python.

- 3-way data for the same example can add a third dimension of time for the different temperature reading in the different locations at different times on the third mode.
- 2-way data in which columns describe features against entities in rows such as student marks in different subject matrices as rank two tensors, such that the student identity is in mode 1, and subjects in mode 2, and values are the marks. The school grade can also be added as another mode and so forth.
- Brain-Computer Interface (BCI) based on EEG signals are naturally multi-mode due to the data recording mechanism. For example, signals are recorded by multiple sensors (electrodes) in multiple trials and epochs for multiple subjects and with different tasks, conditions..., and so forth. This dataset can be represented in rank n tensors to enable multi-way multi-block data analysis techniques.
- Magnetic resonance imaging (MRI), functional MRI, PET, and MEG datasets are also naturally multi-mode. For example, A NIfTI file for a typical MRI scan store the voxel values in an array of numbers. The coordinates for a single voxel within a NIfTI image volume can be specified as a 3-dimensional index (x, y, z) or a 4-dimensional index (x, y, z, t) for time. Then the subject is another mode, then the aim of the experiment is another, the resolution and so forth. Similar datasets can be found at https://openneuro.org/.
- Examples from psychometrics are provided by (Kiers and Mechelen, 2001) in their overview of three-way component analysis techniques. The overview is a good introduction to three-way methods, explaining when to use three-way techniques rather than two-way (based on an ANOVA test), how to preprocess the data, guidance on choosing the rank of the decomposition and an appropriate rotation and methods for presenting the results.

Some datasets will be produced initially in tensor form but usually in multiple files, and a tensorisation step will always be required. Python notebooks accompanying this book, such as "tensorisation.ipynb" and "multi-wayExamples.ipynb", contain sample tensorisation tailored to particular datasets and analysis requirements. These implementations are very simple for illustration purposes. Many opportunities for generalisations, quantisation, sampling, aggregation and optimisation can be achieved. Tensorisation applied in these examples is so far artistic. It might be a talent that can be enhanced by practice and exposure to different datasets, preprocessing requirements and analysis requirements. The thesis in (Debals, 2017) presents a more formal introduction to tensorisation as suitable for BSS and clustering problems. The discussion is rather theoretical, leaving many implementation details to the programmer's creativity.

The opposite of tensorisation can be achieved, as explained in this chapter's first section below. This happens when the data is naturally in tensor form, but the analyst needs to matricise or vectorise it for 2-way analysis. For example, an N-mode tensor can be unfolded or matricised into a matrix in N ways for each mode. The n-mode matricisation of $\mathcal{X} \in \mathbb{R}^{I_1, I_2, \cdots, I_N}$ is denoted as $\mathcal{X}_{(n)} \in \mathbb{R}^{I_n, I_1 \times \cdots \times I_{n-1} \times I_{n+1} \times \ldots \times I_N}$ and is taken by keeping the nth mode as the first mode/rows and concatenating the slices of the rest of the modes as columns into an extended matrix (Kolda and Bader, 2009).

Keeping these datasets in their original tensor-form structure and order as collected maintains the characteristics that will help estimate a manifold representative of the intrinsic structure that might get lost during the transformations such as vectorisation or matricisation. These transformations are meant to enable linear algebra analysis at the expense of losing the remarkable power of higher-order instruments that are not available in the lower order. This power is not a result of the generation of more data, as it is the result of the structure of the data in the higher order as it is naturally collected in different experiments and different domains and dimensionality (Smilde, Bro and Geladi, 2004). These heterogeneous and multi-aspect data are multimodal, measured using different sensors (experiments or data collection measures), and subject to different kinds of errors and uncertainties.

Some representation analysis and pre-processing might be needed for any dataset to enable multi-way analysis based on the problem definition and data collection methods. Tensor summation notation representation preserves the multilinearity of data as it comes in nature (Mangan, 2008). Chapter four will explain further details on the summation notation.

If the complete tensor object in a full format is created in memory, it will require huge memory, and analysing a high dimensional space will suffer from the curse of dimensionality. However, since the non-empty elements of a tensor object are often highly correlated with neighbouring elements in most applications of interest, these tensor objects are highly constrained and limited to a subspace, a manifold of intrinsically low dimension (Zhang, Li and Wang, 2005). Methods of feature extraction, dimensionality reduction, or decomposition/factorisation transform a high-dimensional data set into a low-dimensional equivalent representation while retaining most of the variance and interactions among the elements, capturing the underlying structure or the actual physical phenomenon modelled. Pair-wise interactions do not capture the multi-way interactions by the cancellation of effects and lack of interpretation clarity. In Python code in "multi-wayExamples.ipynb", examples of pivot tables in matrix form were difficult to interpret when more features were added. However, pivot tables can provide a mean to achieve an extra mode on value categories of a specific feature, such as age groups (a mode of children from 0 to 6, 7-14 teens, 15-22, and so forth) from the age feature, to partition the data during tensorisation. In comparison, the tensorisation captures every pair-wise and higher multi-way interaction.
In summary, tensors are defined as vectors that contain collections of components with magnitude and direction but in higher-dimensional space. Tensors can describe a function that houses the transformations of these components on a discrete high-dimensional grid capturing their interactions as the basis of these coordinates change (Charles Van Loan *et al.*, 2009). Chapter five will explain further the coordinate and basis change in representation theory. Not all multidimensional arrays are tensors. However, scalars, vectors, matrices or n-dimensional arrays are tensors and subject to multi-way analysis when their structures can transform to different coordinates (reference axes or scale) than those they are measured on, maintaining their properties, such as invariance, covariance, contravariance, and some form of distance measure or neighbourhood as explained in chapter two.

3.1 N-D Arrays / Tensor definition

3.1.1 Tensor Definition

Having seen why stacking more columns in the same matrix is not good in the motivational problem in chapter 1 illustrated in Matrix-High-DImensional-DF.ipynb, we can now increase the number of indices and use the original data arrangements in tensors.
Tensors are defined to be higher-order matrices of N dimensions, so we need n indices to scan the elements of the tensor by its given shape vector or bounds. A tensor $\mathcal{A} \in \mathbb{R}^{I_1, I_2, \ldots, I_n}$ is an element of the tensor product of N vector spaces, such that the corresponding multi-dimensional array is $\mathcal{A}(i_1, \ldots, i_n)$, in which the index $i_k \in [1, I_\text{k}]$ or $[0, I_\text{k} - 1]$ for computer scientists and:

- **Index:** i_k represents the index along the kth dimension, known as mode;
- **Order:** N is the order of A, i.e. the number of modes/dimensions/ways as illustrated in Figure 12;
- **Size:** I_k represents the size along the kth mode, while the tensor shape is the vector $[I_1, I_2, \ldots, I_N]$. The size of a tensor is the range of values an index can take for a dimension of the tensor. For example, a tensor $\mathcal{X} \in \mathbb{R}^{3,4,5,6}$ is of order 4, size 3 in mode-1, size 4 in mode-2, size 5 in mode-3 and size 6 in mode-4, and can have $3 \times 4 \times 5 \times 6 = 360$ values, and also denoted as having shape vector [3, 4, 5, 6].
- **Fibres:** The mode-j vectors of $\mathcal{A}$ are defined as the I_j dimensional vectors obtained from $\mathcal{A}$ by varying the index I_j, while keeping all the other indices fixed as shown in Figure 13 a, b, c and d.
- **Slices:** The mode-j slice of $\mathcal{A}$ is defined as an (N−1)th-order tensor obtained by fixing the mode-j index of $\mathcal{A}$ to be in $\mathcal{A}$ (:, ..., :, I_j, :, ..., :) as shown in Figure 13 e, f and g.

- **Blocks:** block matrices are Hierarchical/nested matrices represented by tensors. An example of order four is shown in Figure 14 *(a)*.
- **Tensor Product:** A tensor $\mathcal{A} \in \mathbb{R}^{I_1, I_2, \dots, I_n}$ is composed of the outer product of N vectors: $\mathcal{A} = a(1) \circ a(2) \circ \dots \circ a(N)$, where $a^{(k)}$ is the k-dimensional vector corresponding to the kth mode in the tensor. This is illustrated for a tensor of order three in Figure 14 *(b)*.
- **Rank-1 tensor:** is an n-way tensor object that can be strictly decomposed as the tensor product of n vectors. A tensor decomposition expresses a tensor in terms of a sequence of sums and products operating on simpler multi-way tensor objects. These methods will be explained in chapter four (Kolda and Bader, 2009; Lu, Plataniotis and Venetsanopoulos, 2014).

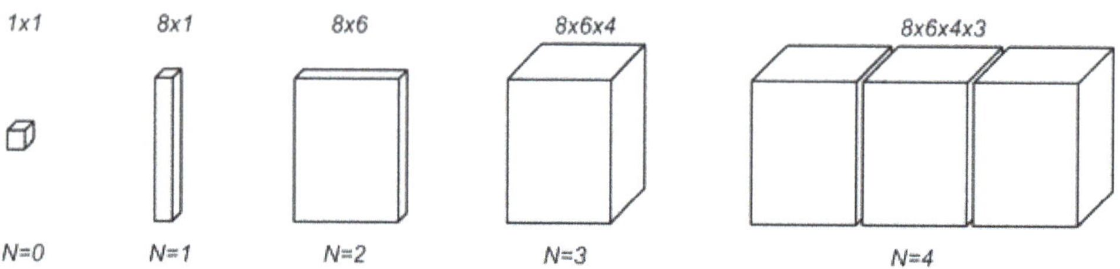

Figure 12: Illustration of tensors of order N = 0, 1, 2, 3, 4. (Lu, Plataniotis and Venetsanopoulos, 2014)

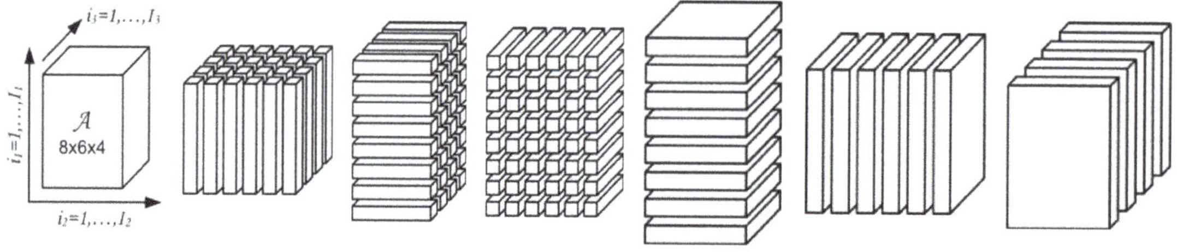

Figure 13: Illustration of the mode-n vectors/fibres and mode-n slices: (a) a tensor $\mathcal{A} \in \mathbb{R}^{8\times 6\times 4}$, (b) the mode-1 vectors or fibers, (c) the mode-2 vectors or fibers, and (d) the mode-3 vectors or fibers, (e) the mode-1 slices $\mathcal{A}_{i::}$, (f) the mode-2 slices $\mathcal{A}_{:i:}$, and (g) the mode-3 slices: $\mathcal{A}_{::i}$.

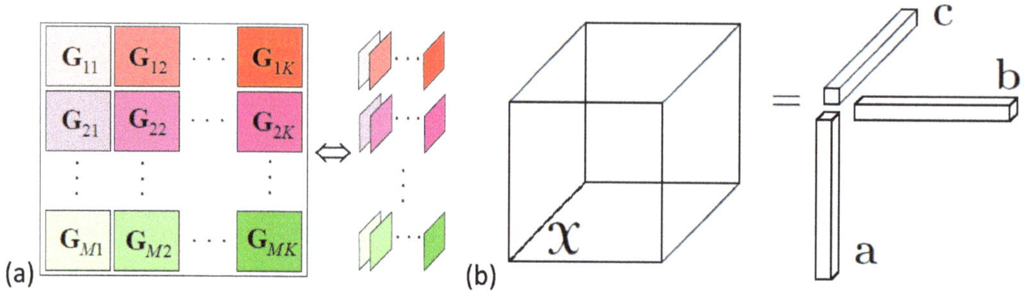

Figure 14: (a) A block matrix represented as a 4th-order tensor (b) Rank-one third-order tensor, $\mathcal{X} = a \circ b \circ c$.

3.1.2 Tensor Indexing

In general, there are two methods for tensors' indexing and the tensorial equations. These are the Einstein notation, and the simple flat multidimensional indexing.

3.1.2.1 Einstein Notation

The direct/ Einstein (symbolic, coordinate-free) notation (The Python NumPy function: np.einsum uses Einstein notation to express tensor contractions). This notation uses subscripts for contra-variants components of a vector (the usual representation, and superscripts for covariant components, to represent an operation concisely using known information about the tensors involved, such as their dimensionality and shape/size. This notation is suitable for Riemannian space, a smooth manifold or Minkowski space, which combines three-dimensional Euclidean space and time into a four-dimensional manifold where the space-time interval between any two events is independent of the inertial frame of reference in which they are recorded.
For example, the usual vector v representation is the contravariant components = [4, 2, 6] with basis vector $\vec{e}_1, \vec{e}_2, \vec{e}_3 = [1, 1, 1]$, such that $\vec{v} = v^1\vec{e}_1 + v^2\vec{e}_2 + v^3\vec{e}_3 = 4 \times 1 + 2 \times 1 + 6 \times 1, |v| = \sqrt{(4 \times 1)^2 + (2 \times 1)^2 + (6 \times 1)^2} = \sqrt{56} = 7.48$. These are contra-variant because an increase of basis to [2,2,2] leads to a decrease of the contra-variant components to v=[2, 1, 3], $v = 2 \times 2 + 1 \times 2 + 3 \times 2, |v| = \sqrt{(2 \times 2)^2 + (1 \times 2)^2 + (3 \times 2)^2} = \sqrt{56} = 7.48$. A contravariant vector is a tangent vector representing the position, displacement, velocity, acceleration, and others given some unit of measure, ruler or coordinate basis as defined above, and the difference with the basis is a distance in space. Increasing the unit of measure from meters to kilometres will decrease the component values in a vector representing a series of measurements. These measurements are often representing the Euclidean space, and the basis are the canonical basis e^i. This is why they are called contravariant vectors and are denoted by superscripts for the components and subscripts for the basis. In Physics, these are called the solid state or the real or direct space or coordinates, and it is the original measurements that we measure data with. The Euclidean space requires orthogonality between the coordinates, therefore the dot product alternative definition of $\langle \vec{e}_i, \vec{e}_j \rangle = \|\vec{e}_i\| \|\vec{e}_j\| \cos \theta$, using θ = 90, will always produce zero for any two Eucleadiean basis vectors.
The crystallographers and physics community needed to study the natural occurrence of crystals of different metals and in different shapes, leading to defining the Miller indices in which the angles need not be 90 degrees to define a good coordinate to measure the origin point and a place of a face in a given crystal as shown in Figure 15 as explained in (Glazer, 2021). The lengths a, b, c along x, y and z axes, define the angles, α, β, and γ in the left figure, while the right figure shows the grey plane intersecting the three axes at a/h, b/k and c/l. The grey plane is then indexed using Miller indices as (hkl). All transformations over points in crystal corners in $\mathbb{R}^3$are considered to form a manifold of these points in the dual basis as described below. As the referenced book describes, known transformations are rotations, reflections, translation, and inversion. Crystals are formed of a group of atoms or molecules of different types bonding together and repeating periodically (but sometimes aperiodically) in a defined structure that can be measured against a lattice (coordinate space with unit basis). For example, Iron (Fe) and Copper (Cu) crystals have a structure that repeats one atom over a 3D lattice. Solids such as Sodium chloride (NaCl) crystals repeat an arrangement of Sodium (Na) and Chlorine (Cl) atoms, and Diamonds repeat two carbon atoms, C1 and C2, over the 3D lattice. As discussed in chapter five, symmetries reduce the complexity and provide known transformation matrices.

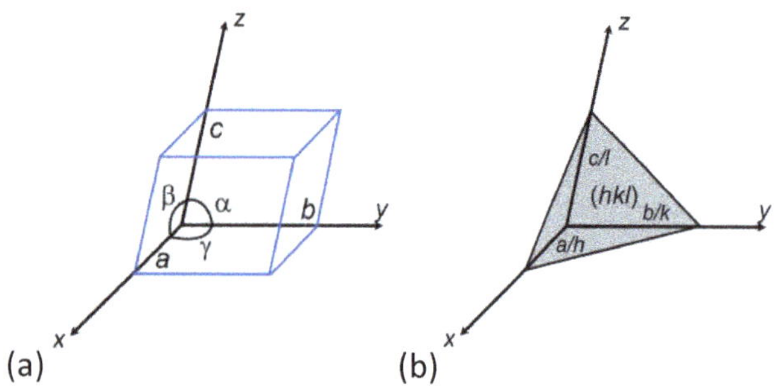

Figure 15: Miller indices. (a) Right-hand convention for choice of axes. (b) Definition of a plane (Glazer, 2021).

The dual representation of the vector v finds the dual basis that represents the same vector equivalently using a mapping function. This dual representation needs to capture the momentum or wave periodicity known as the cotangent representation as a gradient/derivative of the mapping function f = [Δ_xf, Δ_yf, ...]. A transformation of the derivative is inverse to the transformation of the basis/coordinate system, such that an increase in the basis will increase the new components' values and vice versa. This is why they are called covariant vectors and are denoted by subscripts for the components and superscripts for the basis. The dual basis $\vec{b}^1, \vec{b}^2, \vec{b}^3$ are defined such that $\vec{b}^\alpha \cdot \vec{b}_\beta = g(\vec{b}^\alpha, \vec{b}_\beta) = \delta^\alpha_\beta$, where g is the metric tensor mapping from the real/direct basis to the dual basis, and the mixed Kronecker delta δ is defined later in the chapter. For the crystallographers' example above, the dual space measures the diffraction/scattering of waves, such as x-rays as they pass through the solid crystal planes. A simplification of diffraction is the reflection of these waves over the crystal planes acting as mirrors. This will be further simplified below as coordinates functions extracting one axes value from a vector.
Resuming the Eienstian notation, a summation index, when repeated twice or more across the tensors involved in the operation, such as $a_i x_i$, means i is the summation index of all possible values for vectors a and x. This can be written as $a_i x^i$, indicating that a is a covariant vector (can be thought of as a row vector with lower indices) and x is a contravariant vector/covector (can be thought of as a column vector with upper indices). This means they transform covariantly and contravariantly, respectively, with the change of basis. The variance was explained in chapter two, and the change of basis and more examples will be explained later in this chapter. The upper index for a column vector goes from up to down, and the lower index for a row vector goes from left to right. $A_{ji}x_i$ means i is the summation index, and j is a second index to matrix A. This is more concise than writing $\sum_i A_{ji} x_i$. The summation index, also called the dummy index, should have the same range of values for tensors involved in the operation. The non-dummy indices are called free indices and take their ranges from the shape/size of the tensor and are used once in a term. The free index is fixed in the operation where a dummy variable is used, such that $A_{ji}x_i$ for j = 3, and i takes all available values in its range, such as $A_{ji}x_i = A_{31}x_1 + A_{32}x_2 + A_{33}x_3$.
Some examples are as follows (more explanation using tensor notation will follow):

- **Vector Space V with elements v:** $v^i e_i$ written in terms of basis vectors. The basis elements are written with lower indices, and components or vector coefficients are written with upper indices.
- **Inner product:** $a \cdot x = a_i x^i$
- **Kronecker delta:** given the vector space V, its dual space, is V* has dual basis e_i^*, the Kronecker delta is defined as: $< e_i^*, e_j > = e^i(e_j) = \delta_{ij} = \begin{cases} 1 & if\ i = j \\ 0 & if\ i \neq j \end{cases} = \delta^i_j$, here the dual basis elements are written with upper indices.
- **Cross product:** $a \times x = \sum_{i=1}^N a^i e_i \times \sum_{j=1}^N x^j e_j = a^i e_i \times x^j e_j = (a^i x^j)(e_i \times e_j) = a^i x^j \varepsilon_{ij}^k e_k$, where $(e_i \times e_j) = \varepsilon_{ij}^k e_k$ and $\varepsilon_{ij}^k = \delta^{kl} \varepsilon_{lij}$, ε_{ij}^k is the permutation component as the Levi-Civita symbol, and δ^{kl} is the Kronecker delta of the indices kl (1 when equal and zero otherwise).

- **Outer Product:** $A_j^i = a^i x_j = (ax)_j^i$, i and j are different and are not eliminated by multiplication
- **Matrix-Vector Multiplication:** $u = A \cdot x \rightarrow u_i = (Ax)_i = \sum_j A_{ij} x^j \rightarrow u^i = A_j^i x^j$
- **Matrix-Matrix Multiplication:** $C = A \cdot B \rightarrow C_{ik} = (AB)_{ik} = \sum_j A_{ij} B_k^j \rightarrow C_k^i = A_j^i B_k^j$

3.1.2.2 Multidimensional Indexing

The index (component) notation is adopted by Python NumPy arrays higher dimensional tensors, tensorly package and scikit-tt package. This notation is suitable for Euclidean space and uses subscripts only.

3.1.3 Tensor Transformations

The mode-n matricization,$mat(\mathcal{X})_n$, also defined as mode-n unfolding $\mathcal{X}_{[n]}$of a tensor $\mathcal{X} \in \mathbb{R}^{I_1, I_2, I_3 \dots, I_N}$, is defined as follows:

$$mat(\mathcal{X})_n = \mathcal{X}_{[n]} = \mathcal{X}_{mn} \in \mathbb{R}^{I_n, I_1 \times I_2 \dots \times I_{n-1} \times I_{n+1} \dots \times I_N}$$

Where the matrix element is indexed with two indices (i, j), the first is from 1 to I_n, and the second j from 1 to:

$$\prod_{k=1, k \neq n}^{N} i_k$$

The mode-n vectorisation of a tensor, $\mathcal{X} \in \mathbb{R}^{I_1, I_2, I_3 \dots, I_N}$, is defined as follows:

$$vec(\mathcal{X})_n = \mathcal{X}_{vn} \in \mathbb{R}^{I_n \times I_1 \times I_2 \dots \times I_{n-1} \times I_{n+1} \dots \times I_N}$$

Which is a mode-n matricization, followed by vertical stacking of the matrix in one column vector. For example,

given $\mathcal{X} \in \mathbb{R}^{2,2,2} = \begin{bmatrix} \begin{bmatrix} 1 & 3 \\ 2 & 4 \end{bmatrix} \begin{bmatrix} 5 & 7 \\ 6 & 8 \end{bmatrix} \end{bmatrix}$

mode-1 matricization of $\mathcal{X} = \begin{bmatrix} 1 & 2 & 3 & 4 \\ 5 & 6 & 7 & 8 \end{bmatrix}$

mode-1 vectorisation of $\mathcal{X} = \begin{bmatrix} 1 \\ 5 \\ 2 \\ 6 \\ 3 \\ 7 \\ 4 \\ 8 \end{bmatrix}$.

An essential property of vectorisation of two tensors $\mathcal{X}, \mathcal{Y}$, is that $vec(\mathcal{X})^T vec(\mathcal{Y}) = trace(\mathcal{X}^T \mathcal{Y})$.

The n-unfolding of a tensor, $\mathcal{X} \in \mathbb{R}^{I_1, I_2, I_3 \dots, I_N}$ creates a matrix $\in \mathbb{R}^{I_n \times I_1 \times I_2 \dots \times I_{n-1}, I_{n+1} \times \dots \times I_N} = \mathbb{R}^{m \times l}$, such that $m = \prod_{j=1}^{n} I_j$ and $l = \prod_{j=n+1}^{N} I_j$ that is defined as follows:

$$\mathcal{X}_{<n>}(i_1 \dots i_n, i_{n+1} \dots i_N) = \mathcal{X}(i_1 i_2 \dots i_N)$$

where the first n indices enumerate the rows of $\mathcal{X}_{<n>}$, and the last N - n indices for its columns.

The tensor n-rank of a tensor, $\mathcal{X} \in \mathbb{R}^{I_1, I_2, I_3 \dots, I_N}$ namely $rank_n(\mathcal{X})$ is the column rank of the n-unfolding $\mathcal{X}_{<n>}$ such that it computes the number of dimensions in the vector span by n-mode of $\mathcal{X}$.

The tensor rank, namely rank($\mathcal{X}$), is defined to be the minimum number of the sum of rank-one tensor that can exactly factorise tensor $\mathcal{X}$.

3.1.4 Tensor Element-wise operations

Element-wise tensor operations such as addition, subtraction, Hadamard product and division are implemented in NumPy and presented in the python notebook ch3.ipynb, along with other examples used below. The transposition of a tensor is as follows: For a given tensor $\mathcal{X} \in \mathbb{R}^{I_1, I_2, I_3 \dots, I_N}$, the transpose is defined as: $\mathcal{X}^T \in \mathbb{R}^{I_N, I_{N-1}, I_{N-2} \dots, I_1}$.

3.1.5 Tensor Products

The element-wise product followed by a summation is the scalar product (a generalisation of the **inner or dot product**) of two same-sized tensors $\mathcal{X}, \mathcal{Y} \in \mathbb{R}^{I_1, I_2, \dots, I_N}$ results in a scalar value, which is defined as follows:

$$z = \langle \mathcal{X}, \mathcal{Y} \rangle = \langle vec(\mathcal{X}), vec(\mathcal{Y}) \rangle = \sum_{i_1=1}^{I_1} \sum_{i_2=1}^{I_2} \dots \sum_{i_n=1}^{I_N} \mathcal{X}(\mathrm{i}_1, \mathrm{i}_2, \dots \mathrm{i}_n) . \mathcal{Y}(\mathrm{i}_1, \mathrm{i}_2, \dots \mathrm{i}_n) = x^T y$$

Where y is the vectorised form of $\mathcal{Y}$, and x is vectorised $\mathcal{X}$. Similarly, the Frobenius norm is extended in the higher dimension as:

$\|\mathcal{X}\|_F = \sqrt{\langle \mathcal{X}, \mathcal{X} \rangle}$ when the origin is zero, it is the length, but a distance between $\mathcal{X}$ and $\mathcal{Y}$ tensors: $dist(\mathcal{X}, \mathcal{Y}) = \|\mathcal{X} - \mathcal{Y}\|_F = \sqrt{\langle \mathcal{X}, \mathcal{Y} \rangle}$

The outer product for $\mathcal{X} \in \mathbb{R}^{I_1, I_2, \dots, I_P}$ with $\mathcal{Y} \in \mathbb{R}^{J_1, J_2, \dots, J_Q}$ results in a tensor $\in \mathbb{R}^{I_1, I_2, \dots, I_P, J_1, J_2, \dots, J_Q}$ computed as: $\mathcal{C} = \mathcal{X} \circ \mathcal{Y}$ such that $c_{i_1, \dots, i_p, j_1, \dots, j_Q} = x_{i_1, \dots, i_p} y_{j_1, \dots, j_Q}$

The contracted product for $\mathcal{X} \in \mathbb{R}^{I_1, \dots, I_M, J_1 \dots, J_P}$ with $\mathcal{Y} \in \mathbb{R}^{I_1, \dots, I_M, K_1, \dots, K_Q}$ with equal size along the first M modes results in a tensor $\in \mathbb{R}^{J_1 \dots, J_P, K_1 \dots, K_Q}$ computed by:

$$c_{j_1 \dots, j_P, k_1 \dots, k_Q} = \langle \mathcal{X}, \mathcal{Y} \rangle_{1, \dots, M, 1, \dots, M (j_1 \dots, j_P, k_1 \dots, k_Q)} = \sum_{i_1=1}^{I_1} \dots \sum_{i_M=1}^{I_M} x_{i_1, \dots, i_M, j_1 \dots, j_P} y_{i_1, \dots, i_M, k_1 k_1, \dots, k_Q}$$

The results' entries are the summing of the product of the two input tensors along with the common indices. The inner/dot product is a special case of the contracted product when all modes are common, producing a scalar only as $c = \langle \mathcal{X}, \mathcal{Y} \rangle_{1, \dots, M, 1, \dots, M}$. Similarly, the outer product is a special case of the contracted product when no modes are common such that for $\mathcal{X} \in \mathbb{R}^{J_1 \dots, J_P}$ with $\mathcal{Y} \in \mathbb{R}^{K_1, \dots, K_Q}$: $\mathcal{C} = \mathcal{X} \circ \mathcal{Y} = \langle \mathcal{X}, \mathcal{Y} \rangle_{0,0(j_1 \dots, j_P, k_1 \dots, k_Q)}$.

The Tensor products are extensions to matrix multiplication that apply the dot product in a given order of the inputs (along axis 1/rows of the first matrix and axis 0/columns of the second input that need to be conforming) to produce an output on the intersecting index in the output relative to the input indices used. The extension to higher dimensions requires the specification of the conforming axis to apply the product from the inputs, which will decide the position in the output where the result will be placed. The tensor Dot product can be used in different ways, and it is implemented as a function in the NumPy package. Below is the definition, followed by several examples.

Tensor n-mode Products: for $\mathcal{X} \in \mathbb{R}^{I_1, I_2, \dots, I_N}$ with matrix U $\in \mathbb{R}^{J, I_n}$, where n is a mode from the N modes of the first tensor, resulting in tensor $\in \mathbb{R}^{I_1, I_2, \dots, I_{n-1}, \mathrm{J}, I_{n+1} \dots, I_N}$, and is computed as follows:

$$(\mathcal{X} \times_n U)_{\mathrm{i}_1, \mathrm{i}_2, \dots \mathrm{i}_{n-1}, \mathrm{j}, \mathrm{i}_{n+1}, \dots, \mathrm{i}_N} = \sum_{i_n=1}^{I_N} x(\mathrm{i}_1, \mathrm{i}_2, \dots \mathrm{i}_N) u_{j i_n}$$

The n-mode product of a tensor $\mathcal{X}$ with a matrix U is related to a change of basis in the case when a tensor defines a multilinear operator. This is equivalent to pre-multiplying each mode-n vector of $\mathcal{X}$ by U. Thus, the mode-n product above can be written using the mode-n unfolding as $\mathcal{C}_{(n)} = \mathrm{U}\, \mathcal{X}_{(n)}$ where each entry of $\mathcal{C}$ is defined as the sum of products of corresponding entries in $\mathcal{X}$ and **U**. This is also called tensor contraction because the resulting tensor dimension is the sum of the dimensions of the original two tensors minus the dimension of the contraction. The Numpy package tensordot function sums the products of both input tensors' elements (components) over the axes specified by the third argument "axis", which designates the axes along which to perform the reduction (multiplication/addition). When axis = 0, each instance of both input tensors is a scalar input to the tensor product $\otimes$, producing a shape that concatenates input shapes. When axis = 1, or (1, 1), each instance from both inputs is a vector that is used in the tensor dot product. When axis = 2, which is the default, it will do double tensor contractions, producing a scalar. To sum over more than one axis, the third argument specifies one sequence to apply on both inputs or two sequences of the same length to apply on each of the inputs in order, indicating which axis to sum over as one and others as zero. For an N-D tensor, if we set axes argument = N, then we will multiply both tensors element-wise and then sum all values to get a single scalar result.

For vectors: $v = \begin{bmatrix}10\\2\\-6\end{bmatrix}, u = \begin{bmatrix}-3\\0\\-2\end{bmatrix}$, a mode-0 product is defined as $vu^T = \begin{bmatrix}10\\2\\-6\end{bmatrix} \times [-3 \quad 0 \quad -2] = \begin{bmatrix}-30 & 0 & -20\\-6 & 0 & -4\\18 & 0 & 12\end{bmatrix}$, which is the cross-product defined earlier.

The Numpy package does not have an unfold function in one implementation, but the Tensorly package has. This can be produced in Python as a mode-0 tensordot operation. Mode-0 means the vectors along the zeroth axis in both inputs. Since the first vector is a column vector, then each element is a vector to apply the dot product with the zeroth axis vectors of the second vector. Since the second vector is a row vector, then the mode-0 returns this row vector every time. This will be a scalar multiplication between each mode-0 from the first vector (scalar) and the only row from mode-0 from the second vector.

A mode-1 product is defined as $v^T u = [10 \quad 2 \quad -6] \times \begin{bmatrix}-3\\0\\-2\end{bmatrix} = -18$, which is the dot product defined earlier. This can be produced in Python as mode-1 tensordot operation, which applies the dot product on the first axis of v, which is a row vector now after transpose, and the first axis of u, which is the column vector. In vectors, there are no more modes to attempt except 0 and 1.

For matrices example using tensordot, the matrix multiplication example of gas distribution presented in chapter one, we set the axis argument =1, or (1, 0), specifying clearly that vectors along axis=1 (which is each instance of (2,3) in this example) from first input is used as input to the dot product with vectors along last one axis from second input: so that will give us four vectors of length 3, and perform the dot product as follows:

$$\mathrm{P} \in \mathbb{R}^{2\times3} \times_1 \mathrm{S} \in \mathbb{R}^{3\times4} = \begin{bmatrix}0.5 & 0.2 & 0.3\\0.0 & 0.4 & 0.6\end{bmatrix} \times \begin{bmatrix}0.4 & 0.6 & 0.0 & 0.0\\0.0 & 0.7 & 0.3 & 0.0\\0.0 & 0.5 & 0.0 & 0.5\end{bmatrix}$$

$$= \begin{bmatrix} [0.5 \quad 0.2 \quad 0.3] \times \begin{bmatrix}0.4\\0.0\\0.0\end{bmatrix} & [0.5 \quad 0.2 \quad 0.3] \times \begin{bmatrix}0.6\\0.7\\0.5\end{bmatrix} & [0.5 \quad 0.2 \quad 0.3] \times \begin{bmatrix}0.0\\0.3\\0.0\end{bmatrix} & [0.5 \quad 0.2 \quad 0.3] \times \begin{bmatrix}0.0\\0.0\\0.5\end{bmatrix} \\ [0.0 \quad 0.4 \quad 0.6] \times \begin{bmatrix}0.4\\0.0\\0.0\end{bmatrix} & [0.0 \quad 0.4 \quad 0.6] \times \begin{bmatrix}0.6\\0.7\\0.5\end{bmatrix} & [0.0 \quad 0.4 \quad 0.6] \times \begin{bmatrix}0.0\\0.3\\0.0\end{bmatrix} & [0.0 \quad 0.4 \quad 0.6] \times \begin{bmatrix}0.0\\0.0\\0.5\end{bmatrix} \end{bmatrix}$$

$$= \begin{bmatrix}0.20 & 0.59 & 0.06 & 0.15\\0.00 & 0.58 & 0.12 & 0.30\end{bmatrix} \in \mathbb{R}^{2\times4}$$

To apply tensordot across axis 2 on both inputs, we take the last two axes of P, with the first two axes of S, it will return each scalar and multiply with each scalar in the second input, but require that the number of elements in both input tensors matches. Therefore it will not work in the above example but will work on similar shape inputs as below and sum all products:

$$\mathrm{P} \times_2 \mathrm{S} = \begin{bmatrix}0.5 & 0.2 & 0.3\\0.0 & 0.4 & 0.6\end{bmatrix} \times \begin{bmatrix}0.4 & 0.6 & 0.0\\0.0 & 0.7 & 0.3\end{bmatrix} = 0.78$$

To apply tensordot across the axis 0 on both inputs, it will perform the dot product for every instance of P with every instance of S, which will result in an expansion in the form of the cross product on the higher dimension and produce an output shape that concatenates the shape of both inputs.

$$\mathrm{P} \times_0 \mathrm{S} = \begin{bmatrix}0.5 & 0.2 & 0.3\\0.0 & 0.4 & 0.6\end{bmatrix} \in \mathbb{R}^{2\times3} \times \begin{bmatrix}0.4 & 0.6 & 0.0\\0.0 & 0.7 & 0.3\end{bmatrix} \in \mathbb{R}^{2\times3}$$

$$= \begin{bmatrix} \begin{bmatrix} 0.5 \times \begin{bmatrix} 0.4 & 0.6 & 0.0 \\ 0.0 & 0.7 & 0.3 \end{bmatrix} & 0.2 \times \begin{bmatrix} 0.4 & 0.6 & 0.0 \\ 0.0 & 0.7 & 0.3 \end{bmatrix} & 0.3 \times \begin{bmatrix} 0.4 & 0.6 & 0.0 \\ 0.0 & 0.7 & 0.3 \end{bmatrix} \end{bmatrix} \\ \begin{bmatrix} 0.0 \times \begin{bmatrix} 0.4 & 0.6 & 0.0 \\ 0.0 & 0.7 & 0.3 \end{bmatrix} & 0.4 \times \begin{bmatrix} 0.4 & 0.6 & 0.0 \\ 0.0 & 0.7 & 0.3 \end{bmatrix} & 0.6 \times \begin{bmatrix} 0.4 & 0.6 & 0.0 \\ 0.0 & 0.7 & 0.3 \end{bmatrix} \end{bmatrix} \end{bmatrix}$$

$$= \begin{bmatrix} \begin{bmatrix} \begin{bmatrix} 0.2 & 0.3 & 0.0 \\ 0.0 & 0.35 & 0.15 \end{bmatrix} & \begin{bmatrix} 0.08 & 0.12 & 0.00 \\ 0.00 & 0.14 & 0.06 \end{bmatrix} & \begin{bmatrix} 0.12 & 0.18 & 0.00 \\ 0.00 & 0.21 & 0.09 \end{bmatrix} \end{bmatrix} \\ \begin{bmatrix} \begin{bmatrix} 0.0 & 0.0 & 0.0 \\ 0.0 & 0.0 & 0.0 \end{bmatrix} & \begin{bmatrix} 0.16 & 0.24 & 0.00 \\ 0.00 & 0.28 & 0.12 \end{bmatrix} & \begin{bmatrix} 0.24 & 0.36 & 0.00 \\ 0.00 & 0.42 & 0.18 \end{bmatrix} \end{bmatrix} \end{bmatrix} \in \mathbb{R}^{2\times3\times2\times3}$$

To reproduce the example in Figure 16 using NumPy tensordot, while having different shapes for the two input tensors $\mathcal{A} \in \mathbb{R}^{8,6,4}$ and $U \in \mathbb{R}^{3,8}$, the axes argument can be a sequence of (0, 1). This will produce dot products between mode-1 vectors of $\mathcal{A}$ ($\in \mathbb{R}^{8}$) by $U \in \mathbb{R}^{3,8}$ (which is a projection to a higher dimension) to obtain a vector $b \in \mathbb{R}^{3}$, as the differently shaded vector indicates in the right of the figure, producing an output $\in \mathbb{R}^{3,6,4}$. The tensordot NumPy implementation produced the output shape $\in \mathbb{R}^{6\times4\times3}$, because of reversing the indices.
The tensorly python package has a tensor mode dot function as "tenalg.mode_dot", which only contracts a specified axis in the mode argument and concatenates all other shape vectors in inputs to create the output shape. So, only mode =0 can work in **Error! Reference source not found.** For example, as axis=0 in the first input has the s ame shape "8" as axis=1 in the second input, and the output is of shape $\in \mathbb{R}^{3\times6\times4}$ as intended in (Kolda and Bader, 2009; Lu, Plataniotis and Venetsanopoulos, 2014).

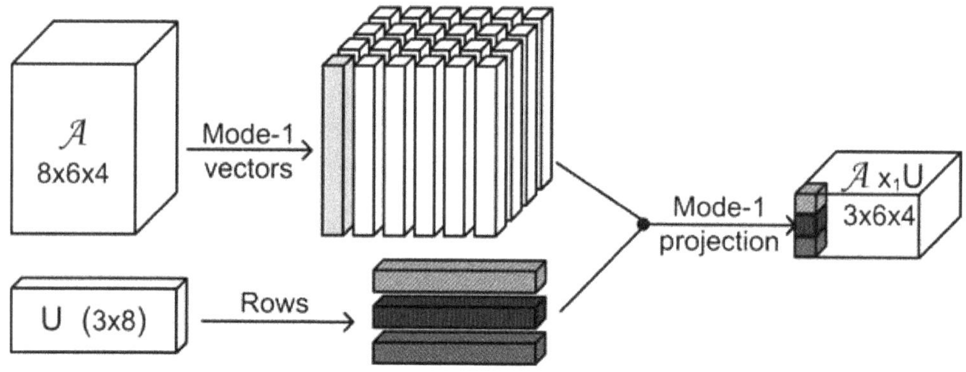

Figure 16: Visual illustration of the mode-n (mode-1) multiplication

The Kronecker product for $A \in \mathbb{R}^{I,J}$with matrix $U \in \mathbb{R}^{K,L}$results in a block tensor $\in \mathbb{R}^{IK,JL}$ computed by scalar multiplication of every element in the first tensor with the full tensor as a block of the second tensor:

$$A \otimes U = \begin{bmatrix} a_{1,1}U & \cdots & a_{1,J}U \\ \vdots & \ddots & \vdots \\ a_{I,1}U & \cdots & a_{I,J}U \end{bmatrix}$$

It can be computed as column-wise Kronecker product as follows:

$$A \otimes U = \left[a_1 \otimes u_1, a_1 \otimes u_2, \; a_1 \otimes u_3 \; \ldots \; a_1 \otimes u_L, \; a_2 \otimes u_1, \ldots \; a_J \otimes u_{L-1}, a_J \otimes u_L\right]$$
$$= [vec(u_1 a_1^T), vec(u_2 a_1^T)], vec(u_3 a_1^T), \ldots \; vec(u_L a_1^T), vec(u_1 a_2^T), \ldots, vec\left(u_{L-1} a_J^T\right), vec\left(u_L a_J^T\right)$$

The mixed-product property of Kronecker product states that if X, Y, A and B are conformable matrices whose dimensions are suitable for multiplications such that the matrix product XY and AB can be formed, then we have $(X \otimes A)(Y \otimes B) = XY \otimes AB$.
Kronecker product is defined for higher order tensors such as $\mathcal{A} \in \mathbb{R}^{I_1,\ldots,I_N}$ and $\mathcal{U} \in \mathbb{R}^{J_1,\ldots,J_N}$ to yield a tensor $\in \mathbb{R}^{I_1J_1,\ldots,I_NJ_N}$.
This is implemented in the Numpy package as "kron" function, producing a composite array made of blocks of the second tensor scaled by the first tensor. For the same previously defined v and u vectors:

$$v\otimes u = \begin{bmatrix}10\\2\\-6\end{bmatrix}\otimes\begin{bmatrix}-3\\0\\-2\end{bmatrix} = [10\times[-3 \quad 0 \quad -2] \quad 2\times[-3 \quad 0 \quad -2] \quad -6\times[-3 \quad 0 \quad -2]]$$

$$= [-30 \quad 0 \quad -20 \quad -6 \quad 0 \quad -4 \quad 18 \quad 0 \quad 12]$$

For the gas distribution matrices example:

$$P \in \mathbb{R}^{2\times3} \otimes S \in \mathbb{R}^{3\times4} = \begin{bmatrix}0.5 & 0.2 & 0.3\\0.0 & 0.4 & 0.6\end{bmatrix} \otimes \begin{bmatrix}0.4 & 0.6 & 0.0 & 0.0\\0.0 & 0.7 & 0.3 & 0.0\\0.0 & 0.5 & 0.0 & 0.5\end{bmatrix} =$$

$$= \begin{bmatrix} 0.5\times\begin{bmatrix}0.4 & 0.6 & 0.0 & 0.0\\0.0 & 0.7 & 0.3 & 0.0\\0.0 & 0.5 & 0.0 & 0.5\end{bmatrix} & 0.2\times\begin{bmatrix}0.4 & 0.6 & 0.0 & 0.0\\0.0 & 0.7 & 0.3 & 0.0\\0.0 & 0.5 & 0.0 & 0.5\end{bmatrix} & 0.3\times\begin{bmatrix}0.4 & 0.6 & 0.0 & 0.0\\0.0 & 0.7 & 0.3 & 0.0\\0.0 & 0.5 & 0.0 & 0.5\end{bmatrix} \\ 0.0\times\begin{bmatrix}0.4 & 0.6 & 0.0 & 0.0\\0.0 & 0.7 & 0.3 & 0.0\\0.0 & 0.5 & 0.0 & 0.5\end{bmatrix} & 0.4\times\begin{bmatrix}0.4 & 0.6 & 0.0 & 0.0\\0.0 & 0.7 & 0.3 & 0.0\\0.0 & 0.5 & 0.0 & 0.5\end{bmatrix} & 0.6\times\begin{bmatrix}0.4 & 0.6 & 0.0 & 0.0\\0.0 & 0.7 & 0.3 & 0.0\\0.0 & 0.5 & 0.0 & 0.5\end{bmatrix} \end{bmatrix}$$

$$\begin{bmatrix} 0.20 & 0.30 & 0.00 & 0.00 & 0.08 & 0.12 & 0.00 & 0.00 & 0.12 & 0.18 & 0.00 & 0.00\\ 0.00 & 0.35 & 0.15 & 0.00 & 0.00 & 0.14 & 0.06 & 0.00 & 0.00 & 0.21 & 0.09 & 0.00\\ 0.00 & 0.25 & 0.00 & 0.25 & 0.00 & 0.10 & 0.00 & 0.10 & 0.00 & 0.15 & 0.00 & 0.15\\ 0.00 & 0.00 & 0.00 & 0.00 & 0.16 & 0.24 & 0.00 & 0.00 & 0.24 & 0.36 & 0.00 & 0.00\\ 0.00 & 0.00 & 0.00 & 0.00 & 0.00 & 0.28 & 0.12 & 0.00 & 0.00 & 0.42 & 0.18 & 0.00\\ 0.00 & 0.00 & 0.00 & 0.00 & 0.00 & 0.20 & 0.00 & 0.20 & 0.00 & 0.30 & 0.00 & 0.3\,0 \end{bmatrix} \in \mathbb{R}^{6\times12}$$

The Khatri-Rao product for $A \in \mathbb{R}^{I,K}$ with matrix $U \in \mathbb{R}^{J,K}$ requires having an equal number of columns in input tensors such that a column-wise Kronecker product of the input tensors results in a tensor that $\in \mathbb{R}^{IJ\times K}$.

$$A \odot U = [a_1\otimes u_1 \quad a_2\otimes u_2 \quad \dots \quad a_K\otimes u_k]$$

Tensorly package has a Khatri-Rao product function, but Numpy does not have one, but a fully vectorised version can be implemented as follows:

```
def khatri_rao(a, u):
    c = a[...,:,np.newaxis,:] * u[...,np.newaxis,:,:]
    # collapse the first two axes
    return c.reshape((-1,) + c.shape[2:])
```

Khatri-Rao product is defined for each mode in the higher-order tensors such as given $\mathcal{A} \in \mathbb{R}^{I_1,\dots,I_N}$ and $\mathcal{U} \in \mathbb{R}^{J_1,\dots,J_N}$ where for which $I_n = J_n$, then $\mathcal{A} \odot_n \mathcal{U} = \mathcal{C} \in \mathbb{R}^{I_1J_1,\dots,I_{n-1}J_{n-1},I_n,I_{n+1}J_{n+1},\dots,I_NJ_N}$ with entries $\mathcal{C}(:,\dots,:,i_n,:,\dots,:) = \mathcal{A}(:,\dots,:,i_n,:,\dots,:)\otimes\mathcal{U}(:,\dots,:,i_n,:,\dots,:)$.

The scientific Python package "SciPy" implements the Khatri-Rao product "scipy.linalg.khatri_rao" as the Kronecker product of every column of the first tensor by the second tensor. It does not work for vectors. For the gas distribution matrix example, the number of columns of the arrays should match, so a transpose on the second matrix results in the following:

$$A \in \mathbb{R}^{2,3} \odot U^T \in \mathbb{R}^{4,3} = \begin{bmatrix}0.5 & 0.2 & 0.3\\0.0 & 0.4 & 0.6\end{bmatrix} \otimes \begin{bmatrix}0.4 & 0.0 & 0.0\\0.6 & 0.7 & 0.5\\0.0 & 0.3 & 0.0\\0.0 & 0.0 & 0.5\end{bmatrix} =$$

$$\begin{bmatrix} [0.5 \quad 0.2 \quad 0.3]\otimes\begin{bmatrix}0.4 & 0.0 & 0.0\\0.6 & 0.7 & 0.5\\0.0 & 0.3 & 0.0\\0.0 & 0.0 & 0.5\end{bmatrix} \\ [0.0 \quad 0.4 \quad 0.6]\otimes\begin{bmatrix}0.4 & 0.0 & 0.0\\0.6 & 0.7 & 0.5\\0.0 & 0.3 & 0.0\\0.0 & 0.0 & 0.5\end{bmatrix} \end{bmatrix}$$

$$= \begin{bmatrix} 0.20 & 0.00 & 0.00 \\ 0.30 & 0.14 & 0.15 \\ 0.00 & 0.06 & 0.00 \\ 0.00 & 0.00 & 0.15 \\ 0.00 & 0.00 & 0.00 \\ 0.00 & 0.28 & 0.30 \\ 0.00 & 0.12 & 0.00 \\ 0.00 & 0.00 & 0.30 \end{bmatrix}$$

The direct sum of tensors is defined for the Nth-order tensors $\mathcal{A} \in \mathbb{R}^{I_1,\dots,I_N}$ and $\mathcal{U} \in \mathbb{R}^{J_1,\dots,J_N}$ yields a tensor $\mathcal{C} \in \mathbb{R}^{(I_1+J_1),\dots,(I_N+J_N)}$,
with entries $\mathcal{C}(k_1,\dots,k_N) = \mathcal{A}(k_1,\dots,k_N)$ if $1 \le k_n \le I_n, \forall n$,
$\mathcal{C}(k_1,\dots,k_N) = \mathcal{U}(k_1 - I_1,\dots,k_N - I_N)$ if $I_n < k_n \le I_n + J_n, \forall n$,
and $\mathcal{C}(k_1,\dots,k_N) = 0$, otherwise (see Figure 17(a)).

Partial mode-n sums for tensors is defined for the Nth-order tensors $\mathcal{A} \in \mathbb{R}^{I_1,\dots,I_N}$ and $\mathcal{U} \in \mathbb{R}^{J_1,\dots,J_N}$ for which $I_n = J_n$, then $\mathcal{A} \oplus_n \mathcal{U} = \mathcal{C} \in \mathbb{R}^{(I_1+J_1),\dots,(I_{n-1}J_{n-1}),I_n,(I_{n+1}J_{n+1}),\dots,(I_NJ_N)}$ with entries $\mathcal{C}(:,\dots,:,i_n,:,\dots,:) = \mathcal{A}(:,\dots,:,i_n,:,\dots,:) \oplus \mathcal{U}(:,\dots,:,i_n,:,\dots,:)$ (see Figure 17(c)).

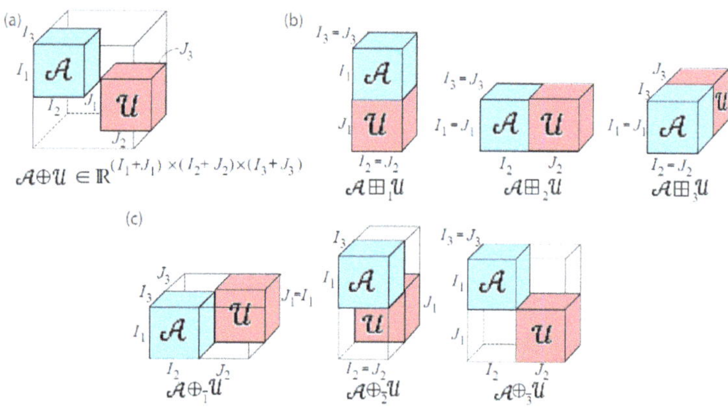

Figure 17: Illustration of the direct sum, partial direct sum and concatenation operators of two 3rd-order tensors. (a) Direct sum (b) Concatenations along mode-1,2,3. (c) Partial (mode-1, mode-2, and mode-3) direct sum.

Concatenation of Nth-order tensors along mode-n of tensors $\mathcal{A} \in \mathbb{R}^{I_1,\dots,I_N}$ and $\mathcal{U} \in \mathbb{R}^{J_1,\dots,J_N}$, for which $I_m = J_m$, $\forall m \neq n$ yields a tensor $\mathcal{C} \in \mathbb{R}^{I_1,\dots,I_{n-1},(I_n+J_n),I_{n+1},\dots,I_N} = \mathcal{A} \boxplus_n \mathcal{U}$ with subtensors $\mathcal{C}(i_1,\dots,i_{n-1},:,i_{n+1},\dots,i_N) = \mathcal{A}(i_1,\dots,i_{n-1},:,i_{n+1},\dots,i_N) \oplus \mathcal{U}(i_1,\dots,i_{n-1},:,i_{n+1},\dots,i_N)$
as illustrated in Figure 17(b).

3D convolution for two 3rd-order tensors $\mathcal{A} \in \mathbb{R}^{I_1,I_2,I_3}$ and $\mathcal{U} \in \mathbb{R}^{J_1,J_2,J_3}$, yields a tensor $\mathcal{C} \in \mathbb{R}^{(I_1+J_1-1),(I_2+J_2-1),(I_3+J_3-1)} = \mathcal{A} * \mathcal{U}$, with entries: $\mathcal{C}(k_1,k_2,k_3) = \sum_{j_1}\sum_{j_2}\sum_{j_3}\mathcal{U}(j_1,j_2,j_3)\mathcal{A}(k_1-j_1,k_2-j_2,k_3-j_3)$ as illustrated in Figure 18 for 2D convolution.

Partial (mode-n) convolution for two tensors $\mathcal{A} \in \mathbb{R}^{I_1,\dots,I_N}$ and $\mathcal{U} \in \mathbb{R}^{J_1,\dots,J_N}$, yields a tensor $\mathcal{C} \in \mathbb{R}^{I_1J_1,\dots,I_{n-1}J_{n-1},(I_n+J_n-1),I_{n+1}J_{n+1},\dots,I_NJ_N} = \mathcal{A} \boxdot_n \mathcal{U}$, the subtensors of which are $\mathcal{C}(k_1,\dots,k_{n-1},:,k_{n+1},\dots,k_N) = \mathcal{A}(i_1,\dots,i_{n-1},:,i_{n+1},\dots,i_N) * \mathcal{U}(j_1,\dots,j_{n-1},:,j_{n+1},\dots,j_N)$, where $k_1 = i_1j_1$, ..., and $k_N = i_Nj_N$.

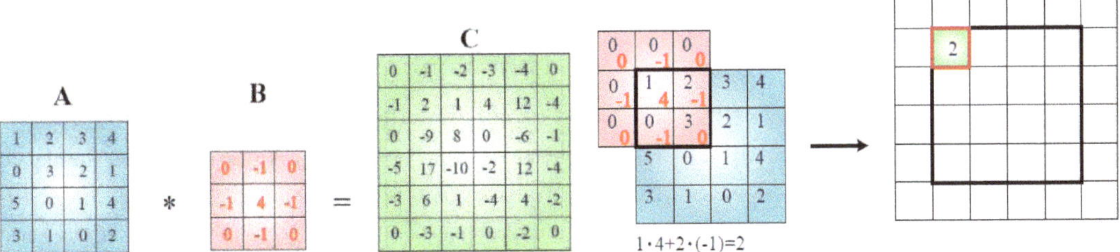

Figure 18: Illustration of the 2D convolution operator, performed through a sliding window operation along both the horizontal and vertical index (Cichocki et al., 2016, p. 1).

3.1.6 Orthonormal Tensor

Given $\mathcal{A} \in \mathbb{R}^{N}$, such that N=($N_1$, N_2, ... N_d)^T, we split $\mathcal{A}$ into two subtensors, the first is $\mathcal{A}_1 \in \mathbb{R}^{N'}$, such that N'=($N_{k1}$, N_{k2}, ... N_{ke})^T, and the second is $\mathcal{A}_2 \in \mathbb{R}^{N''}$, such that N''=($N_{l1}$, N_{l2}, ... N_{lf})^T, such that e+f =d. $\mathcal{A}$ is orthonormal with respect to the $\mathcal{A}_1$ if the N' -matricization of $\mathcal{A}$ ($\mathcal{A}_{N'} = mat(\mathcal{A})_{N'}$) satisfies
$\mathcal{A}_{N'} \cdot (\mathcal{A}_{N'})^T = \mathcal{A}_{N''} \cdot (\mathcal{A}_{N''})^T = I \in \mathbb{R}^{N',N'}$. It is necessary that:

$$\prod_{i=1}^{e} N_{ki} \leq \prod_{i=1}^{f} N_{li}$$

This is illustrated in Figure 19 using a graphical notation similar to the Tensor Networks notation that will be explained in chapter four. $\mathcal{A}$ is orthonormal with respect to $\mathcal{A}_2$ if the N'' -matricization of $\mathcal{A}$ ($\mathcal{A}_{N''} = mat(\mathcal{A})_{N''}$) satisfies $\mathcal{A}_{N''} \cdot (\mathcal{A}_{N''})^T = \mathcal{A}_{N'} \cdot (\mathcal{A}_{N'})^T = I \in \mathbb{R}^{N'',N''}$.
Knowing that a tensor is orthonormal makes its decomposition easier, as explained for matrices in chapter two.

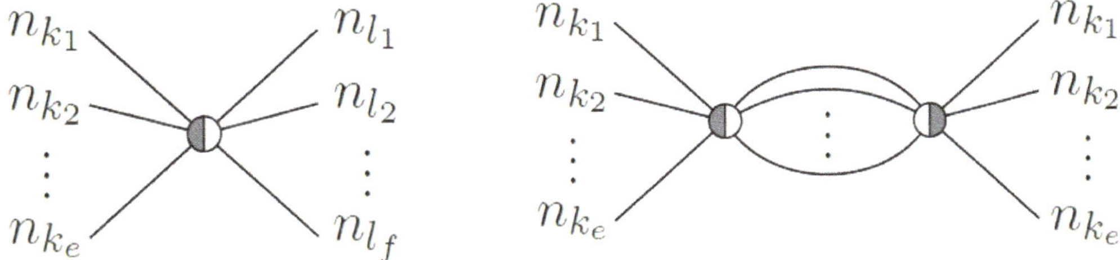

Figure 19: Orthonormal tensors: (a) Graphical representation of a tensor $\mathcal{A} \in \mathbb{R}^{N}$, which is orthonormal with respect to the set N'=(N_{k1}, N_{k2}, ... N_{ke})$^T \subset$ N. (b) Tensor multiplication of $\mathcal{A}$ and $\mathcal{A}^T$. The result is the identity tensor $I \in \mathbb{R}^{N' \times N'}$ (Gelß, 2017).

3.2 Multilinear Algebra

The tensor operations presented in the previous section are the foundation for Multilinear algebra expressed in Euclidean geometry. This section will discuss non-linear functions, followed by a summary of differential geometry on manifold visualizations. These will help visualise the algorithmic concepts discussed in this book and the literature.

3.2.1 Non-Linearly Separable Datasets

Data is a matrix of entities in m rows and n features in columns. A point p in the dataset is a row vector of all features describing one entity in the n-dimensional space. The number of the features N is the dimensionality of the dataset $\mathbb{R}^n$, in which the data vectors form the vector space of the problem with basis e_i $0 \leq i < N$, defined as:

$$e_1 = \begin{bmatrix} 1 \\ 0 \\ \vdots \\ 0 \\ 0 \end{bmatrix}, e_2 = \begin{bmatrix} 0 \\ 1 \\ \vdots \\ 0 \\ 0 \end{bmatrix}, \ldots, e_{n-1} = \begin{bmatrix} 0 \\ 0 \\ \vdots \\ 1 \\ 0 \end{bmatrix} e_n = \begin{bmatrix} 0 \\ 0 \\ \vdots \\ 0 \\ 1 \end{bmatrix}$$

Any dataset can be described as the Manifold M in $\mathbb{R}^n$ that contains all points (rows) in the dataset. Chapter one explains that machine learning aims to approximate a function describing a given dataset. The equation can be linear, such that the linear regression/classification method explained in chapter one will provide a good approximation. When data is not linearly separable in classification, or fits a linear line in regression, a curve equation can be the one that describes its dynamics. Curves can be defined in the non-Euclidian space, such as hyperbolic geometry and elliptic geometry, which this section will focus on and can also be defined in Riemannian geometry, which the next section and chapter five will dive more into it.

Curves equations are described as one of the four types of conic sections, which are the intersections of the surface of the cone with a plane at different angles. Figure 20 shows the sections as cuts through a cone described in Wikipedia. Each type is described by a focus point, directrix line, and eccentricity ratio. Eccentricity is the constant multiple that describes the distance between all the points on the curve of the conic section. The focus point is multiples of the eccentricity constant of the distance to the directrix line. Although it is not considered a conic section anymore, the first type is the circle. Circles are generated when the cutting plane is parallel to the plane of the generating circle of the cone. It is a particular type with a focus point, to which all the points on the circumference are of equal distance and no directrix line; hence, eccentricity is equal to zero. The second type is the ellipse, with eccentricity equal to ½, forming a closed curve inside the cone. The third type is the parabola with eccentricity equal to one. The fourth type is the hyperbola, with eccentricity equals two.

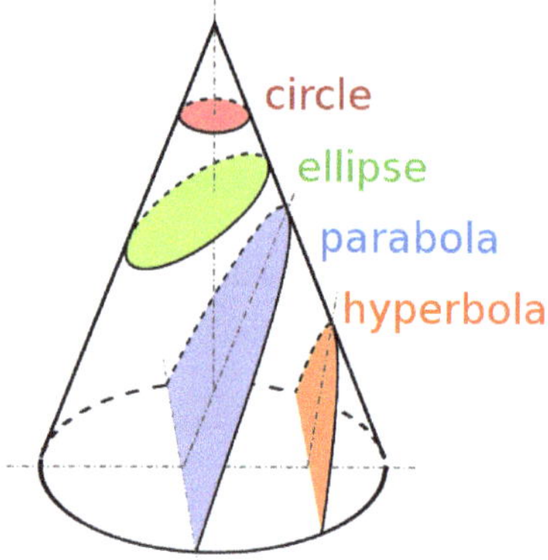

Figure 20: Curves as conic sections.

A quadratic equation of degree two can describe a non-linear decision plane, forming an arc or curve. A polynomial equation of degree two can also be represented algebraically using a matrix. For example, given a dataset as in the first two columns below, can define a system of equations in the third column:

x	y	
-1	3	$w_0 - 1w_1 + 1w_2 = 3$
0	1	$w_0 + 0w_1 + 0w_2 = 1$
1	1	$w_0 + 1w_1 + 1w_2 = -1$

2	4	$w_0 + 2w_1 + 4w_2 = 1$
3	6	$w_0 + 3w_1 + 6w_2 = 3$

This dataset X fits a parabola. The equation of the parabola is: $y = w_0 + w_1x + w_2x^2$. We can use the normal equation. The following matrix X contains an extra first-column vector as constant 1, a second-column vector as the given x variable/feature, and a third-column vector as x^2. Given y, we can infer w (three parameters weights or coefficients to infer):

$$X = \begin{bmatrix} 1 & -1 & 1 \\ 1 & 0 & 0 \\ 1 & 1 & 1 \\ 1 & 2 & 4 \\ 1 & 3 & 9 \end{bmatrix}, w = \begin{bmatrix} w_0 \\ w_1 \\ w_2 \end{bmatrix}, y = \begin{bmatrix} 3 \\ 1 \\ -1 \\ 1 \\ 3 \end{bmatrix}$$

$$X^TXc = \begin{bmatrix} 1 & 1 & 1 & 1 & 1 \\ -1 & 0 & 1 & 2 & 3 \\ 1 & 0 & 1 & 4 & 9 \end{bmatrix} \begin{bmatrix} 1 & -1 & 1 \\ 1 & 0 & 0 \\ 1 & 1 & 1 \\ 1 & 2 & 4 \\ 1 & 3 & 9 \end{bmatrix} \begin{bmatrix} w_0 \\ w_1 \\ w_2 \end{bmatrix} = \begin{bmatrix} 1 & 1 & 1 & 1 & 1 \\ -1 & 0 & 1 & 2 & 3 \\ 1 & 0 & 1 & 4 & 9 \end{bmatrix} \begin{bmatrix} 3 \\ 1 \\ -1 \\ 1 \\ 3 \end{bmatrix} = X^Ty$$

$$= \begin{bmatrix} 5 & 5 & 15 \\ 5 & 15 & 35 \\ 15 & 35 & 99 \end{bmatrix} \begin{bmatrix} w_0 \\ w_1 \\ w_2 \end{bmatrix} = \begin{bmatrix} 7 \\ 7 \\ 33 \end{bmatrix}$$

Now, we can solve by Gaussian Elimination as follows:

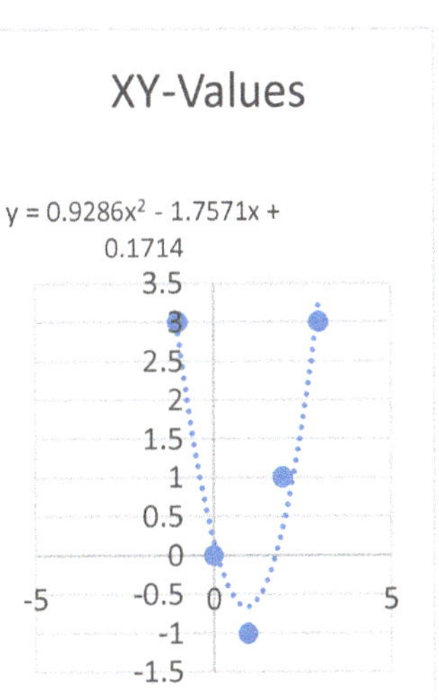

1. Form the Augmented Matrix: $\left[\begin{array}{ccc|c} 5 & 5 & 15 & 7 \\ 5 & 15 & 35 & 7 \\ 15 & 35 & 99 & 33 \end{array}\right]$

2. $r_1 \div 5$ $\left[\begin{array}{ccc|c} 1 & 1 & 3 & 1\frac{2}{5} \\ 5 & 15 & 35 & 7 \\ 15 & 35 & 99 & 33 \end{array}\right]$

3. -5 * r_1 +r_2 and -15 * r_1 +r_3. $\left[\begin{array}{ccc|c} 1 & 1 & 3 & 1\frac{2}{5} \\ 0 & 10 & 20 & 0 \\ 0 & 20 & 54 & 12 \end{array}\right]$

4. $r_2 \div 10$ $\left[\begin{array}{ccc|c} 1 & 1 & 3 & 1\frac{2}{5} \\ 0 & 1 & 2 & 0 \\ 0 & 20 & 54 & 12 \end{array}\right]$

5. -20 * r_2 +r_3. $\left[\begin{array}{ccc|c} 1 & 1 & 3 & 1\frac{2}{5} \\ 0 & 1 & 2 & 0 \\ 0 & 0 & 14 & 12 \end{array}\right]$

6. $r_3 \div 14$ $\left[\begin{array}{ccc|c} 1 & 1 & 3 & 1\frac{2}{5} \\ 0 & 1 & 2 & 0 \\ 0 & 0 & 1 & \frac{6}{7} \end{array}\right]$

We can continue by back-substitution with $w_2 = \frac{6}{7}$

$w_1 + 2(\frac{6}{7}) = 0 \rightarrow w_1 = -1\frac{5}{7}$

$w_0 + (-1\frac{5}{7}) + 3(\frac{6}{7}) = 1\frac{2}{5} \rightarrow w_0 = \frac{19}{35}$

$$\begin{bmatrix} w_0 \\ w_1 \\ w_2 \end{bmatrix} = \begin{bmatrix} \frac{19}{35} \\ -1\frac{5}{7} \\ \frac{6}{7} \end{bmatrix} = \begin{bmatrix} 0.54 \\ -1.71 \\ 0.86 \end{bmatrix}$$

These are not precisely the coefficients calculated by the chart to identify the trend line on the parabola. However, they produce the least squared error as $\frac{32}{35}$ as shown below:

X-Values	Y-Values	Predicted Y	Error	Error^2
-1	3	$3\frac{4}{35}$	$\frac{-4}{35}$	$\frac{16}{1225}$
0	1	$\frac{19}{35}$	$\frac{16}{35}$	$\frac{256}{1225}$
1	-1	$\frac{-11}{35}$	$\frac{-24}{35}$	$\frac{576}{1225}$
2	1	$\frac{19}{35}$	$\frac{16}{35}$	$\frac{256}{1225}$
3	3	$3\frac{4}{35}$	$\frac{-4}{35}$	$\frac{16}{1225}$

The excel plot might use a more computationally efficient least squared error minimisation than the normal equation, in which computational complexity is $O(n^{2.4})$ to $O(n^3)$. The most efficient alternative is the gradient descent algorithm, with computational complexity $O(kn^2)$, and k is the number of iterations (Carter, 1995).
We can expand the normal degree to a higher degree polynomial m for n data points as follows:

$$x = \begin{bmatrix} 1 & x_1 & x_1^2 & \cdots & x_1^m \\ 1 & x_2 & x_2^2 & \cdots & x_2^m \\ \vdots & \vdots & \vdots & \ddots & \vdots \\ 1 & x_{n-1} & x_{n-1}^2 & \cdots & x_{n-1}^m \\ 1 & x_n & x_n^2 & \cdots & x_n^m \end{bmatrix}, w = \begin{bmatrix} w_0 \\ w_1 \\ \vdots \\ w_{n-1} \\ w_n \end{bmatrix}, y = \begin{bmatrix} y_0 \\ y_1 \\ \vdots \\ y_{n-1} \\ y_n \end{bmatrix}$$

Some datasets are difficult to estimate their curve functions. To know which conic section is represented by a dataset with the equation $6x^2 + 15y^2 + 19xy = 1$, a substitution T: $u = 2x + 3y$; $v = 3x + 5y$, clears the mixed term 19xy from the quadratic form $6x^2 + 15y^2 + 19xy$ and we get, $uv = 1$. This is achieved by diagonalisation. Then using the substitution S: $w = u + v$; $z = u - v$, we have the equation $w^2 + z^2 = 4$, which is a hyperbola equation. These compose linear mapping from $S \circ T: \mathbb{R}^2 \to \mathbb{R}^2$, which is a multiplication of the matrices A and B, capturing the linear transformation T and S, respectively. These are:

$$A = \begin{bmatrix} 2 & 3 \\ 3 & 5 \end{bmatrix}, \quad B = \begin{bmatrix} 1 & 1 \\ 1 & -1 \end{bmatrix}, \quad \text{then} \quad S \circ T = BA = \begin{bmatrix} 1 & 1 \\ 1 & -1 \end{bmatrix} \begin{bmatrix} 2 & 3 \\ 3 & 5 \end{bmatrix} = \begin{bmatrix} 1 \times 2 + 1 \times 3 & 1 \times 3 + 1 \times 5 \\ 1 \times 2 - 1 \times 3 & 1 \times 3 - 1 \times 5 \end{bmatrix} = \begin{bmatrix} 5 & 8 \\ -1 & -2 \end{bmatrix}.$$

More details about linear maps, diagonalisation, and various applications can be found in (Chahal, 2018). Chapter five focuses on mapping functions and achieving better representation on a new coordinate basis.
Global polynomial optimization is achieved in Tensor form using tensor decomposition approaches (Marmin, Castella and Pesquet, 2020). This is useful for various function approximation applications for multilinear functions, non-linear functions with polynomials, matrix-matrix multiplication, and systems of polynomial equations.

Python notebook Classification_Linear_NonLinear.ipynb shows examples of non-linearly separable datasets solved by different SVM kernel functions and other linear and non-linear algorithms, as discussed in chapter two. When the non-linear solution is complex, zooming into any arc enough will approximate it as a line and can be solved linearly or in lower dimensions.

3.2.2 Differential Geometry on Manifolds

This section explains some mathematical preliminaries referenced in the following sections and chapters. The Riemannian space or Riemannian Manifolds describe curvatures in higher dimensions and provide geometric properties to facilitate the partial differential equations used in many Machine Learning (ML) algorithms. Some visualisations of these concepts are presented at https://youtube.com/playlist?list=PLbRB7u42hOE8rMlvShBxxiSdBdh9yQQL . Since ML and Data science perspectives are the main focus of this book, we will cover the essentials of how calculus on Manifolds is applied in deriving some of the basic algorithms and explains their behaviour. Calculus on Manifolds is better explained by the derivation steps and visualisations, such as the style adopted in (Fortney, 2018). This book's main aim is to show how these concepts affect the behaviour of the functions in the higher space. Here, we will summarise the main findings relevant to ML rather than how they are derived and all interesting mathematical properties.

Any equation dynamics are best captured in the form of the rate of change that is calculated using calculus methods. Plotting any dataset against the x-y coordinate partially visualises its dynamics. As the data increases in dimensionality, simple plotting will not be feasible. Alternatively, we learn a manifold, which is defined abstractly as a Euclidean space embedded locally in the higher dimensional space $\mathbb{R}^n$ for some value for n. Manifolds spaces are collections of data points, while vector spaces are collections of vectors with linear transformation functions defined on them. Physically, not all transformations are feasible for a dataset, so learning a manifold representing the given points only, reduces the dimensionality. Then, we can algebraically work with gradients of the data to understand its dynamics in the dual space. Gradients are partial first derivatives that are slopes of lines tangent to the graph of the function at a certain point.

Manifolds' data points are assumed to have local Euclidean space on which an equation of neighbourhood can retrieve equally spaced points using Euclidean distance measures and on which parallelism and perpendicular relationships can be identified. Figure 21 (a) shows an example of Euclidean space on $\mathbb{R}^2$ on which a parallel transport from v_p = (2, 1) at point p to point q is done, and parallel vectors are created. Another example is that the distance from point a to point b is measurable using the Euclidean distance metric. Figure 21 (b) shows an $\mathbb{R}^2$ Manifolds represent the earth map on which point p is at the north pole and point q is on the equator. Neither distance nor parallelism can be calculated using Euclidean metrics. Root Mean Square Error (RMSE) is based on the Euclidean metric; hence all our optimisation algorithms, once fed with a new data structure for tensors, will also need to choose a suitable metric. A Minkowski metric is defined on 4-D spacetime as $\eta(v_1, v_2) \equiv x_1x_2 + y_1y_2 + z_1z_2 - t_1t_2$. Otherwise, a **Riemannian metric** can be used instead, such as the **Fisher metric** based on the Fisher information matrix that uses KL divergence as a distance measure. The KL divergence is a measure of dissimilarity between two distributions, and the Fisher information Matrix is the **Hessian Matrix** of the **KL divergence** at the point where two distributions are equal. These will be further explained in the last subsection of this section while discussing Tensors on Manifolds. Some preliminary definitions that are needed while working with Manifolds are as follows:

- **Coordinate maps** $\varphi_i : U_i \rightarrow \mathbb{R}^n$ are defined on an *n*-dimensional **manifold** space *M* that can be entirely covered by a collection of **local coordinate neighbourhoods** U_i with one-to-one mappings φ_i.
- **A coordinate patch** or a **chart** refers to both U_i and φ_i, (U_i, φ_i)
- **A coordinate system or an atlas of M {(Ui, ϕ i)}** is defined as the set of all the charts. The atlas of the world map is a collection of charts.

- Since the U_i cover all of M, we write that $M = \cup U_i$. Also, since φ_i is one-to-one, it is invertible, so φ_i^{-1} exists and is well-defined.
- If two charts have a non-empty intersection, $U_i \cap U_j \neq \emptyset$, then the functions $\varphi j \circ \varphi_i^{-1}: \mathbb{R}^n \rightarrow \mathbb{R}^n$ are called **transition functions**.
- A **differentiable manifold** is a set M, together with a collection of charts (U_i, φ_i), where $M = \cup U_i$, such that every mapping $\varphi j \circ \varphi_i^{-1}$, where $U_i \cap U_j \neq \emptyset$, is differentiable.

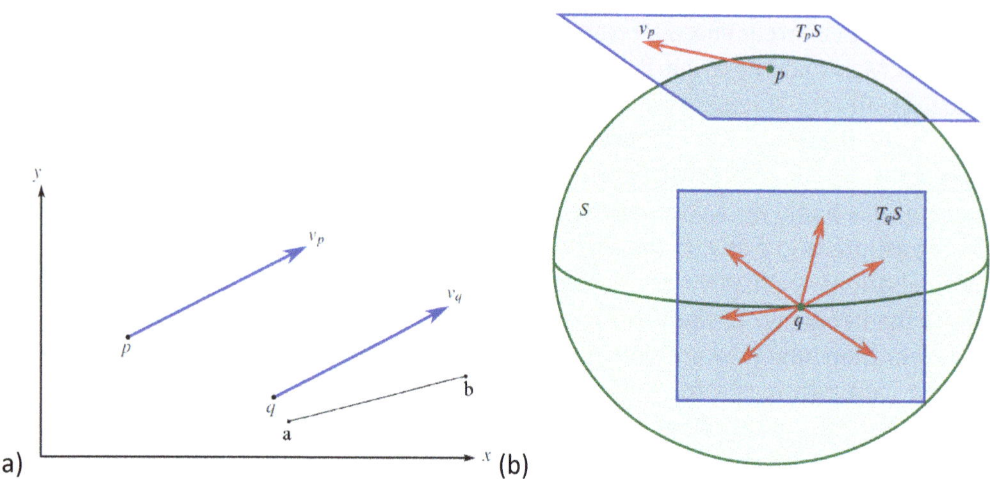

Figure 21: (a) The vector $2e_1 + e_2$ drawn at two different points p and q in the manifold $\mathbb{R}^2$. These two vectors are parallel to each other using a parallel transport from v_p to point q. A straight line between two points a and b in the manifold $\mathbb{R}^2$. It is unclear which of the vectors at q is parallel to the vector at p (Fortney, 2018).

This defines the **Manifold** as space covered by coordinate charts that are invertible and provide continuous mappings to some subset of $\mathbb{R}^n$. A manifold of a dataset connects the data points of the dataset using a coordinate chart basis calculated from their rate of change rather than a specific coordinate system. This will be clearer by the end of this section.

Set of all vectors v_p going through a data point p in Manifold M, forms a **tangent space** that is denoted by T_pM or $Tp\mathbb{R}^n$. Figure 21 (b) shows a green sphere $S \subset \mathbb{R}^3$ on which $\mathbb{R}^3$ vectors are embedded in the tangent spaces at a point p and point q, which are the blue $\mathbb{R}^2$ tangent plane (or hyperplane for higher dimensions) to the manifold at these points. The Whitney embedding theorem states that any reasonably nice manifold can be embedded into $\mathbb{R}^n$ for some sufficiently large n. The basis of the T_pM space is the **partial differential operator** $\frac{\delta}{\delta x_i}$, or simplified to $\boldsymbol{\delta x_i}$, which is equivalent to basis vectors e_i explained in chapter one, such as units of the coordinates of this space. In $\mathbb{R}^3, Tp\mathbb{R}^3 = span \left\{ \frac{\delta}{\delta x^1}\bigg|_p, \frac{\delta}{\delta x^2}\bigg|_p, \frac{\delta}{\delta x^3}\bigg|_p \right\}$. For vector $v \in Tp\mathbb{R}^3 = v^1 \frac{\delta}{\delta x^1} + v^2 \frac{\delta}{\delta x^2} + v^3 \frac{\delta}{\delta x^3}$. The Einstein summation notation representation is $v^i \frac{\delta}{\delta x^i}$ for $\mathbb{R}^n$. As we can see, vectors have coefficients with upper indices. For every point in a manifold M, we have its own tangent space. The collection of these tangent spaces of all points in a manifold is called the tangent bundle. As defined in chapter one, a vector field is an operator on which vector spaces are defined. Vector fields also describe a section of the tangent bundle of a manifold mapping a vector to a point; this will be further explained below. For each coordinate neighbourhood of M we have a coordinate system $(x_1, \ldots, x_n)$, which allows us to write a vectors field as $v = v^i(x_1, \ldots, x_n)\, \delta_{x^i}$, where the v^i are real-valued functions on M. A vector field is illustrated in Figure 22(a).

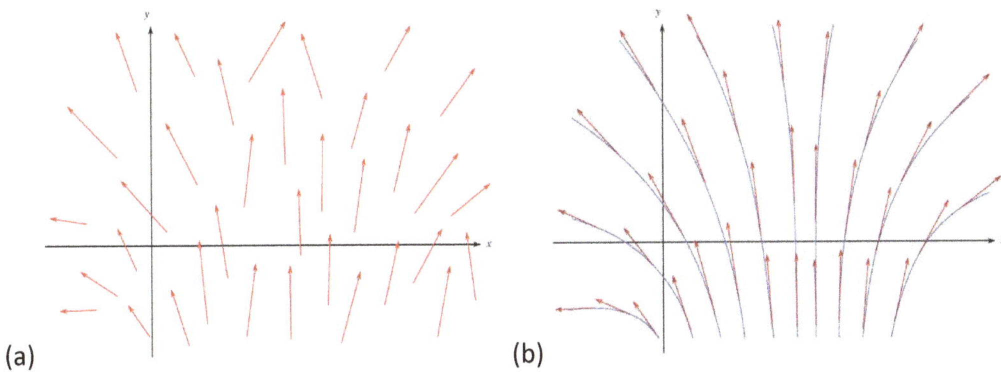

Figure 22: (a) A vector field drawn on the manifold $\mathbb{R}^2$. (b) A smooth vector field is drawn on the manifold $\mathbb{R}^2$. In both, each of the vectors shown are an element of a tangent space and not actually in the manifold $\mathbb{R}^2$(Fortney, 2018).

Tangent vectors are defined as smooth curves $\gamma: (-\epsilon, \epsilon) \subset \mathbb{R} \to M$ such that $\gamma(0) = p \in$ M and ϵ is just some small positive number, to avoid embedding M into some larger space $\mathbb{R}^n$ in order to have tangent Euclidean vectors v_p. The parameter that γ depends on can be estimated as the time to avoid having sharp corners in a curve. If two curves have the same range close to p and have the same parametrization close to p, they are called equivalent $\sim$, such as when you zoom in, they will be linear, not curves. The set of all equivalent curves is called an equivalence class: $[\gamma_1] \equiv \{\gamma | \gamma \sim \gamma_1\}$. Each equivalence class of curves at a point p, $[\gamma]_{p,}$ is defined to be a tangent vector at p. This defines the tangent space as independent of any bigger space $\mathbb{R}^n$ the manifold is embedded in as $TpM = \{[\gamma]_p | \gamma: (-\epsilon, \epsilon) \subset \mathbb{R} \to M \; and \; \gamma(0) = p\}$. Going back to correlating these equivalent curves to the vector at point v_p, in the equivalence class definition $v_p = [\gamma]_p$, $\gamma(0) = p$, and we have$[(\gamma_1(t), \dots, \gamma_n(t))]$. Taking the derivative of γ with respect to time and evaluating the derivative at time t = 0, calculates v_p, $v_p = [\gamma']_p = [\gamma]'_p = [(\gamma'_1(t), \dots, \gamma'_n(t))]_p = [(\gamma_1(t), \dots, \gamma_n(t))]'_p$. This is calculated from the Jacobian matrix of the mapping $\gamma: (-\epsilon, \epsilon) \to M$ as $\begin{bmatrix} \gamma'_1(t=0) \\ \vdots \\ \gamma'_n(t=0) \end{bmatrix} = \begin{bmatrix} \left.\frac{\partial \gamma_1(t)}{\partial t}\right|_{t=0} \\ \vdots \\ \left.\frac{\partial \gamma_n(t)}{\partial t}\right|_{t=0} \end{bmatrix}$. Only the different classes of curves are important integral curves as will be explained below, forming different tangent vectors X, such as $X = \left.\frac{df(\gamma(t))}{dt}\right|_{t_0} = \sum_{i=1}^n \left.\frac{\delta f}{\delta x_i}\right|_p \left.\frac{dx^i(\gamma(t))}{dt}\right|_{t_0} = \sum_{i=1}^n X^i \left.\frac{\delta}{\delta x_i}\right|_p$. The following will continue using vectors but will use curves when needed.

In Figure 22(b), a smooth vector field is illustrated, which changes smoothly as you vary the point, such that it is possible to find curves on the manifold that all the vectors in the vector field are tangent to the curves. The vector field v is called smooth if each of the functions $v^i(x_1, \dots, x_n)$ is differentiable an infinite number of times with respect to the arguments $x_1, \dots, x_n$. This means that there exists a function $\gamma: \subset \mathbb{R} \to M$ of a parameter t, such as time for continuity, defined as $\gamma(t) = (\gamma^1(t), \dots, \gamma^n(t))$ that are differentiable at each point p in the Manifold M: $\left.\frac{d\gamma(t)}{dt}\right|_p = v_p$, which is the system of n differential equations $\frac{d}{dt}\gamma^i = v^i$. These integral curves are used below in the directional derivatives to measure the rate of a change of a function f over any curve γ passing through point p.

A **dual vector** is an object that eats a vector and spits out a number $\mathbb{R}^n \to \mathbb{R}$. The set of all dual vectors of a vector space V is the **dual space** V*. For example, given basis e_i, then vector v can be expressed as combinations of e_i as $v = \sum_{i=1}^n v^i e_i$, its dual vector is $\tilde{v} = e^i(v) = v^i$, which is the coordinate function or the projection of v on a specific coordinate i. This makes e^i the basis for the dual space V* denoted below as $\mathbf{d}_{\mathbf{xi}}$. A dual vector $\tilde{v}$ is a one-to-one and onto map to v as $\tilde{v}(w) = \langle v. w \rangle$. This dot product is the metric dual of v.

The **dual space** can also be denoted by $(\mathbb{R}^n)^*$, is the set of all functionals T on $\mathbb{R}^n \to \mathbb{R}$ satisfying two properties: i) T(v+w) = T(v) + T(w), and ii) T(c.v) = c. T(v). The dual space of the T_pM is the set of all differential one forms, which will be defined below, in the tangent space through point p in Manifold M and is denoted by $(TpM)^*$. $(TpM)^*$ is the **cotangent space** and has basis coordinates from the **differentials d_{xi}**, which picks the ith component of the vector $v_p \in TpM$. v_p is the projection of the v_p vector on the ith coordinate. Therefore $d_{xi}(v_p)$ is equivalent to v_i. This makes the differential one forms in the $(TpM)^*$space to be acting as coordinate functions. For example, given a point p = (2, 3), the cartesian coordinate functions $\mathbb{R}^2 \to \mathbb{R}$ are x(p) = 2, and y(p) = 3. A point exists in any other coordinate system, such as polar, spherical, or cylindrical. The same p point is mapped to the polar coordinate system using mapping functions $r = \sqrt{x^2+y^2}$, and $\theta = arctan\left(\frac{x}{y}\right)$, and inverse mapping functions are: x= r cos(θ) and y = r sin(θ). Working in the cotangent space using coordinate functions enables a coordinate-free approach in which the most suitable coordinate system is used for any dataset. A transformation of components is achieved for point p in two charts, x and y. Then their coordinate vectors transform with the Jacobian of the coordinate transformation x↦y $\left(\Lambda^i_{j'}\right)$: $\frac{\delta}{\delta y^i} = \sum_{j=1}^n \frac{\delta x^i}{\delta y^i}\frac{\delta}{\delta x^{j'}}$, and inverse mapping $\Lambda^{j'}_i = \left(\Lambda^i_{j'}\right)^{-1}$. This is why in the tangent vector space, the $\frac{\delta}{\delta x^j}$ is the coordinate basis. For a vector v in a vector space with basis e_i is represented as v^ie_i , and covector ω after a change of basis to e_i^* is defined as $\omega(v_1, \dots, v_n) = sgn(\pi)\cdot \omega\left(v_{\pi(1)}, \dots, v_{\pi(n)}\right)$ for any permutation of the n elements. When ω is acting on vector v, it is defined as $\omega = \omega e_i^* = \omega(v) = \sum_{i=1}^n \omega_i v^i$. The transformation to the cotangent space is a change of basis that is captured from the Jacobian matrix. For example in $\mathbb{R}^2$,$\omega_x^i\left(\frac{\delta}{\delta x^j}\right) = \delta_j^i$, and $\omega_y^i\left(\frac{\delta}{\delta y^j}\right) = \delta_j^i$, which is the inverse of the tangent vector space, as $\omega_y^i = \sum_{j=1}^n \frac{\delta y^i}{\delta x^j}\,\omega_x^j$, providing the cotangent vector space coordinate basis as $dy^j = \sum_{j=1}^n \frac{\delta y^i}{\delta x^j}\,dx^j$, which is generally expressed as dx^i. For example, the cartesian to polar change of basis can be achieved using the Jacobian matrix determinant as:

$$\begin{vmatrix} \frac{\partial x}{\partial r} & \frac{\partial x}{\partial \theta} \\ \frac{\partial y}{\partial r} & \frac{\partial y}{\partial \theta} \end{vmatrix} = \begin{vmatrix} \cos\theta & -\mathrm{r}\sin\theta \\ \sin\theta & r\cos\theta \end{vmatrix} = r\ \cos^2\theta + r\sin^2\theta = r;\ \text{therefore, } dx\, dy = r\, dr\, d\theta.$$

Figure 23 illustrates the relationships between the manifold $\mathbb{R}^3$, the tangent space $Tp\mathbb{R}^3$, and the cotangent space $T_p^*\mathbb{R}^3$. Although the cotangent space $T_p^*\mathbb{R}^3$ is attached to the manifold at the same point p that the tangent space $Tp\mathbb{R}^3$ is attached, for illustration, it is shown above the tangent space. In $\mathbb{R}^3$, $T_p^*\mathbb{R}^3 = Span\left\{dx^1|_p, dx^2|_p, dx^3|_p\right\}$. For differential form $\alpha \in T_p^*\mathbb{R}^3 = \alpha_1 dx^1 + \alpha_2 dx^2 + \alpha_3 dx^3$. The Einstein summation notation representation is $\alpha_i dx^i$ for $\mathbb{R}^n$ with α_i as real numbers. As we can see, covectors, that is, differential forms, also called coordinate functions, have coefficients with lower indices. Other notations and conventions need to be understood from every reference.

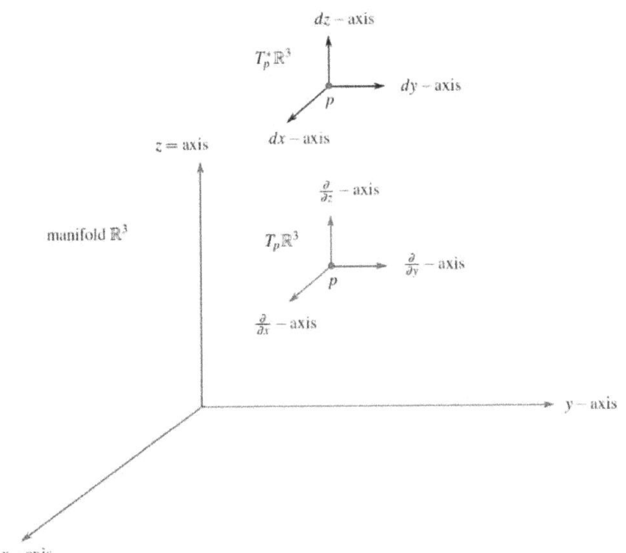

Figure 23: An illustration of the manifold $\mathbb{R}^3$ along with the tangent space $Tp\mathbb{R}^3$ "attached" to the manifold at point p. The dual space $Tp^*\mathbb{R}^3$ is drawn above the tangent space which it is dual to. Notice the different ways the axis are labelled (Fortney, 2018).

Differential forms start from zero-forms as normal functions/functionals that take scalar, produce a real number, and go up to k-forms. A differential one-form $\alpha : T_p\mathbb{R}^n \to \mathbb{R}$, is defined as linear functional on the set of tangent vectors in $\mathbb{R}^n$ at each point p, it takes one vector as input and produces a real number that is its length (1-d volume) as projected on $\mathbb{R}$. Differential two-forms take two vectors and produce a real number representing the area of the parallelogram formed by the input vectors; three-forms take three vectors and produce their volume, up to differential k-forms that take k-vectors and produce a real number representing the higher dimensional volume. Different subspace projections will be illustrated as we proceed. K here represents the number of coordinates (subspaces) used in the projection, which could be the whole dimensionality of the space n or lower down to 1.

Figure 24 illustrates two ways to visualise differential one-form $\alpha = \alpha_1 d_x + \alpha_2 d_y + \alpha_3 d_z$ in the tangent space (left) and in the dual / cotangent space $Tp^*\mathbb{R}^3$ (right). Notice each coordinate is isolated with its coefficient. The left graph shows the result of the one-form acting on the vector $v_p \in Tp\mathbb{R}^3$ as the projection in the $\frac{\delta}{\delta x_1}\Big|_p \frac{\delta}{\delta x_2}\Big|_p \frac{\delta}{\delta x_3}\Big|_p$ −plane. The differential df_p is the linear approximation of the function f at the point p. In other words, the differential df_p "encodes" the tangent plane of f at p. Figure 25 shows the formula for the tangent plane T to the function f (x, y) at the point (x_0, y_0) as $T(x,y) = f(x_0, y_0) + \frac{\delta f}{\delta x}\Big|_{(x_0, y_0)} - (x - x_0) + \frac{\delta f}{\delta y}\Big|_{(x_0, y_0)} -$ $(y - y_0)$. The figure shows vector v with end points in $\mathbb{R}^2$ is $(x_0 + v_1, y_0 + v_2)$. The tangent plane is the closest linear approximation of f at p. df_p can be thought of as the linear approximation of the function f at the point p. This is written as $df = \frac{\delta f}{\delta x}dx + \frac{\delta f}{\delta y}dy = \left[\frac{\delta f}{\delta x}, \frac{\delta f}{\delta y}\right]$ in $\mathbb{R}^2$ and extended to $\mathbb{R}^n$as $df = \frac{\delta f}{\delta x_1}dx_1 + \frac{\delta f}{\delta x_2}dx_2 + \dots \frac{\delta f}{\delta x_n}dx_n = \left[\frac{\delta f}{\delta x_1}, \frac{\delta f}{\delta x_2}, \dots, \frac{\delta f}{\delta x_n}\right]$ which is the gradient vector of f, *grad(f)* or $\nabla(f)$.

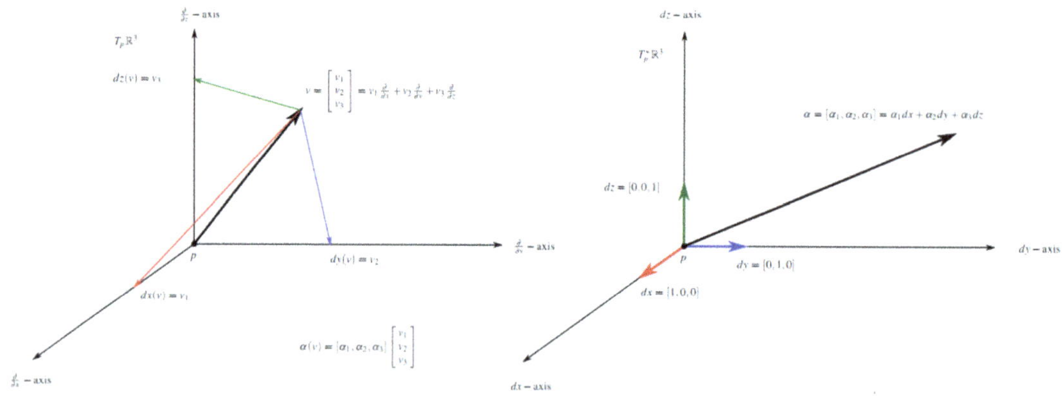

Figure 24: Two different ways to visualize a differential one-form. As a linear combination of the projections onto the axes of the tangent space $Tp\mathbb{R}^3$ (left) or as dual-vectors/ co-vectors / row vectors in the cotangent space $Tp^*\mathbb{R}^3$ (right) (Fortney, 2018).

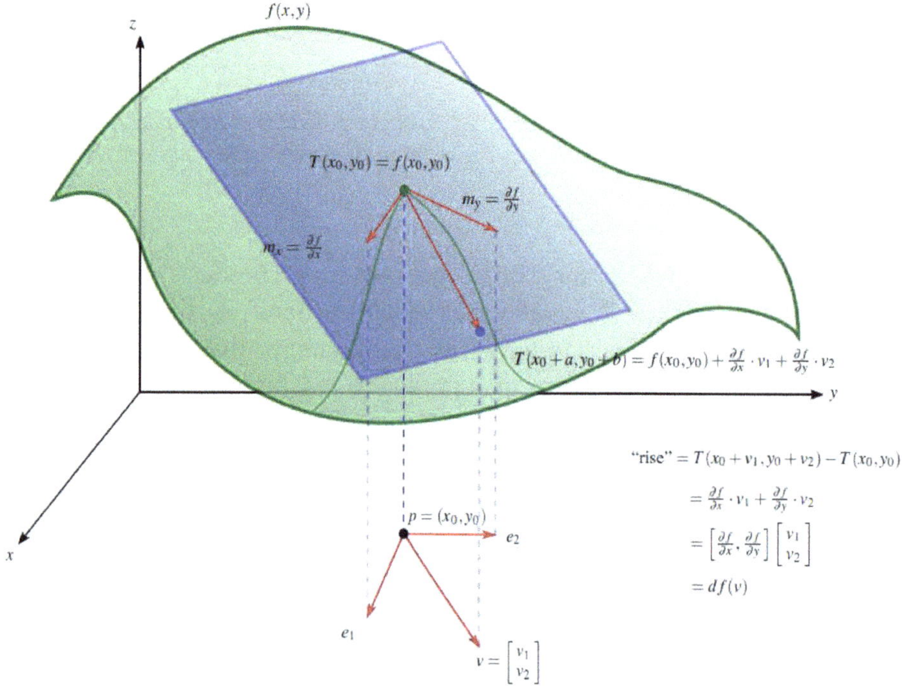

Figure 25: The differential df_p takes a vector v_p at some point p in Manifold $\mathbb{R}^2$ and produces a number which is the rise of the tangent plane to the graph of the function as it moves from p along the vector v_p. The illustration shows the projection on the tangent space and its equivalence with the basis coordinates at the bottom (Fortney, 2018).

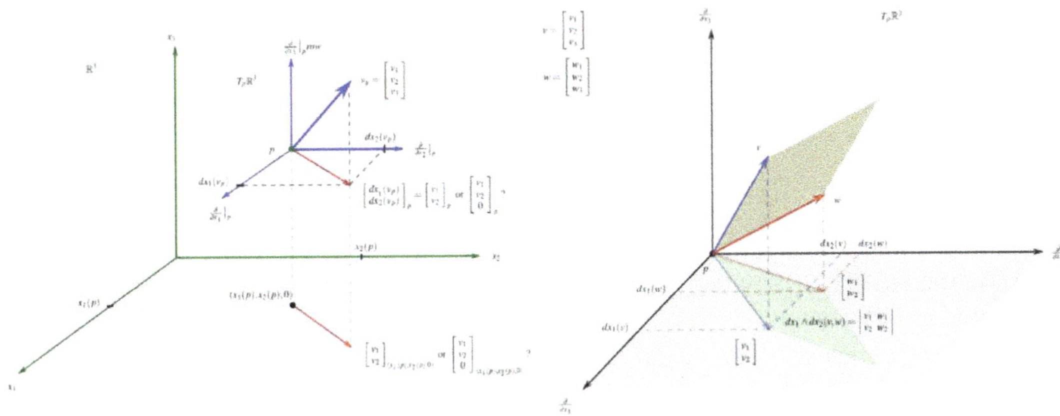

Figure 26: Projecting on lower dimensions (left). The parallelepiped spanned by v and w (brown) is projected onto the $\frac{\delta}{\delta x_1}\Big|_p \frac{\delta}{\delta x_2}\Big|_p$ *-plane in* $Tp\mathbb{R}^3$ *(right). We want* $dx_1 \wedge dx_2$ *to find the volume of this projected area (Fortney, 2018).*

Figure 26 (left) shows the spaces that various vectors belong to by taking point p in $\mathbb{R}^3$, and vector v_p from point p = $\begin{bmatrix} v_1 \\ v_2 \\ v_3 \end{bmatrix}$, then showing different projections, such as = $\begin{bmatrix} dx_1(v)_p \\ dx_2(v)_p \\ 0 \end{bmatrix}_p$ in the tangent space $Tp\mathbb{R}^3$ or at point p in Manifold $\mathbb{R}^3$, $\begin{bmatrix} dx_1(v)_p \\ dx_2(v)_p \\ 0 \end{bmatrix}_{(x_1(p),x_2(p),0)}$ at point $(x_1(p), x_2(p), 0)$ in Manifold $\mathbb{R}^3$, $\begin{bmatrix} dx_1(v)_p \\ dx_2(v)_p \end{bmatrix}$ in the 2-d plane $\frac{\delta}{\delta x_1}\Big|_p \frac{\delta}{\delta x_2}\Big|_p$ of $Tp\mathbb{R}^3$, or $\begin{bmatrix} dx_1(v)_p \\ dx_2(v)_p \end{bmatrix}_{(x_1(p),x_2(p),0)}$ at the point $(x_1(p), x_2(p), 0)$in the xy-plane of $\mathbb{R}^3$.

Figure 26 (right) illustrates the wedge product of two one-forms to produce the area of the plane formed by two vectors on $\mathbb{R}^3$, the space of two-forms on $\mathbb{R}^3$ is denoted as $\Lambda^2(\mathbb{R}^3)$. It shows the result of the one-form acting on the vector $v_p \in Tp\mathbb{R}^3$as the projection of $v_p \in \mathbb{R}^3$ in the $\frac{\delta}{\delta x_1}\Big|_p \frac{\delta}{\delta x_2}\Big|_p$ −plane of $\in Tp\mathbb{R}^2$. Given two vectors v and w, in the figure, the area (2-d volume) is calculated using the wedge product $\wedge$ defined by the determinant of the matrix formed by the appropriate elements of the vectors. For example:

$$v = \begin{bmatrix} 1 \\ 2 \\ 3 \end{bmatrix}, w = \begin{bmatrix} 4 \\ 5 \\ 6 \end{bmatrix} \text{ then, } dx_1 \wedge dx_2 \left(\begin{bmatrix} 1 \\ 2 \\ 3 \end{bmatrix} \begin{bmatrix} 4 \\ 5 \\ 6 \end{bmatrix} \right) \equiv \begin{vmatrix} dx_1(v)_p & dx_1(w)_p \\ dx_2(v)_p & dx_2(w)_p \end{vmatrix} = \begin{vmatrix} 1 & 4 \\ 2 & 5 \end{vmatrix} = (1)(5)\text{- } (4)(2) = -3,$$

if we calculate $dx_2 \wedge dx_1 \left(\begin{bmatrix} 1 \\ 2 \\ 3 \end{bmatrix} \begin{bmatrix} 4 \\ 5 \\ 6 \end{bmatrix} \right) \equiv \begin{vmatrix} dx_1(v)_p & dx_1(w)_p \\ dx_2(v)_p & dx_2(w)_p \end{vmatrix} = \begin{vmatrix} 2 & 5 \\ 1 & 4 \end{vmatrix} = (2)(4)\text{- } (5)(1) = 3$. Therefore, the wedge product of two one-forms is defined in terms of the determinant of the appropriate vector projections. Similarly, the matrix determinant can derive the volume of other plane projections in higher dimensions. To generalise in the $\mathbb{R}^n$, given $v_1, v_2, \ldots, v_n$ vectors, the wedge product of n one-forms is defined as:

$$dx_1 \wedge dx_2 \wedge \ldots.\wedge dx_n(v_1, v_2, \ldots v_n) \equiv \begin{vmatrix} dx_1(v)_1 & dx_1(v)_2 & \ldots & dx_1(v)_n \\ dx_2(v)_1 & dx_2(v)_2 & \ldots & dx_2(v)_n \\ \vdots & \vdots & \ddots & \vdots \\ dx_n(v)_1 & dx_n(v)_2 & \ldots & dx_n(v)_n \end{vmatrix}$$

Another formula for the determinant is given in (Fortney, 2018) as:

$$\begin{vmatrix} a_{11} & a_{12} & \cdots & a_{1n} \\ a_{21} & a_{22} & \cdots & a_{2n} \\ \vdots & \vdots & \ddots & \vdots \\ a_{n1} & a_{n2} & \cdots & a_{nn} \end{vmatrix} = \sum_{\sigma \in S_n} sgn(\sigma) \prod_{i=1}^{n} a_{\sigma(i)i}$$

Then

$$dx_1 \wedge dx_2 \wedge \ldots . \wedge dx_n(v_1, v_2, \ldots v_n) = \sum_{\sigma \in S_n} sgn(\sigma) \prod_{j=1}^{n} dx_{\sigma(i_j)}(v_j)$$

Where S_n is The set of permutations of {1, ...,n} with n! elements in it and particular permutation is denoted as σ such that $a_{\sigma(i)i}$ is the permuted row for column i.
There are many algebraic properties, such as:

- if we have any two of the one-forms being the same, that is, $i_j = i_k$ for some $j \neq k$ then we have two rows that are the same, which gives a value of zero $dx_i \wedge dx_i = 0$.
- if $i \neq j$ and we switch dx_i and dx_j that the wedge product changes sign, $dx_i \wedge dx_j = -dxj \wedge dxi$. This defines the anti-symmetric property of the wedge product.

We can also find the wedge products of n-forms on subspaces projections of $\mathbb{R}^n$. Figure 27 illustrates an example of two vectors v and w in $\mathbb{R}^3$ projected on three 2-d planes in $Tp\mathbb{R}^3$and then summed up: $(dx \wedge dy + dy \wedge dz + dz \wedge dx)(v, w) = dx \wedge dy(v, w) + dy \wedge dz(v, w) + dz \wedge dx(v, w)$. To generalise for $\mathbb{R}^n$, the two forms on n-dimensional manifolds are defined by finding projections of the two vectors v, w on the appropriate two-dimensional subspaces of $Tp\mathbb{R}^n$, forming the two-dimensional parallelepipeds; their volumes are then scaled by the appropriate factor and then summed. The only distinction is that $Tp\mathbb{R}^n$ has $\frac{n(n-1)}{2}$ distinct two-dimensional subspaces. This is denoted as $\Lambda_p^2\mathbb{R}^n$, and generalised for $\Lambda_p^k\mathbb{R}^n$ for 0 <=k <= n. For example, zero-forms in $\mathbb{R}^3$: $\Lambda^0\mathbb{R}^3 = span\ \{1\}$, which is one-dimensional functions on $\mathbb{R}^3$; another example is $\Lambda^3\mathbb{R}^3 = \text{span}\ \{\text{dx} \wedge \text{dy} \wedge \text{dz}\}$, which is one-dimensional three-forms in $\mathbb{R}^3$, with basis given by {dx ∧ dy ∧ dz}. Since the three-form dx ∧ dy ∧ dz projects three vectors u, v,w onto the $\delta x \delta y \delta z$ -subspace of $Tp\mathbb{R}^3$, which is the whole $Tp\mathbb{R}^3$. $\Lambda^2\mathbb{R}^3$is illustrated in Figure 27 as two-forms on $\mathbb{R}^3$, with basis given by { dx ∧ dy, dy ∧ dz, dz ∧ dx} projects the two vectors v,w onto the 2-d planes: $\delta x \delta y$ -plane, $\delta y \delta z$ -plane and $\delta z \delta x$ -plane as subspaces of $Tp\mathbb{R}^3$. Another example is given as $\Lambda_p^3\mathbb{R}^4$ as three-forms in $\mathbb{R}^4$ with basis given by $\{ dx_1 \wedge dx_2 \wedge dx_3, dx_1 \wedge dx_2 \wedge dx_4, dx_1 \wedge dx_3 \wedge dx_4, dx_2 \wedge dx_3 \wedge dx_4\}$ projects the three vectors u, v,w onto the 3-d planes of $\delta x_1 \delta x_2 \delta x_3$, illustrated in Figure 28, and also $\delta x_1 \delta x_2 \delta x_4$, $\delta x_1 \delta x_3 \delta x_4$, $\delta x_2 \delta x_3 \delta x_4$ as subspaces of $Tp\mathbb{R}^4$.

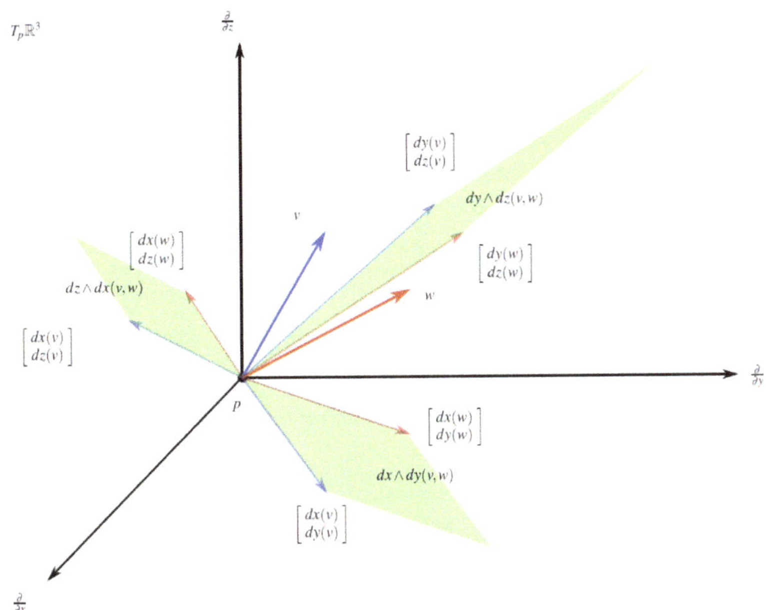

Figure 27: The action of the two-forms dx ∧ dy + dy ∧ dz + dz ∧ dx on two vectors v and w, projected on the three plans: $\left.\frac{\delta}{\delta x}\right|_p \left.\frac{\delta}{\delta y}\right|_p$-plane, $\left.\frac{\delta}{\delta y}\right|_p \left.\frac{\delta}{\delta z}\right|_p$-plane, $\left.\frac{\delta}{\delta z}\right|_p \left.\frac{\delta}{\delta x}\right|_p$-plane in $Tp\mathbb{R}^3$, and then summed up (Fortney, 2018).

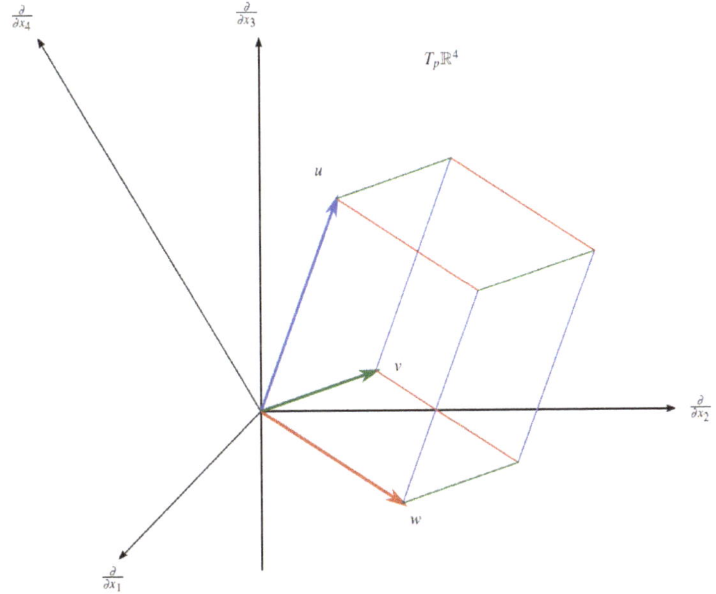

Figure 28: Illustration of three vectors u, v,w onto the 3-d planes of $\delta x_1 \delta x_2 \delta x_3$, as a subspace of $Tp\mathbb{R}^4$ (Fortney, 2018).

For arbitrary k-forms in $\Lambda^k\mathbb{R}^n$. The notation can be simplified such that we do not write all the elements of the basis of $\Lambda^k\mathbb{R}^n$. For example, for arbitrary two-forms in $\Lambda^2\mathbb{R}^3$, we can define $\alpha = a_{12}dx_1 \wedge dx_2 + a_{23}dx_2 \wedge dx_3 + a_{31}dx_3 \wedge dx_1$. We can then generalise to $\Lambda^k\mathbb{R}^n$ as $\alpha = \sum_I a_I dx^I$, such that I stands for elements in the set of k increasing indices $i_1, i_2, \ldots, i_k$, where $1 \leq i_1 < i_2 < \cdots < i_k \leq n$, defined as $I \in J_{(k,n)} = \{(i_1, i_2, \ldots, i_k) | 1 \leq i_1 \leq i_2 \leq \ldots \leq i_k \leq n\}$. Other examples:

- For arbitrary three-forms in $\Lambda^3\mathbb{R}^4$, $I \in J_{3,4} = \{123, 124, 134, 234\}$, we can define $\alpha = \sum_I a_I dx^I = a_{123}dx^{123} + a_{124}dx^{124} + a_{134}dx^{134} + a_{234}dx^{234} = a_{123}dx_1 \wedge dx_2 \wedge dx_3 + a_{124}dx_1 \wedge dx_2 \wedge dx_4 + a_{134}dx_1 \wedge dx_3 \wedge dx_4 + a_{234}dx_2 \wedge dx_3 \wedge dx_4$, such that $dx^{123} = dx_1 \wedge dx_2 \wedge dx_3$ and so forth.
- For arbitrary two-forms in $\Lambda^2\mathbb{R}^4$, $I \in J_{2,4} = \{12, 13, 14, 23, 24, 34\}$, we can define $\alpha = \sum_I a_I dx^I = a_{12}dx^{12} + a_{13}dx^{13} + a_{14}dx^{14} + a_{23}dx^{23} + a_{24}dx^{24} + a_{34}dx^{34} = a_{12}dx_1 \wedge dx_2 + a_{13}dx_1 \wedge dx_3 + a_{14}dx_1 \wedge dx_4 + a_{23}dx_2 \wedge dx_3 + a_{24}dx_2 \wedge dx_4 + a_{34}dx_3 \wedge dx_4$, such that $dx^{12} = dx_1 \wedge dx_2$ and so forth.

Given $\alpha \in \Lambda^k\mathbb{R}^n$, and $\beta \in \Lambda^l\mathbb{R}^n$, where $\alpha = \sum_I a_I dx^I$ and $\beta = \sum_J b_J dx^J$defined as above, then $\alpha \wedge \beta = \sum_I (a_I dx^I) \wedge \sum_J (b_J dx^J) = \sum a_I b_J dx^I \wedge dx^J = \sum_K (\sum_{I \cup J, I, J\ are\ disjoint} \pm a_I b_J) dx^K$. If I and J are disjoint then we have $dx^I \wedge dx^J = \pm dx^K$ where K = I ∪ J, but is reordered to be in increasing order and elements with repeated indices are dropped.
For example, given $\alpha \in \Lambda^2\mathbb{R}^8 = \sum_I a_I dx^I = 5dx_1 \wedge dx_2 - 6dx_2 \wedge dx_4 + 7dx_1 \wedge dx_7 + 2dx_2 \wedge dx_8$, where I has the elements of the set {12, 24, 17, 28} as a ⊂ $J_{2,8}$ and the coefficients are $a_{12} = 5$, $a_{24} = -6$, $a_{17} = 7$, and $a_{28} = 2$. Given also, $\beta \in \Lambda^3\mathbb{R}^8 = \sum_J b_J dx^J = 3dx_3 \wedge dx_5 \wedge dx_8 - 4dx_5 \wedge dx_6 \wedge dx_8$, where I has the elements of the set {358, 568} as a ⊂ $J_{3,8}$ and the coefficients are $b_{358} = 3$, and $b_{568} = -4$, then $I \cup J = \{12358, 24358, 17358, 28358, 12568, 24568, 17568, 28568\}$. Both 28358 and 28568 repeat the 8, since $dx_2 \wedge dx_8 \wedge dx_3 \wedge dx_5 \wedge dx_8 = 0$ and $x_2 \wedge dx_8 \wedge dx_5 \wedge dx_6 \wedge dx_8 = 0$, then we can drop them. K, after having the indices in increasing order, will be K = $\{12358, 23458, 13578, 12568, 24568, 15678\}$. Therefore, $\alpha \wedge \beta = \sum_K (\sum_{I \cup J, I, J\ are\ disjoint} \pm a_I b_J) dx^K = a_{12}b_{358}dx^{12358} + a_{24}b_{358}dx^{23458} + a_{17}b_{358}dx^{13578} + a_{12}b_{568}dx^{12568} + a_{24}b_{568}dx^{24568} + a_{17}b_{568}dx^{15678}$.
The general formula is given as $\alpha \wedge \beta\, (v_1, v_2, \dots v_{k+l}) = \frac{1}{k!l!} \sum_{\sigma \in S_{k+l}} sgn(\sigma) \alpha(v_{\sigma(1)}, v_{\sigma(2)}, \dots v_{\sigma(k)}) \beta((v_{\sigma(k+1)}, v_{\sigma(k+2)}, \dots v_{\sigma(k+l)})$, this means that σ is a(k+l)–shuffle.
In tensor form, this is expressed as $\alpha \wedge \beta = \frac{(k+l)!}{k!l!} \mathcal{A}(\alpha \otimes \beta)$, where $\mathcal{A}$ is the skew-symmetrisation (or anti-symmetrisation) operator that takes a tensor and returns its differential form as skew-symmetric and ⊗ is the tensor product as defined earlier. This is also called anti-symmetric multilinear covectors because it takes a number of vectors and gives a number, changing sign if we reorder its input vectors. This completes the definition of the wedge product of n-forms as calculating the volume of the parallelopiped formed by the n input vectors as column vectors in the matrix from which the determinant is calculated. Other operators can be defined as follows:

- **The inner product between vector and k-form**: given vector v and k-form α, their inner product is defined as: $i_v\alpha\, (v_1, v_2, \dots v_{k-1}) = \alpha\, (v, v_1, v_2, \dots v_{k-1})$, i.e. the resulting (k-1)-form puts the vector v in front.
- **The inner product between vector and two added k-forms**: given vector v and two k-form α & β, their inner product is defined as: $i_v(\alpha + \beta) = i_v\alpha + i_v\beta$.
- **The inner product between two vectors and k-form**: given two vectors v & w, and k-form α, their inner product is defined as: $i_{(v+w)}\alpha = i_v\alpha + i_w\alpha$.
- **Inner Product between two k-forms**: Given two one-forms α, β in $\mathbb{R}^3$: which $\in \Lambda^1\mathbb{R}^3 = \text{span}\{dx, dy, dz\} = Tp^*\mathbb{R}^3$, which is three-dimensional vector space, such that $\alpha = adx + bdy + cdz = [a, b, c], \beta = rdx + sdy + tdz = [r, s, t]$, their inner product is defined as:

$$\langle \alpha, \beta \rangle = \langle [a, b, c], [r, s, t] \rangle \equiv [a, b, c] \begin{bmatrix} 1 & 0 & 0 \\ 0 & 1 & 0 \\ 0 & 0 & 1 \end{bmatrix} [r, s, t]^T = [a, b, c] \begin{bmatrix} r \\ s \\ t \end{bmatrix} = ar + bs + ct$$

  - Another example: given two two-forms η, ξ in $\mathbb{R}^3$: $\Lambda^2\mathbb{R}^3 = \text{span}\{dx \wedge dy, dy \wedge dz, dz \wedge dx\}$, which is a three-dimensional vector space such that $\eta = a(dx \wedge dy), b(dy \wedge dz), c(dz \wedge dx) = [a, b, c], \xi = r(dx \wedge dy), s(dy \wedge dz), t(dz \wedge dx) = [r, s, t]$; their inner product remains defined as previously but on different coordinates:

$$\langle \eta, \xi \rangle = \langle [a,b,c],[r,s,t] \rangle \equiv [a,b,c] \begin{bmatrix} 1 & 0 & 0 \\ 0 & 1 & 0 \\ 0 & 0 & 1 \end{bmatrix} [r,s,t]^T = [a,b,c] \begin{bmatrix} r \\ s \\ t \end{bmatrix} = ar + bs + ct$$

- **Hodge star operator**: or Hodge star dual operator takes a k-form in $\mathbb{R}^n$ to (n-k)-form as: $*: \Lambda^k \mathbb{R}^n \to \Lambda^{n-k} \mathbb{R}^n$, such that α *in* $\Lambda^k \mathbb{R}^n$ *has an equivalent* $* \alpha$ *in* $\Lambda^{n-k} \mathbb{R}^n$ *such that* $\alpha \wedge \beta = \langle * \alpha, \beta \rangle \sigma$ for all β, where <., .> is the inner product that associates a real number to a pair of vectors or differential forms, here both are $\Lambda^{n-k} \mathbb{R}^n$, and σ is the n-dimensional volume form. Notice that <., .> if containing a one-form and a vector, it is canonical pairing between them as used earlier. This means that the Hodge star takes an n-form as input and uses the inner product of the n-k forms (which produces a scalar) to multiply with an n-form σ. This unique mapping between α and $* \alpha$ is valid for any chosen β. The derivation is lengthy, but interesting symmetry is noticed as $*1 = dx \wedge dy$, $dx = *dy$, $*dy = dx$ in $\mathbb{R}^2$, $*1 = dx \wedge dy \wedge dz$, $*dx = dy \wedge dz$, $*dy = dz \wedge dx$, $*dz = dx \wedge dy$ in $\mathbb{R}^3$, $*1 = dx^1 \wedge dx^2 \wedge dx^3 \wedge dx^4$, $*dx^1 = dx^2 \wedge dx^3 \wedge dx^4$, $*dx^2 = dx^1 \wedge dx^3 \wedge dx^4$, $*dx^3 = dx^1 \wedge dx^2 \wedge dx^4$, *and* $*dx^4 = dx^1 \wedge dx^2 \wedge dx^3$ in $\mathbb{R}^4$, and so forth. Also, the Hodge star operator can be applied to k-forms in $\mathbb{R}^n$, and higher such as $*(dx \wedge dy \wedge dz) = 1$ *in* $\mathbb{R}^3$, $*(dx^1 \wedge dx^2)$ as two forms in $\mathbb{R}^{n>=2}$, $*(dx^1 \wedge dx^3)$ as two forms in $\mathbb{R}^{n>=3}$, $*(dx^1 \wedge dx^2 \wedge dx^3)$ as three forms in $\mathbb{R}^{n>=3}$, $*(dx1 \wedge dx2 \wedge dx3 \wedge dx4)$ as four forms in $\mathbb{R}^{n>=4}$and so forth for any value of k <= any value for n, both > 0.

The intuition behind these different spaces, and their implications in machine learning, is focused on multi-way associations of n features' weights on the function output that is estimated to represent a dataset. This means instead of learning a weight for each feature/column/dimension in the dataset, you can learn a combined weight for every n-k permutation of the features, where 0 <=k <= n, and then reduce the dimensionality by ignoring the irrelevant mapping and focus on the strongly correlated mapping with the output. From the 1 to n-dimensional, the Hodge star operator uses symmetry to reduce the number of combinations required. For example, a price of a house can be a function of many features. These features are combined in multiple different factors that can be estimated. A neighbourhood factor might be combined from the distance of the nearest business area, area pollution measures, demographics of people, crime rate, and many other features related to the quality of the neighbourhood. Some other groups of features might be combined as house-specific features, such as the number of rooms, land area, built land area, renovations, number of floors, and others. Standardisation unifies the unit of measures in a dataset such that the net weight of each feature is not affected by the different measures used in collecting the data. Also, combining together different features forming one coordinate against the remaining coordinates for the remaining combinations, then estimating a weight for each new coordinate, reveal the multi-way correlations of the dataset.

3.2.2.1 Directional Derivatives

In chapter one, real-valued functions' **total derivative** $f: \mathbb{R} \to \mathbb{R}$ was introduced to describe the rate of change of the function output with respect to the displacement of a point and the slope of the tangent line at the given point. If the function is differentiable, then the total derivative is known as the gradient. This is a directional derivative in the direction of only one variable.
Also, in chapter one, the **partial/directional derivative** was defined for multivariable functions as $f: \mathbb{R}^n \to \mathbb{R}$ in the direction of a specific variable displacement, treating other variables as constants. This calculates the rate of change of the function output as the function moves in the direction of the variable used in the differentiation. A partial derivative has more options in the direction and needs a vector v_p from point p to define it, such as $df(v_p) = v_p[f] = \lim_{t \to 0} \frac{f(p+tv_p)-f(p)}{f}$, where d is the operator that, given a function f (zero-form that takes a scalar and produces a scalar) as input, yields a one-form output (that takes one vector and produces a scalar). The directional derivative is the dot product of the gradient with the desired direction. The Jacobian matrix is the

matrix of all partial derivatives explaining all ways the output and input are related, providing a total derivative from the partials. It approximates the function for a given point and estimates the change as the function moves along a vector from this point. This is achieved by the dot product of the Jacobian matrix with this vector yielding a vector. This vector is in the new Manifold with a new coordinate system; therefore, the Jacobian matrix is a mapping function between two coordinate systems.

Exterior differentiation d is the extended directional derivative when given zero-forms, as in vector calculus. In a coordinate-free approach, when given one-forms and higher k-forms, exterior differentiation extends the vector derivative by contracting the differential form by a given vector v, yielding a k+1-form output. Vector v provides the direction of the displacement required for the differentiation.

The local (in-coordinates x_i) exterior derivative of k-form α (which itself is defined as differential forms) is $d\alpha = \sum df_i \wedge dx_i$ where $f_i$are functions or zero-forms. For example, given $\alpha = f_1 dx + f_2 dy$ is a one-form on the manifold $\mathbb{R}^2$ for some functions $f_1, f_2 : \mathbb{R}^2 \to \mathbb{R}$, then:

$$d\alpha = df_1 \wedge dx + df_2 \wedge dy$$

$$= \left(\frac{\delta f_1}{\delta x} dx + \frac{\delta f_1}{\delta y} dy\right) \wedge dx + \left(\frac{\delta f_2}{\delta x} dx + \frac{\delta f_2}{\delta y} dy\right) \wedge dy$$

$$= \frac{\delta f_1}{\delta x} \underset{= 0}{\overset{dx \wedge dx}{\Longleftrightarrow}} + \frac{\delta f_1}{\delta y} \underset{= -dx \wedge dy}{\overset{dy \wedge dx}{\Longleftrightarrow}} + \frac{\delta f_2}{\delta x} dx \wedge dy + \frac{\delta f_2}{\delta y} \underset{= 0}{\overset{dy \wedge dy}{\Longleftrightarrow}}$$

$$= \left(\frac{\delta f_2}{\delta x} - \frac{\delta f_1}{\delta y}\right) dx \wedge dy$$

Given two vectors $v = v_1 \frac{\delta}{\delta x} + v_2 \frac{\delta}{\delta y} = \begin{bmatrix} v_1 \\ v_2 \end{bmatrix}$ and $w = w_1 \frac{\delta}{\delta x} + w_2 \frac{\delta}{\delta y} = \begin{bmatrix} w_1 \\ w_2 \end{bmatrix}$, then $d\alpha(v, w) = \left(\frac{\delta f_2}{\delta x} - \frac{\delta f_1}{\delta y}\right) dx \wedge dy(v, w)$

$$= \left(\frac{\delta f_2}{\delta x} - \frac{\delta f_1}{\delta y}\right) \begin{vmatrix} dx(v) & dx(w) \\ dy(v) & dy(w) \end{vmatrix}$$

$$= \left(\frac{\delta f_2}{\delta x} - \frac{\delta f_1}{\delta y}\right) \begin{vmatrix} v_1 & w_1 \\ v_2 & w_2 \end{vmatrix}$$

$$= \left(\frac{\delta f_2}{\delta x} - \frac{\delta f_1}{\delta y}\right) (v_1 w_2 - w_1 v_2)$$

$$= v_1 w_2 \frac{\delta f_2}{\delta x} - v_1 w_2 \frac{\delta f_1}{\delta y} - w_1 v_2 \frac{\delta f_2}{\delta x} + w_1 v_2 \frac{\delta f_1}{\delta y}$$

Exterior differentiation with constant vector fields is illustrated in Figure 29. The one form α on the manifold $\mathbb{R}^n$ is a mapping $\alpha : T_p\mathbb{R}^n \to \mathbb{R}$, with a given vector v on the manifold $\mathbb{R}^n$, then for each $p \in \mathbb{R}^n$, we have $\alpha_p(v_p) \in \mathbb{R}$ is a real number. Therefore $\alpha(v)$ is a function on the manifold $\mathbb{R}^n$, with input as point p and output as real numbers. This is denoted < α, v>, where the notation <·, ·> means the canonical pairing between a one-form/covector and a vector. This can be < α, (v_1, v_2, ... v_k)> for k-form α.

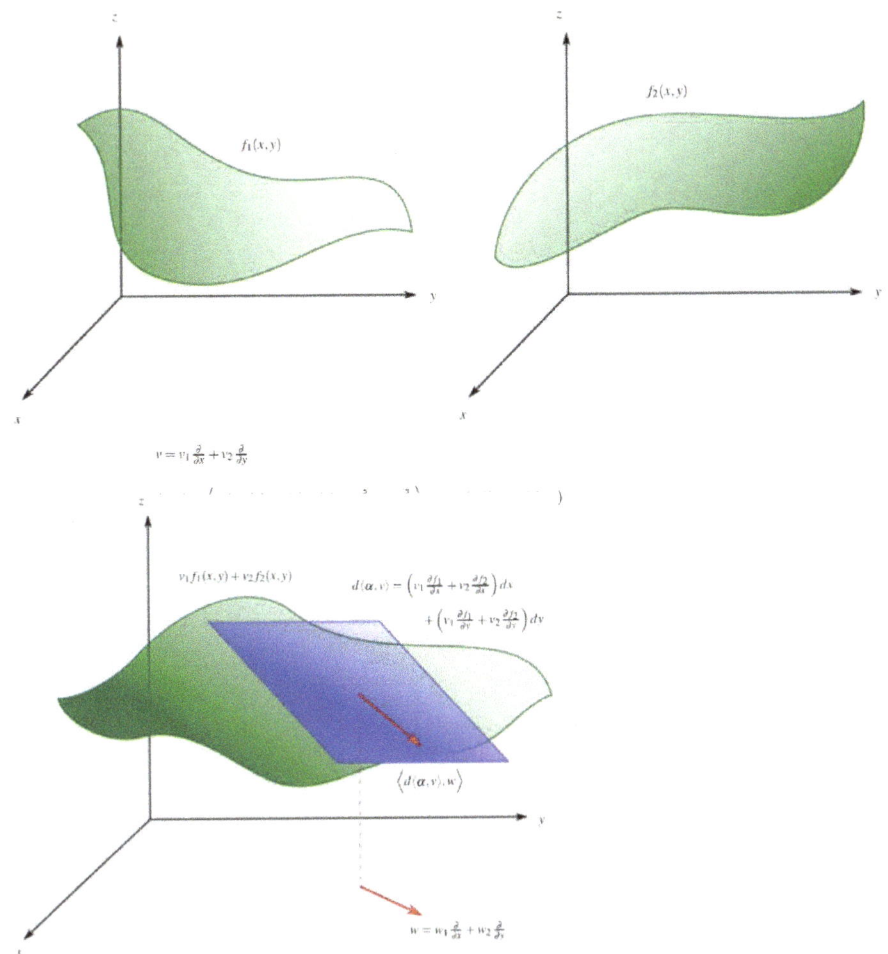

Figure 29: The one-form $\alpha(x,y) = f_1(x,y)\,dx + f_2(x,y)\,dy$ on the manifold $\mathbb{R}^2$ is made up of two functions $f_1, f_2 \colon \mathbb{R}^2 \to \mathbb{R}$, shown above. Once we are given a vector field v on a manifold in $\mathbb{R}^3$, here the constant vector field $v = v_1\delta x + v_2\delta y$, then this can be used to find the real-valued function $< \alpha, v > = v_1 f_1 + v_2 f_2$, which can be viewed as a linear combination of the two functions f_1, f_2. The directional derivative of this function can then be found in the direction of another given vector $w = w_1\delta x + w_2\delta y$. Here the differential d<α, v> in essence encodes the information about the tangent plane to the function $< \alpha, v >$, shown in green (Fortney, 2018).

The global (coordinate-free or invariant) exterior differentiation formula works well in any coordinates such as cartesian, polar, spherical, cylindrical, etc. Given 2-form α, the global exterior derivative is defined as $d\alpha\,(v,w) = v[\alpha(w)] - w[\alpha(v)] - \alpha([v,w])$, where v[f] is one notation for the directional derivative of f in the direction of v, [v,w] is the lie-bracket of two vector fields v and w, which is defined by [v,w] = vw - wv. Lie brackets will be further explained in chapter 5. This is extended to the k-form as $d\alpha\,(v_0, v_1, \dots, v_k) = \sum_i (-1)^i\, v_i[\alpha(v_0, v_1, \dots \hat{v}_i, \dots, v_k)] + \sum_{i<j} (-1)^{i+j}\, \alpha([v_i, v_j], (v_0, v_1, \dots \hat{v}_i, \dots, \hat{v}_j \dots, v_k))$, such that the hat of a vector means omitting the vector. The derivation can be found in (Fortney, 2018).

For example, given non-constant vector fields $f, g \colon \mathbb{R}^2 \to \mathbb{R}$, the exterior differentiation is defined as $df = \frac{\partial f}{\partial x}dx + \frac{\partial f}{\partial y}dy$ and $dg = \frac{\partial g}{\partial x}dx + \frac{\partial g}{\partial y}dy$, their wedge product is

$$df \wedge dg = \left(\frac{\partial f}{\partial x}dx + \frac{\partial f}{\partial y}dy\right) \wedge \left(\frac{\partial g}{\partial x}dx + \frac{\partial g}{\partial y}dy\right)$$

$$= \frac{\partial f}{\partial x} dx \wedge \left(\frac{\partial g}{\partial x} dx + \frac{\partial g}{\partial y} dy \right) + \frac{\partial f}{\partial y} dy \wedge \left(\frac{\partial g}{\partial x} dx + \frac{\partial g}{\partial y} dy \right)$$
$$= \frac{\partial f}{\partial x}\frac{\partial g}{\partial x} \underset{= 0}{\underleftrightarrow{dx \wedge dx}} + \frac{\partial f}{\partial x}\frac{\partial g}{\partial y} dx \wedge dy + \frac{\partial f}{\partial y}\frac{\partial g}{\partial x} \underset{= -dx \wedge dy}{\underleftrightarrow{dy \wedge dx}} + \frac{\partial f}{\partial y}\frac{\partial g}{\partial y} \underset{= 0}{\underleftrightarrow{dy \wedge dy}}$$
$$= \frac{\partial f}{\partial x}\frac{\partial g}{\partial y} dx \wedge dy - \frac{\partial f}{\partial y}\frac{\partial g}{\partial x} dx \wedge dy$$
$$= \left(\frac{\partial f}{\partial x}\frac{\partial g}{\partial y} - \frac{\partial f}{\partial y}\frac{\partial g}{\partial x} \right) dx \wedge dy$$
$$= \underset{Jacobian}{\underleftrightarrow{\begin{vmatrix} \frac{\partial f}{\partial x} & \frac{\partial f}{\partial y} \\ \frac{\partial g}{\partial x} & \frac{\partial g}{\partial y} \end{vmatrix}}} \underset{Area\ form}{\underleftrightarrow{dx \wedge dy}}$$

You can see how this extends to $f, g, h: \mathbb{R}^3 \to \mathbb{R}$, we have:

$$df \wedge dg \wedge dh = \underset{Jacobian}{\underleftrightarrow{\begin{vmatrix} \frac{\partial f}{\partial x} & \frac{\partial f}{\partial y} & \frac{\partial f}{\partial z} \\ \frac{\partial g}{\partial x} & \frac{\partial g}{\partial y} & \frac{\partial g}{\partial z} \\ \frac{\partial h}{\partial x} & \frac{\partial h}{\partial y} & \frac{\partial h}{\partial z} \end{vmatrix}}} \underset{Volumn\ form}{\underleftrightarrow{dx \wedge dy \wedge dz}}$$

For example, given $x = r\cos(\theta) and\ y = r\sin(\theta)$, then

$$dx \wedge dy = \begin{vmatrix} \frac{\partial x}{\partial \theta} & \frac{\partial x}{\partial r} \\ \frac{\partial y}{\partial \theta} & \frac{\partial y}{\partial r} \end{vmatrix} d\theta \wedge dr = \begin{vmatrix} \frac{\partial r\cos(\theta)}{\partial \theta} & \frac{\partial r\cos(\theta)}{\partial r} \\ \frac{\partial r\sin(\theta)}{\partial \theta} & \frac{\partial r\sin(\theta)}{\partial r} \end{vmatrix} d\theta \wedge dr$$
$$= \begin{vmatrix} -r\sin(\theta) & \cos(\theta) \\ r\cos(\theta) & \sin(\theta) \end{vmatrix} d\theta \wedge dr = (-r\sin^2(\theta) - r\cos^2(\theta)) d\theta \wedge dr$$
$$= -r d\theta \wedge dr$$

This describes a polar change of coordinates. Another example of coordinate change is given the new coordinates as u = x + y and v = x – y to map points in the plane $\mathbb{R}^2_{xy} \to \mathbb{R}^2_{uv}$, such that the area in an xy-plane:

$$dx \wedge dy \left(\underset{vectors\ in\ xy-plane}{\underleftrightarrow{\begin{bmatrix} 1 \\ 0 \end{bmatrix}_{(0,0)}, \begin{bmatrix} 0 \\ 1 \end{bmatrix}_{(0,0)}}} \right) = \begin{vmatrix} 1 & 0 \\ 0 & 1 \end{vmatrix} = 1 \text{ and}$$

$du \wedge dv \left(\underset{mapped\ vectors\ in\ uv-plane}{\underleftrightarrow{\begin{bmatrix} 1 \\ 1 \end{bmatrix}_{(0,0)}, \begin{bmatrix} 1 \\ -1 \end{bmatrix}_{(0,0)}}} \right) = \begin{vmatrix} 1 & 1 \\ 1 & -1 \end{vmatrix} = -2$, we can define $du \wedge dv$ in terms of $dx \wedge dy$ as $du = d(x + y) = dx + dy$, and $dv = d(x - y) = dx - dy$, then $du \wedge dv = (dx + dy) \wedge (dx - dy)$, then simplified to $du \wedge dv = -2dx\ + dy$. The inverse mapping is as follows: $x = \frac{1}{2}(u + v)$, and $y = \frac{1}{2}(u - v)$, then $dx = d\left(\frac{1}{2}(u + v)\right) = \frac{1}{2}du + \frac{1}{2}dv$ and $dy = d\left(\frac{1}{2}(u - v)\right) = \frac{1}{2}du - \frac{1}{2}dv$, then $dx \wedge dy = \left(\frac{1}{2}du + \frac{1}{2}dv\right) \wedge \left(\frac{1}{2}du - \frac{1}{2}dv\right)$, then simplified to $dx \wedge dy = -\frac{1}{2}du \wedge dv$. The volume of mapped vectors, as shown in Figure 30, is double the size as expected from the equations above, and the negative sign is because of the counter-clockwise rotation.

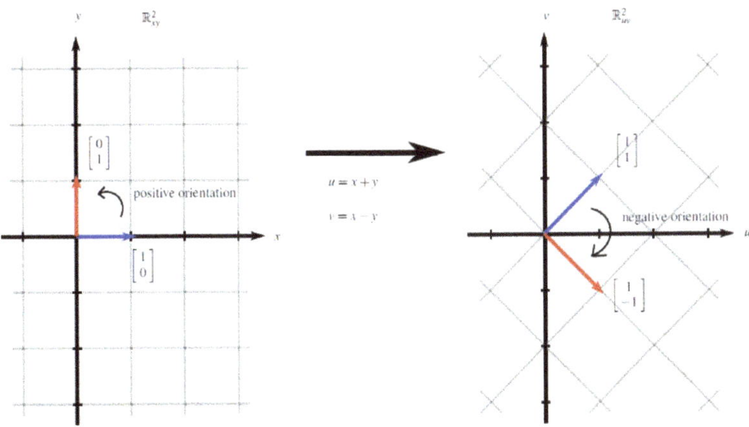

Figure 30: The basis vectors in the xy-plane mapped to two vectors in the uv-plane. Notice the orientation changes

The above examples implicitly rely on a specific coordinate system using a single coordinate patch (U_i, ϕ_i). However, a general manifold does not have a single coordinate system. Instead, it has an atlas {(U_i, ϕ_i)} of coordinate patches (U_i, ϕ_i). The same argument and computation can be done on each of the many coordinate patches. This means that on each of the many coordinate patches, there is a formula that gives the exterior derivative of a differential form d_{Ui}, as long as that form is written in the coordinates of that particular coordinate patch. For $U_i \cap U_j \neq \emptyset$, if d_{Ui} exists and is unique on Ui and d_{Uj} exists and is unique on U_j, then on $U_i \cap U_j$ we must have $d_{Ui} = d_{Uj} = d$. Since this is true on the intersection of all coordinate patches, then we have d existing and unique globally, that is, over $M \ = \cup \ U_i$.

Push-forward of a vector moves it from one manifold to another or the same manifold with a different coordinate system. This is often called tangent mapping. Given the coordinate change $\mathbb{R}^2_{xy} \rightarrow \mathbb{R}^2_{uv}$, mapping function $f(x, y) = (x + y, x - y) = (u, v)$ explained above, we can use the Jacobian Matrix to do the mapping from a point in $\mathbb{R}^2_{xy}$ to a point in $\mathbb{R}^2_{uv}$. Given a point p = (1, 1) and v_p from this point = (1, 2), we evaluate the Jacobian Matrix $D_p f \colon D_p \mathbb{R}^2_{xy} \rightarrow D_{f(p)} \mathbb{R}^2_{uv}$ for point (x, y):

$$\begin{vmatrix} \frac{\partial u}{\partial x} & \frac{\partial u}{\partial y} \\ \frac{\partial v}{\partial x} & \frac{\partial v}{\partial y} \end{vmatrix}_{(x,y)} = \begin{vmatrix} \frac{\partial (x+y)}{\partial x} & \frac{\partial (x+y)}{\partial y} \\ \frac{\partial (x-y)}{\partial x} & \frac{\partial (x-y)}{\partial y} \end{vmatrix}_{(x,y)} = \begin{vmatrix} 1 & 1 \\ 1 & -1 \end{vmatrix}_{(x,y)},$$

then apply the mapping on v_p: to get its mapping (push-forward) in $\mathbb{R}^2_{uv}$ for the mapped point f(p):

$$D_p f . v_p = \begin{vmatrix} 1 & 1 \\ 1 & -1 \end{vmatrix}_{(1,1)} \cdot \begin{bmatrix} 1 \\ 2 \end{bmatrix}_{(1,1)} = \begin{bmatrix} 1.1 + 1.2 \\ 1.1 \pm 1.2 \end{bmatrix}_{f(1,1)} = \begin{bmatrix} 3 \\ -1 \end{bmatrix}_{f(1,1)} = \begin{bmatrix} 3 \\ -1 \end{bmatrix}_{(2,0)},$$

this push-forward changed the basis from point (1, 1) to the mapped point (2,0). This is generalised as the Jacobian mapping at point p as: $D_p f =$

$$\begin{vmatrix} \left.\frac{\partial f_1}{\partial x_1}\right|_p & \left.\frac{\partial f_1}{\partial x_2}\right|_p & \cdots & \left.\frac{\partial f_1}{\partial x_n}\right|_p \\ \left.\frac{\partial f_2}{\partial x_1}\right|_p & \left.\frac{\partial f_2}{\partial x_2}\right|_p & \cdots & \left.\frac{\partial f_2}{\partial x_n}\right|_p \\ \vdots & \vdots & \ddots & \vdots \\ \left.\frac{\partial f_n}{\partial x_1}\right|_p & \left.\frac{\partial f_n}{\partial x_2}\right|_p & \cdots & \left.\frac{\partial f_n}{\partial x_n}\right|_p \end{vmatrix}$$

Pull-back of a differential form moves it from one manifold to another manifold or the same manifold with a different coordinate system. This is often called the cotangent mapping $D^*_p f$, and is dual to the push-back of vectors. Given the coordinate change $\mathbb{R}^2_{xy} \rightarrow \mathbb{R}^2_{uv}$, mapping function f explained above,

$$\xLeftarrow[\text{pull-back of } (du \wedge dv)]{D^*_p f.(du \wedge dv),}$$

$$\begin{vmatrix}1 & 1\\ 1 & -1\end{vmatrix}.(dx \wedge dy)_p\left(\begin{bmatrix}1\\0\end{bmatrix}_p, \begin{bmatrix}0\\1\end{bmatrix}_p\right) = (du \wedge dv)_{f(p)}\left(D_pf.\begin{bmatrix}1\\0\end{bmatrix}_p, D_pf.\begin{bmatrix}0\\1\end{bmatrix}_p\right)$$

$\overleftrightarrow{\text{vectors in } D_p\mathbb{R}^2_{xy}}$ $\overleftrightarrow{\text{push-forward of vectors in } D_p\mathbb{R}^2_{xy} \to D_{f(p)}\mathbb{R}^2_{uv}}$

$\overleftrightarrow{=(-2)(1)=-2}$ $\overleftrightarrow{=-2}$

This is simplified to $-2dx \wedge dy = du \wedge dv$ such that the $-2dx \wedge dy$ is the pull-back of $du \wedge dv$. This is generalised to $\mathbb{R}^n$, given the mapping function (change in basis) $\varphi: \mathbb{R}^n_{(x_1,\dots,x_n)} \to \mathbb{R}^n_{(\varphi_1,\dots,\varphi_n)}$ and a volume form $d\varphi_1 \wedge \dots \wedge d\varphi_n$, the pull-back is defined as (omitting the point p):

$$D^*\varphi.(d\varphi_1 \wedge \dots \wedge d\varphi_n) = \begin{vmatrix} \frac{\partial\varphi_1}{\partial x_1} & \frac{\partial\varphi_1}{\partial x_2} & \cdots & \frac{\partial\varphi_1}{\partial x_n} \\ \frac{\partial\varphi_2}{\partial x_1} & \frac{\partial\varphi_2}{\partial x_2} & \cdots & \frac{\partial\varphi_2}{\partial x_n} \\ \vdots & \vdots & \ddots & \vdots \\ \frac{\partial\varphi_n}{\partial x_1} & \frac{\partial\varphi_n}{\partial x_2} & \cdots & \frac{\partial\varphi_n}{\partial x_n} \end{vmatrix} dx_1 \wedge \dots \wedge dx_n$$

This is for mapping between Manifolds of the same dimensions and for volume forms only, not the general differential forms. A general map $\varphi: \mathbb{R}^n \to \mathbb{R}^m$ is defined as $\varphi(x_1, \dots, x_n) = \varphi^1(x_1, \dots, x_n), \dots, \varphi^m(x_1, \dots, x_n)$, the Jacobian $D\varphi = \begin{vmatrix} \frac{\partial\varphi_1}{\partial x_1} & \frac{\partial\varphi_1}{\partial x_2} & \cdots & \frac{\partial\varphi_1}{\partial x_n} \\ \frac{\partial\varphi_2}{\partial x_1} & \frac{\partial\varphi_2}{\partial x_2} & \cdots & \frac{\partial\varphi_2}{\partial x_n} \\ \vdots & \vdots & \ddots & \vdots \\ \frac{\partial\varphi_m}{\partial x_1} & \frac{\partial\varphi_m}{\partial x_2} & \cdots & \frac{\partial\varphi_m}{\partial x_n} \end{vmatrix}$ and input k-form $\alpha \in \Lambda^k\mathbb{R}^n$, the pull-back yields a k-form $\in \Lambda^k\mathbb{R}^m$ that is defined as follows:

$$(D^*\varphi.\alpha)(v_1, \dots, v_k) \equiv \alpha(D\varphi.v_1, \dots, D\varphi.v_k)$$

For the above simple linear mapping example, we have: $D^*\varphi.(vdu + udv) = 2xdx + 2ydy$. The derivation and more examples of other coordinate mappings can be found in (Fortney, 2018).

In chapter one, vector spaces are defined as the set of vectors, including the zero vector and another vector that, when added or multiplied by a scalar, produces vectors that belong to this space. **Vector fields** are defined above as sections of manifolds because they provide a mapping between each vector in a given vector space and a point. In $\mathbb{R}^3$, a vector field $\mathbb{F}$ is defined as $\mathbb{F}$ = P(x, y, z)i, Q(x, y, z)j, R(x, y, z)k, such that $P, Q, R: \mathbb{R}^3 \to \mathbb{R}$ and I, j, k are the unit vectors in x, y, and z coordinates, defined as e_1, e_2, and e_3, respectively. The operator Δ is defined as $\Delta = \frac{\partial}{\partial x}e_1 + \frac{\partial}{\partial y}e_2 + \frac{\partial}{\partial z}e_3$, which is the gradient when applied on a function (zero-form), turning it into a vector field: $\Delta f = \frac{\partial f}{\partial x}i + \frac{\partial f}{\partial y}j + \frac{\partial f}{\partial z}k = \frac{\partial f}{\partial x}\frac{\partial}{\partial x} + \frac{\partial f}{\partial y}\frac{\partial}{\partial y} + \frac{\partial f}{\partial z}\frac{\partial}{\partial z}$.

In chapter one, the **integration in the vector calculus** was defined using the Riemann sums operator $\int f(x)dx$. Similarly, we can define the **integration of differential forms** as a generalisation of the vector calculus integration to differential forms. For example, in $\mathbb{R}^2$, we integrate the differential form $\alpha = f(x,y)\, dx \wedge dy$, as

$\int\int f(x,y)\, dx \wedge dy$, which keeps track of the orientation (order/sign of the coordinates) and generalises to $\mathbb{R}^n$ as $\int \dots \int f(x_1, \dots, x_n)\, dx_1 \wedge \dots \wedge dx_n$. In the coordinate-free approach, the integration over differential forms works when given a mapping $\mathbb{R}^n_{x_1,\dots,x_n} \xrightarrow{\phi} \mathbb{R}^n_{\phi_1,\dots,\phi_n}$ and is defined as :

$\int_R f(x_1, \dots, x_n)\, dx_1 \wedge \dots \wedge dx_n = \int_{\phi(R)} f \circ \phi^{-1}(\phi_1, \dots, \phi_n)\, T^*\phi^{-1}.(dx_1 \wedge \dots \wedge dx_n)$, such that the left-hand side shows the integral taking place in $x_1, \dots, x_n$ − coordinates and integrates the function $f(x_1, \dots, x_n)$ over the region R using the volume form $dx_1 \wedge \dots \wedge dx_n$ associated with the $x_1, \dots, x_n$ − coordinates. The right-hand side shows the region we are integrating over in $\mathbb{R}^n_{\phi_1,\dots,\phi_n}$ as its image $\phi(R)$. The function $f \circ \phi^{-1}$ is a function in the variables $\phi_1, \dots, \phi_n$, and pull-back of the area-form $T\phi^{-1}.(dx_1 \wedge \dots \wedge dx_n)$, and not the area form $d\phi_1 \wedge \dots \wedge d\phi_n$, which is essential when a change of variables is needed.

Divergence measures how vector fields vary, diverge or spread out at a given point. This is defined for vector field $\mathbb{F}$ as the dot product of the gradient Δ with the vector field $\mathbb{F}$ in cartesian coordinates (x, y, z):

$$div\ \mathbb{F} = \Delta.\mathbb{F} = \left(\frac{\partial}{\partial x}e_1 + \frac{\partial}{\partial y}e_2 + \frac{\partial}{\partial z}e_3\right).(Pe_1 + Qe_2 + Re_3) = \frac{\partial P}{\partial x} + \frac{\partial Q}{\partial y} + \frac{\partial R}{\partial z}$$

The flux of the vector field $\mathbb{F}$ through the surface S is a measure of vector flow over a surface. This can measure fluid flow over a surface, electricity flow, magnetic field flow, and others. To abstract this flow without fluid density or other physical interpretations for a given problem, the flux at each point *p* on the surface *S* we have that $\mathbb{F}_p.\hat{n}_p$ is a real number. That is, we can think of $\mathbb{F}.\hat{n}$ as a real-valued function on *S*, $\mathbb{F}.\hat{n} : S \rightarrow \mathbb{R}$, which means we can easily integrate it over the surface *S*.

$$Flux\ of\ \mathbb{F} = \lim_{|\Delta S| \to 0} \sum_i \mathbb{F}.\hat{n}\Delta S = \int_S \mathbb{F}.\hat{n}dS$$

dS comes from the *ΔS*, which represents the area-form of a small bit of surface *S*.

This derives the divergence at a given point in a surface as follows. Given a small three-dimensional region *V* about the point *(x_0, y_0, z_0)* with boundary *∂V* and volume *ΔV* the divergence of $\mathbb{F}$ at *(x_0, y_0, z_0), and ∂V* is a closed surface like a sphere with no edges, *and* the normal vector $\hat{n}$ point outwards from the *∂V* surface, is defined by:

$$div\ \mathbb{F} = \lim_{\Delta V \to 0} \frac{1}{\Delta V} \int_{\partial V} \mathbb{F}.\hat{n}dS$$

In cylindrical coordinates (r, θ, z), the divergence of vector $field\ \mathbb{F} = \mathbb{F}_r e_r + \mathbb{F}_\theta e_\theta + \mathbb{F}_z e_z$ is defined as: $div\ \mathbb{F} = \frac{1}{r}\frac{\partial(r\mathbb{F}_r)}{\partial r} + \frac{1}{r}\frac{\partial \mathbb{F}_\theta}{\partial \theta} + \frac{\partial \mathbb{F}_z}{\partial z}$.

In spherical coordinates (r, θ, ϕ), the divergence of vector field $\mathbb{F} = \mathbb{F}_r e_r + \mathbb{F}_\theta e_\theta + \mathbb{F}_\varphi e_\varphi$ is defined as: $div\ \mathbb{F} = \frac{1}{r^2}\frac{\partial(r^2\mathbb{F}_r)}{\partial r} + \frac{1}{r\sin(\theta)}\frac{\partial(\sin(\theta)\mathbb{F}_\theta)}{\partial \theta} + \frac{1}{r\sin(\theta)}\frac{\partial \mathbb{F}_\varphi}{\partial \varphi}$.

Curl also measures how vector fields vary, such as the "circulation" per unit area of vector field $\mathbb{F}$ over an infinitesimal path around some point. For the same vector field defined above for the cartesian coordinates, the curl is defined as the cross product for the same operator Δ defined above and the vector field:

$$curl\ \mathbb{F} = \Delta \times \mathbb{F} = \left(\frac{\partial R}{\partial y} - \frac{\partial Q}{\partial z}\right)i + \left(\frac{\partial P}{\partial z} - \frac{\partial R}{\partial x}\right)j + \left(\frac{\partial Q}{\partial x} - \frac{\partial P}{\partial y}\right)k$$

Given S as a surface bounded by the closed curve C = ∂S, ΔS is the area of that surface, $\hat{n}$ is the unit normal vector to that surface, the s in ds is the infinitesimal arc length element, and the surface area ΔS shrinks to zero about the point (x_0, y_0, z_0), and $\hat{t}$ as the unit
tangent vectors to *C*. Then, the curl $\mathbb{F}$ at a point (x_0, y_0, z_0) is defined as:

$$\hat{n}.curl\ \mathbb{F} = \lim_{|\Delta S| \to 0} \frac{1}{\Delta S} \int_C \mathbb{F}.\hat{t}ds$$

The definition of curl derives the Stokes' theorem. Given any surface S, not necessarily in a plane, whose boundary is the closed curve C, we can break up the surface into sub-surfaces S_i with boundaries C_i, if two C_i share an edge, the terms cancel out, and we end up with the Stokes theorem stated below.
In cylindrical coordinates (r, θ, z), the curl of vector field $\mathbb{F} = \mathbb{F}_r e_r + \mathbb{F}_\theta e_\theta + \mathbb{F}_z e_z$ is defined as: $curl\ \mathbb{F} = (curl\ \mathbb{F})_r e_r + (curl\ \mathbb{F})_\theta e_\theta + (curl\ \mathbb{F})_z e_z$, where:

$(curl\ \mathbb{F})_r = \frac{1}{r}\frac{\partial \mathbb{F}_z}{\partial \theta} - \frac{\partial \mathbb{F}_\theta}{\partial z}$,

$(curl\ \mathbb{F})_\theta = \frac{\partial \mathbb{F}_r}{\partial z} - \frac{\partial \mathbb{F}_z}{\partial r}$, and

$(curl\ \mathbb{F})_z = \frac{1}{r}\frac{\partial (r\mathbb{F}_\theta)}{\partial r} - \frac{1}{r}\frac{\partial \mathbb{F}_r}{\partial \theta}$

In spherical coordinates (r, θ, φ), curl of vector field $\mathbb{F} = \mathbb{F}_r e_r + \mathbb{F}_\theta e_\theta + \mathbb{F}_\varphi e_\varphi$ is defined as:
$curl\ \mathbb{F} = (curl\ \mathbb{F})_r e_r + (curl\ \mathbb{F})_\theta e_\theta + (curl\ \mathbb{F})_\varphi e_{z\varphi}$, where:

$(curl\ \mathbb{F})_r = \frac{1}{r\sin(\theta)}\frac{\partial(\sin(\theta)\mathbb{F}_\varphi)}{\partial \theta} - \frac{1}{r\sin(\theta)}\frac{\partial \mathbb{F}_\theta}{\partial \varphi}$,

$(curl\ \mathbb{F})_\theta = \frac{1}{r\sin(\theta)}\frac{\partial \mathbb{F}_r}{\partial \varphi} - \frac{1}{r}\frac{\partial (r\mathbb{F}_\varphi)}{\partial r}$, and

$(curl\ \mathbb{F})_\varphi = \frac{1}{r}\frac{\partial (r\mathbb{F}_\theta)}{\partial r} - \frac{1}{r}\frac{\partial \mathbb{F}_r}{\partial \theta}$

The gradient of function f is the vector field:
$grad\ f = \Delta . f = \frac{\partial f}{\partial x} i + \frac{\partial f}{\partial y} j + \frac{\partial f}{\partial z} k$, this can be a dot product with a vector u to give the directional derivative in the direction of u: $gradf.u = u[f]$.
The Laplacian of a function f is defined to be $div(grad\ f) = \nabla \cdot (\nabla f) = \nabla \cdot \nabla f = \nabla^2 f$, which is the divergence of the gradient that is the trace (tr) of the function's Hessian, H(f). tr(H(f)) is the sum of the eigenvalues of the Hessian and is invariant of change of basis and a measure of the function curvature. More on this will be discussed in chapter five.
The **flat ♭ and the sharp ♯** operators use musical isomorphisms because the symbols are taken from musical note notations. The flat ♭ in musical notes means "lower the pitch", and sharp ♯ means "raise the pitch". Similarly, the ♭ isomorphism means "lower the indices" by going from the tangent space TpM to the cotangent space Tp^*M, such that a vector v is mapped as in $v^\flat : v^I \frac{\partial}{\partial x^I} \to v_i dx^i$. The ♯ isomorphism means "raise the indices" by going from the cotangent space Tp^*M to the tangent space TpM, such that a differential form α is mapped as in $\alpha^\sharp : \alpha_i dx^i \to \alpha^I \frac{\partial}{\partial x^I}$.
Given a vector field $\mathbb{F} = P\frac{\partial}{\partial x}, Q\frac{\partial}{\partial y}, R\frac{\partial}{\partial z}$, we will define a **Hodge star mapping** ($*\circ \flat$) as first flattening the vector field to get a one-form and then Hodge staring that one-form to get a two-form: $(* \circ \flat)\mathbb{F} = *(\mathbb{F}^\flat) = *\left(\left(P\frac{\partial}{\partial x}, Q\frac{\partial}{\partial y}, R\frac{\partial}{\partial z}\right)^\flat\right) = *(Pdx + Qdy + Rdz) = Pdy \wedge dz + Q\, dz \wedge dx + R\, dx \wedge dy$.

3.2.2.2 Summary of Mappings & Generalised Stokes Theorem:

In chapter 9 in (Fortney, 2018), relationships between differential calculus and vector calculus are summarised in this diagram in Figure 31 for $\mathbb{R}^3$. The mappings between each space are shown in the arrows. It is obvious that the identity (id) mapping is used between continuous function and the zero form on the same Manifold because they describe the same thing. The grad mapping applies the gradients of a continuous function to provide the tangent bundle. The differential operator moves the one-form differentials to their two-form equivalent, while the flat operator ♭ move the tangent bundle to the two-form equivalent.

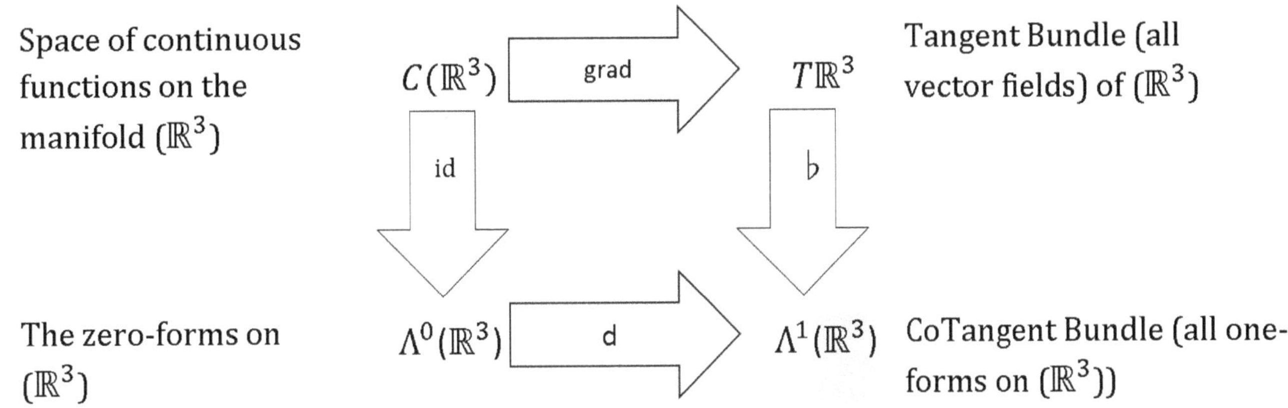

Figure 31: Illustration of relationships between differential calculus and vector calculus

The "diagram commutes" from C($\mathbb{R}^3$) to $\Lambda^1(\mathbb{R}^3)$ through two paths: $C(\mathbb{R}^3) \xrightarrow{(grad)} T\mathbb{R}^3 \xrightarrow{\flat} \Lambda^1(\mathbb{R}^3)$ and C($\mathbb{R}$^3) $\xrightarrow{\text{id}} \Lambda^0(\mathbb{R}^3) \xrightarrow{\text{d}} \Lambda^1(\mathbb{R}^3)$. In other words, given a continuous function f, we have $(grad\ f\ )^\flat = d\big(id(f)\big) = df$. The left-hand side says that flattening the gradient of the continuous function is equivalent to the exterior derivative of the function.

$$\Delta f = \frac{\partial f}{\partial x}i + \frac{\partial f}{\partial y}j + \frac{\partial f}{\partial z}k = \frac{\partial f}{\partial x}\frac{\partial}{\partial x} + \frac{\partial f}{\partial y}\frac{\partial}{\partial y} + \frac{\partial f}{\partial z}\frac{\partial}{\partial z}$$

$$(\Delta f)^\flat = \frac{\partial f}{\partial x}dx + \frac{\partial f}{\partial y}dy + \frac{\partial f}{\partial z}dz$$

$$df = \frac{\partial f}{\partial x}dx + \frac{\partial f}{\partial y}dy + \frac{\partial f}{\partial z}dz = (\Delta f)^\flat$$

Another commuting diagram shown in Figure 32 shows two paths that illustrate that given a vector Field $\mathbb{F} \in T\mathbb{R}^3$, the differential of flattened $\mathbb{F}$ is equivalent to Hodge star of the flattened curl of $\mathbb{F}$: $d(\mathbb{F}\hat{}\ \flat\ ) = *\ ((curl\ \mathbb{F})^\flat\ ) = (*\circ \flat\ )(curl\ \mathbb{F})$. You can work out the mapping operators on the arrows to derive this identity or check the detailed derivation steps in (Fortney, 2018).

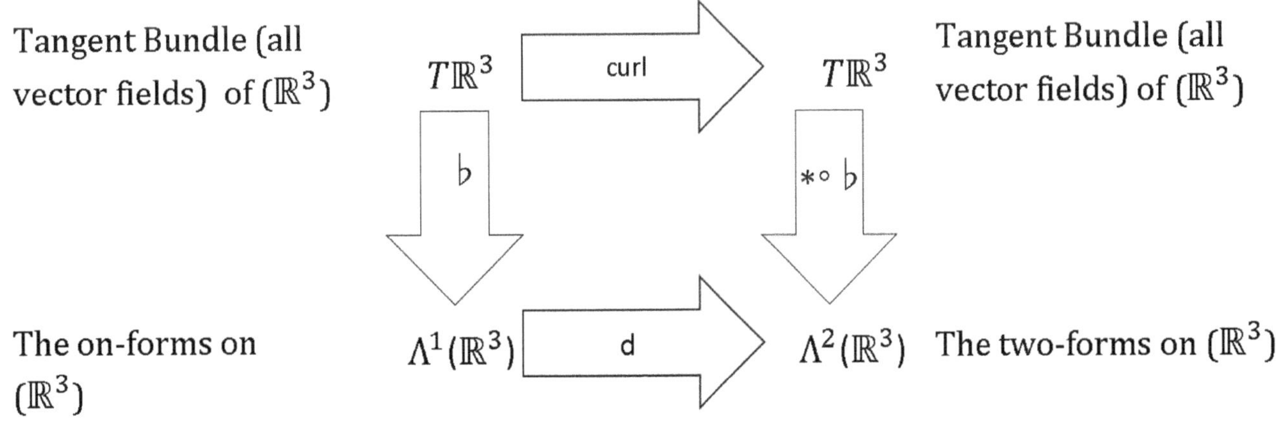

Figure 32: Another commuting diagram

Another commuting diagram shown in Figure 33 shows two paths that illustrate that given a vector Field $\mathbb{F} \in T\mathbb{R}^3$, the Hodge star of divergence of $\mathbb{F}$ is equivalent to the differential of the Hodge star of the flattened $\mathbb{F}$: $*\,(div\ \mathbb{F}) = d\big((* \circ\ \flat\,)\mathbb{F}\big) = d\big(*\,\mathbb{F}^{\flat}\,\big)$. You can work out the mapping operators on the arrows to derive this identity or check the detailed derivation steps in (Fortney, 2018).

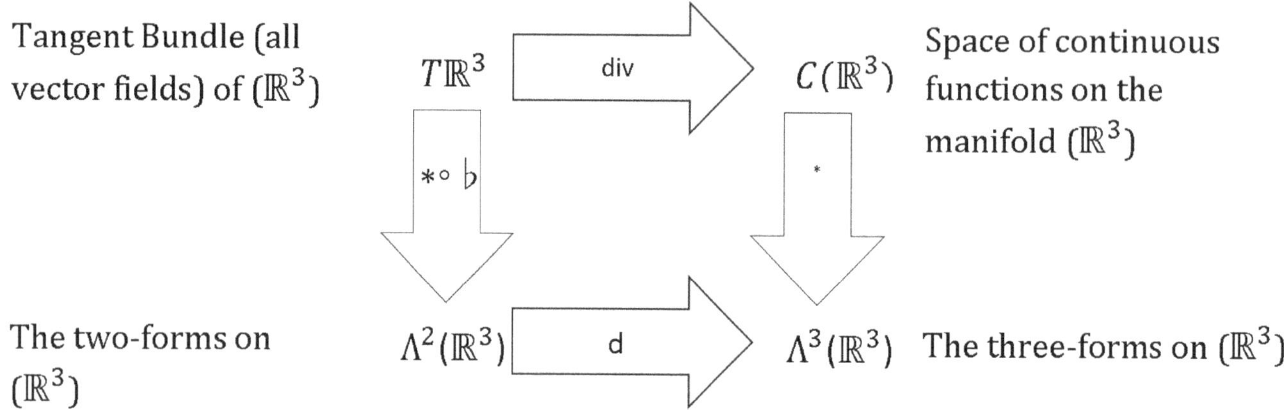

Figure 33: Another commuting diagram

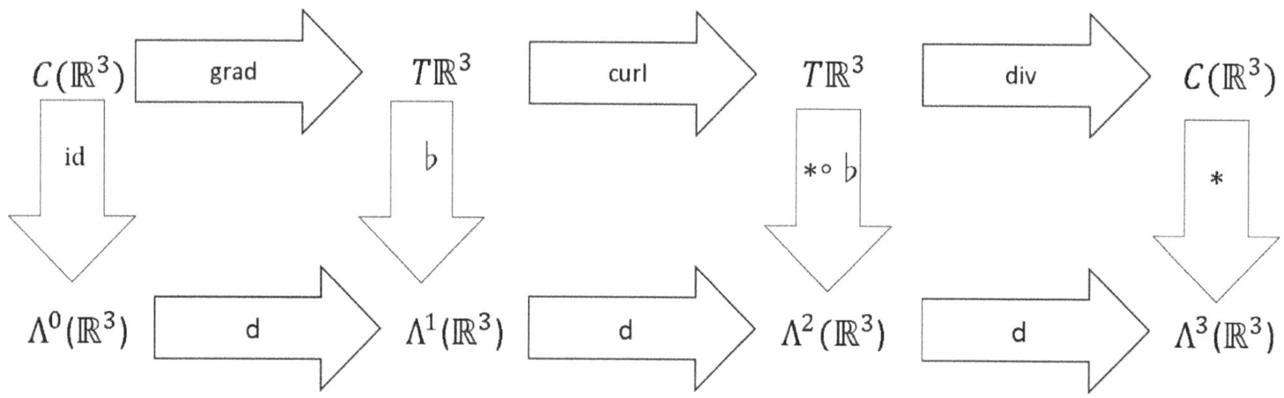

Figure 34: Connecting the three commuting diagrams

Figure 34 connects the three commuting diagrams together, illustrating that the three vector calculus operators: the gradient, the curl and the divergence on top, are all different forms of exterior differentiations on the bottom of the diagram. The vector calculus cannot be generalised to $\mathbb{R}^n$, while the differential calculus can.

Poncaré lemma is a powerful tool for the study of manifolds. It states that every closed form on $\mathbb{R}^n$ is exact. A differential form α is closed if $d\alpha = 0$. A differential k-form α is exact if there is another k-1-form differential form β such that $\alpha = d\beta$.

The following identities from vector calculus can be written in terms of the exterior derivative as follows from the Poncaré lemma: $\nabla \times (\nabla f) = 0 \leftrightarrow d(df) = 0$ and $\nabla \times (\nabla F) = 0 \leftrightarrow d(d\alpha) = 0$.

The fundamental theorem of line integrals, given a curve C, given by $c(s) = (x(s), y(s), z(s))$ with endpoints $c(a) = (x(a), y(a), z(a))$, and $c(b) = (x(b), y(b), z(b))$, where a, b $\in \mathbb{R}$ and a $\leq$ b, then the fundamental theorem of line integrals is given by $\int (grad\ f).ds = f\big(c(b)\big) - f\big(c(a)\big)$, $grad\ f$ produces the vector field $\mathbb{F}$, and flattening it is equal to the differential of it as $(grad\ f)^{\flat} = df$. We can also write the boundary of curve C as $\partial C = \{c(b) - c(a)\}$. Combining these, we can write the theorem of line integral as: $\int_C\ df = \int_{\partial C} f$.

Also, since f is a zero-form, which we could denote as α, and C is a one-dimensional manifold M we could rewrite the fundamental theorem of line integrals as: $\int_M d\alpha = \int_{\partial M} \alpha$.

The **vector calculus version of Stokes' theorem** states that: $\int_S \; curl\, F.\hat{n}dS = \int_{\partial S} F.\acute{c}(s)ds$.

Similar to the line integral, the right-hand of Stokes' theorem can be rewritten in terms of $\int_{\partial S} F^{\flat}$ And similar derivation of the left-hand side, and by replacing the vector field $\mathbb{F}$ by the vector field curl $\mathbb{F}$, to reach: $\int_S \; curl\, \mathbb{F}.dS = \int_S *((curl\, \mathbb{F})^{\flat}) = \int_S \; d(\mathbb{F}^{\flat})$.

Since $\mathbb{F}^{\flat}$ is a one-form α, and S is a two-dimensional manifold M, which means we have arrived again at the Stokes' theorem as above: $\int_M d\alpha = \int_{\partial M} \alpha$.

The **vector calculus version of the divergence theorem** states that: $\int_V \; div\, \mathbb{F}\, dV = \int_{\partial V} \mathbb{F}.dS$.

Again, the integrand on the left-hand side is equivalent to $*\,(div\, \mathbb{F})$, which can be rewritten as $d((* \circ \; \flat)\mathbb{F})$, and the right-hand side is equivalent to the right-hand side as follows: $\int_V \; d(* \circ \; \flat)\mathbb{F}) \; = \int_{\partial V} * \,(\mathbb{F}^{\flat})$.

Writing the three-dimensional manifold V as M and the three two-form $(* \circ \; \flat)\mathbb{F}$ as α, we have the divergence theorem as the generalised Stokes Theorem above: $\int_M d\alpha = \int_{\partial M} \alpha$.

This means that the line integrals, Stokes theorem, and the divergence theorem are all special cases of what is called the generalized Stokes theorem. At this stage, calculus on manifolds is introduced well enough, and the reader is ready to study differential geometry if required. Differential geometry is important for machine learning to achieve independence in the representation of the dataset. These are called the non-parametric models, such as kernels, Gaussian processes, Bayesian non-parametric, and VC dimensions. Chapter five will explain further representation theory and its applications in machine learning. A more advanced representation invariance, such as homotopy, can be encodable in deep learning (Haarmann *et al.*, 2014)
Python notebook ch3.ipynb show examples of calculus in differential geometry operations on manifolds using the Sympy (Python symbolic math) package as its current implementation while writing the book. Other Python packages provide various functions from differential geometry, and geometric statistics, such as the following:

- The Geomstats: https://geomstats.github.io/.
- The Geometric Algebra: https://galgebra.readthedocs.io/.

3.2.3 Tensors on Manifolds/Tensor Transformation Rules

Tensors in general are defined in Physics as functions which eat a certain number of vectors (known as the rank r of the tensor) and produce a number. These input vectors are Nd-arrays indices, and the output number is the value stored in this index location. This is very much the definition of differential forms. The multilinearity in Tensors means that the tensor function is linear in each of its r arguments in terms of the values of the functions/components on the r basis vectors. For example, a rank-2 tensor eats two vectors, v and w, such that multilinearity means:
$T(v_1 + cv_2, w) = T(v_1,w) + cT(v_2,w)$
$T(v, w_1 + cw_2) = T(v,w_1) + cT(v,w_2)$
For vector basis/coordinate for our vector space, say $\hat{x}, \hat{y}$, and $v = v_x\hat{x} + v_y\hat{y}$, $w = w_x\hat{x} + w_y\hat{y}$, then

$$T(v,w) = T(v_x\hat{x} + v_y\hat{y}, w_x\hat{x} + w_y\hat{y}) = v_xT(\hat{x}, w_x\hat{x} + w_y\hat{y}) + v_yT(\hat{y}, w_x\hat{x} + w_y\hat{y})$$
$$= v_xw_xT(\hat{x},\hat{x}) + v_xw_yT(\hat{x},\hat{y}) + v_yw_xT(\hat{y},\hat{x}) + v_yw_yT(\hat{y},\hat{y})$$

Which reduces to coordinate projections on different combinations of the coordinates. The components $(v_x w_x, v_x w_y, \ldots)$ are the tensors evaluation on the coordinate system $(T(\hat{x},\hat{x}), T(\hat{x},\hat{y}), \ldots)$ or denoted $(T_{x,x}, T_{x,y}, \ldots)$. This derives the tensor transformation laws to the new coordinate system, as reevaluating the new components on the basis of the new coordinate $\hat{x}', \hat{y}'$, using mapping A. Then deriving the new components is performed as $\hat{x}' = A_{x',x}\hat{x} + A_{x',y}\hat{y},\ \hat{y}' = A_{y',x}\hat{x} + A_{y',y}\hat{y}$. This is interpreted as not affecting the action of Tensor T, as it exists independently of its coordinate system, and its components can be reevaluated in terms of the new coordinate system as the matrix multiplication:

$$T(v,w) = \begin{bmatrix} v_x & v_y \end{bmatrix} \begin{bmatrix} T_{x,x} & T_{x,y} \\ T_{y,x} & T_{y,y} \end{bmatrix} \begin{bmatrix} w_x \\ w_y \end{bmatrix}$$

For an example from Physics that has applications in computer graphics, robotics navigation control and others, the moment of Inertia tensor I is a quantity that determines the rotational force (torque) required to achieve the required angular acceleration, as explained in the second law of motion. It is a scalar for a rotation around an axis perpendicular to a plane (2D rotation), $I = mr^2 = \int (r^2) dm$, where m is the object mass, and r is the distance to the rotational axis. To freely rotate around three axes, creating a 3D rotation, the Intertia I becomes a symmetric 3x3 matrix (2nd rank tensor) that captures the fact that a torque around one axis can create acceleration on other axes. It is derived as,

$$I = \begin{bmatrix} \int (r_z^2 + r_y^2) dm & -\int (r_x^2 + r_y^2) dm & -\int (r_x^2 + r_z^2) dm \\ -\int (r_y^2 + r_x^2) dm & \int (r_z^2 + r_x^2) dm & -\int (r_y^2 + r_z^2) dm \\ -\int (r_z^2 + r_x^2) dm & -\int (r_z^2 + r_y^2) dm & \int (r_x^2 + r_y^2) dm \end{bmatrix}$$

This matrix can be factored into a rotational matrix R (which is the Eigenvectors of I matrix) and diagonal matrix D (the eigenvalues of I matrix), I=RDR^T. Applying this tensor on two copies of an angular velocity vector w produces the Kinetic Energy KE computed as $KE = \frac{1}{2} I(w,w) = \frac{1}{2} \begin{bmatrix} w_x & w_y & w_z \end{bmatrix} \begin{bmatrix} I_{xx} & I_{xy} & I_{xz} \\ I_{yx} & I_{yy} & I_{yz} \\ I_{zx} & I_{zy} & I_{zz} \end{bmatrix} \begin{bmatrix} w_x \\ w_y \\ w_z \end{bmatrix}$

The I Inertia tensor can also be used as a linear operator that can be applied on the angular velocity vector w to produce the angular Momentum $L = Iw = \begin{bmatrix} I_{xx} & I_{xy} & I_{xz} \\ I_{yx} & I_{yy} & I_{yz} \\ I_{zx} & I_{zy} & I_{zz} \end{bmatrix} \begin{bmatrix} w_x \\ w_y \\ w_z \end{bmatrix}$.

Tensors on a manifold are defined as multilinear mapping:

$$T: \underbrace{T^*M \times \ldots \times T^*M}_{r\ contravariant\ degree} \times \underbrace{TM \times \ldots TM}_{s\ covariant\ degree} \rightarrow \mathbb{R}$$

$$T(\alpha_1, \ldots \alpha_r, v_1, \ldots, v_s) \rightarrow \mathbb{R}$$

This map T takes r one-forms and s vectors as input and produces a real number. This means this tensor of rank (r, s), i.e. r contravariant degrees and s covariant degrees.

Rank-1 Tensors are either covariant tensors or contravariant tensors.

$T: TM \rightarrow \mathbb{R}$ is a Rank (0, 1)-tensor, also called a **rank-1 covariant tensor**. It is a linear mapping of a **vector to a real number**, which is equivalent to the **differential one-form** explained previously. This means that $T \in T^*M$, and expressed in terms of its components $T_i$and basis vectors dx^i as $T = T_1 dx^1 + \cdots + T_n dx^n = \sum_{i=1}^{n} T_i dx^i = T_i dx^i$. A change of basis/coordinate functions from $(x^1, \ldots, x^n)$ to $(u^1, \ldots, u^n)$ using n functions on the same Manifold as: $u^i(x^1, \ldots, x^n) = u^i$ for i from 1 to n. The new components in the new coordinates are $T = \tilde{T}_1 du^1 + \cdots + \tilde{T}_n du^n$. This transformation mapping is captured in the Jacobian, and the transformed components can be calculated as follows:

$$\begin{bmatrix} \tilde{T}_1 \\ \vdots \\ \tilde{T}_n \end{bmatrix} = \begin{bmatrix} \frac{\partial x^1}{\partial u^1} & \cdots & \frac{\partial x^n}{\partial u^1} \\ \vdots & \ddots & \vdots \\ \frac{\partial x^1}{\partial u^n} & \cdots & \frac{\partial x^n}{\partial u^n} \end{bmatrix} \begin{bmatrix} T_1 \\ \vdots \\ T_n \end{bmatrix}$$

Such that $\tilde{T}_i = \frac{\partial x^j}{\partial u^i} T_j$. The tensor T itself does not change, but its coordinate basis and components change.

$T: T^*M \to \mathbb{R}$ is a Rank (1, 0)-tensor, also called a **rank-1 contravariant tensor**. It is a linear mapping of a **one-form paired with a vector $< \alpha, v >$ to a real number**, which is equivalent to the **vector field** explained previously. It is expressed in terms of its components and basis $\frac{\partial}{\partial x^i}$ as: $T = T^1 \frac{\partial}{\partial x^1} + \cdots + T^n \frac{\partial}{\partial x^n} = \sum_{i=1}^n T^i \frac{\partial}{\partial x^i} = T^i \frac{\partial}{\partial x^i}$. Notice that the components of the previous covariant tensor were indicated with lower indices, and the components of this contravariant tensor are indicated by upper indices when using Einstein summation notation. Previously the i in $\frac{\partial x^j}{\partial u^i}$ is regarded as a lower index of the whole term even though it is an upper index of *u because it is in the denominator*, while the *j* is considered an upper index of the term because it is in the numerator.

To transform the basis of this contravariant tensor from $\frac{\partial}{\partial x^i}$ to $\frac{\partial}{\partial u^i}$, we need the mappings from the Jacobian matrix to compute the new components, such as:

$$\begin{bmatrix} \tilde{T}^1 \\ \vdots \\ \tilde{T}^n \end{bmatrix} = \begin{bmatrix} \frac{\partial u^1}{\partial x^1} & \cdots & \frac{\partial u^1}{\partial x^n} \\ \vdots & \ddots & \vdots \\ \frac{\partial u^n}{\partial x^1} & \cdots & \frac{\partial u^n}{\partial x^n} \end{bmatrix} \begin{bmatrix} T^1 \\ \vdots \\ T^n \end{bmatrix}$$

Such that $\tilde{T}^i = \frac{\partial u^i}{\partial x^j} T^j$. The basis elements of T^*M transform as follows:

$$\begin{bmatrix} du^1 \\ \vdots \\ du^n \end{bmatrix} = \begin{bmatrix} \frac{\partial u^1}{\partial x^1} & \cdots & \frac{\partial u^1}{\partial x^n} \\ \vdots & \ddots & \vdots \\ \frac{\partial u^n}{\partial x^1} & \cdots & \frac{\partial u^n}{\partial x^n} \end{bmatrix} \begin{bmatrix} dx^1 \\ \vdots \\ dx^n \end{bmatrix}$$, such that $du^i = \frac{\partial u^i}{\partial x^j} dx^j$

For Rank-2 tensors, we have three possibilities:

sPossibility 1 is a **(0, 2)-Tensors (Rank-Two Covariant Tensor).** This is defined as $T: TM \times TM \to \mathbb{R}$, such that two-forms are a subset. It takes two vectors and produces a real number. $T \in T^*M \times T^*M = span\{dx^i \otimes dx^j | 1 \leq i,j, \leq n\}$. If M is an $\mathbb{R}^2$Manifold, then $T = T_{11} dx^1 \times dx^1 + T_{12} dx^1 \times dx^2 + T_{21} dx^2 \times dx^1 + T_{22} dx^2 \times dx^2 = \sum_{i=1}^n \sum_{j=1}^n T_{ij} dx^i \otimes dx^j = T_{ij} dx^i \otimes dx^j$. It is obvious how this generalises to $\mathbb{R}^n$Manifold. For a change of basis mapping from $(x^1, \ldots, x^n)$ to $(u^1, \ldots, u^n)$, given the appropriate Jacobian matrix, we have the $T = \tilde{T}_{kl} du^k \otimes du^l$ such that the transformed components are calculated as $\tilde{T}_{kl} = \frac{\partial x^i}{\partial u^k} \frac{\partial x^j}{\partial u^l} T_{ij}$. Two forms are a subset of these general Rank-2 covariant tensors because two forms have the special property that $dx^i \wedge dx^j(v,w) = -dx^i \wedge dx^j(w,v)$, and this generalises such that k-form is a skew-symmetric rank k covariant tensor $\wedge^k(M) \subset T^*M \otimes \ldots \otimes T^*M$. If a Tensor has components with opposite signs when two indices are swapped, such as $T(v_1, \ldots, v_i, \ldots, v_j, \ldots, v_k) = -T(v_1, \ldots, v_j, \ldots, v_i, \ldots, v_k)$ this property is satisfied, then these tensors are skew-symmetric or anti-symmetric.

Possibility 2 is a **(2, 0)-Tensors (Rank-Two Contravariant Tensor).** This is defined as $T: T^*M \times T^*M \to \mathbb{R}$. It takes two one-forms and produces a real number. $T \in TM \times TM = span\{\frac{\partial}{\partial x^i} \otimes \frac{\partial}{\partial x^j} | 1 \leq i,j, \leq n\}$. Again, if M is an $\mathbb{R}^2$Manifold, then $T = T^{11} \frac{\partial}{\partial x^1} \otimes \frac{\partial}{\partial x^1} + T^{12} \frac{\partial}{\partial x^1} \otimes \frac{\partial}{\partial x^2} + T^{21} \frac{\partial}{\partial x^2} \otimes \frac{\partial}{\partial x^1} + T^{22} \frac{\partial}{\partial x^2} \otimes \frac{\partial}{\partial x^2} = \sum_{i=1}^n \sum_{j=1}^n T^{ij} \frac{\partial}{\partial x^i} \otimes \frac{\partial}{\partial x^j} = T^{ij} \frac{\partial}{\partial x^i} \otimes \frac{\partial}{\partial x^j}$. It is obvious how this generalises to $\mathbb{R}^n$Manifold. For a change of basis mapping from $(x^1, ..., x^n)$ to $(u^1, ..., u^n)$, given the appropriate Jacobian matrix, we have the $T = \tilde{T}^{kl} \frac{\partial}{\partial u^k} \otimes \frac{\partial}{\partial u^l}$ such that the transformed components are calculated as $\tilde{T}^{kl} = \frac{\partial u^k}{\partial x^i} \frac{\partial u^l}{\partial x^j} T^{ij}$.

Possibility 3 is **(1, 1)-Tensors (Mixed-Rank Covariant-Contravariant Tensor).** This is defined as $T: T^*M \times TM \rightarrow \mathbb{R}$. It takes one vector and a one-form and produces a real number. $T \in TM \times T^*M = span\{\frac{\partial}{\partial x^i} \otimes dx^j | 1 \leq i, j, \leq n\}$. Again, if M is an $\mathbb{R}^2$Manifold, then $T = T_1^1 \frac{\partial}{\partial x^1} \otimes dx^1 + T_2^1 \frac{\partial}{\partial x^1} \otimes dx^2 + T_1^2 \frac{\partial}{\partial x^2} \otimes dx^1 + T_2^2 \frac{\partial}{\partial x^2} \otimes dx^2 = \sum_{i=1}^n \sum_{j=1}^n T_j^i \frac{\partial}{\partial x^i} \otimes dx^j = T_j^i \frac{\partial}{\partial x^i} \otimes dx^j$. It is obvious how this generalises to $\mathbb{R}^n$Manifold. For a change of basis mapping from $(x^1, ..., x^n)$ to $(u^1, ..., u^n)$, given the appropriate Jacobian matrix, we have the $T = \tilde{T}_l^k \frac{\partial}{\partial u^k} \otimes du^l$ such that the transformed components are calculated as $\tilde{T}_l^k = \frac{\partial u^k}{\partial x^i} \frac{\partial x^j}{\partial u^l} T_j^i$.

Back to the **general rank (r, s) tensors**: $T: T^*M \times ... \times T^*M \times TM \times ... TM \rightarrow \mathbb{R}$, which is an element of $T \in TM \otimes ... \otimes TM \otimes T^*M \otimes ... \otimes T^*M = span\{\frac{\partial}{\partial x^{i_1}} \otimes ... \otimes \frac{\partial}{\partial x^{i_r}} \otimes dx^{j_1} \otimes ... \otimes dx^{j_s} | 1 \leq i_1, ..., i_r, j_1, ..., j_s \leq n\}$, and it is expressed in terms of its components and basis as then $T = T_{j_1,...,j_s}^{i_1,...,i_r} \frac{\partial}{\partial x^{i_1}} \otimes ... \otimes \frac{\partial}{\partial x^{i_r}} \otimes dx^{j_1} \otimes ... \otimes dx^{j_s}$.Again, an invertible change of basis from $(x^1, ..., x^n)$ to $(u^1, ..., u^n)$, given the appropriate Jacobian matrix, we have the $T = \tilde{T}_{l_1,...,l_s}^{k_1,...,k_r} \frac{\partial}{\partial u^k} \otimes ... \otimes \frac{\partial}{\partial u^{k_r}} \otimes du^{l_1} \otimes ... \otimes du^{l_s}$, such that the transformed components are calculated as $\tilde{T}_{l_1,...,l_s}^{k_1,...,k_r} = \frac{\partial u^{k_1}}{\partial x^{i_1}} \cdots \frac{\partial u^{k_r}}{\partial x^{i_r}} \frac{\partial x^{j_1}}{\partial u^{l_1}} \cdots \frac{\partial x^{j_s}}{\partial u^{l_s}} T_{j_1,...,j_s}^{i_1,...,i_r}$. Given a mapping φ : M →M, the pull-back of a rank (0, t)-tensor T at the point p is defined similarly to the pull-back of differential forms as: $(\varphi^* T_{\varphi(p)})_p(v_{1_p}, ..., v_{t_p}) = T_{\varphi(p)}(\varphi * v_{1_p}, ..., \varphi * v_{t_p})$. For any tensors T and S, we have $\varphi^*(T \otimes S) = \varphi^* T \otimes \varphi^* S$, which means that pull-backs distribute over tensor products, $\varphi^*(T + S) = \varphi^* T + \varphi^* S$, which means that pull-backs distribute over addition, $\varphi^*(T \wedge S) = \varphi^* T \wedge \varphi^* S$, which means that pull-backs distribute over wedge products.

The Euclidean metric is the dot product, and earlier, the Minkowski metric on $\mathbb{R}^4$ was defined. Both are (2, 0) tensors. The following definitions are needed to define a metric tensor g:

- Like smooth vector fields discussed previously, **smooth tensors** need to be infinitely differentiable in the arguments.
- **Symmetric tensor:** given tensor g and two vector fields v and w, the tensor g is symmetric if $g(v, w) = g(w, v)$.
- **Non-degenerate tensor:** Tensor g is called non-degenerate at point p, if $g_p(v_p, w_p) = 0$. g is a non-degenerate tensor if it is non-degenerate at every point p ∈ M.
- A manifold with such a tensor g is called a **pseudo-Riemannian manifold,** and the tensor g is called the metric or sometimes the **pseudo-Riemannian metric**. If the metric g also has one additional property, that *g(v,w)* ≥ 0 for all vector fields *v* and *w,* then it is called a **Riemannian metric,** and the manifold is called a **Riemannian manifold**.

A metric on the manifold M is a **smooth, symmetric, non-degenerate, rank-two covariant** tensor g, which we can write as a matrix. Metric tensors are generally denoted with a lowercase g. The metric tensor g gives an inner product on every vector space TpM in the tangent bundle of M. The inner product of $v_p, w_p \in TpM$ is given by $g(v_p, w_p)$. Most often, the inner product of two vectors is denoted with $<\cdot, \cdot>$ where $< v_p, w_p > \equiv g(v_p, w_p)$. For basis vectors $< \frac{\partial}{\partial x^i}, \frac{\partial}{\partial x^j} > \equiv g\left(\frac{\partial}{\partial x^i}, \frac{\partial}{\partial x^j}\right) = g_{ij}$, which is a (1,1)-tensor. Being (1,1)-tensor enables defining a map L from a given space to its dual, such as $\mathbb{R}^n \rightarrow (\mathbb{R}^n)^*$. The tensor metric can be expressed as a matrix:

$$g(v, w) = [v^1 \quad ... \quad v^n] \begin{bmatrix} g_{11} & \cdots & g_{1n} \\ \vdots & \ddots & \vdots \\ g_{n1} & \cdots & g_{nn} \end{bmatrix} \begin{bmatrix} w^1 \\ \vdots \\ w^n \end{bmatrix}$$

When $g_{ij} = \delta_{ij}$, which is the Kronecker delta, then g is the Euclidean metric, which is the Euclidean inner product, and matrix $[g_{ij}]$ is none other than the identity matrix.

The length/norm of a vector v_p is calculated as: $\|v_p\| \equiv \sqrt{|g(v_p, w_p)|}$

Given two points p and q in the same coordinate patch of M that are connected by a curve $\gamma: [a, b] \subset \mathbb{R} \rightarrow M$ where $\gamma(a) = p$ and $\gamma(b) = q$. The curve $\gamma(t)$ has tangent velocity vectors $\dot{\gamma}(t)$ along the curve. To ensure the tangent velocity vectors actually exist at the endpoints, the curve needs to be extended a tiny amount ϵ to $(a - \epsilon, b + \epsilon) \subset \mathbb{R}$. The **length of the curve γ** from p to q is defined to be $L(\gamma) = \int_a^b \sqrt{|g(\dot{\gamma}(t), \dot{\gamma}(t))|}\, dt$.

The distance between points p and q is defined in terms of the minimum piecewise continuous curve connecting them as $d(p, q) = \inf_{\gamma} L(\gamma)$, where inf is the infimum operator for the lower limit of lengths of curves in this instance.

If the Manifold is defined with a metric on it, it should be used. If it is not defined with a metric, then distances are not a valid measure.

Given a Riemannian Manifold M and a tensor metric g defined on the tangent space TpM at each point p, this tensor g is the Riemannian metric for this Manifold.

Back to the example from Physics, given an Inertia matrix, a rigid body with origin at O, time-dependent body fixed axis $K = \{\hat{x}(t), \hat{y}(t), \hat{z}(t)\}$ in $\mathbb{R}^3$, an ith particle in the rigid body has mass m_i and position vector r_i with $[r_i]_K = (x_i, y_i, z_i)$ relative to O, and let $r_i^2 \equiv g(r_i, r_i)$, then the (2,0)-moment of Inertia tensor is $I_{(2,0)} = \sum_i m_i \left(r_i^2\, g - L(r_i) \otimes L(r_i)\right)$. The (1,1)-moment of Inertia tensor is $I_{(1,1)} = \sum_i m_i \left(r_i^2\, I - L(r_i) \otimes r_i\right)$. Some common components are defined as $I_{xx} = \sum_i m_i \left(y_i^2 + z_i^2\right)$, and $I_{xy} = -\sum_i m_i x_i y_i$ as seen from the 3x3 Inertia matrix earlier in this section. This matrix showed the entanglement caused by having a spin around one axis affecting the spin around the others. A 2-particle system would create a tensor of order 6 to maintain the $\mathbb{R}^3$ position vector of each particle. Rotation is usually in the $\mathbb{C}^3$ space. Combining rotation of 2 particle system would create a nine-dimensional Hilbert space of Complex space $\mathbb{C}^3 \otimes \mathbb{C}^3$, with the required basis. For complete derivation, check the book (Jeevanjee, 2011). More on Hilbert spaces will be presented in chapter five.

The Lie derivative applies to all forms of tensors, while the global (coordinate-free) exterior differentiation applies to differential forms only as subsets of tensors.

To introduce the Lie derivative, we need to revisit integral curves. Integral curves γ are curves on the manifold M that are considered as a family of mappings from each time step to the next in the same manifold M to itself. We begin by fixing some time t_0 as our zero time at point p. Then, for each time t, we have a mapping $\gamma(t)$ that sends $\gamma(t_0)$ to $\gamma(t_0 + t)$, such that $p = \gamma(t_0) \rightarrow \gamma_t(p) = \gamma(t_0 + t)$. It can also be between Manifolds or to another copy of M: $M \rightarrow M$, which would be a push-forward defined as: $T_p\gamma_t = \gamma_{t*}: T_pM \rightarrow T_{\gamma_t(p)}M$. A pull-back would be $T_p^*\gamma_t = \gamma_t *: T_{\gamma_t(p)}^*M \rightarrow T_p^*M$. Given that at some point p, the mapping takes us to point q, $\gamma_t(p) = q$, we can define the inverse mapping $\gamma_t^{-1}(q) = p$, which is sometimes denoted $\gamma_{-t}(q) = p$, which makes the push forwards defined as: $T_p\gamma_t^{-1} = T_p\gamma_{-t} = \gamma_{-t*}: T_qM \rightarrow T_{\gamma_{-t}(q)}M$.

Lie derivative of a vector field w in the direction of v at the point p: $(\mathcal{L}_v w)_p = \lim_{t \to 0} \frac{T_p\gamma_{-t} \cdot w_{\gamma_t(p)} - w_p}{t} = \frac{d}{dt}\left((\gamma_{-t})^* \cdot w_{\gamma_t(p)}\right)\Big|_0$.

Lie derivatives of one-forms α, in the direction of v at point p : $(\mathcal{L}_v \alpha)_p = \lim_{t \to 0} \frac{T^*\gamma_{-t} \cdot \alpha_{\gamma_t(p)} - \alpha_p}{t} = \frac{d}{dt}\left((\gamma_t)^* \cdot \alpha_{\gamma_t(p)}\right)\Big|_0$.

Lie derivative of functions as zero-forms $(\mathcal{L}_v f)_p = \lim_{t \to 0} \frac{T^*\gamma_{-t} \cdot f_{\gamma_t(p)} - f_p}{t} = \frac{\partial f}{\partial \gamma^i}\Big|_{\gamma(t_0)} \frac{\partial \gamma^i}{\partial t}\Big|_{t_0} = v_p[f]$.

Lie derivative of tensors: Given the rank (r, s) tensor T defined above and that the tensor is in a single coordinate chart on a manifold, it is possible to patch coordinate charts together. The tensor pulls back by γ_t is defined as: $(\gamma_t^* T)_p(\alpha_1, \dots, \alpha_r, v_1, \dots, v_s) = T_{\gamma_t(p)}(\gamma_{-t}^*\alpha_1, \dots, \gamma_{-t}^*\alpha_r, \gamma_{-t}^*v_1, \dots, \gamma_{-t}^*v_s)$. The Lie derivative of a tensor is then defined as: $(\mathcal{L}_v T)_p = \lim_{t \to 0} \frac{\gamma_t^* T_{\gamma_t(p)} - T_p}{t} = \frac{d}{dt}(\gamma_t^* T_{\gamma_{t(p)}})\Big|_0$. This leads to several identities with other operators that facilitate the computation and provide valuable properties. For more details, refer to Appendix A in (Fortney, 2018).

Summary

This chapter should have enabled the reader to see tensors as elementary mathematical objects that transform in a coordinate-free approach. For example, tensor fields in a vector space or on a curved manifold undergo linear transformations under changes in the space coordinates. The Jacobian matrix of the mapping functions is used to transform the coefficients in one coordinate system/basis to another. Differentiation is defined for the different object types. The trace of the Hessian matrix is the Laplacian of a function, which measures the function's curvature as the divergence of its gradient invariant of change of basis. Going through this chapter while executing the code in the ch3.ipynb, editing it to try new examples, and checking the help of the functions for different parameters' options, should make the material easier to visualise and manipulate for various applications. This is not meant to be a math book, but AI is dependent entirely on mathematical findings. A few iterations through this chapter will make many of these concepts more intuitive than it looks from the first reading.

3.3 Multilinear Subspace Learning (MSL)

As we discussed in chapter two, finding a lower-dimensional structure in a given dataset reduces computational requirements turning an intractable solution into a tractable one, reducing noise, and explaining the data dynamics or interactions more clearly. In the higher dimensions, the dimensionality curse is the main obstacle and the need for finding an approximate structure that preserves the non-linear dynamics is even more important. Figure 35 illustrates the computational requirements of the covariance matrix of a vectorised 3-dimensional video dataset, with the first two dimensions being spatial rows and columns of 128 x 88 dimensionality and a time third dimension of 20 frames. The LSL vectorisation in (a) results in a large covariance matrix of 189 GB memory fingerprint and the resulting processing time. The MSL tensor-based analysis of three smaller covariance matrices results in 95.8KB of memory fingerprint and reduced processing time (Lu, Plataniotis and Venetsanopoulos, 2011).

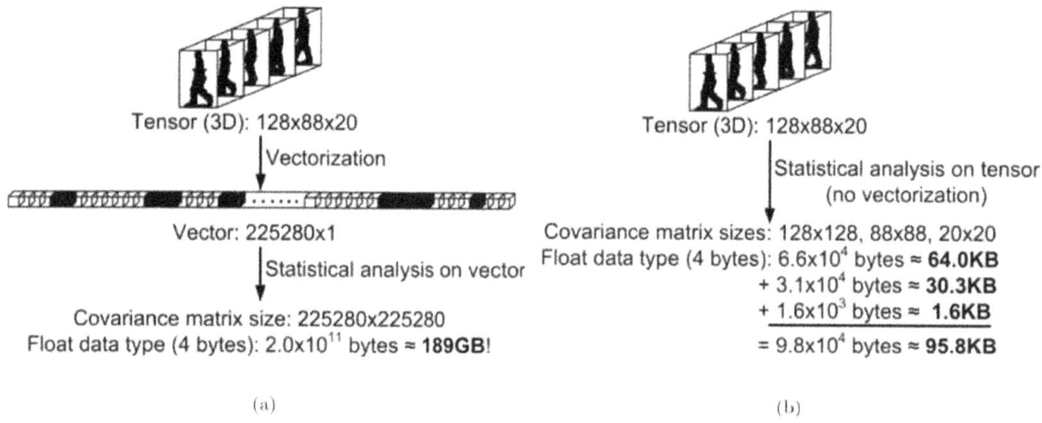

Figure 35: Vector-based analysis in (a) versus tensor-based analysis (b) of a 3D video object covariance matrix (Lu, Plataniotis and Venetsanopoulos, 2011).

As shown in Figure 35, linear subspace learning (LSL) vectorisation is performed by the product of the number of dimensions in each mode. The multilinear subspace learning (MLS) tensor-based analysis is performed by the sum of dimensions in each mode. This reduces the degree of freedom and creates a sparse/compact grid-like structure that preserves the multi-way interactions across the different modes. Consequently, this reduces or solves the small sample size (SSS) problem containing many features, which makes LSL ill-posed (Lu, Plataniotis and Venetsanopoulos, 2014).

3.3.1 Vector-Vector Projection vs Tensor Projection Performance

In chapter one, matrices were defined as performing linear transformations on vectors. These linear transformations are considered projections because it maps a vector $x \in \mathbb{R}^{I_1}$ to another vector $u \in \mathbb{R}^{I_2}$ that could be in a higher or lower-dimensional space using a projection Matrix M $\in \mathbb{R}^{I_1 \times I_2}$ such that $u = M^T x = x \times_1 M^T$ **(Lu, Plataniotis and Venetsanopoulos, 2011).**

Tensor Projections are based on the Tucker decomposition, as explained next chapter, and are a generalisation of the vector projections in the higher dimensions. It takes as input an N-dimensional (N-way) tensor object $\chi \epsilon\, \mathbb{R}^{I_1, I_2, \ldots, I_N}$ and project it to another dimension, such as $\chi \epsilon\, \mathbb{R}^{P_1, P_2, \ldots, P_N}$, where $P_j \leq I_j$ for j = 1, ..., N, using N projection matrices. For example, a matrix (2-way tensor) $\chi \epsilon\, \mathbb{R}^{I_1, I_2}$ is projected to a lower dimension $U \epsilon\, \mathbb{R}^{P_1, P_2}$ using two projection matrices $M_1 \in \mathbb{R}^{I_1, P_1}, M_2 \in \mathbb{R}^{I_2, P_2}: U = \chi \times_1 M_1^T \times_2 M_2^T = M_1^T \chi M_2$. In the higher order, this is generalised to $M_j \in \mathbb{R}^{I_j \times P_j}\, for\, j = 1, \ldots N,\; U = \chi \times_1 M_1^T \times_2 M_2^T \times_3 \ldots \times_N M_N^T$. Figure 36 shows example $\chi \epsilon\, \mathbb{R}^{8,6,4}$ vectorised in (a) and using a vector to vector projection to lower dimension, then as a tensor to tensor projection in (b), then as a tensor to vector projection in (c), where EMP stands for elementary multilinear projection.

The tensor-to-vector projections are based on the CANDECOMP/PARAFAC model, as will be explained in the next chapter. It is a special case of the tensor-to-tensor projections in which the lower dimension shape vector is $P_j = 1$ for j=1...N. For example, a 2-way tensor (matrix) can be projected to a vector of scalars using two projection matrices (or unit vectors since the number of the columns is 1) as $U = \chi \times_1 m_1^T \times_2 m_2^T = m_1^T \chi m_2$. Unit vectors mean their norm $\|m_j\|$ is equal to 1. Figure 37 shows a $\chi \epsilon\, \mathbb{R}^{8,6,4}$ projection to vector using EMP. In the higher dimension, it is considered the inner product between χ with the result of the outer product of the projection vectors: $U = \langle \chi, m_1^T \circ m_2^T \circ \ldots \circ m_N^T \rangle = \langle \chi, M \rangle\, for\, M = m_1^T \circ m_2^T \circ \ldots \circ m_N^T$.

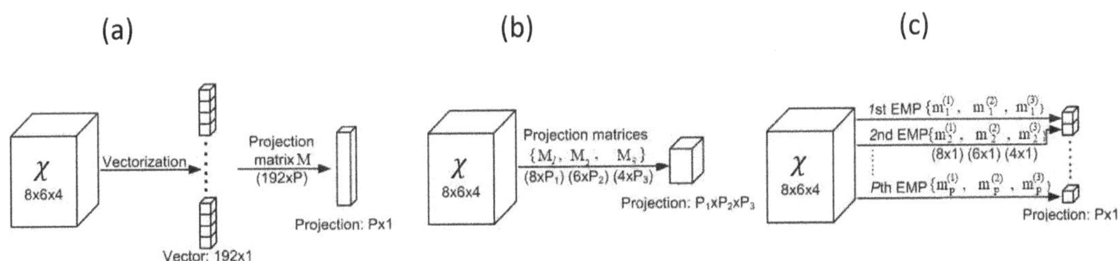

Figure 36: Illustration of (a) vector-to-vector projection, (b) tensor-to-tensor projection, (c) tensor-to-vector projection (Lu, Plataniotis and Venetsanopoulos, 2011).

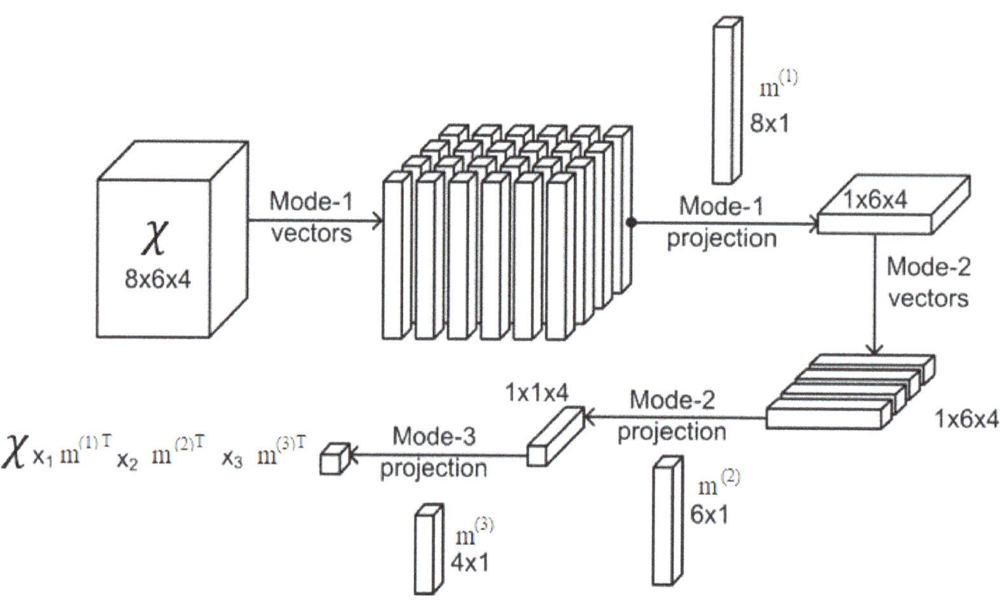

Figure 37: Illustration of an elementary multilinear projection (Lu, Plataniotis and Venetsanopoulos, 2011).

From the examples above, you can see that the vector-to-vector projections (VVP) vectorise a tensor to create a one-dimensional vector of elements $P = \prod_{j=1}^{N} P_j$ different elements/scalars (all elements of the tensor causing the dimensionality curse). That is then linearly mapped into the output vector using one of the linear subspace learning methods in chapter two to reduce the dimensionality by estimating a weight (parameter) to every element. However, in the tensor-to-tensor projection (TTP) (and the special case of tensor-to-vector projections - TVP), each element in χ is projected by each column in the projection matrices M_j, such that there are shared columns in the projection matrices by estimating $P = \sum_{j=1}^{N} I_j$ parameters. This reduces the model's number of parameters, hence reducing its complexity. Table 2 compares the different projection methods on different input and output sizes and shows that tensor-to-tensor projections (TTP) require the fewest number of parameters to estimate than both tensor-to-vector (TVP) and the high dimensional vector-to-vector projections (VVP). In TTP, a tensor object A is projected to a smaller tensor of size P1 × P2 × P3. This multilinear projection can be carried out through P_N mode-n multiplications Table 3 summarises the comparison of LSL and VVP methods and MSL using TVP and TTP methods on various criteria such as representation, accuracy and complexity.

Table 2: Number of parameters to be estimated by three multilinear projections for N=2D, I_N = 10, Pn = 3. (Lu, Plataniotis and Venetsanopoulos, 2011)

Input	Output	VVP	TVP	TTP
$\prod_{n=1}^{N} I_N$	P	$P\prod_{n=1}^{N} I_N$	$P\sum_{n=1}^{N} I_N$	$P\sum_{n=1}^{N} P_N \times I_N$
10 × 10	4	400	80	40 (Pn = 2)
100 × 100	4	40,000	800	400 (Pn = 2)
100 × 100 × 100	8	8,000,000	2400	600 (Pn = 2)
$\prod_{n=1}^{4} 100$	16	1,600,000,000	6400	800 (Pn = 2)

Table 3: Linear versus multilinear subspace learning.

Comparison	Linear subspace learning	Multilinear subspace learning
Representation	Reshape into vectors	Natural tensorial representation
Structure	Break natural structure	Preserve natural structure
Parameter	Estimate a large number of parameters	Estimate fewer parameters
SSS problem	More severe SSS problem	Less SSS problem
Massive data	Hardly applicable to massive data	Able to handle massive data
Optimization (in most cases)	Closed-form solution	Suboptimal, iterative solution

Python notebook ch3.ipynb shows examples of the different projection methods discussed in this section and the parameters' numbers for each.

3.3.2 Scatter Matrices in the higher dimensions

As we have seen in chapter two, finding a lower-dimensional structure required pair-wise covariance or scatter matrices. A tensor object $\chi \in \mathbb{R}^{I_1, I_2, \ldots, I_N}$ is a dataset containing M samples, each described with N features with shape vector (I_1, I_2, ... I_N). The scatter matrix in the higher-dimensional tensor objects suitable for TTP is defined per mode as follows:
$S_{T_\chi}^{(n)} = \sum_{m=1}^{M} (\chi_{m(n)} - \bar{\chi}_{(n)})(\chi_{m(n)} - \bar{\chi}_{(n)})^T$, where $\bar{\chi} = \frac{1}{M}\sum_{m=1}^{M} \chi_m$, and $\chi_{m(n)}, \bar{\chi}_{(n)}$ are the mode-n unfolding of χ_m and $\bar{\chi}$, respectively. For a prelabeled dataset, the between-class scatter is defined as: $S_{B_\chi}^{(n)} = \sum_{c=1}^{C} M_c (\bar{\chi}_{c(n)} - \bar{\chi}_{(n)})(\bar{\chi}_{c(n)} - \bar{\chi}_{(n)})^T$, where C is the number of classes, M_c is the number of samples for class c, c_m is the class label for the mth sample, $\chi_{c(n)}$ is the n-mode of χ_c samples in class c, $\bar{\chi}_{(n)}$is the n-mode $\bar{\chi}$ of the tensor means, and the class mean tensor is defined as: $\bar{\chi}_c = \frac{1}{M_c}\sum_{m=1, c_m=c}^{M} \chi_m$. The within-class scatter matrix is defined as: $S_{W_\chi}^{(n)} = \sum_{m=1}^{M} (\chi_{m(n)} - \bar{\chi}_{c_m(n)})(\chi_{m(n)} - \bar{\chi}_{c_m(n)})^T$, where $\bar{\chi}_{c_m(n)}$ is the mode-n unfolding of $\bar{\chi}_{c_m}$, which is the mean of the class of sample m.
For TVP, scalar-based scatters are defined as degenerate equations similar to those above, using vectors instead of matrices and scalars instead of vectors.

Chapter 4: Tensors Structures and Decomposition

Chapter one, accompanying source code, has introduced why tensors are essential for high dimensional dataset representations enabling multi-way analysis that is not possible when high dimensional data are vectorised or metricised. Representing tensors in full dimensionality suffers from the dimensionality curse. This chapter will start with tensor decomposition methods that factorise the high-dimensional tensor space into the most dominating components in each dimension, providing low-rank compression. These components can be represented in memory using sparse factor matrices and low-order core tensors, called factors or blocks. The most common tensor decomposition algorithms that will be covered are CP and Tucker.
Then, the second section will introduce graphical tensor notations as graph data structures. This section explains how a network of tensors can be contracted into one tensor using graphical notation and Einestien indices. Then the third section will introduce tensor networks as decomposition algorithms that represent large-scale tensors hierarchically using lower-rank core tensors. We can work with networks of tensors, such as each tensor representing a multi-way dataset; particular indices/features in a tensor connect to other indices/features in another multi-way dataset tensor representation as summation indices enabling contraction or left as free indices in the final tensor shape. The final tensor shape is the dataset a machine learning or deep learning algorithm should use, identifying some indices/features as predictors and others as target/outcome variables. We can also work with tensor networks that are a factorisation of a given large tensor. The following section then introduces two tensor Network decomposition approaches. Tensor Train (TT) decomposition reduces the complexity of the tensor decomposition algorithms presented in chapter three when working on large tensors. TT uses permutations of tensor dimensions doing sequential multilinear products over latent tensor cores. Tensor Ring (TR) decomposition optimises the operations of TT by doing circular multilinear products over a sequence of low-dimensional tensor cores. TT and TR reduce a large-scale optimisation problem to tractable, more minor problems (lower-order smaller core tensors of order at most 3), similar to how ALS reduces a non-convex problem to convex subproblems. TT and TR methods build on Hierarchical Tucker methods in which lower-order rank core tensors form a tree representing the large tensor.

The chapter will then conclude with applications. The first application applies tensor completion by using tensor decomposition methods, and the other introduces tensor regression methods. Then, a final section will introduce artificial neural networks (ANN) and how they can benefit from tensor higher-order representations of data and the tensor decomposition algorithms.

4.1 Tensor Decomposition Methods

The previous chapter explained the projection to a lower dimension as the Multilinear subspace learning (MSL) method. In this chapter, learning the projection matrices that effectively capture the dataset structure and optimising the representation of the approximate learned structure to the high dimensional one is explained. Low-rank matrix factorization presented in chapter two does not enable the recovery of the underlying components. In contrast, some tensor decompositions, such as CP decomposition, provide an essentially unique decomposition suitable for many problems, such as Blind Source Separation (BSS) and others. The general framework requires the following steps:

1. Decide the learning paradigm: supervised, unsupervised, semi-supervised, or active learning.
2. Choose the multilinear projection to employ: VVP, TVP, or TTP.
3. Define the criterion to be optimized: such as maximising scatter measures as practised in LSL.

4. The order of tensor representation: 2-D, 3-D, or 4-D are the most natural choices, but some datasets or applications require higher orders.
5. The additional model/constraints to be imposed: PCA maximises the variance captured as the optimisation criteria while keeping orthogonality between PCs as the constraints (uncorrelated). ICA assumes independent sources mixed in the received dataset. Other constraints, optimisation objectives, and assumptions can be extended to each mode in the higher dimension or even in the interactions between modes (Lu, Plataniotis and Venetsanopoulos, 2011).

4.1.1 CANDECOMP/PARAFAC (CP)

As explained in chapter two, the SVD of a matrix is computed by $X = USV^T = \sigma_1 u_1 v_1^T + \sigma_2 u_2 v_2^T + \cdots + \sigma_r u_r v_r^T$. This can be expressed as the summation of outer products of the vectors of the most dominating columns in U, and most dominating rows in V, in the order of the singular values σ from the highest σ_1 to the lowest given rank σ_r, which are diagonalized in S as illustrated in Figure 38.

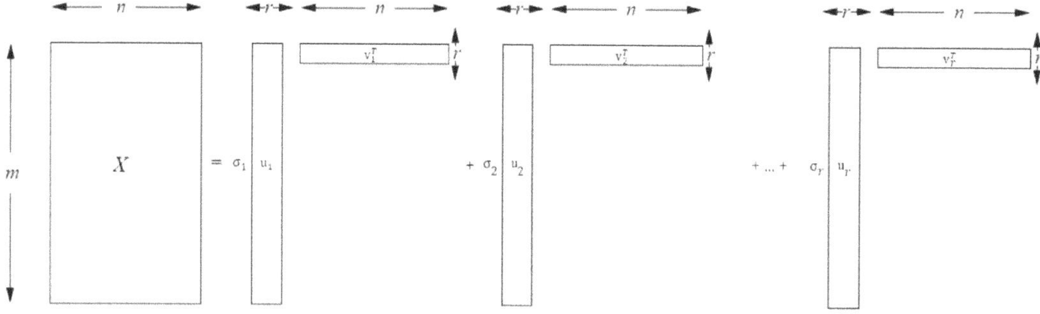

Figure 38: 2-way SVD generalised to enable the higher order SVD

This enables the approximate reconstruction of matrix χ as $\hat{\chi}$ from its dominant components:

$$\hat{\chi} = \sum_{j=1}^{r} \sigma_j u_j v_j^T$$

This means matrix $\hat{\chi}$ is a linear combination of the rank one vectors of the two dimensions of the given matrix χ. The higher-order representation of this process is illustrated in Figure 39 for 3 dimensions. The most dominating components in each dimension are represented as rank-one vectors along with each mode, the multiplication with the singular values is absorbed in the factor vectors, and the summation of their outer products forms the reconstruction.

Hitchcock, in 1927 proposed the idea of the polyadic form of a tensor, i.e., expressing a tensor as the sum of a finite number of rank-one tensors as the Canonical Decomposition (CANDECOMP). This was later redefined in the psychometrics community as parallel factors (PARAFAC), which is an approximation technique suitable for matrices that have a collection of the same number of columns and different rows. CP is the acronym used to denote both CANDECOMP/PARAFAC. PARAFAC relaxes some of the CP constraints and fits the covariance matrices' cross-products to the original data. CP factorises a tensor χ using the outer product $\circ$ of rank-1 vectors across each mode, for R as the tensor rank. For a tensor of order 3, this is defined as follows:
$\chi \in \mathbb{R}^{I,J,K} = \sum_{r=1}^{R} a_r \circ b_r \circ c_r \approx \sum_{r=1}^{R} a_{ir} b_{jr} c_{kr}$ for all $a_r \in \mathbb{R}^I$, $b_r \in \mathbb{R}^J$, and $c_r \in \mathbb{R}^K$.
This is defined as the Khatri-Rao product $\odot$ for the matrix-form on each mode as follows: $\chi_{(1)} \approx A(C \odot B)^T$, $\chi_{(2)} \approx B(C \odot A)^T$, $\chi_{(3)} \approx C(B \odot A)^T$. This is concisely expressed as $\chi \approx \hat{\chi} = [\![\lambda; A, B, C]\!] = \sum_{r=1}^{R} \lambda_r a_r \circ b_r \circ c_r$. This three-way model is expressed as the frontal slices of χ. It is often useful to assume that the columns of A,

B, and C are normalized to length one with the weights absorbed into the vector $\lambda \in \mathbb{R}^R$ that can be added to the equation as shown.

The N dimensions generalisation is defined as $\chi \in \mathbb{R}^{I_1, I_2, \ldots, I_N} \approx [\![\lambda; A^{(1)}, A^{(2)}, \ldots, A^{(N)}]\!] = \sum_{r=1}^{R} \lambda_r\, a_r^{(1)} \circ a_r^{(2)} \circ \ldots a_r^{(N)} = \Lambda \times_1 A^{(1)} \times_2 A^{(2)} \ldots \times_N A^{(N)}$., where $\Lambda \in \mathbb{R}^{r,r,\ldots,r}$ is a diagonal core tensor such that $\lambda_r = \Lambda_{r,r,\ldots,r}$.

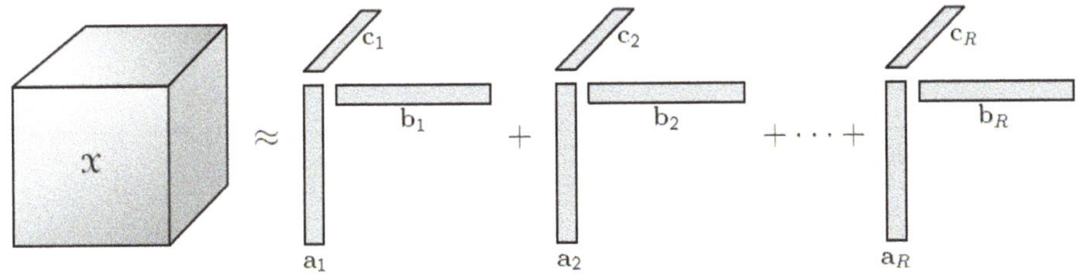

Figure 39: The CANDECOMP/PARAFAC decomposition of a third-order tensor.

Just like the matrix rank is defined as the fewest number of linearly independent columns, the tensor rank should be defined similarly, but this will be NP-hard to identify the rank computationally. Iteratively, the tensor rank is computed as the fewest number of rank-one tensors that generate the approximated tensor as their sum with the smallest error $\|\chi - \hat{\chi}\|^2$, i.e. the fewest number of components in the exact CP decomposition with R = rank(χ). Finding the tensor rank is an NP-hard problem, and methods like Alternating Least Squares (ALS) are used. The method is based on fixing A and B to solve C, then fixing A & C to solve B, then fixing B and C to solve A, and repeating until convergence, which is defined as the case when the error is not significantly decreasing. ALS reduces a non-convex optimisation problem to convex subproblems.

Repeat Until Convergence:

$$\min_{A} \sum_{ijk} \left(x_{ijk} - \sum_{l} a_{il}\, b_{jl} c_{kl} \right)^2 = \min_{A} \left\| X_{(1)} - A(C \odot B)' \right\|_F^2 , such\ that (C \odot B) = \sum_{i=1}^{r} c_i \otimes b_i$$

$$\min_{B} \sum_{ijk} \left(x_{ijk} - \sum_{l} a_{il}\, b_{jl} c_{kl} \right)^2 = \min_{B} \left\| X_{(1)} - B(C \odot A)' \right\|_F^2 , such\ that (C \odot A) = \sum_{i=1}^{r} c_i \otimes a_i$$

$$\min_{C} \sum_{ijk} \left(x_{ijk} - \sum_{l} a_{il}\, b_{jl} c_{kl} \right)^2 = \min_{C} \left\| X_{(1)} - C(B \odot A)' \right\|_F^2 , such\ that (B \odot A) = \sum_{i=1}^{r} b_i \otimes a_i$$

A sample algorithm is defined as follows for a 4th-Order Tensor (Ji *et al.*, 2019), where χ_{mx} is mode x vectorisation of tensor Y:

Input: *The 4th-order tensor* $\chi \in \mathbb{R}^{I,J,k,L}$
Output: *Factor matrices A,B,C,D and the core tensor Λ*
Steps:
Initialize A,B,C,D and CP rank R, where R ≤ min{IJ , JK, IK};
while *the iteration threshold does not reach or the algorithm has not converged,* ***do***
$A = \chi_{m1}[(D \odot_R C \odot_R B)^T]$;
Normalize column vectors of A to unit vector;
$B = \chi_{m2}[(D \odot_R C \odot_R A)^T]$;
Normalize column vectors of B to unit vector;
$C = \chi_{m3}[(D \odot_R B \odot_R A)^T]$;
Normalize column vectors of C to unit vector;
$D = \chi_{m4}[(C \odot_R B \odot_R A)^T]$;
Normalize column vectors of D to unit vector;

Save the value of the norms of the R column vectors in the factor matrix C to the core tensor Λ;
end while
***return** Factor matrices A, B, C, D and the core tensor Λ*

CP can be generalised to N order as:

***Input:** N-order tensor $\chi \epsilon \mathbb{R}^{I_1, I_2, \ldots, I_N}$, tensor rank R*
***Output:** coefficients $\lambda_{n}{}_{n=1}^{N}$, factor matrices $A^n \epsilon \mathbb{R}^{I_n, R}{}_{n=1}^{N}$*
Initialize: randomly initialize $A^n{}_{n=1}^{N}$
repeat
for n = 1, …, N do
$$T_n = A^{(1)^T} A^{(1)} * \ldots * A^{(n-1)^T} A^{(n-1)} * A^{(n+1)^T} A^{(n+1)} * \ldots * A^{(N)^T} A^{(N)}$$
$$A^{(n)} = \chi_{(n)} (A^{(N)} \odot \ldots \odot A^{(n+1)} \odot A^{(n-1)} \odot \ldots \odot A^{(1)}) T_n$$
end for
until the convergence criterion is satisfied

Generally, the CP decomposition has a computational complexity of O(NIr), where N is the dimension, $I \in \mathbb{R}^N$ is a vector of the shape of the tensor, and r is the rank, such that $r \ll N$. This is linear to tensor order. For example, the discretization of the 5-variate (columns) dataset over 100 sample points (rows) on each axis would yield 100^5 = 10,000,000,000 sample points, while a rank-2 CP representation would require only $5 \times 2 \times 100 = 1000$ sample points. It is also worth noting that CP optimization is difficult for high-order tensors, converges slowly, may produce an unstable estimation of its components, and generally, factor matrices can be arbitrarily reordered and scaled.
Example CP applications:

- Time-varying electroencephalographic (EEG) spectrum arranged as a three-dimensional array with modes corresponding to time, frequency, and channel, were compared to space/time ICA and PCA in (Miwakeichi *et al.*, 2004).
- Vowel-sound data where different individuals (mode 1) spoke different vowels (mode 2) and the formant (i.e., the pitch) was measured (mode 3) in (Harshman, 1970).
- Multi-subject fMRI data were analysed with a three-way extension of independent component analysis (ICA) and CP, and the differences in terms of the higher-order statistical properties were identified in (Stegeman, 2007).

4.1.2 Tucker Decomposition

The Tucker decomposition is the most cited and is considered a higher-order (or multi-way) PCA. It decomposes a tensor into a core tensor (not a diagonal core tensor of weights as in CP decomposition) multiplied by a factor matrix along each mode. This enables capturing the arbitrary interaction of factors among each mode independently from each other (mixed modes). For a given tensor $\chi \epsilon \mathbb{R}^{I_1, I_2, \ldots, I_N}$, it is computed using mode-n multiplication of $\mathcal{G} \in \mathbb{R}^{R_1, R_2, \ldots, R_N}$ as the core tensor such that the values R_k denotes the rank along the kth mode, and $A^{(k)} \in \mathbb{R}^{I_k, R_k}$ as the orthogonal factor matrices for each mode k. Given an order-3 tensor, its Tucker decomposition is defined as:

$$\chi \in \mathbb{R}^3 \approx \mathcal{G} \times_1 A \times_2 B \times_3 C$$

It is defined using outer products on the vector level as follows:
$\chi \approx \sum_{i=1}^{R_1} \sum_{j=1}^{R_2} \sum_{k=1}^{R_3} g_{ijk} a_i \circ b_j \circ c_k$
The scalar representation is defined as follows:

$$x_{ijk} \approx \sum_{i=1}^{R_1} \sum_{j=1}^{R_2} \sum_{k=1}^{R_3} g_{ijk} a_i \, b_j c_k$$

And the compact form is $[\![\mathcal{G}; A,\ B,\ C]\!]$, where.
The N-Dimensional generalisation is $X \in \mathbb{R}^{I_1, I_2, \dots, I_N}$ as $\chi \approx [\![\mathcal{G}; A^{(1)},\ A^{(2)}, \dots, A^{(N)}]\!]$, such that $\hat{\chi}$ is estimated from $\hat{x}_{i_1 i_2 \dots i_N} = \sum_{r_1=1}^{R_1} \dots \sum_{r_n=1}^{R_N} \dots g_{r_1 \dots r_n} \; a_{i_1 r_1}^{(1)} \circ a_{i_2 r_2}^{(2)} \circ \dots \; a_{i_n r_n}^{(N)}$.

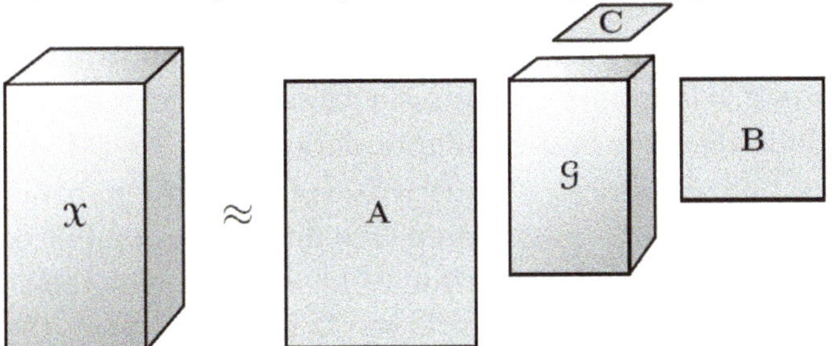

Figure 40: The Tucker decomposition of a third-order tensor.

This can be expressed in matrix form by unfolding χ and G and using the Kronecker product $\otimes$ as follows: $\chi = A^{(n)} \mathcal{G}_{(n)} . \left(A^{(n+1)} \otimes \dots \otimes A^{(N)} \otimes A^{(1)} \otimes \dots . \otimes A^{(n-1)}\right)^T$
The CP decomposition can be considered a special case Tucker decomposition in which the core tensor Λ is super diagonal such that $R_1 = R_2 = \dots R_N$, containing the weights/coefficient along the diagonal describing an interaction between one mode factor matrix and another mode factor matrix. While in Tucker, we have Multiple Linear Ranks (Tucker Rank: (R_1, R_2, ..., R_N)) for each mode, and the core tensor captures the underlying multi-way structure of tensor data. Standard 2-dimensional PCA is a Tucker 1 decomposition by setting the factor matrices to the Identity matrix I and capturing the variance in mode-1 independent of the other modes. Using ALS, Tucker 2 alternates the I matrix to find other modes' variance. The Higher Order SVD (HOSVD) used for tensor compression requires that the factor matrices and the core tensor be all orthogonal. Higher-order Factor Analysis is also considered a special case of the Tucker decomposition.
TensorFaces, which will be reviewed in detail in chapter six, is an example of HOSVD based on the Tucker decomposition. It takes facial images of different people from different angles, lighting, facial expressions, and more modes as required. It is significantly more accurate than PCA face recognition methods and valuable for compression and removing irrelevant effects (Vasilescu and Terzopoulos, 2002).
The Tucker decomposition generally has a computational complexity of $O(NIr + r^N)$, where N is the dimension, $I \in \mathbb{R}^N$ is a vector of the tensor's shape, and r is the rank. This is exponential to tensor order but is more stable and produces a better approximation than CP decomposition. Tucker decomposition does not produce unique factor matrices and can be rotated along each mode.
In ch4.ipynb, Tensorly Python package implementation of CP and Tucker examples are presented. Other Python packages provide tensor decomposition implementation, such as scikit-tt (https://github.com/PGelss/scikit_tt), and HOTTBOX (https://github.com/hottbox/hottbox).

4.1.3 Other Tensor Decomposition Approaches

Other tensor decomposition approaches have been proposed in the literature. These include but are not limited to the following:

- INdividual Differences in SCALing (INDSCAL): the method is a special case of 3-way CP suitable for 3-way tensors that are symmetric in 2 modes. This is implemented in scikit-tensor (https://github.com/mnick/scikit-tensor).
- CANonical Decomposition with LINear Constraints (CANDELINC): the method imposes linear constraints in one or more of the factor matrices, such as being orthonormal or replaced with one that generates the same orthogonal column space. It is useful for large-scale datasets for compression and regularisation. Its applications include multicollinearity in chemometric datasets.
- PARAFAC2 simultaneously decomposes a collection of matrices, with each having an equal number of columns but a different row size, allowing for distinct factors associated with different frontal slices in the first mode. Example Application: PARAFAC2 handles time shifts in resolving chromatographic data with spectral detection. In this application, the first mode corresponds to elution time, the second mode to wavelength, and the third mode to samples.
- DEDICOM is a decomposition into directional components that describe tensor χ as an asymmetric relationship between I objects. Such as I countries, and the I_{ij} is the exports from country i to country j. The method identifies that Latent components in R and groups the I objects accordingly, and factor matrix A is the factor loadings. For example, countries' group interactions can be modelled by applying scaling and rotations as required to maximise the variance across matrix A. Example Application: (Bader, Harshman and Kolda, 2007) applied their ASALSAN method for computing DEDICOM on email communication graphs over time. In this case, x_{ijk} corresponded to the (scaled) number of email messages sent from person i to person j in month k. DEDICOM is also implemented in scikit-tensor.
- PARATUCK2 combines CP and Tucker 2 to generalise DEDICOM to capture the interactions between two sets of interacting objects, similar to PLS in the LSL context.
- Nonnegative variants are suitable for datasets in which the interpretation requires nonnegativity for physical or psychological reasons. Tensorly provides several non-negative tensor decomposition algorithms.

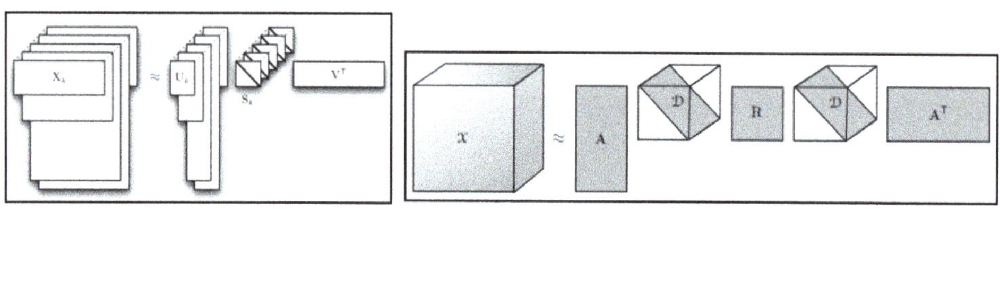

(a) (b)

Figure 41; Parafac2 in (a) and DEDICOM in (b)

The important other tensor decomposition formats that the next section will build on are:

- The Hierarchical Tucker(HT) decomposition decomposes a tensor hierarchically, similar to a binary tree split. In HT decomposition, the core tensor must be less than or equal to the third order, and no more than three-factor matrices can be connected to the core tensor. In tensor networks (explained later), this can be achieved by a hierarchy of nested separation to split a higher-order tensor into lower levels in the tree, such that each tensor has three modes only. For example, given a tensor $\chi \epsilon \mathbb{R}^{I_1, I_2, I_3, \ldots, I_N}$, the objective is to define disjoint subsets u, v such that, u={1, ..., N_0), and v={N_0+1, ... N}, where $t = u \cup v \sqsubset 1,2, \ldots, N$ and 1 <= N_0 <= N. For example, given a fourth-order tensor χ , N_0 = 2, such that u={1,2}, v={3,4}, and the HT is defined as $\chi = \sum_{r_{12}=1}^{R_{12}} \sum_{r_{34}=1}^{R_{34}} g_{r_{12} r_{34}}^{(1234)} \; a_{r_{12}}^{(u)}(x_1, x_2) \circ a_{r_{34}}^{(v)}(x_3, x_4)$, such that $a_{r_{12}}^{(u)}(x_1, x_2) = \sum_{r_1=1}^{R_1} \sum_{r_2=1}^{R_2} g_{r_1 r_2 r_{12}}^{(12)} \; a_{r_1}^{(1)} a_{r_2}^{(2)}$ and $a_{r_{34}}^{(v)}(x_3, x_4) = \sum_{r_3=1}^{R_3} \sum_{r_4=1}^{R_4} g_{r_3 r_4 r_{34}}^{(34)} \; a_{r_3}^{(3)} a_{r_4}^{(4)}$.
- The Tree Tensor Network States (TTNS) format extends HT, creating many disjoint subsets.

Detailed algorithms for computing these decompositions and example applications for tensors of different orders can be found in (Cichocki *et al.*, 2016, p. 1).

Figure 42, Figure 43, and Figure 44 show more MLS algorithms' taxonomies, such as the hierarchy of higher-order PCA-based algorithms as an unsupervised learning method, higher-order LDA-based algorithms as a supervised learning method, and ICA, CCA, PLS higher-order methods, illustrating the projection used, the optimisation criteria, the number of modes it applies to, the model name, and the learning model. Chapters four and eight in (Lu, Plataniotis and Venetsanopoulos, 2014) discuss these algorithms and list their original publications for even more details.

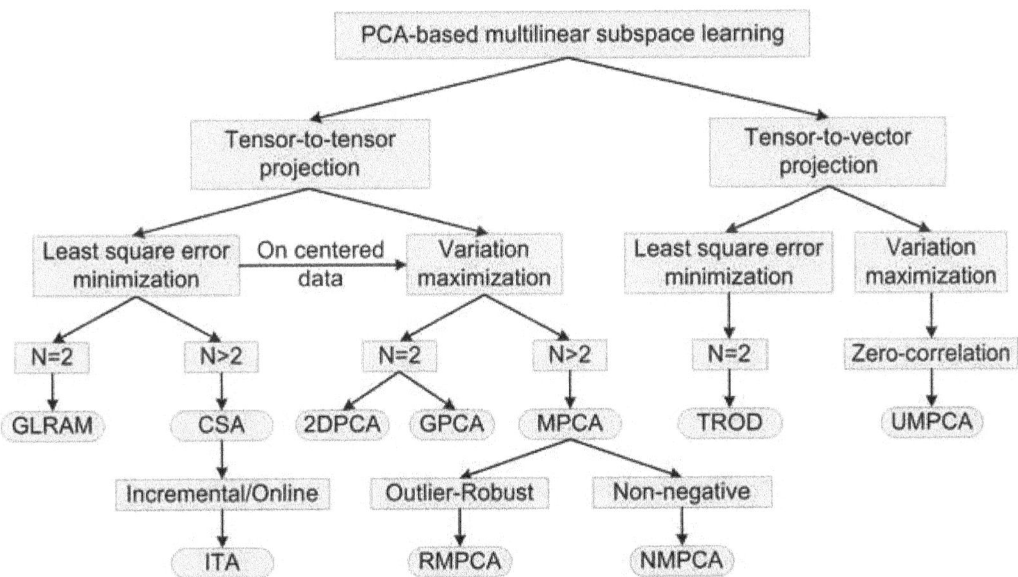

Figure 42: A taxonomy of PCA-based MSL algorithms

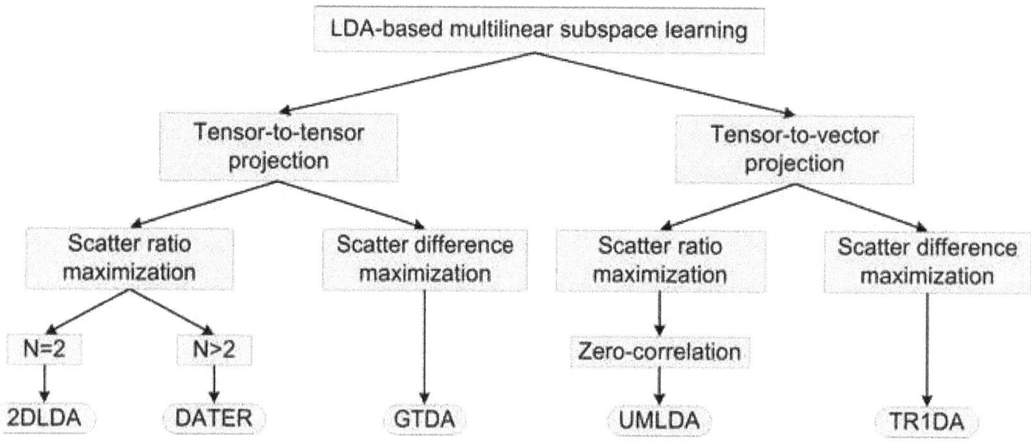

Figure 43: A taxonomy of LDA-based MSL algorithms.

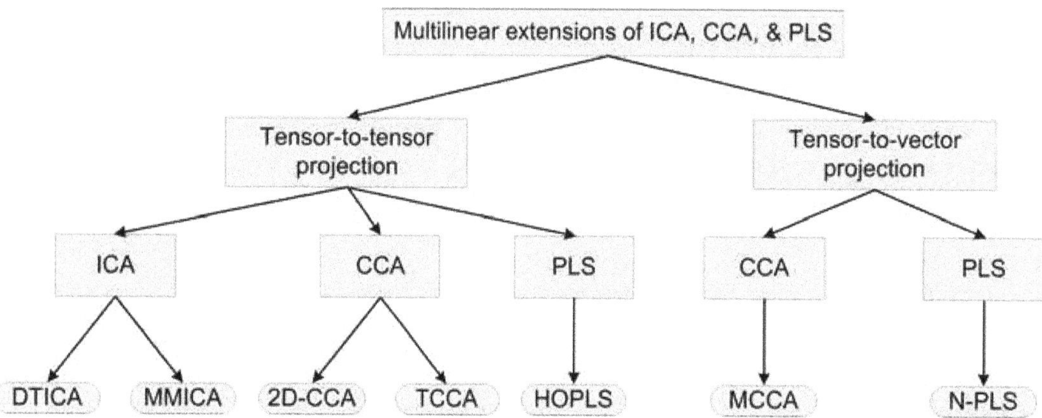

Figure 44: Taxonomy of ICA, CCA, PLS-based MSL algorithms.

Python notebook ch4.ipynb, multi-wayExamples.ipynb and tensorisation.ipynb show examples of the tensor decompositions methods discussed in this section.

4.2 Tensor Graphical Notation

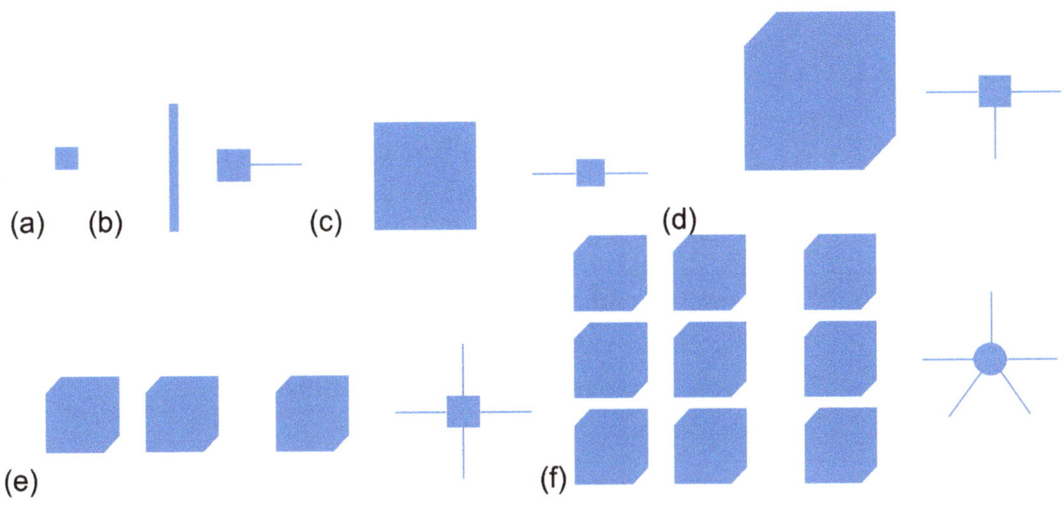

Figure 45: Tensor Network representations for (a) scalar, (b) vector, (c) matrix, and (d) 3-way tensor, (e) 4-way tensor, (f) 5-way tensor.

The graphical tensor notation uses graph data structures of nodes and edges. The graph nodes describe tensors (can be matrices, vectors or even scalars) as a circle, a square, a dot or a polygon such as a pentagon or a hexagon. Each outgoing edge of the tensor represents the index of a particular dimension, and the order is the number of edges. Figure 45 illustrates some tensor possible graphical representations of tensors up to order 5. This notation enables the graphical illustration of Tensor contractions, some of which are listed in Table 4, showing their equations, graphical tensor notation, and some explanations. Tensor contraction is denoted as a connection between two nodes. As explained in chapter one, this is the multilinear product operator between two tensors on a specific mode, which corresponds to the summation over the indices of that mode.

Table 4: Some Tensor contractions illustrations using Tensor Networks Notation

=	$\sum_j A_{ij}\, x_j = \mathrm{b}_i$	Matrix-vector multiplication
=	$\sum_j A_{ij}\, B_{jk} = C_{ik}$	Matrix-Matrix Multiplication
	tr(A) = a	Connecting two index lines of the same tensor corresponds to a trace. This produces a scalar value. Similarly, any network of all tensor indices connected will result in a scalar. Only unpaired indices/edges will count towards the resulting tensor order.
	$A_{ij}B_{ji} = Tr[AB]$=a	Transpose of Matrix-Matrix Multiplication

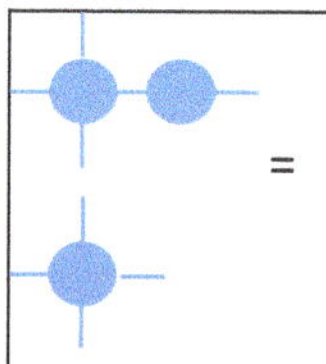 =	$\sum_k \mathcal{T}_{ijkl}\, \mathcal{V}_{km} = \mathcal{R}_{ijml}$	Tensor-Matrix Multiplication
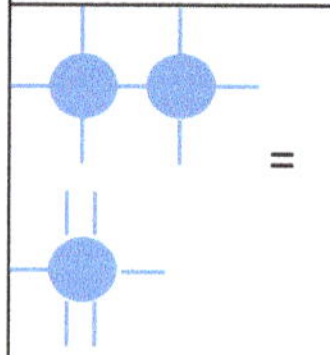 =	$\sum_k \mathcal{T}_{ijkl}\, \mathcal{V}_{kmno} = \mathcal{R}_{ijmnol}$	Tensor-Tensor mode-k Multiplication with the third mode k in the first tensor = first mode of the second tensor. The resulting contracted tensor is shown.
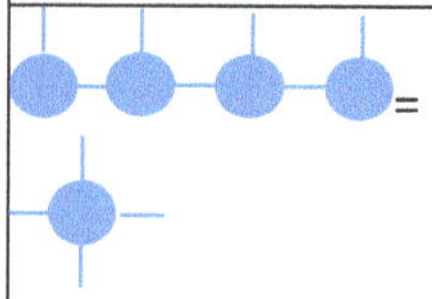 =	$\sum_{\alpha_1,\alpha_2,\alpha_3} \mathcal{A}^{s_1}_{\alpha_1} \mathcal{B}^{s_2}_{\alpha_1,\alpha_2} \mathcal{C}^{s_3}_{\alpha_2,\alpha_3} \mathcal{D}^{s_4}_{\alpha_3} = \mathcal{R}_{s_1 s_2 s_3 s_4}$	Tensor-Tensor Contraction shows upper indices not involved in the contraction and lower indices involved in different contractions.
 = Σ	$CP(\chi_{ijkl}) = \sum_{r=1}^{R} a_r \circ b_r \circ c_r \circ d_r$	The CP decomposition for a 4th-order tensor
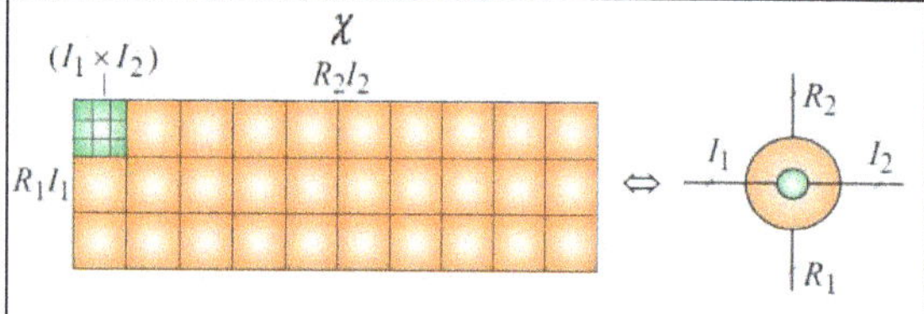 $(I_1 \times I_2)$ χ $R_2 I_2$ $R_1 I_1$ ⇔ R_2 I_1 I_2 R_1		Hierarchical matrix structures, a 4th-order tensor representation for a block matrix $\chi \epsilon\, \mathbb{R}^{R_1 I_1 \times R_2 I_2}$ (a matrix of matrices), which comprises block matrices $X_{r_1,r_2} \epsilon\, \mathbb{R}^{I_1 \times I_2}$
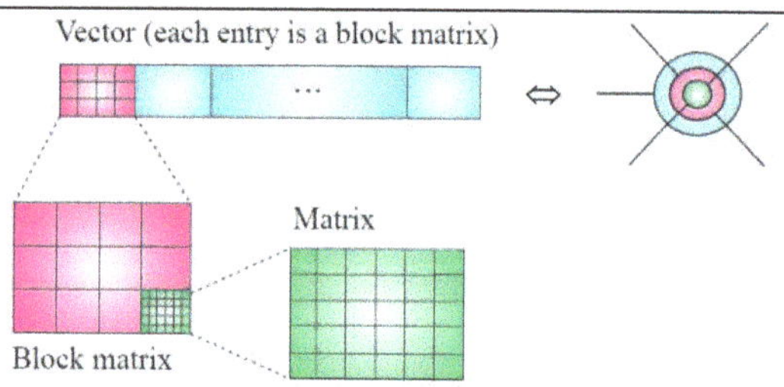 Vector (each entry is a block matrix) ... ⇔ Matrix Block matrix		A 5th-order hierarchical tensor
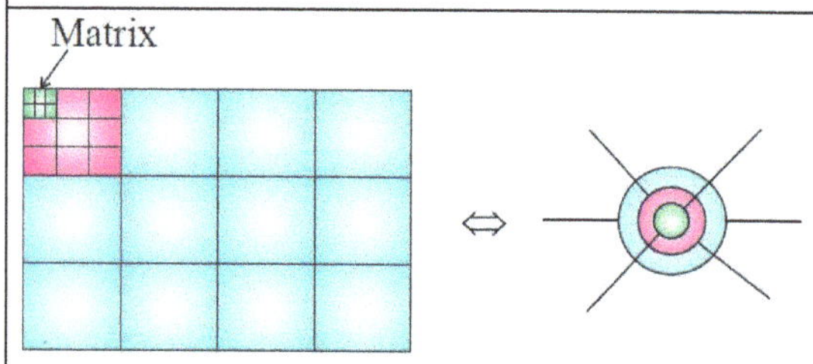 Matrix ⇔		A 6th-order hierarchical tensor

Ingoing or outgoing arrows onto index lines illustrate the Einstein notation showing contravariant/up versus covariant/down indices, respectively. The physics community uses unique tensors' icons to denote different tensor types, such as isometric tensors as triangles and unitary tensors as rectangles. A diagonal line through the middle of the tensor shape illustrates a diagonal tensor. Hyper-edges or multiple indices which are "locked" together can be notated by introducing "Kronecker delta" or "spider" tensors, often notated by small black dots. These tensors can have an arbitrary number of indices, and only diagonal elements are equal to one (*The Tensor Network*, no date). The last three rows in the table represent hierarchical tensors and their graphical representations (Cichocki *et al.*, 2016, p. 1).

The Python notebook ch4.ipynb, used tensortrace application created in a gamemaker studio environment that is available for download from https://www.tensortrace.com/, to graphically create four examples of random networks. Then, the tool generates the python code for their contraction using the ncon Python function ("Network CONtractor") (Pfeifer *et al.*, 2015).

4.3 Tensor Networks

Section one discussed various tensor decomposition algorithms that factorise tensor objects into factor matrices. Tensor Networks (TN) decompose higher-order tensors into sparsely interconnected lower-order core tensors. The lower-order core tensors are the dominant components in the large-scale tensorial dataset. This decomposition enables data approximation that captures the relevant/important/dominating multi-way interactions to compress large-scale data by removing irrelevant information. This decomposition also enables the distributed storage and computation of large-scale tensors. As discussed in chapter two, large-scale high-dimensional datasets often contain subspace of much lower dimensionality embedded in the ample high-dimensional space. TN decomposition learns this subspace approximating the original high dimensional space in full format and distributes it on lower rank cores in sparse format.
For example, an N-variate function $f(x) = f(x_1, x_2, ..., x_N)$ can be approximated by a finite sum of products of individual functions, each depending on only one or a very few variables, such as $f(x_1, x_2, ..., x_N) \approx f^{(1)}(x_1) f^{(2)}(x_2) \dots f^{(N)}(x_N)$. These are coordinate functions, as explained in chapter three. The sparse format reduces the storage requirement from $\prod_{j=1}^{N} I_j$to $\sum_{j=1}^{N} I_j$, which is $\ll I_N$. The sparse format is robust in the presence of noise and missing data and flexible enough to incorporate various constraints as required. TN extends the 2-way (matrix) Component Analysis (2-way CA) methods to multi-way component analysis (MWCA), capturing the relations between the different modes while growing linearly with the dataset size. This decomposition can be performed in tensorial datasets or after tensorising vector or matrix form datasets. All tensor operations after that can be performed on the core tensors. TN formats enable emerging optimisation algorithms such as random coordinate descent (RCD) schemes, sub-gradient methods, alternating direction method of multipliers (ADMM), and proximal gradient descent methods.

There are many algorithms for Tensor Networks. This section will discuss Matrix Product State / Tensor Train and Tensor Rings. Other methods include Matrix Product Operator (MPO), Tree Tensor Network / Hierarchical Tucker, Projected Entangled Pair States (PEPS), and Multi-scale Entanglement Renormalization Ansatz (MERA).

4.3.1 The Tensor Train Decomposition

The Tensor Train (TT) and Tensor Chain (TC) decomposition are special cases of the Hierarchical Tucker Decomposition introduced in section one. In these methods, each core tensor is chained in series and aligned by having the same dimension, and all the factor matrices are unit matrices as leaf nodes. This decomposition transforms a large problem into several tractable small-scale problems. TC connects the last tensor with the first, making all tensors of the same dimension, while TT has its first and last tensors of one less dimension than the intermediate tensors of order 3. The physics communities refer to TC decomposition as the Matrix Product State (MPS) decomposition with periodic boundary conditions (PBC) and the TT decomposition as the MPS decomposition with the Open Boundary Conditions (Oseledets, 2011).

Figure 46: Tensor Train decomposition showing first and last core tensors of order-3 and internal tensors of order4.

Given an Nth-order tensor $\chi \epsilon \mathbb{R}^{I_1, I_2, I_3, \ldots, I_N}$, the TT decomposition is:

$$\chi = \mathcal{A}_1 \times_{3,1} \mathcal{A}_2 \ldots \times_N \mathcal{A}_N$$

Such that each entry in χ is:

$$x_{i_1,\ldots i_N} = \sum_{r_1}^{R_1} \ldots \sum_{r_N}^{R_N} \mathcal{A}_1(r_0, i_1, r_1)\, \mathcal{A}_2(r_1, i_2, r_2) \ldots \mathcal{A}_N(r_{N-1}, i_N, r_N)$$

Where $\mathcal{A}_n \epsilon \mathbb{R}^{R_{n-1}, I_n, R_n}$, $R_0 = R_N = 1$; n = 1, 2, ..., N, such that $\mathcal{A}_1$ and $\mathcal{A}_N$ are of lesser rank than the internal core tensors. The mode ordering of the core tensors is important, and their permutations should be optimised. $\mathcal{A}_1 \times_{3,1} \mathcal{A}_2$means mode-3 from $\mathcal{A}_1$ multiplied by mode-1 from $\mathcal{A}_2$ and similar notation is used elsewhere. The approximately reconstructed tensor from its TT decomposition is $\hat{\chi}$ with each entry is defined in terms of entries in $\mathcal{A}$ as follows:

$$\hat{x}_{i_1, i_2, \ldots, i_N} = \sum_{r_1, r_2, \ldots, r_N = 1}^{R_1, R_2, \ldots, R_N} a^1_{1, i_1, r_1}\, a^2_{r_1, i_2, r_2}\, a^3_{r_2, i_3, r_3} \ldots a^{N-1}_{r_{N-2}, i_{N-1}, r_{N-1}}\, a^N_{r_{N-1}, i_N, 1}$$

Similar to Tucker decomposition, the TT rank is defined for each mode as (R_1, R_2, ..., R_N), where $R_n = rank(\chi_{mcn})$, where m means matricization, c means canonical, and n means mode-n. $\chi_{mcn} = mat(\chi)_{cn}$, such as mat is the mode-n canonical matricisation of the tensor, which extracts n dimensions from the original tensor as the first dimension of the resulting matrix and the remaining (N-n) dimensions as the second dimension. This notation is used in the following equations. The TT rank increases in proportion to the dimension of the original data tensor χ.

Expressing large tensors in their TT decomposition enables tensor operations on the smaller core tensors, reducing the number of parameters to estimate. For example, Given two tensors expressed in their TT core tensors:

$\chi \in \mathbb{R}^{I_1, I_2, \ldots, I_N} = \chi_1 \times_{3,1} \chi_2 \times_{3,1} \cdots \times_{3,1} \chi_N$ with $\chi_n \in \mathbb{R}^{R_{n-1}, I_n, R_n}$ and

$\mathcal{Y} \in \mathbb{R}^{I_1, I_2, \ldots, I_N} = \mathcal{Y}_1 \times_{3,1} \mathcal{Y}_2 \times_{3,1} \cdots \times_{3,1} \mathcal{Y}_N$ with $\mathcal{Y}_n \in \mathbb{R}^{Q_{n-1}, I_n, Q_n}$

For $n = 1, 2, \ldots, N$ and R_n are the tensor's χ TT rank, and Q_n are the tensor's $\mathcal{Y}$ TT rank.

- **Their Hadamard product** is $\mathcal{Z} = \chi \odot \mathcal{Y} = \mathcal{Z}_1 \times_{3,1} \mathcal{Z}_2 \times_{3,1} \cdots \times_{3,1} \mathcal{Z}_N$, where each core tensor $\mathcal{Z}_n \in \mathbb{R}^{R_{n-1}Q_{n-1}, I_n, R_n Q_n} = \chi_n \otimes \mathcal{Y}_n$for n=1, 2... N.
- **Their sum** is $\mathcal{Z} = \chi + \mathcal{Y}$, such that $\mathcal{Z}_n = \begin{bmatrix} \chi_n & 0 \\ 0 & \mathcal{Y}_n \end{bmatrix}$, with the first and last core tensors are defined as $\mathcal{Z}_1 = [\chi_n \quad \mathcal{Y}_n]$ and $\mathcal{Z}_n = \begin{bmatrix} \chi_n \\ \mathcal{Y}_n \end{bmatrix}$. The TT rank of $\mathcal{Z}$ equals the sum of the TT rank of χ and $\mathcal{Y}$: $(R_1 + Q_1, R_2 + Q_2, \ldots, R_n + Q_n)$
- **Their scalar/dot/quantitative product** is $\mathcal{Z} = \mathcal{X} \cdot \mathcal{Y}$, $(\mathcal{Z}_n)_{m1} = \mathcal{X}_{n-1}(\mathcal{Y}_n)_{m1}$ by using cumulative array variable $a_1 = 0$, and subsequent values $a_n = \mathcal{X}_n \times_{1,2} (\mathcal{Y}_n \times_{1m} a_{n-1}) \in \mathbb{R}^{R_n, Q_n}$, for $n = 2, \ldots, N$, such that the last value in the array a_N will be equal to $\mathcal{X} \cdot \mathcal{Y}$ (Oseledets, 2011).

Various methods solve the TT decomposition, including:

1. SVD-based TT algorithm (TT-SVD) performs mode-n matricisation on the input tensor and then performs HOSVD decomposition to compute a minimum possible compression rank.
2. Algorithms based on low-rank matrix decomposition (LRMD) are similar to TT-SVD but simplify the SVD decomposition using matrix cross-approximation or CR decomposition.
3. Restricted Tucker-1 decomposition (RT1D), converting the original input tensor into a 3rd-order tensor and then performing Tucker-1 and Tucker-2 decomposition.
4. A generalised alternating least squares (ALS) algorithm and modified ALS (MALS) algorithm facilitate the self-adaptation of ranks by using SVDs or employing a greedy algorithm.

The TT decomposition has a computational complexity of O(NIr²), where N is the dimension, I ∈ $\mathbb{R}^N$ is a vector of the tensor's shape, and r is the rank. The number of parameters is linear to the tensor order. The increased rank increases the computational complexity, and methods such as TT Trunction are used to approximate the solution using a smaller rank. TT Trunction performs the Nth canonical matricisation of the core tensor and performs a low-rank matrix approximation (SVD and QR). Several modified tensor representations based on TT have been proposed in the literature. These propositions include the quantised tensor-train format (QTT), the block tensor-train format (BTT), and the cyclic tensor-train (CTT). TT representation has been applied to large-scale problems in numerical analysis, such as the optimisation of the Rayleigh quotient, e.g., density matrix renormalisation group (DMRG), and the approximate solution of linear systems, e.g., alternating minimal energy (AME).

TT/MPS are the most popular solutions for tensor networks in 1D. As seen earlier, the factors are linearly connected in 1D. TT and HT do not allow cycles, but TC allows cycles. Various layered tensor networks have been introduced in the literature, enabling an analysis on a 2D lattice or deeper layers to reduce the TT rank by increasing the number of core tensors but with more minor ranks, as illustrated in Figure 47. The 3rd-order core tensors of TT were replaced by 5th-order core tensors in the Projected Entangled Pair States (PEPS) method that connects higher-order tensors to represent a physical state in a two-dimensional network. Also, TT 3rd-order core tensors were replaced by 6th-order core tensors in the Projected Entangled Pair Operators (PEPO) method. The Honey-Comb Lattice (HCL) uses 3rd-order core tensors, and the Multi-scale Entanglement Renormalization Ansatz (MERA) uses 4th-order tensors. The computational complexity increases in proportion to the number of cycles, with MERA generally having a smaller size and dimension, reducing the number of parameters. The cycles explain correlations between variables. These developments are mainly contributed by researchers from quantum physics communities studying the interactions of many particle systems (Ji *et al.*, 2019). MERA is implemented in Python at https://www.tensors.net/mera, MPS Python implementation can be found at https://www.tensors.net/mps, https://www.tensors.net/mps-vumps.

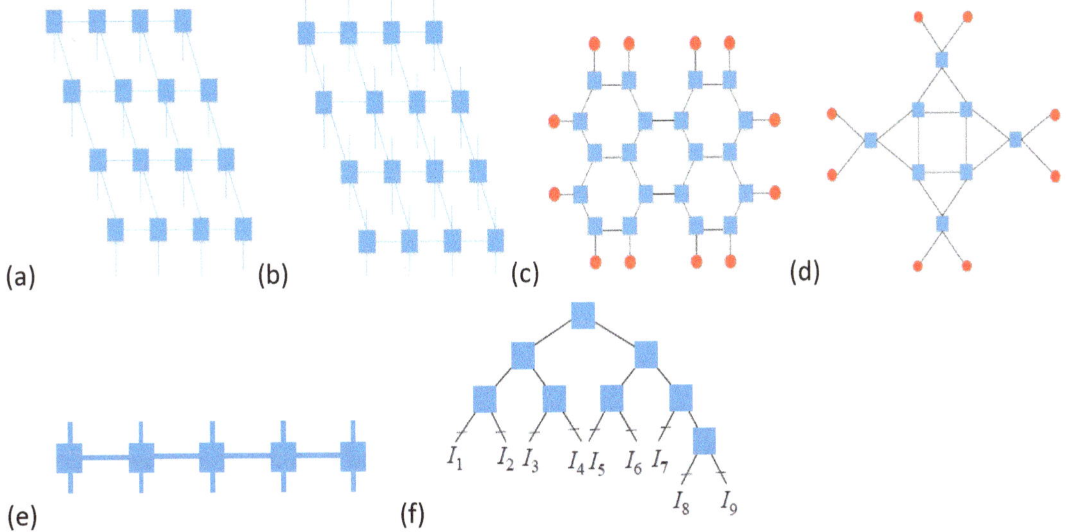

Figure 47: (a) PEPS uses 5th-order core tensors, (b) PEPO uses 6th-order core tensors, (c) HCL uses 3rd-order core tensors, (d) MERA uses 4th-order tensors. The blue rectangle represents core tensors, and the red circle represents factor matrices, (e) MPO of leaf core tensors of order 3, and internal ones of order 4, and (f) TTNS binary tree (Ji et al., *2019).*

TNs enable change of topology while keeping the modes and their interactions intact. HT/TT allows sequential contractions of the core tensors to reduce computational complexity. Algorithms that enable cycles can be modified to eliminate the cycles by contractions and reduce the complexity. Converting tensor networks with cycles to trees reduces the computational complexity as well.

The original TT paper has its Python package "ttpy" Python package published at https://github.com/oseledets/ttpy. The Python notebook ch4.ipynb shows Tensorly Python package implementation of TT. Tensorly also implemented a regression example in TT format, published at https://github.com/tensorly/Proceedings_IEEE_companion_notebooks/blob/master/tt-compression.ipynb. There are other Python packages as well, such as:

- "scikit_tt" is published at (https://github.com/PGelss/scikit_tt/), and its requirements are demonstrated in ch4.ipynb. The TT class has many interesting features, and the package has many examples for solvers, regression, and Data Analysis methods.
- "ttrecipes" Python package is built on top of ttpy. It was built by (Cichocki *et al.*, 2016, p. 1) and published at https://github.com/rballester/ttrecipes. Thet have examples of tensor completion problems and tensor compression.

4.3.2 Tensor Rings

Like tensor chain (TC), Tensor Ring (TR) decomposition employs a circular dimensional permutation invariance and equivalently makes first and last core tensors of similar shape as central core tensors. This decomposition generalises TT decomposition using linear combinations of its core tensors. TR relaxes the constraints that $R_1 = R_{N+1} = 1$, and no dimension permutation optimisation is required, enabling circular multiplications of the trace of all core tensors.

Figure 48:Tensor Ring Illustration showing that only order-3 core tensors are used and connected circularly.

Given an Nth-order tensor $\chi \epsilon\, \mathbb{R}^{I_1, I_2, I_3, \ldots, I_N}$, the TR decomposition is:

$$\chi = \Re(\mathcal{A}_1, \mathcal{A}_2, \ldots \mathcal{A}_N) = \sum_{\alpha_1, \alpha_2, \ldots \alpha_N = 1}^{R_1, R_2, \ldots R_N} a_1(\alpha_{1,}\alpha_2)^\circ a_2(\alpha_{2,}\alpha_3)^\circ \ldots {}^\circ a_N(\alpha_{N,}\alpha_1)$$

Where the TR rank is defined for each mode as (R_1, R_2, ..., R_N), core tensors $\mathcal{A}_n \,\epsilon\, \mathbb{R}^{R_n, I_n, R_{n+1}}$, n = 1, 2, ..., N, and last one $\mathcal{A}_N \,\epsilon\, \mathbb{R}^{R_n, I_n, R_1}$ completes the circular connection with the first one, such that $R_1 = R_{N+1}$. The symbol '∘' denotes the outer product of vectors and $a_k(\alpha_{k,}\alpha_{k+1}) \,\epsilon\, \mathbb{R}^{I_k}$ denotes the$(\alpha_{k,}\alpha_{k+1})^{th}$ mode-2 fibre of tensor $\mathcal{A}_k$. $\mathcal{A}_1$ and $\mathcal{A}_2$ is multiplied along one dimension indexed by $\alpha_{2,}$, which is thus denoted by a connection with the size of that mode (i.e., R_2). This decomposition indicates that the whole tensor can be composed of the sum of rank-1 tensors generated from N vectors taken from each core respectively. The main difference with TT decomposition is the circular dimension permutation invariance such that the TR decomposition of $\chi \epsilon\, \mathbb{R}^{I_1, I_2, I_3, \ldots, I_N} = \Re(\mathcal{A}_1, \mathcal{A}_2, \ldots \mathcal{A}_N)$, if we shift the dimensions of χ k positions to the left as $\overleftarrow{\chi}^k \epsilon\, \mathbb{R}^{I_{n_{k+1}}, \ldots, I_N, I_1, \ldots, I_{n_k}}$, then the TR decomposition of $\overleftarrow{\chi}^k$ is defined as $\overleftarrow{\chi}^k = \Re(\mathcal{A}_{k+1}, \ldots, \mathcal{A}_N, \mathcal{A}_1 \ldots \mathcal{A}_k)$.

In TR decompositions, all shifting is equivalent such that:

$$\chi = \Re(\mathcal{A}_1, \mathcal{A}_2, \ldots \mathcal{A}_N) = \Re(\mathcal{A}_2, \mathcal{A}_3, \ldots \mathcal{A}_N, \mathcal{A}_1) = \cdots = \Re(\mathcal{A}_{k+1}, \ldots, \mathcal{A}_N, \mathcal{A}_1 \ldots \mathcal{A}_k) = \cdots = \Re(\mathcal{A}_N, \mathcal{A}_1 \ldots \mathcal{A}_{N-1})$$

The approximately reconstructed tensor from its TR decomposition is $\hat{\chi}$ with each entry is defined in terms of entries in A as follows:

$$\hat{x}_{i_1,i_2,\dots,i_N} = Tr\{\mathcal{A}_1(i_1)\mathcal{A}_2(i_2) \dots \mathcal{A}_N(i_N)\} = Tr\{\prod_{k=1}^{N} \mathcal{A}_k(i_k)\}$$

where the 'Tr' is the trace function, $\mathcal{A}_k(i_k)$ denotes the i_k th lateral slice matrix of the latent tensor $\mathcal{A}_k$, which is of size $r_k \times r_{k+1}$. Any two adjacent core tensors are of equal dimension r_{k+1} on their corresponding mode.

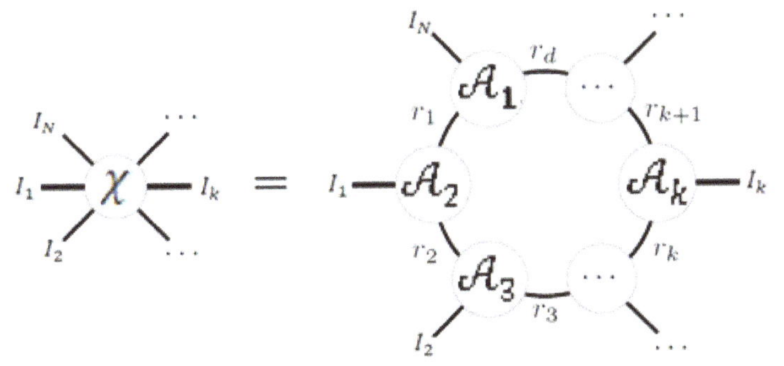

Figure 49: A circular graphical representation of the tensor ring decomposition (Zhao et al.*, 2016)*

Tensors represented in their TR decomposition can perform tensor operations such as those defined for the TT decomposition, including addition, multilinear product, Hadamard product, inner product, and Frobenius norm performed efficiently on each core.
Minimising the ranks and the error solves the TR decomposition:

$$\min_{A_1,\dots,A_N} r$$
$$s.t.: \|\chi - \Re(A_1, A_2, \dots A_N)\|_F \leq \epsilon\|\chi\|_F$$

Several approaches are used in the literature, including:

- TR-SVD is a sequential SVD-based approach. The algorithm uses subchains of the core tensor multiplications formed by n-unfolding and n-mode matricisation steps, then merging into a single core by multilinear products. These subchains form several TT representations on which to apply the TT_SVD algorithm. This approach does not guarantee optimal TR-ranks but converges fast.
- TR-ALS builds on ALS concepts given a fixed pre-defined rank by optimising one core while fixing the others and alternating between them until some defined convergence-stopping criteria. This approach is faster but uses fixed pre-defined ranks.
- ALS-AR also builds on ALS concepts but uses adaptive ranks from initial values that get updated during the iterations to minimise the error.
- BALS is a block-wise ALS algorithm based on truncated SVD on blocks (subchains) formed by merging adjacent core tensors, optimising for one block, and fixing the others while updating the ranks. This algorithm is better at finding the most optimal rank without increasing iterations due to the block-wise optimisation iterations of merged adjacent cores rather than one-by-one.

The number of parameters, and hence the computational complexity in TR representation, is $O(NIr^2)$, which is linear to the tensor order N, similar to TT However, TR is a more generalised, flexible, and powerful representation with usually more minor ranks than TT (Zhao *et al.*, 2016).

The Python notebook ch4.ipynb shows "tednet" Python package that implements various tensor decomposition algorithms, including CP, Tucker2, TT, and TR. Their code and documentation are published at https://github.com/tnbar/tednet. There are several Matlab implementations for TR decomposition, such as https://qibinzhao.github.io/ and https://github.com/oscarmickelin/tensor-ring-decomposition.

4.4 Machine Learning Tensor Decomposition Applications:

This section will present two tensor decomposition machine learning applications. The first one is the tensor completion example, based on CP decomposition. The second application is a class of algorithms to extend regression approaches to tensorial datasets efficiently.

4.4.1 Tensor Completion Application

Tensor completion is an extension to the matrix completion class of problems that aims to interpolate missing values in a dataset from the given values. This is also called inpainting or imputation of missing values. A 3-way association tensor completion application example is presented in (Huang *et al.*, 2021). It is important to understand the dataset and the objective of the analysis that needs to be performed on it. The dataset used in this paper is collected from the HMDD (the Human microRNA Disease Database), which is a database that curates biological lab experiment-supported evidence for human microRNA (miRNA) and disease associations. Auxiliary data are the disease descriptors collected from Medical Subject Heading (MeSH), a comprehensive controlled vocabulary thesaurus about life science, to calculate disease semantic similarity. MicroRNAs (miRNAs) is a small single-stranded non-coding RNA molecule (containing about 22 nucleotides) found in plants, animals, and some viruses that functions in RNA silencing and post-transcriptional regulation of gene expression. They play crucial roles in various biological processes associated with human diseases, such as cell growth and division, tissue differentiation, embryonic development and apoptosis, cell cycle regulation, inflammation, and stress response. For example, miR-129, miR-142-5p, and miR-25 are differentially expressed (found in the human cell in different quantities) between paediatric/children's central nervous system neoplasms and normal tissue, indicating their role in oncogenesis. Identifying potential miRNA-disease associations contributes to understanding the molecular mechanisms of miRNA-related diseases in order to discover new biomarkers and/or develop new therapies. The MiRNA role in disease prominently diverges. For instance, Genetic variants of microRNA (mir-15) may affect miRNAs' expression level, leading to B cell chronic lymphocytic leukaemia. In comparison, circulating miRNAs have the potential to detect breast cancer in the early stage (the quality and quantity changes of circulating miRNAs are associated with the initiation and progression of cancer and can be easily detected by basic molecular biology techniques). The four different types of miRNA-disease associations considered in this paper are illustrated in Figure 50.

Previous work focused on predicting whether a miRNA-disease association exists or not (binary classification/prediction). These methods can be grouped mainly into three categories: (1) methods based on score function, (2) methods based on complex network or graph algorithms, and (3) methods based on machine learning algorithms. Instead of building a binary graph association, this paper presented the dataset in a 3-way structure of miRNA-disease-type triplets as a tensor. It introduced Tensor Decomposition methods to solve the prediction task, such that the type explains the roles of miRNAs in disease development or identification. A miRNA-disease type can be naturally modelled as a binary tensor where every element represents whether the corresponding entry (miRNA, disease, type) exists or not. The authors formulated the multi-type miRNA-disease association prediction as a tensor completion task. Their goal was to complete the tensor for exploring the unobserved triple associations using Tensor Decomposition Methods.

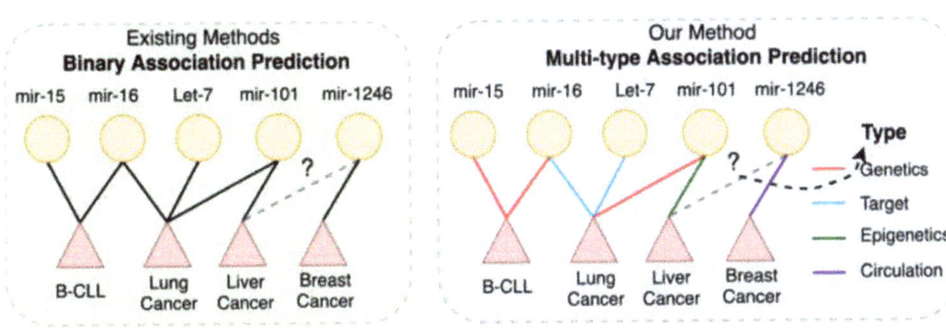

Figure 50: The figure on the left illustrates the binary association graph, and the figure on the right illustrates the MiRNA role in diseases' defined four types

The paper proposed a novel method, Tensor Decomposition with Relational Constraints (TDRC), which incorporates biological features (miRNA-miRNA similarity and disease-disease similarity) as relational constraints to further the existing tensor decomposition methods. TDRC employs the alternating direction method of multipliers (ADMM) framework and resorts to the conjugate gradient (CG) method to avoid computing an inverse matrix in inner iterations of ADMM for lower time complexity.
The authors compared TDRC performance against two previous tensor decomposition methods and a third binary network-based approach:
1) CP decomposition without auxiliary information, as explained earlier in this chapter.
2) Tensor Factorization Using Auxiliary Information (TFAI) considers incorporating auxiliary information into the CP model via introducing graph Laplacian regularizations.
3) NLPMMDA is the latest heterogeneous **N**etwork-based **L**abel **P**ropagation **M**iRNA **M**iRNA **D**isease **A**ssociation method that predicts each type of miRNA-disease association by label propagation on the miRNA-miRNA disease-disease similarity network.
Compared with the NLPMMDA, tensor decomposition-based methods significantly improve because these models dissect the data in a higher dimensional perspective through the tensor decomposition and capture complicated ternary relationships of miRNA-disease-type triples. TFAI works slightly worse on HDMM v3.2 than CP, which may be attributed to its weak ability to incorporate the auxiliary information, while TDRC achieved much better performance as it makes sufficient use of the auxiliary information.
The authors concluded that TDRC could produce better performance while being more efficient. The reconstructed tensor's low-rank property may help further improve the performance. The python code of the paper is found at https://github.com/BioMedicalBigDataMiningLab/TDRC. The mathematical formulation of the paper is as follows and is illustrated in Figure 51:

- Given a set of miRNAs $\mathcal{E} = \{e_1, e_2, \dots, e_m\}$, a set of diseases $D = \{d_1, d_2, \dots, d_n\}$ and a set of association types $\mathcal{R} = \{r_1, r_2, \dots, r_t\}$, the authors constructed a multi-relation bipartite graph $\mathcal{G}$. A triple (e_i, d_j, r_t) as a link in the graph $\mathcal{G}$ denoting an association between the miRNA e_i and the disease d_j with the type r_t .
- $\mathcal{G}$ is a binary three-way tensor $\mathcal{X} \in \{0,1\}^{m \times n \times t}$ with miRNA mode, disease mode, and type mode, where each slice is the adjacency matrix with regard to a type of miRNA-disease association.
- An entry x_{ijt} of the tensor is set to 1 if $(e_i, d_j, r_t) \in \mathcal{G}$. Otherwise, the entries are set to 0.
- The tensor $\mathcal{X}$ is extremely sparse, with many unknown entries, and thus it is challenging to reach the goal only by using known links.
    - Hence, the authors considered biological similarities as auxiliary information to tackle the challenge.

- Given the miRNA-disease-type tensor $\mathcal{X}$, the CP decomposition model can be represented as the following optimization problem (solved by Alternating Least Squares (ALS) method):
    - $\min_{C,P,F} \|\mathcal{X} - [\![C, P, F]\!]\|^2$
    - Here, $\|\cdot\|$ is the norm of a tensor. $C \in \mathbb{R}^{m\times r}$, $P \in \mathbb{R}^{n\times r}$ and $F \in \mathbb{R}^{t\times r}$ are the factor matrices with respect to the miRNA (the ith miRNA is encoded as a vector $c_{i:}$), disease (the jth disease is represented as a vector $p_{j:}$) and type mode in F, which are usually considered as latent representations for the corresponding modes.
- $[\![C, P, F]\!]$ is the reconstructed tensor, and its $(i, j, t)^{th}$ element is calculated by $\sum_l^r c_{il} p_{jl} f_{tl}$
    - where c_{il}, p_{jl} and f_{tl} denote respectively the $(i, l)^{th}$ element of C, the $(j, l)^{th}$ element of P and the $(t, l)^{th}$ element of F. We call r the rank of the approximated tensor $[\![C, P, F]\!]$.
- In general, r is set much lower than min(m, n) so that the low-rank property of the latent representations is enforced.
- Then they added the auxiliary information:
    - MeSH descriptors, the hierarchical relationships of diseases, are represented as Directed Acyclic Graphs (DAGs), where nodes represent the diseases and edges represent the relationships between different diseases to calculate the disease semantic similarity.
    - For a disease d, a DAG denoted as $DAG(d) = (N(d), E(d))$ is constructed, where $N(d)$ is the set of all ancestors of d (including itself) and $E(d)$ is the set of links from ancestor disease to their children.
    - The semantic contribution of disease $d_i \in N(d)$ to disease d can be calculated as:
        - $C(d, d_i) = \begin{cases} 1 & if d = d_i \\ max(\Delta \times C(d, d_j) | d_j \in children\ of\ d_i\} & if d \neq d_i \end{cases}$, where Δ is the semantic contribution factor, and it was set to 0.5 in the paper. Then the semantic value of disease d is defined as: $SV(d) = \sum_{d_i \in N(d)} C(d, d_i)$.
    - Finally, the semantic similarity between the two diseases d_i and d_j is calculated by: $s_{ij}^n = S_{disease}(d_i, d_j) = \frac{\sum_{d \in N(d_i) \cap N(d_j)} (C(d_i, d) + C(d_j, d))}{SV(d_i) + SV(d_j)}$.
    - The miRNA functional similarity between two miRNAs e_i, e_j are calculated as follows:
        - $s_{ij}^m = S_{\text{miRNA}}(e_i, \quad e_j) = \frac{\sum_{d \in \mathcal{D}(e_i)} S_{disease}(d, d_j^*) + \sum_{d \in \mathcal{D}(e_j)} S_{disease}(d, d_i^*)}{|\mathcal{D}(e_i)| + |\mathcal{D}(e_j)|}$, where $\mathcal{D}(e_i)$ represents the set of diseases that are associated with miRNA e_i in at least one association type, $|\mathcal{D}(e_i)|$ is the number of elements in the set $d_i^* = \underset{d_i \in \mathcal{D}(e_i)}{argmax}\ S_{disease}(d, d_i)$.
    - Both similarities are denoted as:
        - $S_m \in \mathbb{R}^{m\times m}$ as the miRNA-miRNA functional similarity matrix with s_{ij}^m as its $(i, j)^{th}$ element.
        - And $S_n \in \mathbb{R}^{n\times n}$ as the disease-disease semantic similarity matrix with s_{ij}^n as its $(i, j)^{th}$ element.
    - A real-valued function $f(x, y) = xMy^T$ is used to approximate the similarity between two miRNAs (or diseases) for high-quality relational learning, where M is a projection matrix, x and y are the row vectors of C (or P).
    - The approximation errors are minimized by:
    - $\min_{C,P,M} \alpha \sum_{i=1}^m \sum_{j=1}^m (s_{ij}^m - c_{i:} M_1 c_{j:}{}^T)^2 + \beta \sum_{i=1}^n \sum_{j=1}^n (s_{ij}^n - p_{i:} M_2 p_{j:}{}^T)^2$
    - The optimization problem is reformulated in matrix form:
    - $\min_{C,P,M} \alpha \|S_m - CM_1C^T\|_F^2 + \beta \|S_n - PM_2P^T\|_F^2$
- Then adding ℓ_2 regularization to the combined optimisation: $\min_{C,P,F,M} \frac{1}{2} \|\mathcal{X} - [\![C, P, F]\!]\|^2 + \frac{\lambda}{2} (\|M_1\|_F^2 + \|M_2\|_F^2) + \frac{\alpha}{2} \|S_m - CM_1C^T\|_F^2 + \frac{\beta}{2} \|S_n - PM_2P^T\|_F^2$

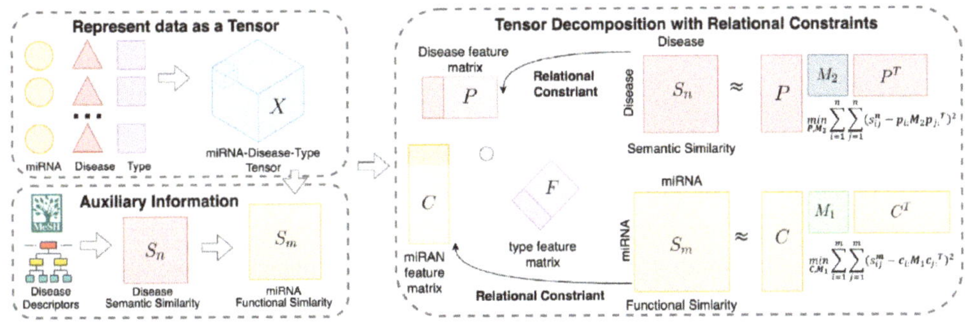

Figure 51: TDRC method to incorporate biological similarities as constraints into the CP model

This application illustrates a method that can be generalised to tensorizing any relational dataset such that there are several types of relationships involved. Example datasets are found in social networks friendships as the two subjects involved, and the type of relationship can be likes, retweets, comments, content sharing, and tagging. A 3-way tensor slice might capture each available relationship by fixing the index of the two subjects involved and varying the relationship index.

4.4.2 Tensor Regression

As chapter one explains, regression is one of the most fundamental supervised machine learning algorithms. It fits a dataset of labels represented as y (dependent/ target/ outcome/ response) as a function of x (independent/ predictor) features. The fitting can be a linear equation such as $y = \epsilon + \sum_{i=0}^{N} w_i x_i$, such that the w is the estimated regression parameters, including w_0 as the bias and $x_0 = 1$. Chapter two explains that it can also be a non-linear regression using a higher degree polynomial equation or any other non-linear parameters such as exponential, trigonometric, and power functions. A multivariate regression model is when x is multiple predictors and y can be multiple responses.

A non-parametric regression model does not assume a specific form of the parameters of the predictors. These algorithms do not need to define a linear or non-linear function to fit the data. They evaluate the mean outcome of the predictor covariates without pre-assumptions and hence misspecification errors. These methods expand to various machine learning algorithms, such as Gaussian Processes (GP), Artificial Neural Networks (ANN), Decision Trees, and Support Vector Regression (SVR). These methods usually require much more sample data than parametric methods (Hou, 2017).

If the dataset is in a matrix form, a regression model will estimate the regression parameters based on the correlation between each feature predictor and the target feature by estimating a parameter value for each predictor. Most classical regression algorithms can be applied to a dataset in tensor after vectorising or matricising the tensor. This is not successful in capturing the multi-way structural information, leading to lower accuracy and higher error. These methods will also use more parameters than tensor regression methods, requiring more storage and computational complexity. This section surveys the tensor regression algorithms that capture the multi-way inherent structures in tensorial data while being more efficient computationally and more accurate in avoiding overfitting. These methods are based on CP and Tucker decompositions of tensors, as presented earlier in this chapter. The tensorial regression models reduce the number of parameters from $O(I^N)$ to O(NIR), where N is the number of modes, I is the number of elements in each mode, and R is the rank, which is usually $R \ll I$. These fewer parameters will be associated with each mode independently. Conversely, the traditional regression models on vectorised or matricised tensorial datasets combine the modes, making the estimated extra parameters challenging to interpret.

A simple tensor regression model is defined as: given an Nth-order tensor $\chi \epsilon \mathbb{R}^{I_1,I_2,I_3,\dots,I_N}$, and the output $\mathcal{Y}$ could be a tensor of any order required to represent the dependent variable(s); the regression equation is:

$$\mathcal{Y} = f(\mathcal{X}) + \epsilon$$

The f function for linear regression can be the dot product defined in the generalised linear tensor regression model as:

$$\mathcal{Y} = \langle \mathcal{X}, \mathcal{B} \rangle + \epsilon$$

Such that the dot product of the predictor and β as the coefficient tensor in the same size as the predictor χ, capturing its tensor covariate, and is added to ϵ as the tensor representation error or bias. It can also be non-linear, as defined in chapter two, by using polynomial equations or other non-linear functions such as exponential, logarithmic, and others. Prediction or reconstruction/interpolation can occur based on a dataset of M samples as follows:

$$\hat{x}_{i_1,i_2,\dots,i_N} = \sum_{k=1}^{M} \langle \chi_{k,} \beta_k \rangle$$

Solving $\langle \mathcal{X}, \mathcal{B} \rangle$ by vectorising, both tensors will produce a huge number of parameters. For example, an MRI dataset $\mathcal{X} \in \mathbb{R}^{128\times128\times128}$ will require 2,097,152 + and five usual covariates parameters to estimate, which is intractable. Using the unsupervised PCA produces the most dominating principal components that are irrelevant to the input, lose the multi-way structural relationship, and are difficult to interpret.

The CP Tensor Regression defines the $\mathcal{B}$ tensor in terms of its rank-R CP decomposition a

$[B_1, B_2, \dots, B_N]$ with $B_n = \left[b_1^{(n)}, \dots, b_R^{(n)}\right] \in \mathbb{R}^{I_n,R}$

such that $y = \langle \mathcal{X}, \mathcal{B} \rangle + \epsilon = \left\langle \mathcal{X}, \sum_{r=1}^{R} b_r^{(1)} \circ b_r^{(2)} \circ \dots b_r^{(N)} \right\rangle + \epsilon$ where y is a scalar output. This reduces the number of parameters from $O(I^N)$ to the scale of O(NIR) while also producing reasonable reconstruction accuracy. For example, the previous MRI example parameters can be reduced to 389 = 5 + 128 × 3 for a rank-1 model and to 1, 157 = 5 + 3 × 128 × 3 for a rank-3 model.

As discussed earlier in this chapter, Tucker decomposition is more flexible than CP and accurately captures the multi-way structural relationships in the core tensors. Tucker Tensor Regression defines the $\mathcal{B}$ tensor in terms of its Tucker decomposition as:

$$\sum_{r_1=1}^{R_1} \dots \sum_{r_n=1}^{R_N} \dots g_{r_1 \dots r_n} b_{r_1}^{(1)} \circ b_{r_2}^{(2)} \circ \dots b_{r_n}^{(N)}$$

such that $y = \langle \mathcal{X}, \mathcal{B} \rangle + \epsilon = \left\langle \mathcal{X}, \sum_{r_1=1}^{R_1} \dots \sum_{r_n=1}^{R_N} \dots g_{r_1 \dots r_n} b_{r_1}^{(1)} \circ b_{r_2}^{(2)} \circ \dots b_{r_n}^{(N)} \right\rangle + \epsilon$ where $\mathcal{G} \in \mathbb{R}^{R_1,R_2,\dots,R_N}$ with entries $\{g_{r_1 \dots r_n}\}_{r_1=1,\dots r_n=1}^{R_1,\dots,R_N}$. The factor matrices are defined as $B_n \in \mathbb{R}^{I_n,R_n}$ along different modes. This reduces the number of parameters from $O(I^N)$ to the scale of $O(NIr + r^N)$, which is higher than the CP regression parameters of O(NIR) but more parsimonious modelling of the input data when $R \ll N$. An example application presented in (Li, Zhou and Li, 2013) shows that for a tensorial dataset representing neuroimaging data as a 3D signal $\mathcal{X} \in \mathbb{R}^{16\times16\times16}$ using a Tucker model with multilinear rank = (2, 2, 5), the number of parameters is 131, while using a 5-component CP regression model yields 230 parameters.

Other tensor regression algorithms are as follows:

1) Linear Tensor Regression Methods:

- Hierarchical Tucker Tensor Regression reduce the $O(NR^3 + NIR)$
- Higher-order partial least squares (HOPLS) model a tensor response from tensor predictors by extracting a small number of common latent variables that capture the maximum covariance, followed by a regression step against them. This is done using block Tucker decompositions of both the predictor and outcome tensors. This model is computationally prohibitive for large tensors. Incremental higher-order partial least squares (IHOPLS) are suitable for infinite online streams of tensors by incrementally

clustering the learned latent variables to summarise previous data in the core tensors and projection matrices.

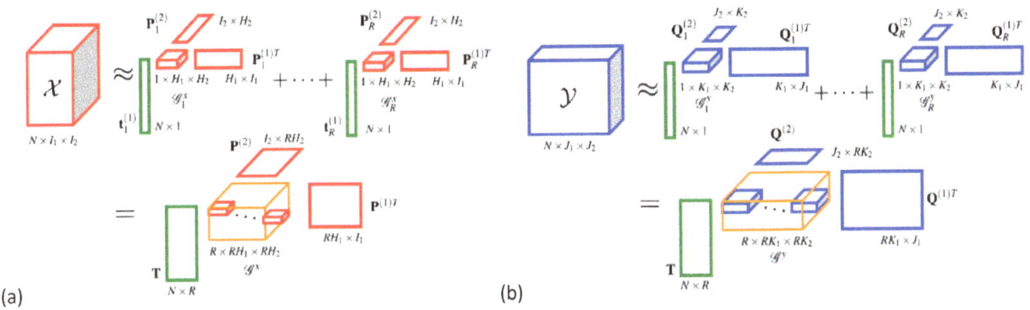

Figure 52: An illustration of high-order partial least squares (HOPLS) for predictor (M+1)th-order tensor $\mathcal{X}$ or order M=2, and and an outcome (L+1) th-order tensor $\mathcal{Y}$ and L=2, such that they couple in the first mode and having equal samples (a) shows HOPLS decomposes $\mathcal{X}$ into a sum of rank-$(1,H_1, \ldots, H_M)$ Tucker blocks, and (b) shows HOPLS decomposes $\mathcal{Y}$ into a sum of rank-$(1,K_1, \ldots, K_L)$ Tucker blocks (Hou, 2017).

- Generalised and Penalised Tensor Linear Regression.
- Bayesian Tensor Linear Regression.
- Online Local Gaussian process for tensor-variate regression (OLGP).

2) Non-Linear Tensor Regression Models:

- Incremental higher-order partial least squares (IHOPLS).
- Recursive higher-order partial least squares (RHOPLS) conduct a consecutive blockwise calculation by merging the new data into the previous low-rank approximation of the model, storing only fewer factors than the complete observation.
- Kernel-based multiblock tensor partial least squares (KMTPLS) predict dependent tensor blocks from a set of independent tensor blocks through the extraction of a small number of common and discriminative latent components by fusing the information from multiple tensorial data sources and unifies the single and multiblock tensor regression scenarios into one general model.
- Kernel-based Tensor Partial Least Squares (KTPLS).
- Kernel-based multiblock tensor partial least squares (KMTPLS).
- Kernel-based higher-order linear ridge regression (KHOLRR).
- Tensor Regression Networks: In deep learning (DL), Convolution Neural Networks (CNN) have been used in regression models. Tensor Regression Layer can update the weight matrix in the last Fully Connected (FC) layer with regression coefficient tensor in low-rank Tucker decomposition format, as shown in Figure 53.

Simple Linear Tensor Regression Methods are solved by approaches such as Rank Minimisation, Alternating Least Squares (ALS), Greedy Low Rank, and Projected Gradient Descent. Various Tensor Regression applications are found in the literature, such as Tensor on Vector Regression, Vector on Tensor Regression, Tensor on Tensor Regression, and Multiple Tensor-on-Tensor Regression.

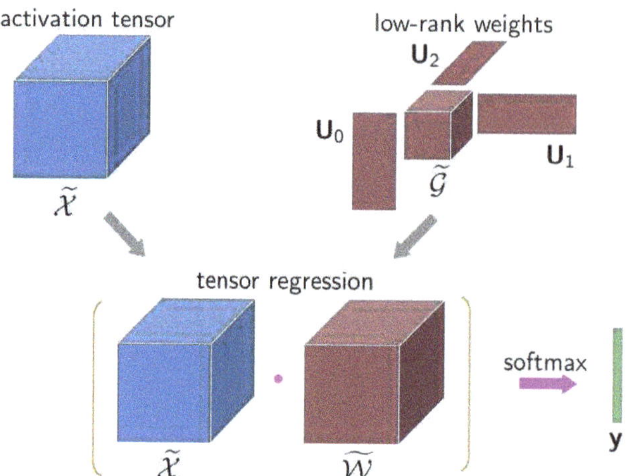

Figure 53: An illustration of tensor regression layer (TRL).

A tensor regression is implemented in the Tensorly package as shown at https://github.com/tensorly/Proceedings_IEEE_companion_notebooks/blob/master/tensor_regression_layer.ipynb. Another implementation is provided by scikit_tt Python package for three different regression algorithms that can be found at https://github.com/PGelss/scikit_tt/blob/master/scikit_tt/data_driven/regression.py. Also, ttrecipes Python package provides a tensor regression and completion implementation that can be found at https://github.com/rballester/ttrecipes/blob/master/ttrecipes/core/completion.py. T3F implements tensor completion as well https://t3f.readthedocs.io/en/latest/tutorials/tensor_completion.html. T3F is built on top of Tensorflow, providing Tensor Train decomposition for neural networks (NN) with Riemannian optimization. More about NN will be explained in the next section and chapter six. There is a collection of tensor completion methods maintained at https://github.com/zhaoxile/reproducible-tensor-completion-state-of-the-art.

4.5 Deep Learning Applications

The tensor decomposition algorithms presented in this chapter are data analysis algorithms that reveal complex relationships from the available data without adding any other machine learning algorithms. Tensor completion and regression discussed in the previous section can already do prediction and classification. Other machine learning algorithms that benefit from these concepts include support tensor machines, canonical correlation analysis, higher-order partial least squares), generalised eigenvalue decomposition, Riemannian optimisation, and the optimisation of deep neural networks. Tensor decomposition models are analogous to machine learning models. Some examples are as follows:

- TT/MPS is analogous to Hidden Markov Models (HMM).
- HT/TTNS is analogous to Deep Learning Neural Networks and Gaussian Mixture Model (GMM).
- PEPS is analogous to Markov Random Field (MRF) and Conditional Random Field (CRF).
- MERA is analogous to Wavelets and Deep Belief Networks (DBN).
- ALS, DMRG/MALS Algorithms are analogous to Forward-Backward Algorithms and Block Nonlinear Gauss-Seidel Methods (Cichocki *et al.*, 2016, p. 1).

For Artificial Neural Networks (ANN) algorithms, many building blocks contribute together to provide the non-parametric performance that requires no pre-defined assumptions about the function to approximate. ANN uses no rule-based programming, such as if statements or pre-defined equations used in classical machine learning (ML) algorithms, such as those used in chapter two methods. ML relied on developing new algorithms to address new problems or suitable feature engineering to inject the algorithms with human knowledge about the dataset. Adding neurons and layers and choice of activation functions and error functions are the methods to capture the complexity of the data structures and their correlations. These functions can be linear or non-linear based on the problem requirement. The construction of the network is massively parallel by definition and enables the employment of supercomputers and very-large-scale-integrated (VLSI) technologies. ANN depends on the forward propagation (mapping) of the input from the input layer, to the estimated output on the output layer, through a computational graph (of any number of layers and neurons per layer), doing the dot products between weights (starting from initial random values) and input connections in every neuron, applying the activation function and passing on to connected neurons in next layer (whether fully connected, convoluted, or other architectures). The estimated output is compared to the expected output to calculate the loss at the output layer. The loss is used to update the weights in backward propagation. The mapping from input to output is adaptive to dynamic changes in a batched dataset or a changing environment in an online learning model and is subject to many hyperparameters, such as the learning rate, the number of epochs, the learning algorithm, choice of activation and loss functions, validation process, convergence criteria, and others.

The human-brain-inspired model is empowered with the kernel methods from statistics introduced in chapter three, which will be further explored in chapter five. ANN is first theorised in the 1940s and implemented in the 1950s with various advancements through the initial decades, but with lousy performance due to the lack of large datasets and computing power. The SVM Kernel approaches were state-of-the-art during these decades. The big data scale datasets available now in the public domain and the exponential growth in computing power are the main reasons ANN picked up again in 2006 to become state of the art in various ML tasks. The computing power that was available to supercomputers in the late 2010s is now available in individual desktops and laptops with multiple cores and GPUs or accessible through dense GPU systems in the cloud. This enabled deeper large networks to be established and trained on large datasets, with increased accuracy sometimes exceeding human performance, such as winning in the Go game against humans. For example, the 2017 Google neural machine translation achieved near human language translation using 100 ExaFLOPS supercomputers to train a network to estimate 8700 million meters. The 100 ExaFLOPs (Exascale = 10^{18} Floating Point Operation per second) supercomputer processing is equivalent to two years of processing on a dual CPU server. The advancement in models' size (number of parameters over many layers and neurons), optimised gradient backpropagation algorithms, sparsification, regularisation, and many more have led to the current trillion parameter models for natural language processing (NLP). NLP models are more challenging than image models because of sequential dependence, semantic ambiguity, and other challenges.

This section introduces ANN in general and how tensor decomposition methods can enhance their performance. Then tensorising a data set example will be presented. Chapter six will discuss other detailed applications.

4.5.1 Introduction to NN

This section briefly describes Artificial Neural Networks (ANNs) to introduce how tensor decomposition methods can be used in these models. Chapter two introduced various dimensionality reduction AI algorithms and dimensionality expansion in the Kernel Trick to learn the data structures in the higher dimensional space. We can view neural networks as kernel machines because of their ability to implicitly learn nonlinear decision boundaries similar to kernel methods, such as support vector machines (SVMs). For example, the input features are transformed through a series of layers in feedforward neural networks using non-linear activation functions. Each layer consists of nodes (neurons) that perform weighted summation and activation. The layers closer to the input capture lower-level features, while deeper layers learn more abstract and high-level representations. The Radial Basis Function (RBF) is also used as an activation function in NN. This kernel machine characteristic of NN enabled desirable features as follows: 1) feature representation in the higher dimension and the infinite space is achieved through the layers of the network, learning complex representations from the trained weights and activation functions; 2) Non-linear decision boundaries are achieved by using non-linear activation functions; 3) The Universal Approximation Theorem states that a feedforward neural network with a single hidden layer containing a sufficient number of neurons can approximate any continuous function to any desired degree of accuracy, similar to the expressive power of kernel machines.

The simplest explanation of ANN, which is relatively more straightforward than many other machine learning algorithms, is that it comprises six steps. 1) The NN takes input data and passes it through the neurons of the input layer by multiplying the data by a set of weights. 2) The weights matrix determines the strength of connections/ influence of one node on another, and biases are associated with each node in the layers that control the node's tendency to be active or inactive. A simple non-linear activation function is applied to the weighted sum of the neuron input to produce the output to the following node. The weights and biases are initialised at the first epoch and then learned during training to optimize the network's performance by minimising a loss function. 3) Then, the results from the neurons in one layer are stacked up to the following layers to capture more complex patterns/interactions. 4) the final layer is designed to produce the required predicted output of the machine learning task. 5) The predicted output is compared to the pre-labelled output to calculate the loss and use the loss to backpropagate through the network, adjusting the weights. 6) The forward/backward process is repeated until convergence. The width (number of neurons) of each hidden layer (not the input and the output layers, as these are specific to the input and output size required), and the depth of the NN, are learned from best practice papers and models specific to the complexity of the data structure and the learning objective.

For more details on these models' theoretical and mathematical foundations, books such as (Haykin, 2009) can be explored. For more programming exercises and essential building blocks of neural networks, books such as (Ekman, 2021) can be explored. The origin of the artificial neuron as a mathematical model is the biological neuron, as illustrated in Figure 54 (a), in which the body of the neuron is a node that performs two functions: it computes the sum of the weighted input signals, and it applies an output function to the sum. The neuron output/activation function is usually non-linear; examples are:

- Converting the neuron's output to a set of discrete values.
- Limiting the range of the output values.
- Normalising the range of output values.

The input layers should have enough neurons for the number of input features. The output layer is based on the objective of the model. If it is classification, then the number of classes of the supervised prelabelled data set is the number of neurons in the output layer or other encoding methods to reduce the number of neurons. If it is a regression model, then one output neurone will contain the estimated predicted outcome continuous value. Adding more hidden layers between input and output, as illustrated in Figure 54 (b, c), enables more complex functions, not just simple monotonic ones, to be estimated. In computer vision, adding more hidden layers can extract more complex shapes, such as object detection. Recurrent connections that take the output of a neuron to the input of a neuron in the same layer (including itself) can be used to implement memory, as illustrated in Figure 54 (d). ANN implement spatial filters for a dataset of pixels of an image, such that nearby pixels will be input to adjacent neurons. For example, a 16x16 image will require an input layer containing 256 neurons that will read the vectorised image data as intensities of grey shade or any other scalar representation. Spatial filters extract local features such as differences of intensity between adjacent pixels in an image, and this local property can be used for tasks like identifying edges in the image. More details about recurrence and convolution will follow.

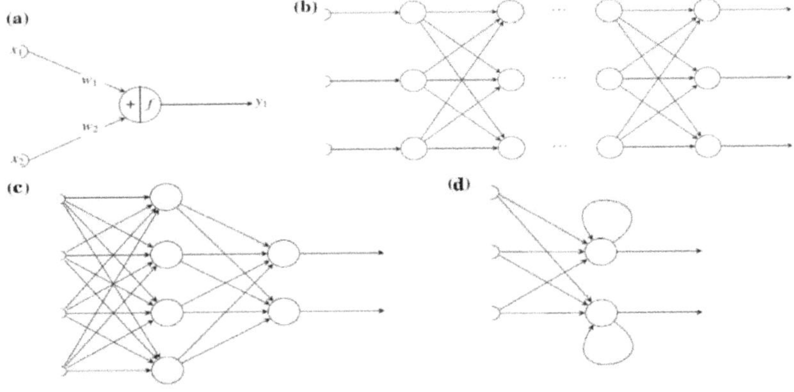

Figure 54: (a) ANN: one neuron with two inputs, (b)Fully Connected Neural network for deep learning such that many hidden layers can be added, (c) Another example of a 3-layer ANN.(d) ANN with memory

The weights/parameters/coefficients of the input features are learned/estimated using various approaches. The main classes of approaches are:

- **Supervised Learning:** The output required for every set of inputs is pre-defined. The network is trained to estimate the weights by reducing a quantified error while learning from a prelabelled training dataset and generalising for unseen datasets by approximating a function of the inputs and the weights: $y = w_1x_1 + w_2x_2 + \dots + w_nx_n,$
- **Reinforcement Learning:** A good output vs bad output is generally defined as using a utility function that generalises the objective without specific details. An environment of the problem specifies possible actions, rewards, and states. The network is trained to maximise the utility function/reward and store the state/action/reward as samples or strategies to learn from in the future. For example, in a collision-avoidance navigation algorithm with an unknown map, in which the utility function is the shortest path, it learns by attempting possible strategies/actions (such as driving forward until an object is sensed ahead, then turning right). All sensed objects' positions are recorded, and better shortest paths are calculated later. Then strategies are updated as the map change, object positions change, and utility function changes.
- **Unsupervised Learning:** There is no specific output, but the inputs have patterns that can be estimated, such as in clustering.

The Hebbian rule updates the ANN connections' weights between two neurons, such as increasing or decreasing them in proportion to the product of their activation:

$$\Delta w_{kj} = \alpha y_k x_j$$

Such that neuron k and neuron j have connection weight w_{kj} with Δw_{kj} is the change of w_{kj}, y_k is the output of neuron k, x_j is the input of neuron j, and α is a constant that defines the speed of learning.

A perceptron is an artificial neuron with a weighted summation unit with inputs $\{x_1, x_2, \dots, x_n\}$ and each x_i is multiplied by a factor w_i before summation. An additional input x_0 has the constant value 1 for setting a bias independent of the inputs. The output is obtained by applying a function f to the addition result. For binary classification, this output can be the sign of the summation indicating a + class or a – class:

$$y = sign\left(\sum_{i=1}^{n} w_i\, x_i\right) = \pm 1$$

Perceptrons are the basic building blocks of deep learning, and the Hebbian learning rule is the basic rule applied in the stochastic gradient descent algorithm using partial derivatives for the high dimensional datasets: $w_i(t+1) = w_i(t) + \eta(\frac{dy}{dx_i})$ that is added or subtracted in the opposite direction of the gradient. The algorithm starts by initialising the weights arbitrability, such as 0.1. Then iteratively update the weights until convergence. The learning phase/iterations are terminated when the model converges. Convergence is defined as reaching 98% of the samples correctly classified or when the magnitudes of the corrections to the weights become small below a specified threshold.

Multiple Layer Perceptrons draw a new decision line boundary by each perceptron that can be simply effective in multiclass classification, such as Multiclass Linear Discriminant Analysis (LDA), or causing the decision boundary to be non-linear such as in Quadratic Discriminant Analysis (QDA). Both LDA and QDA are parametric in that they measure the data against a pre-defined form (linear or quadratic) and similar distributions in each class. ANN does not require these assumptions.

Computing partial derivative for multiple neurons for each dimension in the dataset in multiple layers is computationally expensive. This is solved by using a backpropagation algorithm: 1) The forward pass, where we present one learning example (a row in a dataset) to the network and compare the network output to the desired value (the ground truth). 2) The backward pass, where we compute the partial derivatives with respect to the weights. These derivatives are then used to adjust the weights to make the network output closer to the ground truth. The gradient descent algorithm tracing over a simple network is animated in https://developers-dot-devsite-v2-prod.appspot.com/machine-learning/crash-course/backprop-scroll. Instead of the non-differentiable sign function, the tanh or continuous sigmoid function is used.

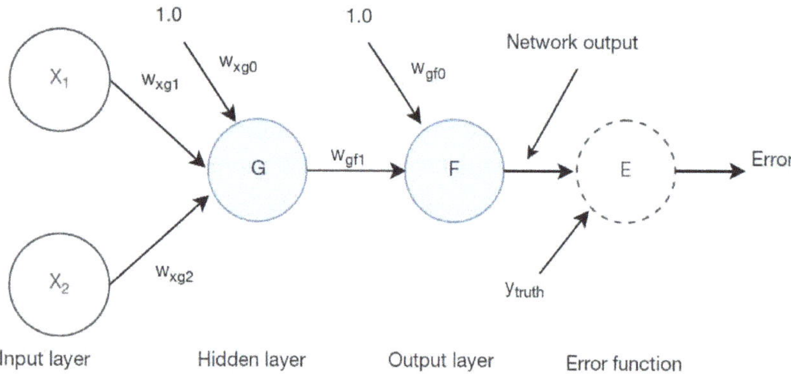

Figure 55: Simple two-layer network used to explain backpropagation. The last unit (dashed) is not a part of the network but represents the error function that compares the output to the ground truth (Ekman, 2021).

Figure 55 shows a two-layer ANN with two inputs and one output for a dataset with m samples. Each sample is applied to the network in each iteration to update the weights. In designing an ANN model, various building blocks need to be put together, such as:

- **The input aggregation functions/activation function in each neurone:** for example, for the ANN in Figure 55: a Sigmoid function can be applied for hidden layer F neuron and a tanh for input layer G neurone, such that the predicted outcome can be computed as: $\hat{y} = Sigmoid(w_{gf0} + w_{gf1}tanh(w_{xg0} + w_{xg1}x_1 + w_{xg2}x_2))$

- **The number of hidden layers** required (and their type) and the number of neurons in each layer, and their connections.
- **The loss/Error Function:** for example: Mean squared error $MSE = \frac{1}{m}\sum_{i=1}^{m}\left(y^{(i)} - \hat{y}^{(i)}\right)^2$
- **The minimisation algorithm of the error function:** for example, the minimisation can be done analytically using calculus, such as computing a composite function by applying the chain rule in calculating the derivatives: $Error\left(w_{gf0}, w_{gf1}, w_{xg0}, w_{xg1}x_1, w_{xg2}x_2\right) = e \circ f \circ z_f \circ g \circ z_g$, where z_f is the activation function of neuron F, and z_g is the activation function of neuron G. The iterative method uses a gradient descent class of algorithms to minimise an error until a threshold is met or a number of iterations are performed.
- **Other parameters to fine-tune**, such as the learning rate, the number of iterations, the convergence criteria, and the regularisation parameter to avoid overfitting. Each implementation comes with default values, but learning fine-tuned values to a particular dataset or task can be achieved using search algorithms.

A simple visualisation can be found at https://aegeorge42.github.io/. Another Multiclass classification ANN is shown in Figure 56. The network takes input from the MNIST dataset of handwritten digits containing 3D arrays of images, where the first dimension selects one of the 60,000 training images or 10,000 test images. The other two dimensions represent the 28×28 pixel (flattened as 784 pixels) values (integers between 0 and 255). Each pixel is fed to one neurone in the input layer. A fully connected network (i.e. each neuron in one layer connects to all neurons in the next layer) with one hidden layer is constructed. One Hot encoding output layer, in which only one is activated to 1 as the estimated class/digit, and the remaining nine neurons/units are zeros (Ekman, 2021).

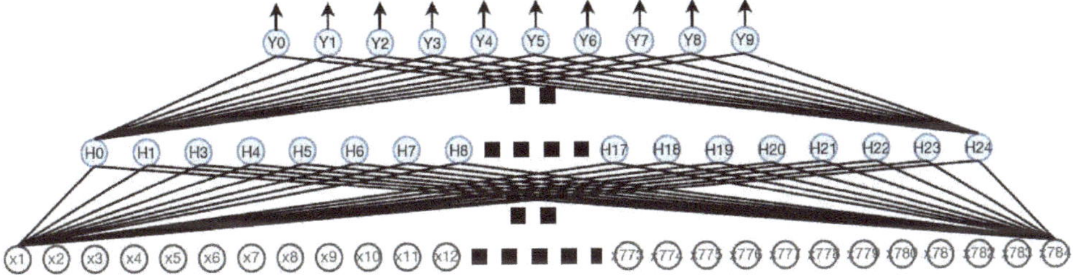

Figure 56: Network for digit classification. A large number of neurons and connections have been omitted from the figure to make it less cluttered. In reality, each neuron in a layer is connected to all the neurons in the next layer (Ekman, 2021).

Researchers have been proposing new NN models to handle different data types, machine learning tasks, and complexity. Major NN architectures are convolutional neural networks (CNN) that are suitable to spatial datasets such as images, maps, or any n-D datasets where the input position is related to the positions of spatially related inputs. CNN complexity is much less than fully connected layers and all other remaining architectures. The remaining models are discussed in the order of increasing complexity in this section. Recurrent Neural Networks (RNN) are suitable for sequential datasets, such as time series, sentences, audio, and video files. There is also Recursive NN which sometimes uses the same acronym (RNN) and is suitable for learning on graphs. There is also long/short-term memory (LSTM) and their variant simplified Gated Recurrent Units (GRUs) that solve the vanishing gradient problems of RNNs. There are also multi-component NNs, such as encoder/decoder models,

Generative Adversarial Neural Networks (GAN), among many others. In the following, some of the significant architectures will be concisely introduced.

4.5.1.1 Feed Forward Neural Networks (FFNNs)

A feedforward neural network is a type of artificial neural network where the nodes are arranged in layers, with each node receiving input from the previous layer. The network processes the input data in a forward direction through the layers until it reaches the output layer. FFNNs are used for image classification, speech recognition, and time-series forecasting applications. FFNNs tasks include Classification, regression, and pattern recognition.

Example Keras Python Source code:

```
from keras.models import Sequential
from keras.layers import Dense

model = Sequential()
model.add(Dense(units=64,activation='relu',
     input_dim=input_dim))
model.add(Dense(units=32, activation='relu'))
model.add(Dense(units=output_dim, activation='softmax'))
```

4.5.1.2 Deep Belief Network (DBN)

Deep Belief Networks (DBNs) are generative models that consist of two main types of layers: the visible layer and the hidden layer(s). The visible layer represents the input data, while the hidden layers capture the higher-level representations of the complex patterns and structures in data.

Here is a possible architecture for a Deep Belief Network:

1. Visible Layer: The visible layer receives the input data, which can be binary, continuous, or categorical. Each node in the visible layer represents a feature or an attribute of the input data.

2. Restricted Boltzmann Machines (RBMs): RBMs are a type of generative stochastic artificial neural network. RBMs are trained to reconstruct the input data by learning the joint probability distribution between the visible and hidden nodes. RBMs use an energy-based model, where the energy of a particular configuration is defined by the weights, biases, and states of the visible and hidden nodes. The energy function represents how well the RBM reconstructs or fits the observed data. RBMs use a probabilistic activation function called the sigmoid function, which maps the input to a value between 0 and 1. RBMs are trained using a technique called Contrastive Divergence (CD) or its variants, such as Persistent Contrastive Divergence (PCD). CD approximates the gradient of the log-likelihood function to update the weights and biases incrementally. The training process aims to minimize the difference between the original input and the reconstructed input generated by the RBM.

3. Unsupervised Pre-training: The DBN is usually trained in a layer-by-layer manner using unsupervised pre-training. Each RBM is trained individually to learn the features of the data at that layer. The weights learned in the RBM are then used to initialize the corresponding layer in the DBN.

4. Fine-tuning: After pre-training, the DBN is fine-tuned using supervised learning techniques, such as backpropagation. The pre-trained weights serve as a good initialization for the network, and the fine-tuning step adjusts the weights to minimize the error between the predicted outputs and the true outputs.

5. Output Layer: The final layer of the DBN is the output layer, which produces the predicted outputs based on the learned representations from the hidden layers. The number of nodes in the output layer depends on the specific task at hand, such as classification or regression.

By stacking multiple RBMs and fine-tuning the network, a DBN can learn hierarchical representations of the input data. DBNs have been widely used in various domains, including image recognition, natural language processing, and recommendation systems for tasks such as feature learning, dimensionality reduction, and collaborative filtering.

Example Keras Python Source code:

```
import numpy as np
from keras.models import Sequential
from keras.layers import Dense
from keras.layers import Dropout

# Define the architecture of the DBN
def build_DBN(hidden_units):
    dbn = Sequential()
    # Add the visible layer
    dbn.add(Dense(units=hidden_units[0],                 activation='relu',
input_shape=(input_dim,)))

    # Add the hidden layers
    for units in hidden_units[1:]:
        dbn.add(Dense(units=units, activation='relu'))
        dbn.add(Dropout(0.2))  # Dropout for regularization

    # Add the output layer
    dbn.add(Dense(units=output_dim, activation='softmax'))
    return dbn

# Set the dimensions of the input and output layers
input_dim = 784  # Example: MNIST dataset with 28x28 pixel images
output_dim = 10  # Example: Classification into 10 classes

# Set the number of hidden units in each layer
hidden_units = [512, 256, 128]  # Example: Three hidden layers with 512, 256,
and 128 units respectively

# Build the DBN model
dbn_model = build_DBN(hidden_units)

# Compile the model
dbn_model.compile(optimizer='adam',          loss='categorical_crossentropy',
metrics=['accuracy'])

# Train the DBN model
```

```
dbn_model.fit(X_train,        Y_train,        batch_size=128,        epochs=10,
validation_data=(X_val, Y_val))

# Evaluate the DBN model
loss, accuracy = dbn_model.evaluate(X_test, Y_test)
print("Test loss:", loss)
print("Test accuracy:", accuracy)
```

In the example above, we first define a function `build_DBN` that takes the list of hidden units as an argument and constructs the DBN model using the Sequential API of Keras. The visible layer is defined with the input dimension, and the hidden layers are added using the specified number of units and the ReLU activation function. Dropout layers are also added for regularization. Finally, the output layer is added with the specified output dimension and softmax activation.

We then set the dimensions of the input and output layers, as well as the number of hidden units in each layer. In this example, we use the MNIST dataset with 784-dimensional input (28x28 pixel images) and a classification task with ten output classes. The DBN model is built using `build_DBN` function, compiled with the Adam optimizer and categorical cross-entropy loss. We then train the DBN model using the `fit` method with the training data (`X_train` and `Y_train`) for a specified number of epochs.

Finally, we evaluate the trained DBN model using the test data (`X_test` and `Y_test`) and print the test loss and accuracy. Note that in this example, you'll need to replace `X_train`, `Y_train`, `X_val`, `Y_val`, `X_test`, and `Y_test` with your actual data. Make sure the input and output dimensions, as well as the hidden unit configuration, are appropriate for your specific task.

4.5.1.3 CNN

ANN input layer uses a neuron per input variable, such as a column in a dataset. This requires flattening a 2D image input, as seen in the MNIST example illustrated in Figure 56. The spatial information that connects a pixel to its eight neighbours spatially on a 2D grid is important to capture. This is what CNN is doing. CNN input layer uses a receptive field of the same size as the convolution filter size that divides an image input, for example (or any spatial data) using the kernel size, the stride (how much overlap in the image between the filter application), and requires padding in case of residuals. There is a 1D convolution to connect a data point to its previous and following data points, but images usually require 2D convolutions, and we also have 3D convolutions for video files with an extra frame/time dimension. A 2D convolution animation of different kernels can be found at https://setosa.io/ev/image-kernels/.

The grid of neurons creates a feature map for the image, such that each layer has multiple output channels. Each neuron acts as a feature/pattern identifier (such as vertical line, horizontal, ... etc.) and is activated if the particular feature is found in the location covered by that neuron's receptive field. This provides translation invariance, i.e. identifying an object found in any particular position in an image by sharing the weights between all neurons in a single channel. The next chapter will discuss translation invariance from different perspectives and other forms of invariance. The sparse connection (each neuron works on its assigned receptive field only) leads to efficient computation costs. CNN layers are stacked such that each layer receives inputs from multiple input channels of the previous layer and produces multiple-output channels, such that a neuron in subsequent layers receives NxMxM inputs (+bias) for N output channels from the previous layer, and the kernel size of MxM. The resolution (number of neurons per channel) of the first convolutional layer is lower than the resolution of the image, and further CNN layers need to be of lower resolution than previous layers. For example, use a stride greater than 1,

or use a max-pooling layer to reduce the size of a layer by combining the output neurons within channels such as every 2×2 neurons output their max value to the next neuron in the next layer. Stacking CNN layers will recognise more complex objects than in the initial CNN layer, where simple vertical/horizontal lines and other kernels are used. CNN layers compute fewer parameters than Fully connected layers. For example, assume an image 32×32×3 and a CNN layer, the weights to learn for the 3×3 kernel is 3*3*3+1 = 28, such that the third factor (3) represents the three channels in the previous layer. The +1 is the bias weight. A fully connected layer would have required 32*32*3+1 = 3,073 weights to learn.
Figure 57 illustrates the receptive fields in 2D convolution over images and the different kernel sizes and strides effect over the convolution through the image size. Figure 58 shows an example CNN network learning the different features by stacking the CNN layers, then flattening to merge the learned objects and produce a class prediction, and also shows the receptive field as it grows deeper by stacking the CNN layers and merging identified objects into more complex objects.
There is an extensive history behind the choice of kernel sizes, layers, and their types in many of the CNN models and classical computer vision concepts that can be reviewed from multiple other references. For online references: there is an article diving into the different types: https://towardsdatascience.com/a-comprehensive-introduction-to-different-types-of-convolutions-in-deep-learning-669281e58215. There is also an article explaining the math: http://d2l.ai/chapter_convolutional-neural-networks/channels.html (Ekman, 2021).

There are also now many pre-trained models that can be used directly or can be tuned to a particular dataset or ML task that can benefit from the learned weights. Using the pre-trained models, the initial layers are the most general, and the later layers are more specific. The final layers can be changed as required to be suitable for a new ML task by selecting which layers to keep and which to remove and adding more layers as required or freeze some layers' weights from being updated during the fine-tuning. For example, VGGNet (16 layers) and GoogLeNet (22 layers) have been close to human-level object identification since 2014, then beaten by ResNet-152 consisting of 152 layers in 2015. Many other pre-trained models on various machine learning tasks can be fine-tuned as required, such as those posted in online repositories like TensorFlow Hub, or TensorFlow specific to Keras, Pytorch Hub, the NGC Catalog , GitHub, and http://paperswithcode.com. There is also a low code/no-code framework for using transfer learning in new applications provided by the NVIDIA TAO Toolkit.

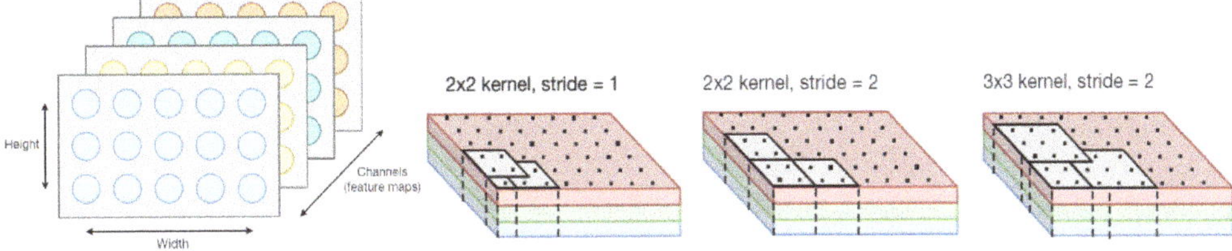

Figure 57: CNN Receptive fields, kernels, strides, multiple channel outputs, sharing weights

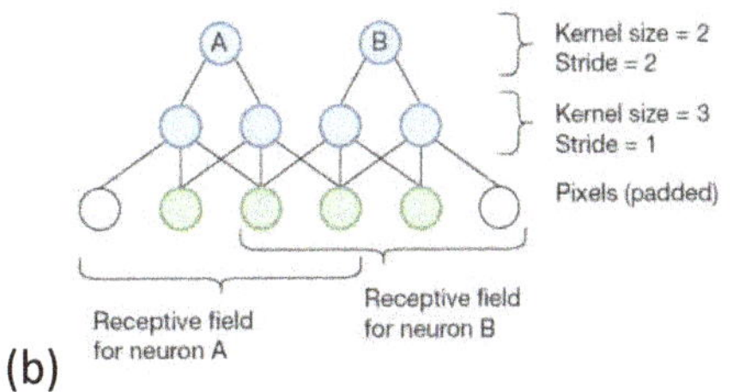

(b)

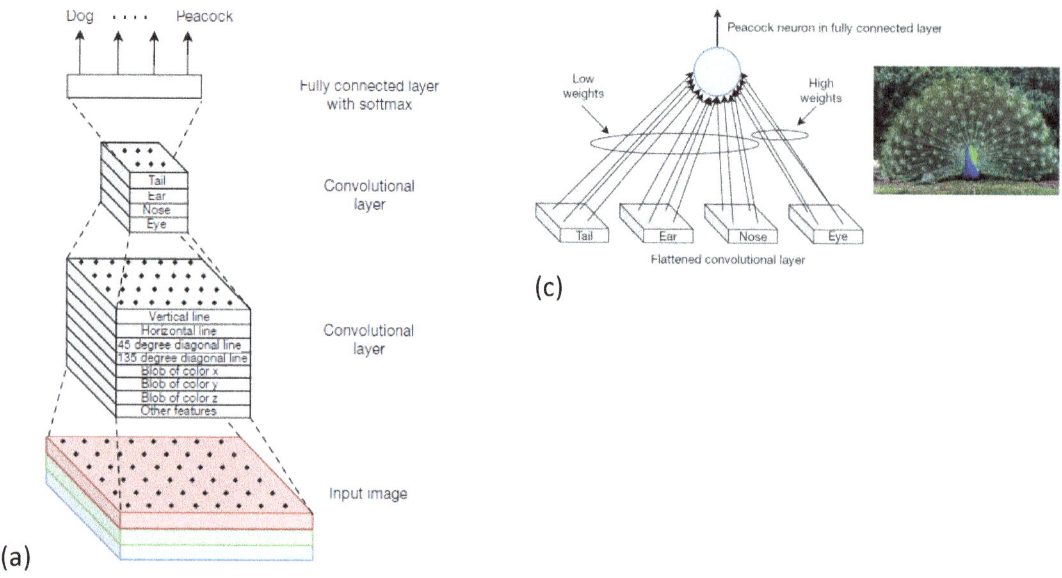

Figure 58: (a) CNN Layers stacking identifying different features, then combining features to identify more complex objects, then flattening using Fully Connected Layer to produce the identified object type (b) The receptive field increases deeper into the network. Although the neurons in the topmost layer have a kernel size of only 2, their receptive fields are four pixels. Note the padding of the input layer. (c) How a neuron in the fully connected layer combines multiple features into an animal classification (Ekman, 2021).

Example Keras Python Source code:

```
from keras.models import Sequential
from keras.layers import Conv2D, MaxPooling2D, Flatten, Dense

model = Sequential()
model.add(Conv2D(filters=32,kernel_size=(3,3),
  activation='relu', input_shape=input_shape))
model.add(MaxPooling2D(pool_size=(2, 2)))
model.add(Flatten())
model.add(Dense(units=128, activation='relu'))
model.add(Dense(units=output_dim, activation='softmax'))
```

4.5.1.4 RNN

A Fully connected RNN layer connects the outputs from a dense layer to the inputs of that same layer, such that the number of inputs (weights) to a single neuron is now a function of both the size of the input vector and the number of neurons in the layer. This enables the weight to learn the interaction with previous values keeping the sequential data dependence such as time series and input value changes over time steps. Multiple recurrent layers can be stacked after each other to create a deep RNN, and a combination of recurrent layers, regular fully connected feedforward layers, and convolutional layers in the same network are also possible based on the machine learning task at hand. For example, for a regression ML task, one neuron is required in the output layer with Linear activation to produce the weighted sum of the predictive features. The regression accuracy measure in the output layer can be the Mean Absolute Error to measure how far a predicted continuous value is from the ground truth. More details about the computation in RNN is illustrated in Figure 59. Bi-directional RNN learns the sequential dependence in both directions (for example, look at future words) by having two RNN layers operating in parallel, but they receive the input data in different directions. Because of the successive weight multiplications over the time steps, RNNs suffer from the vanishing gradient problem (Ekman, 2021).

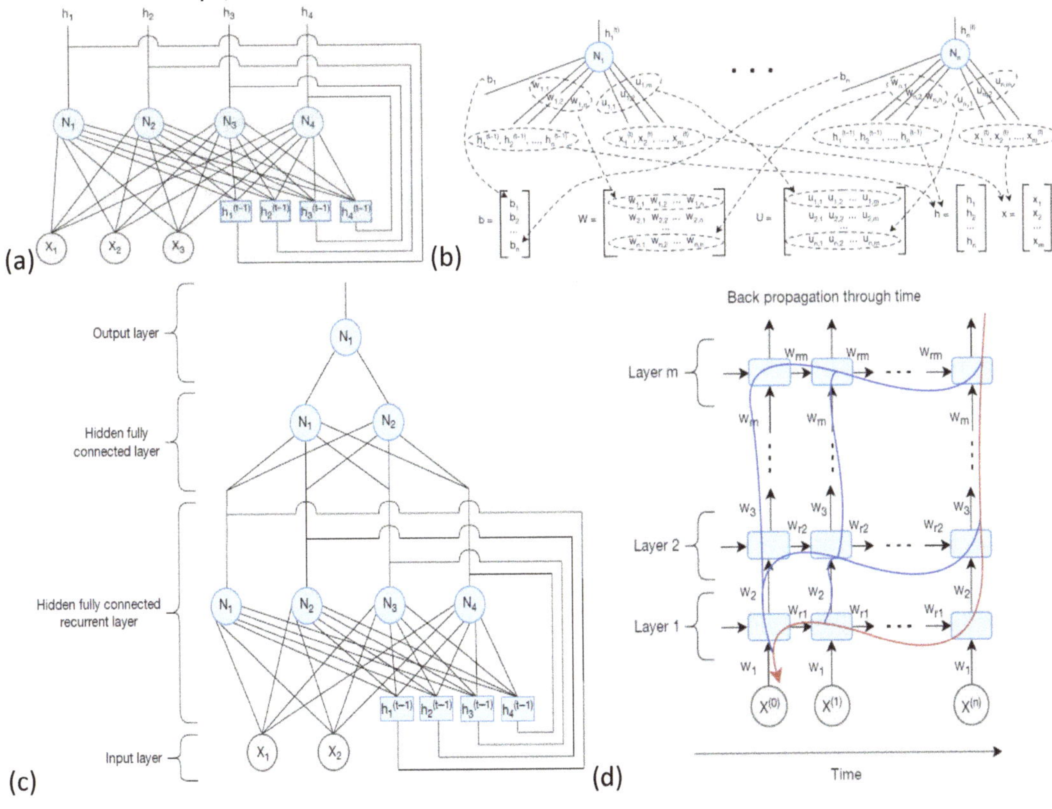

Figure 59 (a) Simple 4-neuron RNN layer with three inputs, reading back their output along with every new input applied to the network (b) The activation function in Dense Layers is: y = tanh(Wx), while in RNN Layers, it is: $h^{(t)} = tanh(Wh^{(t-1)} + Ux^{(t)} + b)$, in which $h^{(t-1)}$ is the previous output and their Weights W, $x^{(t)}$ are current input with their Weights U, and the bias for each neuron to produce the new output $h^{(t)}$ (c) shows a network that learns the book sales prediction from two inputs: historical book sales and overall consumer spending, using dense RNN 4-neurons input layer that read their own output along with the new iteration of new input (time step), such that they continuously update their learned weight (hidden states) with every time step, then pass on their output to a fully connected layer of 2 neurons to simplify the network, then to a final output layer of a single continuous variable using simple linear activation. (d) A flattened through-time RNN (n+1 time-steps in each layer) that shows how the backpropagation through time (BPTT) algorithm takes weight sharing into account when training RNN layers. The figure shows weights connecting the layers and recurrent weights back to the same layer: $w_{r1}, w_{r2}, \ldots, w_{rm}$). The error from the output propagates backward both through the network (vertically) and through time (horizontally) (Ekman, 2021).

Example Keras Python Source code:

```
from keras.models import Sequential
from keras.layers import SimpleRNN, Dense

model = Sequential()
model.add(SimpleRNN(units=64,activation='relu',
     input_shape=(timesteps, input_dim)))
model.add(Dense(units=output_dim, activation='softmax'))
```

4.5.1.5 LSTM

Long Short-Term Memory (LSTM) is a more complex unit that acts as a drop-in replacement for a single neuron in a recurrent neural network (RNN). LSTM addresses the gradient vanishing and exploding problems from training both vertically and horizontally in Deep RNN over long time-steps, and enables capturing attention. If the LSTM is fed long paragraphs of text (or any sequential data), it remembers the key elements of that text or data, while RNN would be more affected by the most recent elements. For intuition on how LSTM works, watch the video at https://www.youtube.com/watch?v=8HyCNIVRbSU. The LSTM cell has no less than five non-linear functions: Three are logistic sigmoid functions known as the gates in the unit, making it a gated unit. Two can be any regular activation functions, with popular choices being tanh and ReLU. It has four weighted sums, so the number of weights is four times as many as in a simple RNN. Multiplying a value by the output of a logistic sigmoid function results in the logistic sigmoid function acting as a gate: 0 to close and 1 to open and capture the value ($X^{(t)}$). tanh activation function is popular because many RNNs are not as deep as feedforward networks without severe vanishing gradient problems. ReLU function can also be used as input and output activation functions in the LSTM. Multiple LSTM cells can be connected into a recurrent network layer, just like a regular RNN, but each neuron has been replaced by the LSTM cell. This results in a network with two sets of states. We have the internal state (c) inside each LSTM cell, and we also have the state (h) in the global recurrent connections, just as in an RNN based on simple neurons. Figure 60 illustrates an LSTM cell, an LSTM layer, and their unrolling over time. The complexity of LSTM is four times the complexity of RNN (learning more parameters); Gated Recurrent Units (GRUs) simplify LSTM cells by not having an internal cell state. GRUs have only a single activation function, and the forget and remember gates are combined into a single update gate. LSTM and GRU are the most popular units used in RNNs, among other variations.

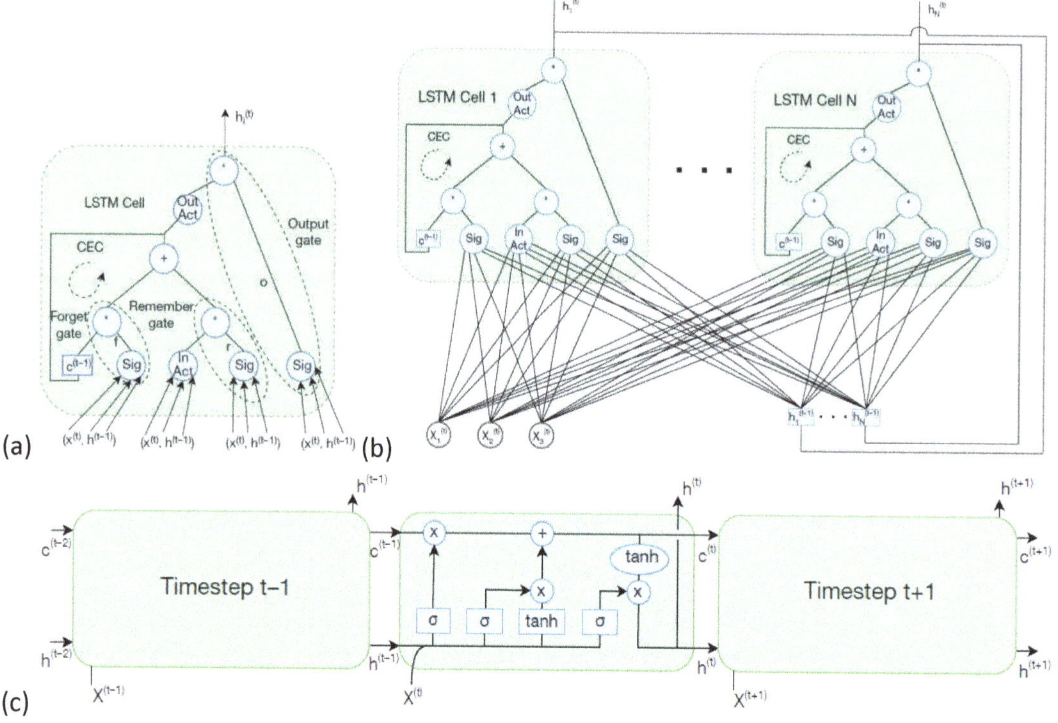

Figure 60: (a) LSTM Cell showing five activations functions and their input and output, (b) LSTM Layer showing connections of LSTM Cells, (c) LSTM unrolled in time

Example Keras Python Source code:

```
from keras.models import Sequential
from keras.layers import LSTM, Dense

model = Sequential()
model.add(LSTM(units=64,activation='relu',
  input_shape=(timesteps, input_dim)))
model.add(Dense(units=output_dim, activation='softmax'))
```

4.5.1.6 Multi-component NNs

Having two networks in one model is useful, and the most popular architectures are the encoder/decoder and the Generative Adversarial Network (GAN).

An autoencoder is an unsupervised neural network model that generates efficient representation latent vectors that describe the network input by reducing the input to a lower-dimensional latent space and then reconstructing the original data from the reduced representation. This requires that the output layer be duplicated from the input layer. Autoencoders are commonly used for applications such as image denoising, dimensionality reduction, and anomaly detection. For example, taking samples of sequences and pass on to hidden layers of fewer neurons and learning how to generate the input again as output (hence the prefix auto). In unsupervised training, the hidden layer weights are updated until convergence forming a lower dimensional representation of the input (embedding). Convergence is achieved when insignificant weight updates are required. Variational autoencoders learn the latent representation (distribution parameters of the latent space of the input) such that it can generate output that interpolates the given input, such as continuing sentences or drawing images.

Example Keras Python Source code for multiple layers autoencoder:

```
from keras.models import Sequential
from keras.layers import Dense

model = Sequential()
model.add(Dense(units=128,activation='relu',
       input_dim=input_dim))
model.add(Dense(units=64, activation='relu'))
model.add(Dense(units=128, activation='relu'))
model.add(Dense(units=input_dim, activation='sigmoid'))
```

An autoencoder may contain one encoder layer and one decoder layer only. An Example of Keras Python Source code would be:

```
from keras.layers import Input, Dense
from keras.models import Model

# Define the input size
input_size = 784

# Define the encoding dimension
encoding_dim = 32

# Define the input layer
```

```
input_data = Input(shape=(input_size,))

# Define the encoding layer
encoded = Dense(encoding_dim, activation='relu')(input_data)

# Define the decoding layer
decoded = Dense(input_size, activation='sigmoid')(encoded)

# Define the autoencoder model
autoencoder = Model(input_data, decoded)

# Define the encoder model
encoder = Model(input_data, encoded)

# Compile the autoencoder model
autoencoder.compile(optimizer='adam',
    loss='binary_crossentropy')

# Train the autoencoder
autoencoder.fit(X_train,      X_train,      epochs=10,      batch_size=256,
    shuffle=True, validation_data=(X_val, X_val))
```

We train the autoencoder by passing the training data X_train as input and target values. During training, the autoencoder learns to reconstruct the input data from the compressed representation.

Sequence to Sequence (Seq2Seq) problems have input sequences to learn from how to produce an output sequence, where the input and output are both variable-length sequences. The encoder network learns the hidden states' representation of an input sequence, such as embedding the input space (a lower dimension generalised equivalent or the context vector) to pass on to the decoder network to learn the corresponding output sequence from samples of prelabelled data. Various stacking models can create an encoder/decoder model, such as RNN encoder to RNN decoder, CNN encoder and CNN decoder, LSTMs, and many combinations based on the objective of the network and type/structure of the input and the output.

```
from keras.models import Model
from keras.layers import Input, LSTM, Dense

# Define the input sequence
encoder_inputs = Input(shape=(input_seq_length, input_dim))

# Define the encoder LSTM
encoder_lstm = LSTM(units=hidden_units, return_state=True)
encoder_outputs,state_h, state_c = encoder_lstm(encoder_inputs)
encoder_states = [state_h, state_c]

# Define the decoder inputs
decoder_inputs = Input(shape=(output_seq_length, output_dim))

# Define the decoder LSTM
decoder_lstm      =      LSTM(units=hidden_units,      return_sequences=True,
          return_state=True)
```

```
decoder_outputs,_,_=decoder_lstm(decoder_inputs,
            initial_state=encoder_states)

# Define the output layer
decoder_dense = Dense(output_dim, activation='softmax')
decoder_outputs = decoder_dense(decoder_outputs)

# Define the Seq2Seq model
model=Model([encoder_inputs, decoder_inputs], decoder_outputs)

# Compile and train the model
model.compile(optimizer='adam',loss='categorical_crossentropy'
        , metrics=['accuracy'])
model.fit([encoder_input_data,decoder_input_data],
      decoder_target_data,batch_size=batch_size,epochs=epochs,
      validation_split=0.2)
```

Seq2Seq models often involve more sophisticated techniques such as attention mechanisms, beam search, and teacher forcing, which are not included in this basic example. Seq2Seq models are commonly used in tasks such as machine translation, such that the input length can be different from the output length, word order and context vary from one language to another, text summarization, chatbots, and speech recognition.

Generative models in Deep learning are similar to the generative models in machine learning; it is about learning the data distribution and how samples are generated in a class rather than just being discriminative among the classes. GANs apply some game theory models, using a generator and discriminator components as players. The generator learns the input data representation and generates new samples, labelled as fake or generated but as close as possible to the genuine/real data. On the other side, the discriminator keeps learning how to identify the generated from real data. Both continuously update their weights to minimise their error. The model is called Adversarial because of the competition between the players to perfect their output. The generator aims to make the discriminator fail, and the discriminator aims to correctly identify generated from real data. GANs applications include Image generation and data synthesis.

Example Keras Python Source code:

```
from keras.models import Sequential
from keras.layers import Dense

generator = Sequential()
# Generator architecture

discriminator = Sequential()
# Discriminator architecture

gan = Sequential([generator, discriminator])
```

The Transformer model is an encoder/decoder model that learns input data representation in the encoder by using multi-head self-attention layers and exposing all encoder states to the decoder to have different weights of the different states. This will be further discussed in chapter six.

Example Keras Python Source code:

```
from keras.models import Sequential
   from keras.layers import Input, Dense
   from keras_transformer import get_model

   model = get_model(
       token_num=token_num,
       embed_dim=512,
       encoder_num=6,
       decoder_num=6,
       head_num=8,
       hidden_dim=2048,
       dropout_rate=0.05,
       attention_activation='relu',
       feed_forward_activation='relu',
   )
```

4.5.2 Tensorisation Benefits

The tensor decomposition methods can be applied in any building block to reduce the number of parameters providing compression of the NN model and capturing multi-way structures that increase the model's expressive power, increasing the accuracy and reducing overfitting. The data can already be collected in tensor forms, such as from multiple experiments or multimodal readings. A vector or matrix form dataset can also be tensorised to tree or chain structures to benefit from the tensorised algorithms. This will be explained in this section.

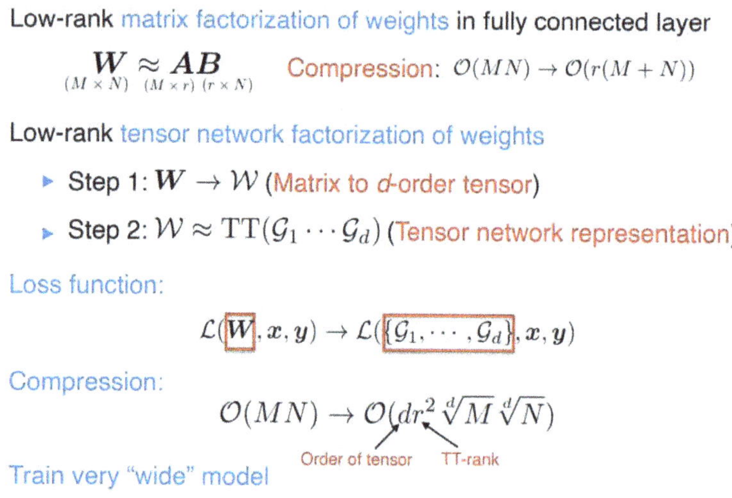

Low-rank matrix factorization of weights in fully connected layer

$\underset{(M \times N)}{\boldsymbol{W}} \approx \underset{(M \times r)}{\boldsymbol{A}}\underset{(r \times N)}{\boldsymbol{B}}$ Compression: $\mathcal{O}(MN) \rightarrow \mathcal{O}(r(M+N))$

Low-rank tensor network factorization of weights

- Step 1: $\boldsymbol{W} \rightarrow \mathcal{W}$ (Matrix to d-order tensor)
- Step 2: $\mathcal{W} \approx \mathrm{TT}(\mathcal{G}_1 \cdots \mathcal{G}_d)$ (Tensor network representation)

Loss function:

$$\mathcal{L}(\boldsymbol{W}, \boldsymbol{x}, \boldsymbol{y}) \rightarrow \mathcal{L}(\{\mathcal{G}_1, \cdots, \mathcal{G}_d\}, \boldsymbol{x}, \boldsymbol{y})$$

Compression:

$$\mathcal{O}(MN) \rightarrow \mathcal{O}(dr^2 \sqrt[d]{M} \sqrt[d]{N})$$

Order of tensor TT-rank

Train very "wide" model

Figure 61: Tensorising Neural Networks (Novikov et al.*, 2015)*

In the first ANN building block, activation and loss function choice can be tensorised, as shown in Figure 61. The standard weighted sum of dot products of input vectors with weight vectors and then aggregating them is suitable for vector and matrix form datasets. A tensorised activation function for a tree data structure can start from the node assigned to a neuron to recursively compute the weighted sum of its children with weight sharing between neurons to reduce the model complexity. This model, called a recursive neuron, is first modelled for binary trees and leads to a higher-order generalised n-ary tree using tensorised aggregation. CP decomposition or Tensor Train (TT) decomposition can further decompose the full format tensor aggregation. Chapter six will introduce more details about tensorised activation functions (Bacciu and Mandic, 2020). The loss function as well can use the decomposed tensor cores of the weights tensor.

In the second ANN building block, the choice of the number of hidden layers and the number of neurons per layer can also benefit from the compressive nature of tensor decompositions algorithms. Tensor Networks can compress the whole Deep Neural Network (DNN) using a suitable tensor decomposition algorithm and then map back to the uncompressed form. Another approach is to update only the final fully connected layer (or specific layers of interest) of a model with a tensor decomposition layer, such as TT. Usually, compressed models benefit from wider fewer layers (shallower networks). Chapter six will also introduce more details about layers' compression (Bacciu and Mandic, 2020).

Back to tensorising datasets, tensor network representations often allow for super-compression of datasets as large as 10^{50} entries, down to the affordable levels of 10^7 or even less. The previous section shows an example of the MNIST dataset of handwritten digits containing images of 28×28 pixels (flattened as 784 pixels) values representing grey shade as integers between 0 and 255. Data in the tensor form can represent a coloured image with pixel values for red content, green content, and blue content as three different values in the (RGB) frames stacked into a 3rd-order tensor. Similarly, a video dataset can include the 3rd-order coloured image frames extended with the time dimension in a 4th-order tensor. This new arrangement of the data will require an alignment of the data slicing into the different epochs. These blocks of tensorised data need to represent the multi-way structures in the dataset identifying latent variables so that the learning iterations can reduce the error.

Domain-transform methods can achieve this representation. The values stored in a given index vector capture interaction between the dimensions/modes. This means symmetric or partially symmetric tensors might be sufficient to capture the inter-mode interactions, ignoring the values in a permuted index (same modes in a different order) in which the value might be redundant. For example, in the EEG dataset, we have F frequency measures collected over T time samples from S channels, forming a 3rd-order tensor. Transforming the domain of this 3rd-order tensor to get the time-frequency decomposition can be achieved using a short-time Fourier transform (STFT) that uses a fixed window size or wavelet transform (WT) that uses variable window sizes inversely proportional to the frequency resolution (high or low). Other transformations can represent data at multi-scale and orientation levels, such as the Gabor, contourlet, or pyramid steerable transformations. More details about the change of basis and representation learning will be discussed in the next chapter.

Furthermore, datasets can contain statistically independent latent variables. Hence, the dataset can be represented by higher-order statistics (cumulants) or by partial derivatives of the observations' Generalised Characteristic Functions (GCF). Using a suitable tensor format, such as the lower-rank core tensors presented in this chapter, enables all the above-discussed transformations and others while keeping the number of parameters smaller. The monograph in (Cichocki *et al.*, 2017, p. 2) provides detailed discussions with examples of various forms of tensorisation that prepare a dataset for a compressed tensorised deep neural network model. This section will present one example in detail.

Chapter one presents tensor vectorisation and matricisation functions and the reverse operation of tensorising a vector or a matrix. The tensorisation depends on considering the vector or matrix as a hierarchical object of data blocks. The segmentation is a process of identifying the index ranges of a block, and then each block range of values becomes the size of the dimension/mode in the resulting tensor. For example, a vector of four elements can be thought of as containing two blocks of each of two elements. This vector can be matricised such that:
M(i,j) = v(i*cols+j), such that M(0,0) = v(0), M(0,1)=v(1), M(1, 0) = v(2), M(1, 1)=v(3).

M matrix is considered a folding of vector v. A higher-order folding yielding tensor $\mathcal{X} \in \mathbb{R}^{I_1 \times I_2 \times \ldots \times I_N}$ is considered a folding of a vector v of length $I_1 \times I_2 \times \ldots \times I_N$, if
$\mathcal{X}(i_1, i_2, \ldots, i_N) = v(i)$, for $0 \leq i_n \leq I_n$for $1 \leq n \leq N$, and for $0 \leq i \leq (I_1 \times I_2 \times \ldots \times I_N)$, $i = 1 + \sum_{n=1}^{N}(i_n - 1)\prod_{k=1}^{n-1} I_k$ as a linear index of $(i_1, i_2, \ldots, i_N)$.
Data or signals come in many structured forms that can be assumed in the tensorisation details. For example, two observations from natural and physical datasets have been helpful. The first observation is that a higher-order folding of a vector of length q^N ($q = 2, 3, \ldots$), sampled from an exponential function $y_k = az^{k-1}$, yields an Nth-order tensor of rank 1. This is called quantisation, such as mapping the continuous, unrestricted data to a quantised discrete restricted set of values. The second observation is that many functions are formed from products and/or sums of trigonometric, polynomial, and rational functions. These can be quantised as shown above to yield (approximate) low-rank tensor train (TT) network formats. These two assumptions can be used in Blind Source Separation (BSS) problem when given a mixture y(t), and it is assumed to be composed of J sources as $y(t) = a_1 x_1(t) + a_2 x_2(t) + \cdots + a_J x_J(t) + n(t)$, where $n(t)$ is added Gaussian noise. Extracting the sources by estimating the mixing matrix A can be done by assuming a higher-order folding $\mathcal{X}$ of the sources with low-rank representations using one of the known tensor decomposition algorithms, such as CP, Tucker, TT, or TR. The multilinearity of this tensorisation keeps the relation between the tensorised mixture $\mathcal{Y}$ and the tensorised sources $\mathcal{X}$ as $\mathcal{Y} = a_1 \mathcal{X}_1 + a_2 \mathcal{X}_2 + \cdots + a_J \mathcal{X}_J + \mathcal{N}$, where $\mathcal{N}$ is the tensorised noise. Decomposing $\mathcal{Y}$ into any TN format, the separate decomposed components will represent the sources up to a scaling ambiguity.

For example, if the mixture signal length was $L = 2^d J^2$, and the sources are contributing to the mixture equally: $a_1\|\mathcal{X}_1\| = a_2\|\mathcal{X}_2\| = \cdots = a_J\|\mathcal{X}_J\|$, we can tensorise the mixture $\mathcal{Y}$ to the dth-order of size $2R \times 2 \times \ldots \times 2 \times 2R$. It is observed that An Nth-order tensor of size
$I_1 \times I_2 \times \ldots \times I_N$, where $I_n \geq 2$, which is reshaped from a sinusoid signal, can be represented by a multilinear rank-$(2,2,\ldots,2)$ tensor. The modulated variants of the Harmonic sinusoidal signals, such as the exponentially decaying signals $\exp(\gamma t)$, are fundamental in many practical applications. Remember that signals such as audio waves are composed of sine waves that are harmonic (periodic) with a given frequency and length. Using a sinusoidal representation will reduce/quantise the representation in the tensorisation step. This tensorisation enables the tensors of $\mathcal{X}_n(t)$ to be represented by tensors in the TT format of rank-$(2,2,\ldots,2)$. In order to separate the J signals $\mathcal{X}_n(t)$ from the mixture $\mathcal{Y}$ (t), the process requires fitting $\mathcal{X}_n$ sequentially to the residual $\mathcal{Y}_n = \mathcal{Y} - \sum_{s \neq n} \mathcal{X}_s$ calculated by the difference between the data tensor $\mathcal{Y}$ and its approximation by the other TT-tensors $\mathcal{X}_s$, where $s \neq n$. Then, a minimisation step of the reconstructed mixtures from $\underset{\mathcal{X}_n}{\operatorname{argmin}}\|\mathcal{Y}_n - \mathcal{X}_n\|_F^2$ for n=1, …, J. In this setup, the signal length L determines the quality of the extraction of the sources and the d value to use in the tensorisation. Other tensorisation methods are suitable for short-length signals, such as multi-way Toeplitz or Hankel tensors (Cichocki *et al.*, 2017, p. 2).
An example of the BSS problem using tensor decomposition is presented in (Böttcher *et al.*, 2018). The authors built a Python Package, “Decompose”, that generalises the PCA, ICA, and NMF solutions to the BSS problem. These methods are built on statistical assumptions that might be found in a dataset or might not be found. Each of them would produce different sources when applied to the same dataset. Expert knowledge is usually needed to identify the correct statistical assumptions of a given dataset in an application domain. The authors built a probabilistic BSS model that estimates the priors of every source, can extend to new prior distributions, scale well to large datasets, assuming each source has a different sparsity level, and efficiently estimates the posterior adapted to the dataset. Their code is published at https://github.com/bethgelab/decompose.

The python notebook ch4.ipynb shows various NN architectures and links to sample tensorial CNN, RNN, and others.

4.6 Summary

All methods discussed earlier are presented in their very introductory intuition. Most of them are computationally expensive for larger tensors. Researchers adopted the Alternating Least Square (ALS) method using approximations of the rank, multiplying the input matrix by random Gaussian matrices, and by iterative methods until convergence. Good approximations have been achieved with very low-rank factors. Many approaches have been proposed to handle large tensors, such as: decomposing only a compressed representation of the original tensor, sparse tensor multiplications for sparse tensors, decomposing a sample (sub-tensor) of the original tensorial data, parallelizing or distributing the decomposition computation, or efficiently using Tensor Networks (Hou, 2017).

Chapter 5: Representation Theory

This chapter discusses when input and/or output data has a structure that a model can benefit from learning its representation using algebraic theories. Representation learning can be unsupervised or semi-supervised to guide learning algorithms and increase their accuracy. The chapter starts with theoretical discussions of abstract algebra foundations required, then how group representation theory is applied in traditional machine learning and neural networks, and then develops to its role in tensor products and their decompositions.

Chapter one introduced machine learning (ML) algorithms using the linear regression example that estimates the weights of an equation that maps the target/dependent variable that could be given in a dataset if prelabelled (supervised) or a state or cluster membership (unsupervised) to the other independent variables of the dataset. This equation, f(x), is called mapping or transformation. Chapter two introduced the importance of dimensionality reduction using projections to orthogonal spaces or embedding or manifold learning. Chapters three and four introduced how this can be done for the multi-way structures using tensor decompositions methods. This chapter introduces representation discovery or learning, which is also a dimensionality reduction and regularisation approach achieved by a change of coordinate systems or basis functions. Dimensionality reduction or representation learning are considered data pre-processing steps to perform before using an ML algorithm. Parametric ML algorithms estimate the input/output mapping function using pre-defined parameters by assuming a particular representation or data distribution, such as fitting a linear or non-linear equation of a given polynomial degree. This is usually attempted using trial and error until a good measure of fitness is achieved. Data visualisation can also help to estimate the appropriate representation manually. The non-parametric machine learning algorithm of the SVM Kernel trick, introduced in chapter two, attempts to learn the representation from the data using kernel methods. This learning will add computational overhead due to permutations having n! elements. However, symmetries that are often found in datasets will reduce the computational overhead. In algebra, we learned how to solve a system of equations, whether linear, quadratic, cubic or even quartic (4th order) equations. Galois, around 1830, showed that each polynomial equation has a finite group of "symmetries" (permutations of its roots that leave its coefficients invariant). The equation is solvable only if its group decomposes in a certain way. A polynomial function of degree five (aka quintic function) in the form $ax^5+bx^4+cx^3+dx^2+ex+f$ of coefficients $(a, b, c, d, e, f) \in \mathbb{R}$ or $\mathbb{C}$, is not solvable because it contains the non-Abelien simple group A_5 of even permutations of five objects. The same applies to equations of a polynomial degree of $n \geq 5$. This is why we need to understand groups and their role in modular arithmetic and in understanding non-Euclidean geometries. Mathematicians continued identifying solutions to finite simple groups and how to generalise them to continuous groups until the Lie Algebra formulated differential equations and their symmetries, forming continuous groups that are generated from infinitesimal elements. This approach made continuous groups decompose into simpler, solvable groups and enabled solving polynomial equations of higher degrees.

A symmetrisation step can be included as a dimensionality reduction or compression technique with an acceptable loss and work as regularisation. Furthermore, the variables in x can be members of one or more groups in the dataset. These groups can be reducible to subgroups and have properties that make learning this equation's coefficients easier. Algebraic group theory, Lie theory, and representation theory (often mean the same thing) and their properties capture symmetries and are often used in the various machine learning algorithms. This will facilitate our understanding and ability to apply and advance these algorithms as required.

The first section introduces abstract algebra as a recent player in machine learning algorithms to achieve modular programming that benefits from symmetries and group decomposition representation, along with python examples. Computer scientists are already familiar with object-oriented inheritance and polymorphism properties. These concepts enable modular programming such that extra functionality is added or existing functionality is eliminated during inheritance from superstructures to substructures. This enables polymorphic methods that operate differently based on the structure of their parameters. This is how algebraic objects are related in a tree structure of inheritance and polymorphism with different operations and properties.

Then, the second section progresses into Harmonic analysis using Fourier Transforms and Wavelet analysis that discovers the representation basis of a given dataset. The Laplace operator will be further explained for its role in revealing symmetries. Then a third section on learning in the Hilbert space using kernel methods will discuss how this can also be performed on group representations of datasets. The fourth section on invariance summarises how all the above methods are actually learning the new invariant subspace basis representing a dataset input or output spaces. A final section on applications of these approaches will discuss various representation learning applications in various domains.

The last chapter presented the BSS problem and how it is solved using tensorisation such that the symmetries and the unique properties of the sinusoidal signals are used to solve the separation. The topics of this chapter will explain another geometric definition of tensors as positive definite symmetric matrices. To understand symmetries, we need to learn abstract algebra. Abstract algebra, as its name suggests, abstracts not only Algebra but also many different tools used in other math topics such as geometry, number theory, and topology, such that the same abstract tools can be used in all of them. Groups are fundamental objects to many abstract objects that build upon them, such as rings, fields, vector spaces and modules. We covered fields and vector spaces in the previous chapters and will focus on the remaining concepts. The main aim is to understand how machine learning algorithms map datasets such as collections of images, problem states in Reinforcement Learning (RL), or words in natural language processing (NLP), into an implicit vector space or group without redundancy and how mappings to output space can be achieved using algebraic methods.

This chapter, again, is full of mathematical definitions and equations. Once again, the aim is not to discuss the derivations, proofs, or all properties. The aim is to familiarise the reader with the wealth of mappings between groups, subgroups, symmetries, reducing groups, composing groups, rings, and modules. Machine learning algorithms employ these concepts by taking advantage of equivalence between computationally expensive structures and their equivalent or approximate representations reducing the computational overload. The material covered in this chapter is summarised from (Stillwell, 2008), (Gilmore, 2005), (Risi Kondor, 2008), (Milne, 2021), (Mahadevan, 2008), and many examples from the Socratica YouTube channel. This chapter cannot be a source to study these concepts thoroughly, but it can serve as an appetiser to expand the reader's horizon and create a unified ML context of these topics.

5.1 Group and Representation Theory

Group theory is a branch of abstract algebra that studies groups satisfying certain axioms, such as the representation theory of symmetric groups.

5.1.1 Group Theory Main Structures

5.1.1.1 Sets

A set is a collection of objects that do not necessarily have any additional structure or properties.

5.1.1.2 Group

A group G is defined as a set of elements such as x, y, with an operation $G \times G \to G$ producing results as xy or $x.y$ as the product of the elements. Multiplication $\times$ and addition $+$ are the most used group operations since division can be rewritten as multiplication with reciprocals, and subtraction can be rewritten as addition with negatives. The operation can be generalised as * for abstractness. A finite group is described by its **order** (number of elements or **cardinality**) as $|G|$ and can be continuous or discrete, and has four axioms: **closure, associativity, identity, and inverse**. The **closure** axiom is defined as the group operation result also being a group member. For multiplication operation groups, $xy \in G$ for all x, y members of G. For addition operation groups, $x + y \in G$. This is generalised/abstracted to $x * y \in G$. The **associativity** axiom is defined such that for any $x, y, z \in G$, also $(xy)z = x(yz) \in G$ in multiplication operations or $(x + y) + z = x + (y + z) \in G$ in addition operations, and abstracted to $(x * y) * z = x * (y * z) \in G$. The **identity element** is defined such that $ex = xe = x \in G$, which is 1 in the multiplication operation and 0 for the addition operation, and abstracted as $e * x = x * e = x \in G$. The **inverse** axiom is defined such that $xx^{-1} = e$ for multiplication operation such that the reciprocal is the inverse or $x + (-x) = e$ for addition operations such that the negative value is the inverse and abstracted as $x * (x^{-1}) = e$. Commutativity axiom as in $(x * y) = (y * x)$ if existing in a group, then it is an Abelian group. Symmetric groups are not Abelian except when their order n is less than or equal to two. A group can be defined by listing its elements and multiplication table or a table showing other operations called the Cayley table.

For example, the Integer numbers group $\mathbb{Z}$ is an infinite group closed under the addition operation to maintain all the above axioms. Given $x, y, z \in \mathbb{Z}$, **closure**: when x=2, y=3, and z=4, then x+y=2+3=5 $\in \mathbb{Z}$; **associativity** $(x + y) + z = x + (y + z)$ is $(2 + 3) + 4 = 2 + (3 + 4) = 9 \in \mathbb{Z}$, **identity element** 0, such that $e * x = x * e = x \in G$ is $0 + 2 = 2 + 0 = 2 \in G$; and **inverse** $x + (-x) = e$ is $2 + (-2) = 0$. We can solve an equation using these axioms, such as:

```
x+3=5                    Integer Under addition
(x+3)+(-3) = 5+(-3)      Inverse
(x+3)+(-3) = 2           Closed Under addition
x+(3+(-3)) = 2           Associativity
x+0=2                    Identity
x=2
```

Other examples for different orders are shown in the following table, starting from order one, the trivial group, which would contain the identity element only. For the different orders, the multiplication/Cayley table starting from the identity element is shown in the table:

Order 1

	e
e	e

Order 2 $\cong \frac{\mathbb{Z}}{2\mathbb{Z}}$(integers mod 2)

	e	a
e	e	a
a	a	e

Order 3, which is the only one $\cong \frac{\mathbb{Z}}{3\mathbb{Z}}$(integers mod 3), isomorphic groups

	e	a	b
e	e	a	b
a	a	b	e
b	b	e	a

There are only four groups of order four; three of them are equivalent, which means only two order four groups up to isomorphism both are Abelian of prime power order: 1) Cyclic group of order four, 2) Klein Viergruppe four group, the product of the quotient group $\frac{\mathbb{Z}}{2\mathbb{Z}}$ with itself (the group of order two explained above multiplied with itself).

The cyclic group of order 4, using additive notation

	0 (identity)	1 (generator)	2	3 (generator)
0	0	1	2	3
1	1	2	3	0
2	2	3	0	1
3	3	0	1	2

The cyclic group of order 4, using multiplication notation

	e (identity)	x (generator)	x^2	x^3 (generator)
e	e	x	x^2	x^3
x	x	x^2	x^3	e

Klein Viergruppe V as isomorphic to: $\frac{\mathbb{Z}}{2\mathbb{Z}} \times \frac{\mathbb{Z}}{2\mathbb{Z}}$

	e	a	b	c
e	e	a	b	c
a	a	e	c	b
b	b	c	e	a
c	c	b	a	e

x_2	x^2	x^3	e	x
x_3	x^3	e	x	x^2

Notice that in all the previous Cayley tables, every row and every column should contain the **identity** element once because of the existence of the **inverse** of every element. **No duplicate** element in any row or column because if there is any, then there is an equivalence (redundancy) between the group elements. If the table is symmetric (if you flip it around the diagonal, you get the same table), then the group is Abelian (commutative) such that a*b=b*a.

5.1.1.3 Rings

A ring extends the group by being a set of elements defined with operations $+/-$ and $\times$. The $+$ operation has negative numbers as inverses such that the subtraction operation is also included. The $\times$ operation has no inverses as the reciprocals are not included in the ring. Rings are commutative under $+$, which is Abelian under addition, and associative under $\times$, such that $a \times (b \times c) = (a \times b) \times c$. Rings' distributive property links both addition and multiplication operations: $a \times (b + c) = a \times b + a \times c$. Elements can be generalised to polynomials and matrices. If a ring is commutative under multiplication, it is a commutative ring. If G has identity 1, it is called a "ring with identity" because rings naturally have zero additive identity. A **Unit** in a ring R is the element $x \in R$ that has a multiplicative inverse $x^{-1} \in R$, such that $x.x^{-1} = 1$. All units in a ring form the **group of units** $R^{\times}$, which is a group under multiplication. In $\mathbb{Z}$ ring, the group of Units is $\mathbb{Z}^{\times} = \{1, -1\}$ since all other multiplicative inverses will yield a fraction. In $\frac{\mathbb{Z}}{12\mathbb{Z}}$ ring, the group of Units is $\left(\frac{\mathbb{Z}}{n\mathbb{Z}}\right)^{\times} = \{1, 5, 7, 11\}$; this can be verified from the Cayley table of the ring. Any integer $\mathbb{Z}$ multiplied by the units' set yields associates, such as for $\mathbb{Z}^{\times}$, the associates are {2, -2}, {3, -3} and so forth. Associates are important in identifying equivalent factorisations and ignoring unit factors. The fundamental theorem of Arithmetic states that every integer n except 0, 1, and -1, has a prime factorisation that is unique up to order and associates. For example, a ring $R = \left\{\begin{bmatrix} a & b \\ c & d \end{bmatrix} \middle| a, b, c, d \in \mathbb{Z}\right\}$ has a unit matrix $\begin{bmatrix} 2 & 7 \\ 1 & 4 \end{bmatrix}$, to which the multiplicative inverse (the matrix inverse) = $\begin{bmatrix} 4 & -7 \\ -1 & 2 \end{bmatrix} \in \mathbb{Z}$, and identity matrix $\begin{bmatrix} 1 & 0 \\ 0 & 1 \end{bmatrix}$. Not all matrices in R have multiplicative inverses and the group of units $R^{\times}$= matrices A with determinant (A)= ±1.

An example of infinite rings is the group of Integer numbers $\mathbb{Z}$ under $+, -, \times$, such that addition, subtraction, and multiplication of two integers yields an integer, but division yields a fraction, which is not an element of $\mathbb{Z}$. Another example is the infinite group of polynomials $f(x) = a_n x^n + a_{n-1} x^{n-1} + \cdots + a_2 x^2 + a_1 x + a_0$ such that addition, subtraction, and multiplication of two polynomials yield a polynomial, but division yields a non-polynomial. The polynomials ring is a commutative ring with identity. Coefficients can be integers, complex numbers, $\frac{\mathbb{Z}}{n\mathbb{Z}}$, matrices, or any ring. Rings can be used in composing rings, such as a ring of polynomials in which the coefficients are rings. A ring of matrices is not commutative because a change in the order of matrix multiplication yield different results.

The quotient group example of $\frac{\mathbb{Z}}{2\mathbb{Z}}$ take the group/ring $\mathbb{Z}$ and divide it by the **normal subgroup/ideal** (both will be defined below) $2\mathbb{Z}$ yielding finite rings. This class of finite rings containing $\frac{\mathbb{Z}}{n\mathbb{Z}}$ groups, except when n is prime p, then $\frac{\mathbb{Z}}{p\mathbb{Z}}$ is a field, which is also a ring. Every field is a ring, but not every ring is a field, as shown in Figure 62.

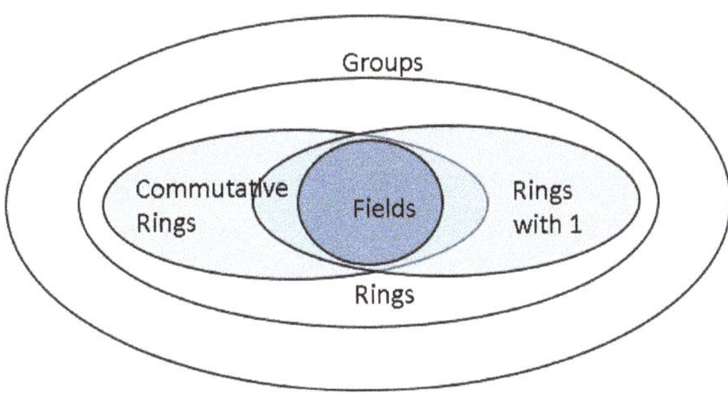

Figure 62: Groups, Rings, and Fields.

5.1.1.4 Fields

Fields are defined in chapter one and redefined in chapter three. Fields $\mathbb{F}$ extend the abstract algebra ring objects as elements on which the four algebraic operations are defined, $+, -, \times, \div$. For abstract algebra generalisation, these operations are redefined as addition, additive inverses, multiplication, and multiplicative inverses. For example, real numbers of fractions $\mathbb{R}$, integer numbers $\mathbb{Z}$, natural numbers $\mathbb{N}$, rational numbers of decimals $\mathbb{Q}$, complex numbers $\mathbb{C}$, and prime fields $\frac{\mathbb{Z}}{p\mathbb{Z}}$ such as $\frac{\mathbb{Z}}{2\mathbb{Z}}, \frac{\mathbb{Z}}{5\mathbb{Z}}, \ldots$, etc., are illustrated in Figure 63, such that ($\mathbb{N} \subset \mathbb{Z} \subset \mathbb{Q} \subset \mathbb{R} \subset \mathbb{F}$), and ($\mathbb{C} \subset \mathbb{F}$).

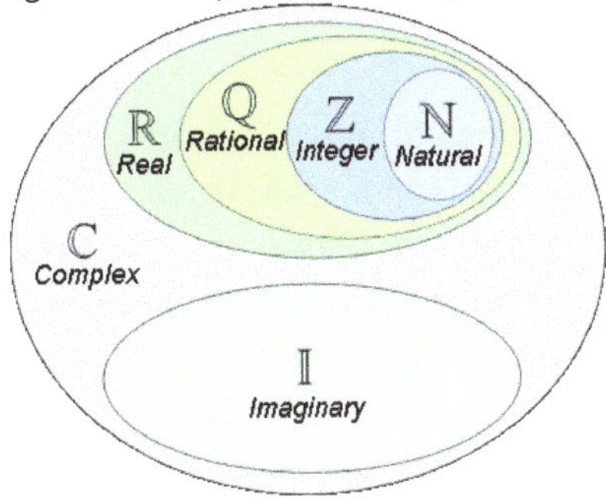

Figure 63:Fields of Numbers as sets/groups/rings, from https://www.mathsisfun.com/sets/number-types.html.

These are all infinite fields because they have all the properties of rings with identity, commutative under multiplication, and include multiplicative inverses. Fields are defined as two groups combined: field $\mathbb{F}$ under addition $\langle \mathbb{F}, + \rangle$ as a commutative group, and Field $\mathbb{F}$ under multiplication $\langle \mathbb{F}^{\times}, \cdot \rangle$ as a commutative group, linking addition and multiplication by the distributive property. Infinite fields can be extended, forming other fields. The integer group $\mathbb{Z}$ can be extended with multiplicative inverses, including fractions, to become the field $\mathbb{Q}$. If we extend $\mathbb{R}$ with an imaginary number to solve equations such as $i^2+1=0$ that needs i^2 to be = -1, and hence i= $\sqrt{-1}$, then this defines the complex numbers field $\mathbb{C}$ as a 2D numbering system. $\mathbb{C} = \mathbb{R} + i_1\mathbb{R}, {i_1}^2 = -1$, which is the largest field that can not be extended, and it is algebraically closed, such as any polynomial equation in $\mathbb{C}$ can be solved in $\mathbb{C}$. $\mathbb{C}$ can be extended by variables such as $\mathbb{C}(x)$ or multivariable such as $\mathbb{C}(x_1, \ldots, x_n)$. Just as much as any vector in $\mathbb{R}^n$ is a linear combination of n basis vector e_i as $v=v_1e_1+ \ldots + v_ne_n$, also, any $\mathbb{C}$ vector is a linear combination of bases, except that each v_i, has 2 components as $v_i=v_{i0}+v_{i1}i$. This means 2N-dimensions are needed to represent a N-dimension $\mathbb{C}$ in $\mathbb{R}$. A change of bases in $\mathbb{R}$ using an invertible transformation matrix A is applied as $e_j = A^i_j e_i$ and the inverse mapping is as $e_i = \left(A^i_j\right)^{-1} e_j = A^j_i e_j$. The same change of basis rules applies to $\mathbb{C}$.

We can construct the quaternions Q from the complex numbers $\mathbb{C}$ as $Q = \mathbb{C} + i_2\mathbb{C}$, such that ${i_2}^2 = -1, i_1 i_2 = -i_2 i_1$, this makes the quaternions a 4D numbering system that can be expressed as $Q = a + bi + cj + dk$ such that $i^2=j^2=k^2=ijk=-1$, and can be represented as an ordered pair binary form of real (a) and vector part v = (b, c, d) $Q = [a \in \mathbb{R}, v \in \mathbb{R}^3]$. The multiplication operation is a non-commutative quaternion product with multiplication identity one, defined similarly to the cross product of unit cartesian vectors as follows:

	1	i	j	k
1	1	i	j	k
i	i	-1	k	-j
j	j	-k	-1	i
k	k	j	-i	-1

A Cayley field can be constructed from quaternions as well as the 3D rotation groups, as explained below. Similar modular construction applies, such as quaternions can have a change of basis and be represented as Complex numbers $\mathbb{C}$ using 2N dimensions and real $\mathbb{R}$ using 4N dimensions. Further expansions, such as the Octonions, are possible, but they are non-associative such that $u(vw) \neq (uv)w$ sometimes and hence not a Field, and cannot be represented in matrix form. With every expansion, some properties are lost. Convergent sequences Limits can also be used to limit $\mathbb{Q}$ to $\mathbb{R}$. For example, finite fields are Galois fields containing a finite number of elements, such as the integer mod p, where p is a prime number.

5.1.1.5 Vector Spaces

Vector spaces are defined in chapter one as well. They have the properties of allowing addition and scaling operations and commutative, including the zero vector, identity element, inverses, and associative. These properties generalise vector spaces as commutative groups under addition operation with the additional operation of scaling with its distributive property. Even scalars can be generalised abstractly from any given Field, not necessarily real numbers. This redefines the vector space to a commutative/Abelian group V containing vectors v as elements, under + operation, that has a field of scalars $\mathbb{F}$, if $v \in V, f \in \mathbb{F} \Rightarrow f.v \in V$ such that $f.v$ is a scaled vector with distributive property $f.(v_1 + v_2) = f.v_1 + f.v_2$, and $(f_1 + f_2).v = f_1.v + f_2.v$, associative property $f_1.(f_2.v) = (f_1 \times f_2).v$ and scaling identity 1. For example, a polynomial of degree 5 or less is a vector space V such that adding two polynomials always keeps or reduces the polynomial degree by cancellations but never increases the degree. Polynomials can be scaled, keeping the degree. Another example of a vector space is the space of continuous functions. Vector spaces are of finite dimensions determined by n, with basis vectors $\{e_1, \dots, e_n\}$, such that Vector components are defined as $V = f_1 e_1 + \dots + f_n e_n$ such that $f_i \in$ field of scalars $\mathbb{F}$, which makes V isomorphic to $\mathbb{F}^n$: $V \cong \mathbb{F}^n$.

5.1.1.6 Modules

The vector spaces are generalised to Modules, such that scalars are not Fields but rings, and the elements of a Module do not need to be vectors. This defines Module M to be an Abelian group of m elements, with Ring R scalars of r elements, such that r.m is a scaled element with distributive property $r(m_1 + m_2) = r.m_1 + r.m_2$, and $(r_1 + r_2).m = r_1.m + r_2.m$, associative property $r_1.(r_2.m) = (r_1.r_2).m$ and scaling identity 1. For example, M is any Abelian group of elements a, with R = $\mathbb{Z}$ scalars, on which the scalar multiplication is defined r.a $\in M$. Every Abelian group is a $\mathbb{Z}$-module. Another example is a Module M of elements as 2x3 matrices = $\left\{\begin{bmatrix} m_{11} & m_{12} & m_{13} \\ m_{21} & m_{22} & m_{23} \end{bmatrix} | m_{ij} \in \mathbb{Z}\right\}$, with R = $\mathbb{Z}$ scalars, and scalar multiplication:

$$r.\begin{bmatrix} m_{11} & m_{12} & m_{13} \\ m_{21} & m_{22} & m_{23} \end{bmatrix} = \begin{bmatrix} r.m_{11} & r.m_{12} & r.m_{13} \\ r.m_{21} & r.m_{22} & r.m_{23} \end{bmatrix}$$

A third example shows that Modules with vector elements can do more than vector spaces, is when the scalars are not defined in $\mathbb{Z}$ but as a Ring of matrix $R = \left\{ \begin{bmatrix} a_{11} & a_{12} & a_{13} \\ a_{21} & a_{22} & a_{23} \\ a_{31} & a_{32} & a_{33} \end{bmatrix} | a_{ij} \in \mathbb{R} \right\}$ which are not sure to be invertible and not commutative but have an identity matrix 3x3. When M= $\mathbb{R}^3 = \{(x, y, z)|x, y, z \in \mathbb{R}\}$ under +, the scalar multiplication r.m = matrix multiplication. Modules can be isomorphic to n copies of Ring scalars R similar to vector spaces, which is called finitely generated. Another finitely generated module that is not n copies of R, is $\mathbb{Z} \times \left(\frac{\mathbb{Z}}{2\mathbb{Z}}\right) \times 4\mathbb{Z}$. In addition, Modules can be infinitely generated, such as the free Modules. This complexity of Modules enables the decomposition of scalar Rings that we can not do with Fields as scalars in Vector spaces.

5.1.1.7 Algebras

A linear algebra A consists of a collection of vectors $v_1, v_2 \dots, v_n \in V$, a collection of fields $f_1, f_2 \dots, f_n \in \mathbb{F}$, a field, and three kinds of operations (α) vector addition, (β) scalar multiplication, and (γ) vector multiplication. For the vector space collection, closure, associativity, identity, inverse, and commutativity hold. Other algebras can be defined based on which properties they hold. For example, an algebra of a set of real n × n matrices forms a real n^2-dimensional vector space under matrix addition and scalar multiplication. An associative algebra adds matrix multiplication to the previous algebra. The first algebra example has a subspace of $n \times n$ symmetric matrices $(S_{ij})^T = S_{ji} = +S_{ij}$. Symmetric matrices matrix multiplication does not yield symmetric matrices output. Symmetrisation of two symmetric matrices, S, and T, is defined as: $[S, T]_+ = ST + TS$. The anti-commutation relation is $[S, \alpha T_1 + \beta T_2]_+ = \alpha[S, T_1]_+ + \beta[S, T_2]_+$. A symmetrisation operation and anti-commutation form an algebra from symmetric matrices. An Anti-symmetrisation operation of two antisymmetric matrices A, and B, such that $A^T = -A$, $A_{ij} = -A_{ji}$, is defined as: : $[A, B] = AB - BA$. The commutation property is defined as $[A, \beta B_1 + \gamma B_2] = \beta[A, B_1] + \gamma[A, B_2]$. The antisymmetric multiplication and the commutation relations form an algebra called Lie Algebra from antisymmetric matrices, provided that the combinatorial antisymmetrisation operation obeys $[A, [B, C]] = [[A, B], C] - [B, [A, C]]$, which identifies the Jacobi identity: $[A, [B, C]] + [C, [A, B]] + [B, [C, A]] = 0$. More details on Lie Algebra will follow. If an Algebra has a norm and a division, it is called a normed division algebra, in which only four exist, the real numbers $\mathbb{R}$, the complex numbers $\mathbb{C}$, the quaternions Q, and the octonions O.

5.1.2 Main Concepts & Definitions

The algebraic structures (group, field, and others mentioned previously) can be mapped into another similar algebraic structure, keeping some or all of its structural properties. A realisation is a mapping into an algebraic structure that can be written down concretely and described analytically. A representation is a mapping into a set of matrices.

The following describes the main concepts and definitions from which many algorithms benefit, such as the conjugate gradient (CG) method (https://scipy-lectures.org/advanced/mathematical_optimization/) used in applying the tensor completion example presented at the end of chapter four. Many algorithms employ these equivalent decompositions to achieve faster computation.

Let us start by defining conjugacy. Two group elements, x and y, are said to be **conjugate**, which means equivalent if there is a $t \in G$ such that $t^{-1}xt = y$. This can partition group G into **conjugacy classes**. For any two x, and y conjugate vectors, any vector parallel to x and y, is also conjugate. The conjugate gradient algorithm uses conjugacy to reduce the number of iterations required to minimise a quadratic equation. Being linearly independent is being orthogonal in a vector space, but conjugacy means a transformation can make two vectors orthogonal in another space (Haykin, 2009).

Hermitian conjugacy denoted as A^*, A^H or $A^\dagger$, is complex square matrices that are equal to their conjugate transpose $A = A^{*T}$. The symmetry is captured such as an element, at i,j indices, is equal to its conjugate, at j, i indices: $a_{ij} = a^*_{ji}$. The adjoint of an operator is the infinite-dimensional generalisation of conjugate transpose, where you find the transpose of an operator (in matrix form, this is done by $A^T_{ij} = A_{ji}$ and then take the complex conjugate of it. This can be done in any order $(A)^*_{ij} = ((A)^T_{ij})^* = ((A_{ij})^*)^T = A^*_{ji}$.
We need to understand subgroups and simple groups to prepare for group decompositions. **Subgroups** are defined as $H \leq G$, when elements of H are subsets of G, and H has a group invertible operation. Any group G has at least two **normal subgroups**, G is a subgroup of itself, and the **trivial group** that contains one identity element $\{e\}$ is a subgroup of any group. A **proper subgroup** is $H < G$, such that both elements are not equal. **Lagrange theorem** states that the order of H divides the order of G: given $H \leq G \Rightarrow |H|$ divides $|G|$. For example, if the number of elements in G, $|G| = 323$, the factors dividing 323 are 1, 17, 19, and 323. The subgroup H containing one element is the identity element, G itself is the subgroup containing all its elements, and there might be two other subgroups containing 17 and 19 elements.
A **simple group** has no other groups except the identity group and is a building block for other groups, such as prime numbers to the Integers group. There are four classes of simple groups defined as follows:

1. An Abelian group of Integer mod p group under addition: $\frac{\mathbb{Z}}{p\mathbb{Z}}, +$, where p is a prime number, which leads to having only two subgroups, the trivial identity group {0}, and the whole group $\frac{\mathbb{Z}}{p\mathbb{Z}}$, which is the definition of a simple group. Because prime numbers are infinite, there is an infinite number of groups in this class.
2. The alternating non-Abelian group A_n was proven to be simple for n≥5, and will be further explained while discussing normal series and their role in solving polynomial equations.
3. Groups of Lie type will be further explained below.
4. 26 Sporadic Groups do not fit into any category, among which a monster group contains 20 out of the 26 groups.

Conjugate subgroup H^t is isomorphic of subgroup H of group G for any element $\in G$. H^x is defined as $H^x\colon \{x^{-1}hx | h \in H, x \in G.\}$. If $H^x = H$, then H is a **normal subgroup or self-conjugate subgroup** $H \trianglelefteq G$. A normal subgroup H of group G is defined such that $H\colon \{x^{-1}hx | h \in H, x \in G.\}$, where x may or may not be in H. All subgroups of cyclic groups are normal, and one subgroup of Abelian groups is normal. An example normal subgroup is $n\mathbb{Z} \trianglelefteq \mathbb{Z}$, such as $2\mathbb{Z} \trianglelefteq \mathbb{Z}$.
Measures of equivalence and similarity will make group decomposition feasible. Isomorphism, homomorphism, kernels, automorphism, and isometry will be defined next. **Isomorphism** is when two groups (having similar structures/equal form) $G \cong G'$ has one-to-one mapping $\emptyset\colon G \rightarrow G'$, such that $\emptyset(x)\emptyset(y) = \emptyset(xy)$ for all $x, y \in G$. This leads to considering both groups as the same group. For example, two groups: G the finite integer mod 4 with addition operation: $\frac{\mathbb{Z}}{4\mathbb{Z}}, +$, and the group H containing elements {1, -1, i, -i} with multiplication operation. The Cayley tables for both groups are defined below and coloured for similarity. The identity element is coloured red; the second element, 1 in the first group, is highlighted in green. It needed a swap between the second and third elements in the second group to match the structure. The third element is highlighted in blue, and the last element is highlighted in magenta. The colour map shows that both groups have the same structure and are isomorphic. Abstractly they are the same group, regardless of the different operations and elements.

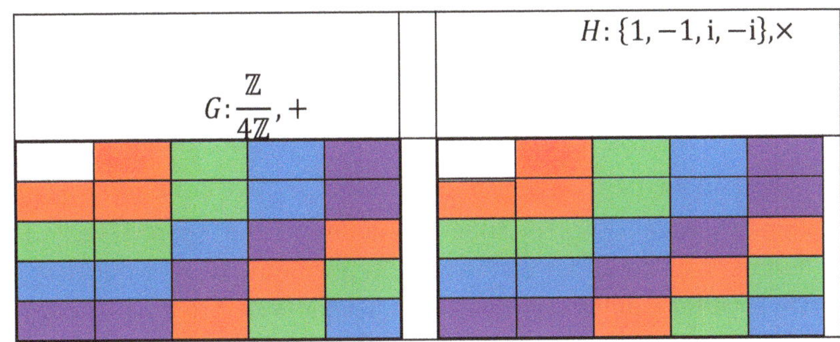

Homomorphism is when mapping between two groups $\emptyset: G \to H$ preserves the same structure such that $\emptyset(x)\emptyset(y) = \emptyset(xy)$ for all $x, y \in G$, but without one-to-one mapping. A homomorphic group is an **embedding** such as a subgroup or a **quotient map**. For example, the infinite integer group with addition operation: $\mathbb{Z}, +$, and the finite integer mod 2 with addition operation: $\frac{\mathbb{Z}}{2\mathbb{Z}}, +$, containing two elements {0, 1}. The first group: $\mathbb{Z}, +$, can be broken into two sets: $\mathbb{Z} = \{evens\} \cup \{odds\}$, such that the operations in the first columns in the following table are defined, and the operations for the second group $\frac{\mathbb{Z}}{2\mathbb{Z}}$, are defined in the second column. If you replace even with zero and odd with 1, then both columns are the same.

$\mathbb{Z}, +$ divided into $\mathbb{Z} = \{evens\} \cup \{odds\}$	$\frac{\mathbb{Z}}{2\mathbb{Z}}, +$
even + even = even	0+0=0(mod 2),
even + odd = odd	0+1=1(mod 2),
odd + even = odd	1+0=1(mod 2),
odd + odd = even	1+1=0(mod 2)

We can define a mapping function between these two groups: $f: \mathbb{Z} \to \frac{\mathbb{Z}}{2\mathbb{Z}} = \begin{cases} 1 \; if \; \mathbb{Z} \; is \; odd \\ 0 \; if \; \mathbb{Z} \; is \; even \end{cases}$.

To generalise this concept to any two groups $G, *$ and $H, \diamond$ with abstract operations, we attempt defining a mapping function between both groups $f: G \to H$ such that for $x, y \in G$, we have $f(x), f(y) \in H$, and $f(x * y) = f(x) \diamond f(y)$, sending identities to identities and inverses to inverses. In the isomorphism example, the mapping for identities is $f: 0_G \to 1_H$ and the mapping for inverses is $f: 1_G \to i_H, f: 3_G \to -i_H$, and this is the inverse of the identity $f: 2_G \to -1_H$. For homomorphism, this function does not need to be one-to-one/injection nor onto/surjection. For isomorphism, it needs to be both 1-1 and onto, which is a bijection. The mapping function does not need to be invertible for both testing for homomorphism and isomorphism. If we can construct such a mapping, these two groups are homomorphic, and if they are of the same cardinality, they are isomorphic. This is very important to identify similar and identical groups and their fundamental building blocks. This is what we did in chapter two to factorise a matrix to decompose into dominant submatrices such as SVD, and we did it in chapter four for tensor factorisation/decomposition as well.

A Kernel of a group homomorphism $f: G \to H$ measures how similar these two groups are, i.e., how far the mapping function is far from a one-to-one function. This is done by mapping all elements in G to the identity element in H. Different mapping functions have different kernels. If f is an isomorphism, then the kernel is the identity element. If f is not an isomorphism, then at least two elements in G map to the identity element in H. This makes the definition of the kernel be: $ker(f) = \{x \in G | f(x) = 1_H\}$. Here is at least one mapping of identities both ways in the kernel in the case of isomorphism as a one-to-one mapping, and there will be more than or equal to two mappings in the kernel in the case of homomorphism. This defines the kernel as a subgroup of G.

Automorphism is when a group is mapped to itself, such that the set of automorphisms of G forms a group under composition, denoted Aut(G). For example, all permutations of a graph, such as the connections of its vertices, remain the same, i.e., maintaining the same graph topology, which is called the automorphism group of this graph.

Isometry groups are the group of transformations of a metric space that leave the metric invariant.

5.1.3 Group Types

Infinite but countable groups, such as the set of integers in $\mathbb{Z}$ under addition operation, and the **cyclic group** of order n, denoted $\mathbb{Z}_n$, or $\frac{\mathbb{Z}}{n\mathbb{Z}}$ or C_n. **The order of an element** $x \in G$, is the smallest positive integer n such that $x^n = e$ and is defined as $|x| = n$. When there is no value for n, then the order of the element is infinite. For multiplication group on non-zero Real numbers $\mathbb{R}$, the order of the identity element $|1| = 1$ because it has no inverse, while $|-1| = 2$ because $(-1)^2 = 1$. Other elements in this group have infinite orders.
Uncountable Topological groups, such as Group G with topology $f(x) = x^{-1}$ as a continuous map $f : G \rightarrow G$; and $g(x, y) = xy$ as a continuous map $g: G \times G \rightarrow G$. A topology is a system of G subsets called open sets that obey certain axioms and are invariant under translation. An example of uncountable topological groups is the Hawaiian earring space, defined as a group of $\mathbb{R}^2$ Eucleadian Circles with centers 1/n for n=1, 2, 3, ...
A compact group is a topological group of open sets that can be covered/bounded with a subset of its elements. A locally compact group is a topological group in which any group element has a compact neighbourhood. A space T is compact if every infinite sequence of points t_1, t_2, ...,($t_i \in$ T) contains a subsequence of points that (a) converges to a point and (b) this point is in T. For example, the real line $\mathbb{R}^1$ is not compact because the sequence of points t_i = i, i = 1, 2,... does not have a convergent subsequence. The circumference of the unit circle in $\mathbb{R}^2$ is compact. The interior of the unit circle is not compact because the sequence of points t_n = 1 – 1/n, n = 1, 2,..., converges to a point on the circumference and, therefore, is not in the original set.
Abelian groups are commutative groups such that $xy = yx$, which are much simpler than the non-commutative groups.
Symmetric groups $\mathbb{S}_n$, is defined as a finite group under function composition ∘ from the n! permutations of a set of degree n, S = {1, 2, ..., n}, such that $|\mathbb{S}_n| = n!$. $\sigma_2\sigma_1$ is the permutation that we get by permuting {1, 2, . . . , n} first according to σ_1 and then, according to σ_2. It is considered as group G acting on set S as a subgroup of $\mathbb{S}_n$ denoted $\mathbb{S}_{|S|}$. Symmetric groups are very important in machine learning and computational algebra because, according to the Cayley theorem, every finite group is a subgroup of a Symmetric group. **The two-line notation** of a permutation places the input on the top row and the output mapping in the bottom row. For example, a permutation σ is defined for $\mathbb{S}_4$ as:
$\sigma = \begin{bmatrix} 1 & 2 & 3 & 4 \\ 1 & 3 & 4 & 2 \end{bmatrix}$, such that $\sigma(1) = 1, \sigma(2) = 3, \sigma(3) = 4, and\ \sigma(4) = 2$. This enables handling permutations as functions and enables function composition. The relations $\sigma_2(\sigma_1(i)) = (\sigma_2\sigma_1)(i)$ for all $\sigma_1, \sigma_2 \in \mathbb{S}_n$ and i = 1, 2, . . . , n, define group operations. For example, if $\sigma_1 = \sigma$ defined above, and $\sigma_2 = \begin{bmatrix} 1 & 2 & 3 & 4 \\ 4 & 3 & 2 & 1 \end{bmatrix}$, then $\sigma_2\sigma_1 = \begin{bmatrix} 1 & 2 & 3 & 4 \\ 2 & 4 & 3 & 1 \end{bmatrix}$ by tracing the mapping from the top row to the bottom row in $\sigma_2$first, then continue from the top row to the bottom row in σ_1. The intermediate step is $\begin{bmatrix} 4 & 3 & 2 & 1 \\ 2 & 4 & 3 & 1 \end{bmatrix}$. $\sigma_2\sigma_1 \neq \sigma_1\sigma_2$ because $\mathbb{S}_4$is not Abelian. Only $\mathbb{S}_1$and $\mathbb{S}_2$ are Abelian.
Cycle notation allows writing a permutation in one line as an ordered subset $s_1, s_2, \ldots, s_k$ of {1, 2, ... , n}, such that $\sigma(s_i) = s_{i+1}$ for i < k and $\sigma(s_k) = s_1$. For example, a permutation σ for $\mathbb{S}_4$ defined above in the cycle notation is (1)(2, 3,4), such that the permutation σ is a product of 2 cycles, the first is one mapping to itself in a 1-cycle, and the second is 2 → 3, 3 → 4, and 4 → 2 in a 3-cycle. 1-cycles can be omitted as they do not change anything. A 2-cycle is a transposition. The order of elements in a cycle is not important as they rotate to reach each other, and the order of the cycles does not matter. Therefore, it is advised to start with the smallest number. If a permutation composition has repeated elements in each permutation mapping cycle, then the order of the cycles will matter. For example $\sigma_2{}^\circ\sigma_1 = (1,4)(2,3)^\circ(2,3,4) \neq \sigma_1{}^\circ\sigma_2 = (2,3,4)^\circ(1,4)(2,3)$.
The **cycle-type** of σ is a list of the lengths of all the cycles making up σ, encoded as a partition on integer n, denoted $\lambda \vdash n$, such as $\lambda = (\lambda_1, \lambda_2, \ldots, \lambda_k)\ with\ \lambda_i \leq \lambda_{i+1}$ for i=1, ..., k-1 such that $n = \sum_{i=1}^{k} \lambda_i$, and k is the partition λ length. The partition of the previous example σ is = (1,3) , k=2, and $\lambda \vdash n$ is $(1,3) \vdash 4$.

A cyclic group G with multiplication operation is defined as generated by one element x in a cyclic way. For example, for $x \in G$, the smallest subset H containing x should contain x, its inverse, the identity element 1, and all powers of x and its inverses: {..., $x^{-4}, x^{-3}, x^{-2}, x^{-1}, 1, x, x^2, x^3, x^4$, ... }. This group is the group generated by $xH = \langle x \rangle$, and when $G = H = \langle x \rangle$, then G is a cyclic group. Another example for the groups with addition operation is the group of the integers $\mathbb{Z}, +$, the smallest subgroup H containing x, is {..., $-4x, -3x, -2x, -x, 1, x, 2x, 3x, 4x$, ... }, and H is cyclic generated by $xH = \langle x \rangle$. We can have finite cyclic groups, such as Integers mod n under addition: $\frac{\mathbb{Z}}{n\mathbb{Z}}, +$. Cyclic groups are fundamental to the theorem of finitely generating Abelian groups, which states that any finitely generated Abelian group can be divided by a finite number of cyclic subgroups.

A symmetric (r, 0) tensor is an (r, 0) tensor whose value is unaffected (invariant) by the interchange (or transposition) of any two of its arguments, $T(v_1, \ldots, v_i, \ldots, v_j, \ldots, v_r) = T(v_1, \ldots, v_j, \ldots, v_i, \ldots, v_r)$ for any i and j. For rank two tensors, the symmetry condition implies $T_{ij} = T_{ji}$. Symmetric (0,r) tensors are defined similarly. You can easily check that the symmetric (r, 0) and (0,r) tensors each form vector spaces, denoted $S^r(V^*)$ and $S^r(V)$ respectively. This also means that these matrices are invariant under any rearrangement of the indices. This is because any rearrangement can be obtained via successive transpositions.

An antisymmetric (or alternating) (r, 0) tensor is one whose value changes sign under transposition of any two of its arguments, i.e., $T(v_1, \ldots, v_i, \ldots, v_j, \ldots, v_r) = -T(v_1, \ldots, v_j, \ldots, v_i, \ldots, v_r)$. Antisymmetric (0,r) tensors are defined similarly, and both sets form vector spaces, denoted $\Lambda^r V^*$ and $\Lambda^r V$ (for r = 1 we define $\Lambda^1 V^* = V^*$ and $\Lambda^1 V = V$). Antisymmetry has the following properties:

1. $T(v_1, \ldots, v_r) = 0$ if $v_i = v_j$ for any $i \neq j$
2. $T(v_1, \ldots, v_r) = 0$ if $\{v_1, \ldots, v_r\}$ is linearly dependent
3. If dim (V) = n, then the only tensor in $\Lambda^r V^*$ and $\Lambda^r V$ for r>n is the 0 tensor

The symmetrisation postulate states that all known particles in nature are either of type fermions, such that their motion states are captured in a symmetric tensor, or type bosons, such that their states are caught in an antisymmetric tensor. This postulate has many consequences that exclude many states from the high dimensional permutations that could be considered otherwise. It is unclear how valid this postulate is for all datasets in all application domains for machine learning, but it is definitely applied in many applications related to Physical motion and is worth checking.

A Lie group is at the intersection of group theory, differential geometry, and linear algebra, named after the Norwegian mathematician Sophus Lie, who studied them in the late 1800s. Lie theory uses calculus to explain linear algebra. Classical Lie groups of geometric rotations in 2, 3 and 4 dimensions use linear algebra concepts and are then transformed to the tangent space to explain their Lie algebras using calculus. Moving back and forth between the group and its algebra, use log (log(1+x)) and exponential (Taylor series, for e^x) functions. The Lie algebra's flat structure captures the Lie groups' curvatures.

They are used to study symmetries and continuous transformations in mathematics and physics. Lie groups play a fundamental role in various areas, including representation theory, differential geometry, and theoretical physics. For example, the special orthogonal group in three dimensions, denoted as SO(3) consists of all 3x3 orthogonal matrices with determinant 1. We can visualize SO(3) as the group of rotations in three-dimensional space as explained further below.

Define the group: SO(3) = {R ∈ ℝ^(3x3) | R^TR = I and det(R) = 1}

Properties: The elements of SO(3) are 3x3 orthogonal matrices, which means they preserve lengths and angles. Additionally, the determinant of each matrix is 1, ensuring that they are proper rotations rather than reflections.

Example element: Let's consider a rotation around the z-axis by an angle θ. The corresponding rotation matrix R is:

$$R = \begin{bmatrix} \cos(\theta) & -\sin(\theta) & 0 \\ \sin(\theta) & \cos(\theta) & 0 \\ 0 & 0 & 1 \end{bmatrix}$$

This homogenous coordinate matrix represents a rotation in the xy-plane by θ radians.

Source Code Example:

Here's a Python code snippet using the NumPy library to demonstrate Lie groups, specifically the special orthogonal group SO(3):

```
import numpy as np

# Define the rotation angle
theta = np.pi / 4  # Rotation by 45 degrees

# Define the rotation matrix
R = np.array([[np.cos(theta), -np.sin(theta), 0],
              [np.sin(theta), np.cos(theta), 0],
              [0, 0, 1]])

# Verify the properties of R
is_orthogonal = np.allclose(np.dot(R.T, R), np.eye(3))
has_determinant_1 = np.isclose(np.linalg.det(R), 1)

print("Is R orthogonal?", is_orthogonal)
print("Does R have determinant 1?", has_determinant_1)
```

The code defines the rotation matrix R corresponding to a rotation in the xy-plane by 45 degrees (π/4 radians). It then verifies the properties of R: orthogonality ($R^TR = I$) and determinant equal to 1. The results indicate whether the matrix satisfies these conditions, confirming its membership in SO(3).

Lie groups are continuous groups with group elements that are 'infinitely close' to the identity, known as 'infinitesimal transformations' or 'generators' or Lie Algebra. The simplest definition is that Lie groups can be parametrised in terms of a certain number of real variables, which define the dimension of the group, such as the surface of a sphere but should also be studied from the algebra-based on an identity element. A maximal torus is formed from the cartesian products of simpler groups. A lie infinite group G is a topological group with operations multiplication and inversion being smooth maps that is also a smooth differentiable manifold with the same topological maps $f(x) = x^{-1}: G \to G$ and $g(x,y) = xy: G \times G \to G$.

The simplest one-dimensional rotation about the origin O (the axis of rotation) through angle θ is represented using multiplication by a complex exponential number: $e^{i\theta} = \cos\theta + i\sin\theta$. The Lie group S^1 is the unit circle (1-dimensional sphere) is the set of all such complex numbers defined with operations of complex numbers multiplication and inversion. S^1 consists of the points at a distance one from the origin in $\mathbb{R}^2$. An $\mathbb{R}^2$ maximal torus is defined as $T^2 = S^1 \times S^1$. In chapter one, the rotation 2x2 matrix R_θ was derived manually from trigonometry rules. A 2D rotation of a plane around the origin O is illustrated in Figure 64. It is a linear transformation that maps the basis vectors (1,0) and (0,1) to (cos θ, sin θ) and (−sin θ, cos θ), respectively.

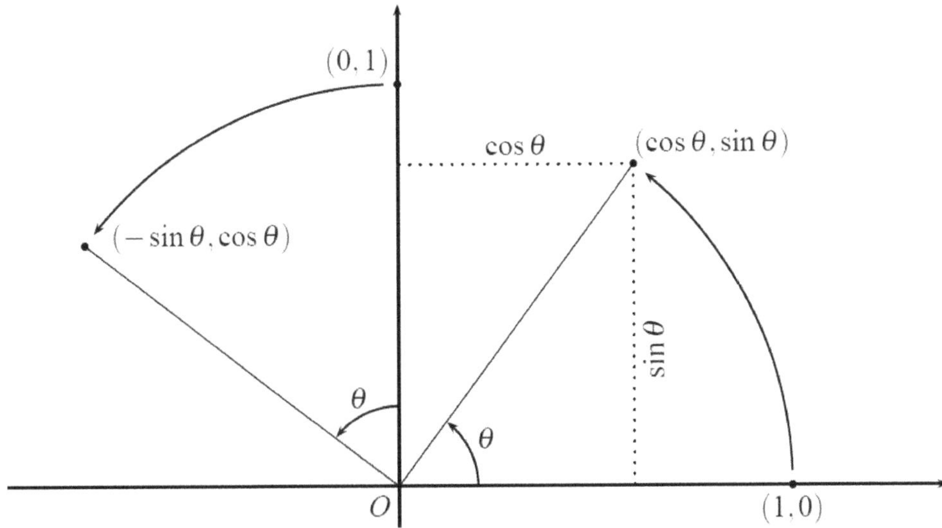

Figure 64: Rotation of the plane through angle θ (Stillwell, 2008) .

R_θ is represented by the matrix $\begin{bmatrix}\cos\theta & -\sin\theta\\ \sin\theta & \cos\theta\end{bmatrix}$, which also represents the complex number $z_\theta = \cos\theta + i\sin\theta$ that we can multiply by any point (x, y) to apply the $\mathbb{R}^2$ rotation. The matrices R_θ, for all angles θ, form a group called the special orthogonal group SO(2) (aka the rotation group, which is equivalent to S^1). S^2 is the ordinary sphere, consisting of the points at a distance one from the origin in $\mathbb{R}^3$. Then S^n is the generalised unit n-spheres consisting of the points at a distance one from the origin in $\mathbb{R}^{n+1}$, from which the S^1, S^2 and S^3 are the only Lie groups and not the higher dimensions n > 3. S^3 is also known as the special unitary group SU(2), which is closely related to SO(3) or 3D rotations. Unitary matrices are the complex counterpart of orthogonal matrices.
Complex numbers in the form a+bi are represented in matrix form as: $\begin{bmatrix}a & -b\\ b & a\end{bmatrix}$ with determinant a^2+b^2. Similarly, quaternions of reals (a, b, c, d) can be represented in matrix form as: $\begin{bmatrix}a+id & -b-ic\\ b-ic & a-id\end{bmatrix}$ with determinant $a^2+b^2+c^2+d^2$. Unit quaternions with determinant equal 1 form the analogue of the sphere, called the 3-sphere S^3, in the space $\mathbb{R}^4$ of all 4-tuples (a,b,c,d) that are used to represent rotations in $\mathbb{R}^3$ using the imaginary 3D part only and omitting the real component. Remember, a quaternion is a + bi + cj + dk, with i, j, k forming three-dimensional space overlooking the real component a. $\mathbb{R}^3$ rotations, for all angles θ, form the group SO(3), which is the product of reflections in planes through O that meet along the rotation axis. $\mathbb{R}^4$ rotations are represented using two quaternions, making SO(4), not a simple Lie group, as it is a direct product of SO(3) with itself. SO(4) is "almost" the same as SU(2)×SU(2).
Generalising rotations in n dimensions in SO(n), the transformation matrices need to preserve the inner product to preserve length and orientation (angle) by having a determinant equal to one. $\mathbb{R}^n$ rotations that fix O are the product of at most n reflections in hyperplanes through O. Many properties and operations define the quaternion/**Hamilton** algebra $\mathbb{H}$ that are considered fundamental to the Lie theory that can be visualised and computed in the $\mathbb{R}^n, \mathbb{C}^n, and\ \mathbb{H}^n$ spaces. $\mathbb{H}^n$ space, which is equivalent to $\mathbb{R}^{4n}$, of ordered n-tuple of quaternions p_i and q_j, preserves the inner product $(p_1, p_2, \ldots, p_n).(q_1, q_2, \ldots, q_n) = p_1\bar{q}_1 + p_2\bar{q}_2, \ldots + p_n\bar{q}_n$. The non-commutative property of quaternions makes the $p_i\bar{q}_i$ different from $\bar{q}_i p_i$, while quaternion matrices are associative and preserve the inner product and lengths. This forms the symplectic group Sp(n) of $\mathbb{H}^n$ matrices such as Sp(1) is the 1x1 unit quaternion matrix in which $\mathbb{H} = \mathbb{R}^4$, and SP(2) of 2x2 quaternion matrices in which $\mathbb{H}^2 = \mathbb{R}^8$. Quaternion matrices can be represented as complex block matrices making Sp(n) a subgroup of U(2n). For detailed properties and proofs, refer to (Stillwell, 2008) for a massive literature of identifications of classical groups and their properties and subgroups.

Another example of a matrix Lie group is a group closed under products, inverses, and nonsingular limits of $n \times n$ matrices M of real numbers that are defined as follows: $= \left\{ A = \left[\begin{bmatrix} a_{11} & \cdots & a_{1n} \\ \vdots & \ddots & \vdots \\ a_{n1} & \cdots & a_{nn} \end{bmatrix} \right] \right\}$, where det(A) ≠0, i.e., the lie group contains the entries of the matrix, forming a vector of n^2 dimensions: $M \rightarrow (a_{11}, a_{12}, \dots, a_{1n}, a_{21}, \dots, a_{2n}, \dots a_{nn}) \in \mathbb{R}^{n^2}$. Taking the space $\mathbb{R}^{n^2}$ and removing all matrices B with determinants equal to zero, we have a manifold. **A lie type group** is similar to a lie group, but it is a finite group that is defined over a finite field. Many groups belong to this category; that is a simple group.

Lie Algebra is the smallest set of properties necessary for a vector space spanned by infinitesimal generators (defined below) to generate a Lie group maintaining its structure. The $\mathbb{R}^n$ Euclidean space is an example of a non-compact Lie group under the addition of vector, and zero vector as the identity with the differential and topological structures of $\mathbb{R}^n$. Lie algebra g is a vector space that is closed under commutators, in the sense that if X and Y ∈ g, then so is [X,Y] ≡ XY – YX. Expanding the commutators lead to satisfying the Jacobi Identity, such that [[X,Y],Z] + [[Y, Z], X] +[[Z, X],Y] = 0, ∀X,Y,Z ∈ g. A compact Lie group example is the circle group $\mathbb{T}$ of complex numbers of unit modulus, forming a group under multiplication.

The Lie group connects components on a manifold in terms of **infinitesimal generators**, which means the smallest value of change ϵ that can be applied multiple times on the coordinates unit basis to generate all components in the manifold. For example, in a one-dimensional Manifold M for a group with a multiplication operation, the identity element is 1, and the tangent vector $\sigma = +1$ is taken as a basis for M. An infinitesimal transformation in the neighbourhood of the identity element is g =1+ $\epsilon\sigma$. If $\epsilon = 0.001$, and we want to represent point 2, then g =1+0.001=0.001, and $g^{693} = 1.999013$ is the closest approximation that generates 2. Using calculus, an exact generator can be used to avoid approximation. Let g_θ be a member of the group labelled by a real number θ, then g_θ is expressed in terms of the exponential function $\exp(\theta, \sigma)$. These exponential maps applied on infinitesimal generators reveal much information about the group's structure. Generalising this to a higher dimension, given a Lie Group (differential Manifold) with basis $T_1, T_2, \dots, T_n$ of Tangent space T_xM, where T_i is the infinitesimal generator for axis i, any element x of G in the neighbourhood of the identity can be written in the form: $x(x_1, \dots, x_n) = \exp(\sum_{i=1}^{n} x_i T_i)$for some $x_1, \dots, x_n \in \mathbb{R}$.

Lie groups are very close to being entirely determined by the behaviour of their one-parameter subgroups; in particular, every element of a Lie group sufficiently close to the identity is contained in a one-parameter subgroup. This association between finite transformations and their infinitesimal versions is precisely the relationship between a Lie group and its Lie algebra. For example, rotation operators transform the orthogonal matrices into antisymmetric matrices.

The Lie bracket abstracts the Lie algebra from the matrix Lie groups to all other Lie groups. A Lie Group, which is a Manifold with tangent space at point x (T_xM), has a Vector space V of directions (infinitesimal generators) along which this point translates along the manifold. The Lie bracket g operation is the vector space V with bilinear map $[.,.]: V \times V \rightarrow V$ turns the Tangent space T_xM into a Lie algebra $\mathcal{L}(V)$, which is the set of all linear operators on V. The exponential mapping of infinitesimal generators tells us that at least locally, $\mathcal{L}$ completely determines the structure of G. This is defined by the bracket [X,Y] for $X, Y \in \mathrm{T}_x\mathrm{M}$ generators for the group, which is calculated as [X,Y](f) = X(Y(f)) – Y(X(f)). This means a generator X acting on another generator Y that would give zero first-order terms ((I+X)(I+Y) = 1+X+Y), and the second-order infinitesimal term is then (XY – YX) independent of parametrisation. The Lie bracket g satisfies the Antisymmetry property [X,Y]=- [Y, X] ∀X,Y ∈ g and the Jacobi identity explained earlier. The Lie bracket encodes the entire Taylor series expansion of the multiplication on the Lie group near the identity, capturing the "local" behaviour of the Lie group.

A differentiable Lie group is a differentiable Manifold M, such that a chart at point $x \in M$ is a homeomorphism φ from an open neighbourhood U of p to an open subset of $\mathbb{R}^n$. Every point of a differentiable manifold is covered by at least one chart. The ith component of φ is a function $[\varphi(x)]_i: U \rightarrow \mathbb{R}$, simplified to φ_i. We say that a function f is differentiable at point x if $f \circ \varphi^{-1}$ is differentiable at φ(x), and use the notation $\frac{\delta}{\delta x^1}$ for $\frac{\delta}{\delta x^1}(f \circ \varphi^{-1})$.

Because of Lie groups desirable properties they have diverse applications in computing. One of these properties is having group structures with closures, associativity, identity and inverse elements, enabling algebriac operations. Lie groups are also smooth manifolds, which means they locally resemble Euclidean spaces. This property allows for the application of differential geometry techniques to analyze and manipulate Lie groups. Each Lie group has a corresponding Lie algebra. The Lie algebra captures the tangent space information of the Lie group, providing a linearized representation. This correspondence allows for the study of Lie groups through their associated Lie algebras. Computer Graphics and Computer Vision: Lie groups play a vital role in computer graphics and computer vision applications. They are employed to model and manipulate 3D transformations, such as rotations, translations, and scaling. Lie groups, particularly the special Euclidean group SE(3), are widely used for rigid body transformations in 3D graphics and robotics. Robotics and Motion Planning: Lie groups find extensive use in robotics and motion planning algorithms. They provide a mathematical framework for modeling and controlling robot manipulators, enabling the efficient representation and computation of robot configurations, kinematics, and dynamics. Lie groups are also employed in path planning algorithms to generate feasible robot motions. Lie groups are increasingly employed in machine learning and deep learning algorithms. They offer a structured representation for certain types of data, such as images, shapes, and signals, allowing for the development of specialized learning architectures. Techniques such as Lie group neural networks leverage the Lie group properties to design models that respect the inherent symmetries and transformations in the data. In computer vision tasks like pose estimation, Lie groups are utilized to represent and estimate the 3D position and orientation of objects in a scene. They enable efficient parameterization and optimization of the pose estimation problem, enabling accurate localization and tracking of objects. Lie groups are employed in numerical optimization algorithms to optimize functions defined on Lie groups. These optimization techniques, such as the trust region method or Gauss-Newton algorithm on Lie groups, exploit the Lie group structure to efficiently search for the optimal solutions (Eade and Drummond, 2013).

5.1.3.1 Classical groups:

These definitions laid down the foundation for the classical groups identified by physicists in an attempt to explain how the universe works. Then further analysed by mathematicians over more than a century in a wealth of literature that can not be explained clearly in a fraction of a chapter. In the previous section, many classical groups are discussed. This section will expand on the groups used in computational graphics applications summarising some of their properties that are useful in understanding the stack of code in which they are used.

When Lie groups arise as groups of matrices (such Lie groups are called **linear groups**), the generators $T_1, T_2, \ldots, T_n$ are themselves matrices, the exponentiation is just matrix exponentiation, and [A, B] is equal to the commutator AB – BA. In chapter one, we have seen how to use **matrices** to solve a system of equations. We can make groups from matrices in two different ways for addition or multiplication operations. The matrix of real numbers $\mathbb{R}$ under addition has the zero matrices as the identity matrix and forms infinite groups that are Abelian and non-Abelian. The matrices under multiplication require matrices that can be multiplied together, so restricting them to $n \times n$ matrices is required, using the $n \times n$ identity matrix, and the inverses need the matrices to have non-zero determinants, making them a General Linear Group $GL_n(\mathbb{R})$. When the determinant is equal to one, it is the Special Linear Group $SL_n(\mathbb{R})$.

The general linear group of vector space V, denoted GL(V), is a Lie group that is formed by the composition of maps of invertible linear transformations on V. When V is finite n-dimensional space, GL(V) is a group of $n \times n$ invertible (nonsingular) matrices of linearly independent rows and linearly independent columns, under matrix multiplication operation. Sometimes the notation used is GL(N, $\mathbb{R}$), or $GL_N(\mathbb{R})$, which means N-dimensional general linear group of real numbers $\mathbb{R}$. For example, a group containing one element as a 2x2 matrix $\begin{bmatrix} a & b \\ c & d \end{bmatrix}$, with $a, b, c, d \in \mathbb{R}$ having determinant $\neq 0$, is a $GL_2(\mathbb{R})$ or GL(2, $\mathbb{R}$), the identity of this group is the 2x2 identity matrix. The subset of these matrices with determinant +1 forms a (sub)group called SL (n). The collection of $n \times n$ unitary matrices U(n) also forms a group under matrix multiplication.

When groups are unitary (preserving inner products/length and orientation by having determinant equals 1), they form U(N+, N-, ℝ) with parameters as positive dimensions and negative dimensions, along with the Field definition. When linear groups are orthogonal (preserve length but not orientation), they form O(N+, N-; ℝ) with the same definitions of the parameters. Orthogonality means that the matrix representing the group has the property $A^{-1} = A^T$, $or\ A^T A = I$,having determinant equals to ± 1. Both U and O groups are denoted for simplicity U(N) and O(N). The Symplectic groups S_p(2N, ℝ) have even dimensions 2N, on ℝ, and ℂ, but not when defined on Quaternions S_p(N,ℚ). There are also the unitary symplectic groups US_p(2N+,2N-; ℝ).
U and O have special subgroups, such as the SU(n) and SO(n), both with determinants equal to 1 . SU(n) is a special unitary group of $n \times n$ unitary matrices. SO(n) is a special orthogonal group that generalises rotation transformation matrices invariant of dimension and geometry. They are known as rotation matrices R(θ) ∈ SO(N) that are cross-product operators (CPO) capturing similarities with interesting properties. U(n) and SU(n) are analgous to O(n) and SO(n) for $\mathbb{C}^n$ numbers with inner products to be evaluated as reals in $\mathbb{R}^{2n}$ defined as the **Hermitian**. AA^T is the inner product of a real matrix A, and $A\bar{A}^T$ is the inner product of complex matrix A, which $\bar{A}$ is the complex conjugate of A. SU(2) is crucial in the theory of angular momentum in quantum mechanics, and SU(3) is fundamental in particle physics.
$R(\theta) \in$ SO(2) as a linear one-parameter Lie abelian and compact group, is generated from a single parameter, the angle θ, and using the Euler equation. As explained earlier, it can be expressed as a complex exponential function as $R(\theta) = \begin{bmatrix} \cos\theta & -\sin\theta \\ \sin\theta & \cos\theta \end{bmatrix} = I_2 \cos\theta + i\sigma_2 \sin\theta = e^{(i\sigma_2\theta)}$, where I_2 is the 2x2 identity matrix. σ_2 is the generator for θ and is obtained by differentiating R(θ), $\sigma_2 = -i\frac{dR}{d\theta}\Big|_{\theta=0} = -i\begin{bmatrix} 0 & 1 \\ -1 & 0 \end{bmatrix} = \begin{bmatrix} 0 & -i \\ i & 0 \end{bmatrix}$. Figure 65(a) illustrates a point rotation on the complex plane.

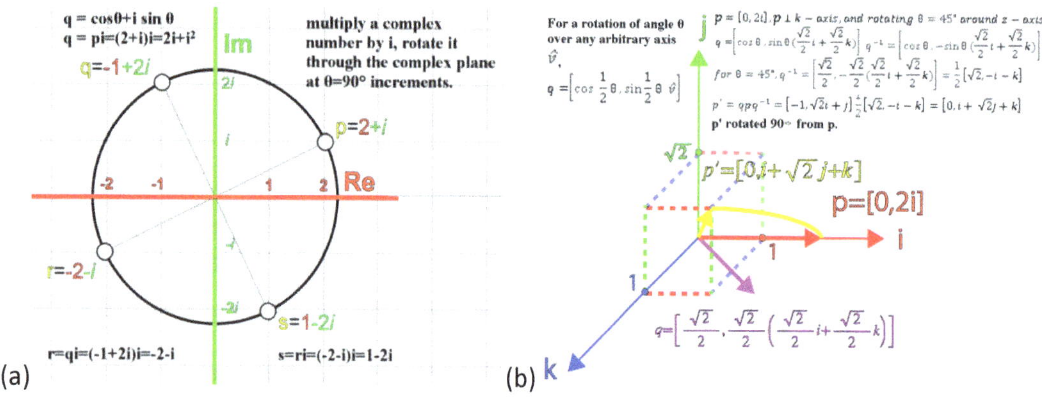

Figure 65: (a) 4 points on a sphere on a complex plane. Starting from point p, each point is generated by multiplying by i, making i a rotation operator for 90-degree rotations. (b) point p rotates 90 degrees around k-axis using quaternion q (Jeremiah, 2012).

Expanding to 3D, we define rotation around each axis independently. A rotation around the z-axis, $R_z(\theta) = \begin{bmatrix} \cos\theta & -\sin\theta & 0 \\ \sin\theta & \cos\theta & 0 \\ 0 & 0 & 1 \end{bmatrix}$, which is generated from $T_z = -i\frac{dR_z(\theta)}{d\theta}\Big|_{\theta=0} = \begin{bmatrix} 0 & -i & 0 \\ i & 0 & 0 \\ 0 & 0 & 0 \end{bmatrix}$. A rotation of angle θ can be generated by successive N applications of smaller angle rotations, $\frac{\theta}{N} = \delta\theta$. The infinitesimal angle $\delta\theta$ may be expanded from $R_z(\delta\theta) = I_3 + i\delta\theta T_z$, to N rotations as $R_z(\theta) = [I_3 + i\delta\theta T_z]^N = \begin{bmatrix} 1 & 0 & 0 \\ 0 & 1 & 0 \\ 0 & 0 & 1 \end{bmatrix} + i\delta\theta\begin{bmatrix} 0 & -i & 0 \\ i & 0 & 0 \\ 0 & 0 & 0 \end{bmatrix} = \begin{bmatrix} 1 & \delta\theta & 0 \\ -\delta\theta & 1 & 0 \\ 0 & 0 & 1 \end{bmatrix}$. As N goes to ∞ , $R_z(\theta) = \lim_{N\to\infty}\left[1 + i\frac{\theta}{N}T_z\right]^N = e^{(i\theta S_z)}$, which identified T_z as generator for R_z. This is solved by the series expansion $e^x = \lim_{n\to\infty}(1+\frac{x}{n})^n = 1 + x + \frac{x^2}{2!} + \frac{x^3}{3!} + \cdots$. Similarly, for the other axes, by differentiating the coordinate rotations: $R_x(\psi) = \begin{bmatrix} 1 & 0 & 0 \\ 0 & \cos\psi & \sin\psi \\ 0 & -\sin\psi & \cos\psi \end{bmatrix}$, and $R_y(\varphi) = \begin{bmatrix} \cos\varphi & 0 & -\sin\varphi \\ 0 & 1 & 0 \\ \sin\varphi & 0 & \cos\varphi \end{bmatrix}$, we get the generators: $T_x = \begin{bmatrix} 0 & 0 & 0 \\ 0 & 0 & -i \\ 0 & i & 0 \end{bmatrix}, T_y = \begin{bmatrix} 0 & 0 & i \\ 0 & 0 & 0 \\ -i & 0 & 0 \end{bmatrix}$. The Lie algebra for these rotation groups has a basis $\{I, T_x, T_y, T_z\}$, and is determined by the single relation $[T_a, T_b] = \epsilon_{abc}T_c$, where ϵ_{abc} is +1 if (a, b, c) is a cyclic shift of (x, y, z); $\epsilon_{abc} = -1$ if it is a cyclic shift of the reverse permutation (z, y, x) and ϵ_{abc} = 0 in all other cases. Then SO(3) has commutators of the basis elements as $[T_x, T_y] = T_z$, $[T_y, T_z] = T_x$, $[T_z, T_x] = T_y$. When the generators are labelled with numbers instead of letters, we can extend to the higher dimensions easy as $[T_i, T_j] = \sum_{k=1}^{3} \epsilon_{i,j,k} T_k$. These are the angular momentum commutation relations of quantum mechanics.

The above θ, ψ, φ are axes' angle of rotations used as parameters to generate the rotation matrices. There is always a single-axis rotation that simplifies any combinations of these three rotations using interpolation. Other parameters to generate these matrices exist, such as the Euler angles and the quaternions. Euler rotations apply three consecutive rotations on each axis using Euler angles. Euler sequential rotations cause problems when two axes are lined up and lose a degree of freedom, causing the "gimbal lock" problem. Quaternions solve this problem, perform rotations in any order, and make interpolation easier. As explained earlier, quaternion has four components representing 4 points on the surface of the sphere, representing the rotation in 3D. The first is usually denoted w, as the unrotated point, and x represents 180-degree rotation around the x-axis. Similarly, the y and z components represent 180-degree rotations around the y- and z-axis.

A quaternion 3D orientation is expressed as as qpq^{-1} of some 3D point p = xi+yj+zk, and q is the orientation quaternion, for example, (0.5+0.5i+0.5j-0.5k), and its inverse q^{-1}= (0.5-0.5i-0.5j+0.5k). This uses the quaternion multiplication properties that extend the complex numbers multiplications. Figure 65(b) illustrates a point p 3D rotation using quaternion q. Because it is difficult to choose these points, most animation and graphics software do not expose their values. However, the blender software exposes the quaternion values. There are many visualisation videos to understand quaternions, such as https://eater.net/quaternions.

This example set of groups (rotation and translation) shows how a lie group can be generated from infinitesimal generators, such as the angular momentum operators/vectors generating rotations and the momentum operator generating translations. They also show how two or more successive transformations can be combined using a different transformation and can be reversed using an inverse transformation.

As explained in the previous section, SO(3) is generalised to $\mathbb{R}^n$ as SO(n). SO(n) is a manifold with various charts that allows a change of basis or coordinate systems. This is generally used in computer graphics and planning the motion of robots or objects in 3D scenes in a series of coordinate system changes between the different coordinate frames of the camera, the robot, and the world. (Olguín Díaz, 2018) explains more details about how these matrices are constructed from the degrees of freedom (represented as infinitesimal generators as explained earlier). For example, three parameters are required in $\mathbb{R}^3$ to construct the nine elements of a rotation matrix using exponential mapping of the cross product of the parameters vector. The symmetry of all possible rotations around the intrinsic axis (the current coordinate frame of the robot or object) or the extrinsic axis (the base frame) creates 24 different possibilities. The Euclidean group, denoted E(n) or ISO(n), is a group of Euclidean isometries such that the transformations (all translations, rotations, and reflections) preserve the Euclidean distance between any two points. The Special Euclidean Group denoted $E^+(3)$, $ISO^+(3)$, or SE(3) of order 3 is a mapping transformation that combines rotation R and a translation d (no reflection) from the parameters of vectors (R, d) on each axis, $SE(3) = \mathbb{R}^3 \times SO(3)$. Their elements represent rigid motion. The Skew Symmetric Group SS(3) of order 3 is a mapping transformation that combines the rotation matrix and the angular velocity.

The projective space P^n, such as those used in image representations, has n+2 basis, the standard basis $e_i = [0, ..., 1, ..., 0]^T$, where only the ith position element is equal to 1, for $1 \le i \le n+1$, and the standard projective basis $e_{n+2}=[1, 1, ..., 1]^T$, where all elements are equal to 1. These projective basis are called homogeneous coordinates. For 3D, we need four coordinates represented using the quaternions. P^n is topologically equivalent to the unit sphere S^n of $\mathbb{R}^{n+1}$, in which the antipodal points have been identified. Antipodal are the quaternions x and −x that represent diametrically opposite points on the n-sphere of unit quaternions. Any point in S^n is represented by the vector $x=[x_1, ..., x_{n+1}]^T$ such that $x = \sum_{i=1}^{n+1} x_i^2 = 1$ is also a point in P^n, with vector -x as the antipodal point of x found in both S^n and P^n. This means all projective spaces are compact spaces, and their differential structures are as simple as the Euclidean ones, such as embedding the sphere units in the higher space, as illustrated in Figure 66. A homography is an isomorphism of projective spaces to enable generalising an image representation invariant of the camera position by projecting a 2D image onto a 3D space, as explained by this OpenCV tutorial on various applications https://docs.opencv.org/4.x/d9/dab/tutorial_homography.html, and applied in data augmentation to achieve more invariance for Deep Learning data representation to reduce overfitting on specific image details such as https://www.tensorflow.org/api_docs/python/tf/keras/preprocessing/image/ImageDataGenerator.

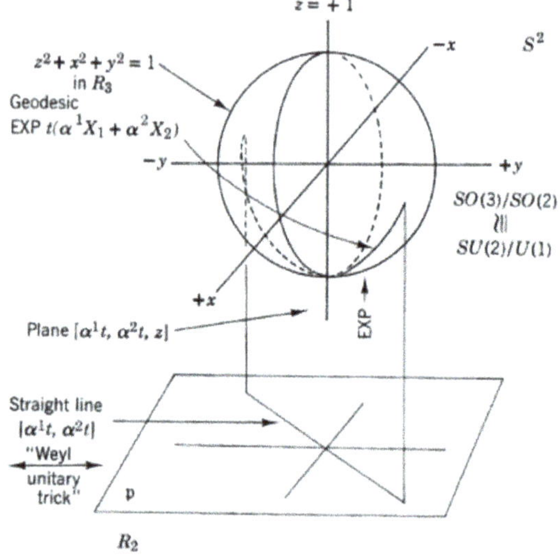

Figure 66: The coset space P=EXPP, originates from SO(3)/SO(2) ≈ SU(2)/U(1) and appears as the surface of a sphere S^2 in $\mathbb{R}^3$ (Gilmore, 2005).

The action of the three-dimensional rotation group SO(3) on the unit sphere S^2 is an example of homogeneous space. Taking any point on S^2, the unit vector e_z pointing along the z-axis, and a rotation matrix R, $\{Re_z | R \in SO(3)\}$ sweeps out the entire sphere, so S^2 is a homogeneous space of SO(3). The isotropy group, in this case, is the subgroup of rotations about the z-axis, which is just SO(2). For example, composing two rotations in sequence, the first R_1 is a $\theta_1$rotation from coordinate frame A to B, ${}^{A}\{R_1\}_B\,(\theta_1)$ and the second R_2 is a θ_2 rotation from coordinate frame B to C ${}^{B}\{R_2\}_C\,(\theta_2)$, using homogenous coordinates is ${}^{A}\{R_1\}_B\,(\theta_1) \times {}^{B}\{R_2\}_C\,(\theta_2)$:

$$= \begin{bmatrix} \cos\theta_1 & \sin\theta_1 & 0 & 0 \\ -\sin\theta_1 & \cos\theta_1 & 0 & 0 \\ 0 & 0 & 1 & 0 \\ 0 & 0 & 0 & 1 \end{bmatrix} \times \begin{bmatrix} \cos\theta_2 & \sin\theta_2 & 0 & 0 \\ -\sin\theta_2 & \cos\theta_2 & 0 & 0 \\ 0 & 0 & 1 & 0 \\ 0 & 0 & 0 & 1 \end{bmatrix} = \begin{bmatrix} \cos\,(\theta_1+\theta_2) & \sin(\theta_1+\theta_2) & 0 & 0 \\ -\sin(\theta_1+\theta_2) & \cos(\theta_1+\theta_2) & 0 & 0 \\ 0 & 0 & 1 & 0 \\ 0 & 0 & 0 & 1 \end{bmatrix}$$

All matrices in this subgroup are the same periodic function of one real variable, θ, given by R(θ) $\in SO(2) = R_1(\theta_1) + R_2(\theta_2) = \begin{bmatrix} \cos\theta & \sin\theta & 0 \\ -\sin\theta & \cos\theta & 0 \\ 0 & 0 & 1 \end{bmatrix}$., i.e. $SO(2)$ is locally isomorphic to $\mathbb{R}^1$. Another $SO(3)$ example combining a rotation θ with a translation d is $\begin{bmatrix} \cos\theta & \sin\theta & 0 & 0 \\ -\sin\theta & \cos\theta & 0 & 0 \\ 0 & 0 & 1 & d \\ 0 & 0 & 0 & 1 \end{bmatrix}$; the set of such matrices is continuously parameterised by these two variables θ and d. Thus, this subgroup is a two-dimensional Lie group, resulting from the Cartesian product $SO(2) \times T(1)$. These groups are differential; their first-order derivative gives an expression of the velocity of a motion, and the higher-order derivative gives an expression of acceleration.

From an algebraic point of view $S^2 \sim= \frac{SO(3)}{SO(2)}$, and generalises to $S^{n-1} \sim= \frac{SO(n)}{SO(n-1)}$. There is also a surjective relationship from SU(2) to SO(3). In other words, SO(3) has SU(2) as a compact connected covering group, and

SU(2) is the double cover of SO(3). This is because the higher n SO have a Lie algebra with a 3 × 3 compact regular representation and can be composed of coset decomposition with respect to a compact subgroup.
It is difficult to explain concisely how these relationships have been identified and how many of them are used in many computational applications without ending up copying existing books. To keep it brief, some groups are composed of simpler groups, simpler groups approximate complex groups, and others can be generated from parameters. For example, there is a Lie algebra isomorphism stemming from the group homomorphism between lower n SU and higher n SO, when SU act on a given vector field such as $SU(2) \cong SO(3)$ and $SU(4) \cong SO(6)$ because of the double cover in the representation. A theory states that nonsemisimple Lie groups can be constructed from semisimple Lie groups by a limiting procedure, and group expansion performs the inverse process. Applications of Lie groups and their algebra leads to a complete listing of all the globally symmetric pseudo-Riemannian spaces, such as the sphere and the hyperboloid, which are the Riemannian symmetric spaces associated with the group SO(3). If this very concise summary of this vast topic motivates you to learn how these are derived and the many properties and applications of expansions and contractions of these algebraic structures, please read full books on the subject such as (Stillwell, 2008), (Gilmore, 2005), (Vince, 2021), (Altmann, 1986), (Jeevanjee, 2011) and (Dixon, 2002).
The SO and SE matrices are implemented in OpenCV Python, such as affine transformations using "getAffineTransform", "getRotationMatrix2D", and the perspective transformations using "getPerspectiveTransform". Peter Corke implemented them in Matlab and partially implemented them in the Python package Robopy (Corke, 2017). Also, Python package PyGeometry implements many of these matrices. RobotPy is also a Robot simulator in Python that its path-planning module builds on top of these matrices.

5.1.3.2 Geometric groups:

The group of symmetries is defined as a group of groups formed from the symmetries of a geometric shape, such that the shape looks the same before and after flipping and rotation. For example, **the dihedral group** is the group of symmetries of a regular n-polygon shape. This group contains 2n symmetries groups, the identity transformation that does nothing e, the θ rotation symmetries such that $\theta = 360°$ for complete rotation, or $\theta = \frac{360°}{n} = \frac{2\pi}{n}$ radians for r single symmetric rotation that move one point to the next point position. Repeated application of r gives n different symmetries to rotate back to the original position, which is the identity: $r^n = e$. The reflection/flip around an axis is another symmetric transformation. For the n-polygon, we have an axis passing through each point that can be used for symmetric reflections. If you flip twice, you return to the identity position: $f^2 = e$. Other symmetries are formed by composing rotations and reflections. This makes the finite dihedral group of symmetries contains 2n symmetries defined as $\{e, r, r^2, \ldots, r^{n-1}, f, r.f, r^2.f, \ldots, r^{n-1}.f\}$. This is non-Abelian such that $r.f \neq f.r$. Some denote this group as D_n for the number of elements in the group, and others denote it as $D_{2n}$for the number of symmetries in the group. For example, the simplest n-polygon is the equilateral triangle where n=3, and the dihedral group of symmetries for it contains six symmetries = $\{e, r, r^2, f, r.f, r^2.f\}$ such that the element order of r is 3, $r^3 = e$, and the element order of f is 2, $f^2 = e$ as shown in Figure 67.

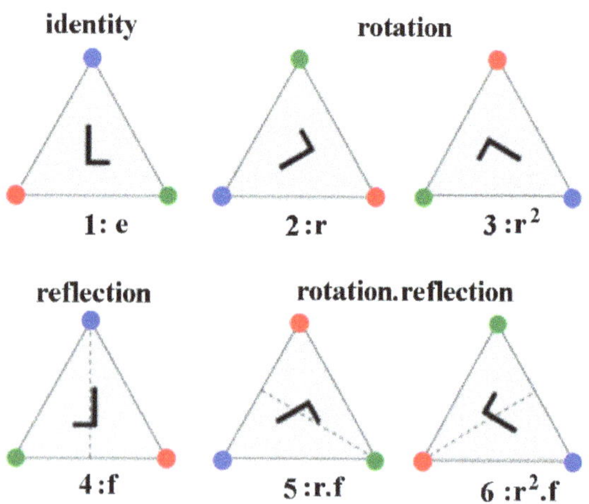

Figure 67: The dihedral group of symmetries for an equilateral triangle.

This goes on for polygons of higher degrees and other shapes. To summarise the group types discussed above, we have:

	Finite Groups	Infinite Groups
Abelian Groups	Integers mod n: $\mathbb{Z}\backslash n\mathbb{Z}$	$\mathbb{Z}, \mathbb{Q}, \mathbb{R}, \mathbb{C}$ under +
Non-Abelian Groups	Symmetric Groups: $\mathbb{S}_n$ for n > 2	Matrices: GL, SO, SU, ...

5.1.4 Group Decomposition

Group decomposition into simpler ones is achieved using various methods. This section will explain some of these methods. Cosets are not subgroups, but they provide a traversal method of group elements, and their elements can be treated as subgroups. The following will explain the difference between cosets and subgroups, how they are used in group decompositions, and how similar methods can be applied to rings and modules.
Left and right cosets of $H < G$ and $x \in G$ are defined as $xH = \{xh|h \in H\}$ as the left coset of x and the set $Hx = \{hx|h \in H\}$ as the right coset of x, both cosets have the same cardinality as H. cosets are not groups and do not have the axioms stated earlier. Any two cosets are either identical or disjoint, and the set of left cosets provides a partition of G, i.e., G of cardinality $|G| = n$ is split into k non-overlapping (disjoint) left cosets of the same cardinality $|H| = d$: $H, x_1H, x_2H, \ldots, x_nH$, such that $d.k = n$, i.e., d divides n: $d|n$. The same can be done using the right cosets. Abelian groups have left cosets the same as the right cosets. If H is a **normal subgroup**, then $xH = Hx$ for any $x \in G$, hence the systems of left and right cosets are the same. This leads to $\frac{G}{H}$ forming a **quotient group** under the operation $(xH)(yH) = (xy)H$, which is not a subgroup of G. Example quotient group $\frac{\mathbb{Z}}{5\mathbb{Z}}$ is explained below. Since non-Abelian groups, when multiplied by one of its elements, gives back the group, also if two cosets have an element in common, they are identical.
An example decomposition of a group G representing a plane $\mathbb{R}^2$ of points (x,y) under vector addition into H as the subgroup of points (0,y). In this case, we use additive notation and write the coset of (x,y) as (x,y)+H = {(x,y) : y ∈ $\mathbb{R}$ }, where x is constant. Then H is the y-axis and the coset (x,y)+H is H translated by the vector (x,y) decomposing G into parallel lines. Different g ∈ G give the same coset gH, such as (1, 0) + H and (1, 1) + H are both the vertical line x = 1 as illustrated in Figure 68.

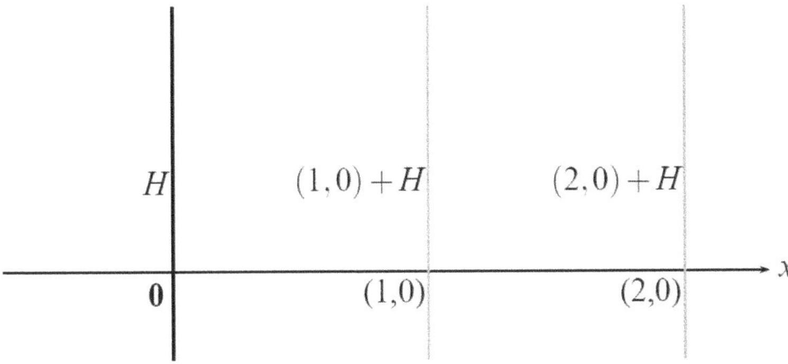

Figure 68: Subgroup H of $\mathbb{R}^2$ and cosets (Stillwell, 2008).

It is important to note the fundamental homomorphism theorem for groups that states that any homomorphism φ of G onto another G' preserving the group structure can be viewed as the special type φ : G→ G/H. The appropriate normal subgroup H of G is called **kernel** of φ: H = ker φ = {g ∈ G : φ(g) = 1}. Then G' is isomorphic to the group G/ker φ of cosets of ker φ, which is also a group and a normal subgroup of G. G' should be simpler or at least not more complicated than G.

A quotient space is defined for the left and right cosets. G/H is the quotient space of left cosets. Similarly, H\G is the quotient space of the right cosets. If H is a normal subgroup of G, then the group of cosets $\frac{G}{H}$ forms a group that is called **factor group/quotient group** and denoted $H \trianglelefteq G$.

Module Arithmetic, founded by Gauss, takes a group of integers, partitions them into a finite number of sets, and handles each set as a new type of number. This is done using **normal subgroups and Quotient groups** in group theory. For example, the quotient group $\frac{\mathbb{Z}}{5\mathbb{Z}}$ is the Integer mod 5 group is composed of the subgroups of remainder r= Integer mod 5, as follows:

r=0	{… , -10, -5, 0, 5, 10, …}
r=1	{… , -9, -4, 1, 6, 11, …}
r=2	{… , -8, -3, 2, 7, 12, …}
r=3	{… , -7, -2, 3, 8, 13, …}
r=4	{… , -6, -1, 4, 9, 14, …}

Applying the group operation on an element from one specific subgroup to an element in another specific subgroup will produce an element in the same third subgroup. These are called congruence classes. For example, in integer mod n group: $\mathbb{Z}/n\mathbb{Z}$, the group with elements a, b, a is congruent to b, if they give the same remainder when divided by n. Another example is the Integers $\mathbb{Z}$ group with addition operation has an infinite number of subgroups: $\mathbb{Z}, 2\mathbb{Z}, 3\mathbb{Z}, 4\mathbb{Z}, 5\mathbb{Z}, \ldots$ Given one subgroup $5\mathbb{Z}$, and all possible remainders to it, we represent $\mathbb{Z}$ group with one disjoint subgroup and four cosets as shown in the table below. Adding an element from the first coset to an element of the third coset yield an element in the fourth coset: $(1 + 5\mathbb{Z}) + (3 + 5\mathbb{Z}) = (4 + 5\mathbb{Z})$. These sets are congruence classes.

$5\mathbb{Z}$ subgroup	r=0	{… , -10, -5, 0, 5, 10, …}
$1 + 5\mathbb{Z}$ coset	r=1	{… , -9, -4, 1, 6, 11, …}
$2 + 5\mathbb{Z}$ coset	r=2	{… , -8, -3, 2, 7, 12, …}
$3 + 5\mathbb{Z}$ coset	r=3	{… , -7, -2, 3, 8, 13, …}
$4 + 5\mathbb{Z}$ coset	r=4	{… , -6, -1, 4, 9, 14, …}

A left transversal A is a set of coset representatives with two distinctive elements $x, y \in A$, $xH \neq yH$ and $\cup_{x \in A} xH = G$. **Right transversals** are defined analogously.
Other types of cosets are two-sided and double cosets. **Two-sided cosets** are sets of the form $x_1Hx_2 = \{x_1hx_2 | h \in H\}$ (with $x_1, x_2 \in G$). **Double cosets** are defined for H_1 and H_2 are both subgroups of G such that $H_1xH_2 = \{h_1xh_2 | h_1 \in H_1, h_2 \in H_2\}$ (with $x \in G$). This forms the **double quotient space** $\frac{H_1 \backslash G}{H_2}$.
Algebraic structures are often constructed from the direct sums or direct products of two or more simpler structures. **The direct product** of two groups G, H, denoted $G \times H$, is the group of pairs $(g, h), g \in G, h \in H$ resulting from the cartesian product defined as $(g_1, h_1)(g_2, h_2) = (g_1g_2, h_1h_2)$. The resulting group contains the identity element $(e_G, e_H)(1_G \in G, 1_H \in H)$ and all elements inverses $(g^{-1}, h^{-1})(g^{-1} \in G, \mathrm{h}^{-1} \in H)$. The group operations are defined on the pairs as given $(a, b), (x, y) \in G \times H$, then $(a, b).(x, y) = (a.x, b.y)$. For example, given G is $\mathbb{Z}$ under addition and H is {1, -1, i, -i} under ×, then $G \times H = \{(x, y) | x \in \mathbb{Z}, y = \pm 1 \; or \; y = \pm i\}$ having identity element (0, 1). A group operation on the pairs (5, -i), (0, 1) = (5+0, -i.1)=(5, -i). This is because the first group operation is the addition, and the second group operation is the multiplication. Another example is the group $\mathbb{R}^2$ under vector addition is the product $\mathbb{R} \times \mathbb{R}$.
This is generalised to $\mathbb{R}^n$ as the direct product $\mathbb{R} \times \mathbb{R} \times \ldots \times \mathbb{R}$, and generalised to direct products of groups of matrices, forming tuples containing elements from each group. For example, the direct product of $G_1 \times G_2 \times G_3 = \{(x, y, z) | x \in G_1, y \in G_2, z \in G_3\}$ produces an $\mathbb{R}^3$ tuple with identity element $(e_{G_1}, e_{G_2}, e_{G_3})$, and abstract group operation as defined for each group $(a, b, c) * (x, y, z) = (a *_{G_1} x, b *_{G_2} y, c *_{G_3} z)$. If any one of the k groups in the direct product is infinite, then the direct product is infinite. If all groups are finite with orders $n_1, n_2, \ldots, n_k$, then the order of the direct product is $n_1 \times n_2 \times \ldots \times n_k$. The order of the direct product is infinite for the product of an infinite number of finite groups. If any one of the groups is non-Abelian, then the direct product is non-Abelian. $\mathbb{R}^2$ group is generalised to $\mathbb{R}^n$, as the direct product of n copies of $\mathbb{R}$. Similarly, the n-dimensional unit torus $\mathbb{T}^n$ is a direct product of n copies of the circle group. Not all groups are composed of the direct product of simpler groups. Other decomposition methods will be explained below.
Semi-direct product of a group H and a subgroup H, denoted $G \rtimes H$, is the group of all ordered pairs $(x, \Lambda)(x \in G, \Lambda \in H)$ with group multiplication defined $(x', \Lambda')(x, \Lambda) = (x'\Lambda'(x), \Lambda'\Lambda)$. The unit element of $G \rtimes H$ is (e_G, e_H) and the inverse of (x, Λ) is $(\Lambda^{-1}(x^{-1}), \Lambda^{-1})$. For example, the isometry group $ISO^+(3)$ of $\mathbb{R}^3$ (excluding reflections), composed of transformations $x \to Rx + b$, where R is a rotation matrix, and b is a translation vector. This group and its generalisations to n dimensions are called the **rigid body motions groups**.
A Normal subgroup N of group G and $x \in G$, partitions group G into several cosets. The elements of these cosets form a **factor group** in which the identity element is the normal subgroup, such that the multiplication of an element in one coset with an element in another coset will produce an element in a third coset: $x_1N.x_2N = \{x.y | x \in x_1N, y \in x_2N\} = x_jN$. A factor group example in which N is the identity element and the rest are the cosets partitioned from G is as follows:

$$\begin{pmatrix} x_6N & x_7N & x_8N \\ x_5N & x_4N & x_3N \\ N & x_1N & x_2N \end{pmatrix}$$

The Normal Series is defined as decomposing finite group G and choosing a proper, normal and maximal subgroup such that it is the biggest normal subgroup in G, denoting it N1, then the next maximal normal proper subgroup N2, and so on until the identity subgroup. This forms the Normal Series: $G \rhd N_1 \rhd N_2 \rhd \cdots \rhd 1$ such that $N_i < G$, and no duplicate subgroups. **The composition series** is a normal series that is as long as possible, similar to the prime factorisation of an Integer. A finite group G can have more than one composition series that are equivalent by having the same lengths and identical factor groups that might need to be rearranged to be isomorphic according to Jordan-Hölder Theorem. The composition series is used in solving equations of polynomial n such as $a_nx^n+a_{n-1}x^{n-1}+\ldots+a_1x+a_0 = 0$ formed as a group S_n. The solution is to decompose S_n into its composition series $S_n \rhd N_1 \rhd N_2 \rhd \cdots \rhd 1$ with abelian factor groups of simple quotient groups $\left(\frac{N_1}{1}, \frac{N_2}{N_1}, \frac{N_3}{N_2}, \ldots\right)$, but this fails when the polynomial degree n is ≥5. When n≥5, the group S_n is decomposed into three groups only, the full group itself, the alternating group, and the trivial identity group: $S_n \rhd A_n \rhd 1$. This leads to having the factor groups be $\left(\frac{S_n}{A_n}, \frac{A_n}{1}\right)$, such that $\frac{S_n}{A_n} \cong \frac{\mathbb{Z}}{2\mathbb{Z}}$, and $\frac{A_n}{1} \cong A_n$, and A_n was proven to be simple for n≥5 and can not be decomposed.

An ideal $I \subseteq R$ to a ring R is like a normal subgroup is to a group, with concepts of partitioning into cosets and kernels of homomorphism. Ideal partition rings into cosets; a collection of cosets are called factor groups or quotient groups. Ideal I must be an additive subgroup of ring R: (I, +)≤ (R, +), should also be closed under multiplication, and for any elements r in R, and i in I, then ir, ri should also be in I, such as cosets R/I form a factor/quotient ring.

A sub-module can be similarly defined to decompose modules, the way normal subgroups and ideals decompose groups and rings, respectively. For example, $3\mathbb{Z}$ is a $\mathbb{Z}$-module, with infinite sub-modules as $6\mathbb{Z}, 9\mathbb{Z}, 12\mathbb{Z}, \ldots$, etc.

Group mappings are identified by different properties as follows:

- **A function on a group** G is a function $f: G \to S$ mapping each group element to a member of some set S, which is primarily a vector field $\mathbb{F}$. If G is a finite group and V is a vector space over $\mathbb{C}$ of dimension |G|, taking any basis of V and labelling the basis vectors with the group elements $\{e_x\}_{x \in G}$, we identify the linear mapping of G elements L(G) with V by mapping each $f \in L(G)$ to the vector $\sum_{x \in G} f(x)e_x$.
- A **G-module** of a group G is a vector space V over a field $\mathbb{F}$ with operation $G \times V \to V$ satisfying: $xv \in V$; $x(\alpha v + \beta w) = \alpha(xv) + \beta(xw)$; $(xy)v = x(yv)$; $ev = v$. A G-module admits a homomorphism $\varphi: G \to GL(V)$.
- **Translating a function on a group,** $f: G \to S$ by $t \in G$, will yield $f^t: G \to S$, given by $f^t(x) = f(t^{-1}x)$, is the left-translate. If G is non-Abelian, we must distinguish the left-translate from the right-translate $f^{(t)}(x) = f(xt^{-1})$.
- **Haar measures** μ is a left-translation and right-translation invariant measure on G by any t $\in G$. Its left-translate is $\mu^t(X) = \mu(\{x \in G | tx \in X\})$, where X is the left-translate. It is unique up to scaling that is usually set so that $\int_G \mu(x) = 1$.
- **A closed set of transformations** turns a bijective mapping into a group by two operations: compositions and inverse, producing elements in the set. Given a set of bijective mappings $T = \{T_i: S \to S\}$ if for any $T_1, T_2 \in T$, their composition $T_2 \circ T_1$ is an element of T, and for any $T_i \in T$, the inverse map T_i^{-1} is also $\in T$ that reverses the transformation T_i.
- **A group G acts on a set S** if, to every group element x, we can associate a function $T_x: S \to S$ (also $T_x(s), x(s), or\ xs$) in such a way that $T_e(s) = s$ for all $s \in S$ and $T_{xy} = T_x\left(T_y(s)\right)$ for all $x, y \in S$ and s ∈ S.
- An **orbit** is what we get when we apply every element of G to s as a subset of S $\{x(s)\}_{s \in S, x \in G}$. The orbits partition S into disjoint subsets. If there is only one orbit, we say that G acts transitively on S.
- **A homogeneous space of group** G is a set S when there is only one orbit, and we fix any $s_0 \in S$, the map $\varphi: G \to S$ given by $x \to xs_0$ is surjective (i.e., sweeps out the entire set S).
- **The isotropy subgroup of group G** is formed from group elements fixing s_0 , which are subgroup $H = \{h \in G | hs_0 = s_0\}$. The Left quotient spaces and homogeneous spaces are just two aspects of the same concept since $xhs_0 = xs_0$ for any $h \in H$ is a one-to-one correspondence between S and the left cosets G/H.

The Groups, Algorithms, and Programming (GAP) is an interpreted language written in C that has Pascal-like syntax and can be compiled. The core GAP system contains built-in capabilities for group theory representation, algorithms, data sets, and many user-contributed packages. They have GAP 4 now, online documentation, and examples, and it can be downloaded from https://www.gap-system.org/Releases/index.html (GAP4, 2022). A Python wrapper to GAP can be found at https://github.com/embray/gappy/. Some elementary abstract algebra routines are implemented in Python, such as sack: https://github.com/johnkerl/sack. Ch5.ipynb uses some examples from sack to illustrate some of the concepts introduced in this section.

5.1.5 Representation Theory

Representation theory is a branch of mathematics that studies how algebraic structures, such as groups, rings, or Lie algebras, act on vector spaces. It provides a way to understand these structures by representing them as linear transformations matrices. A matrix representation ρ of a compact group G over Field $\mathbb{F}$ associated with each element of $x \in G$, a matrix $\rho(x) \in \mathbb{F}^{d_\rho \times d_\rho}$such that $\rho(xy) = \rho(x)\rho(y)$, for all $x, y \in G$, $\rho(e) = I$, $\rho(x^{-1}) = (\rho(x))^{-1}$, d_ρ is the order of the representation. This section explains the representation types and their properties.

Trivial representation is a one-dimensional irreducible constant representation $\rho_{tr}(x) = I \, \forall x \in G$. From one-dimensional to |G|-dimensional are possible based on the complete reducibility theorem.

Equivalent representations are defined for ρ_1, ρ_2, when there is an invertible square matrix T such that $\rho_1(x) = T^{-1}\rho_2(x)T, \forall x \in G$.

The fundamental representation of a Lie group can be thought of as the generators of the group. For example, vector representation is used for G = O(3) or SO(3) acting on vector space V = $\mathbb{R}^3$, and the spinor representation are used for G = SU(2) acting on a vector space V = $\mathbb{C}^2$ ('Spin representation', 2022).

The adjoint representation is based on the Adjoint homomorphism as a map from G to GL(g), where the operator Ad_A for A ∈ G is defined as $Ad_A(X) = AXA^{-1}, X \in g$. This is the Lie algebra of G. The following table summarises this and the previous representation type for some known groups (Jeevanjee, 2011):

Group	Fundamental Representation	Adjoint Representation
SO(3)	vector	vector
O(3)	vector	pseudovector
SU(2)	spinor	vector

Regular representation is the |G|-dimensional representation based on the action of G on itself, such that the representation matrices' rows and columns are labelled by the group elements, the matrix entries of the regular representations are:

$$[\rho_{reg}(x)]_{xy} = \begin{cases} 1, & if\ xy = z \\ 0, & otherwise \end{cases}.$$

A **character** is assigned to each representation $\chi: G \rightarrow C$, such that it is the trace of the representation matrices, $\chi(x) = tr(\rho(x))$, such that equivalent representations will share the same character.

Almost all interesting representations result from tensor products of other, simpler representations. Tensors themselves are elements of tensor product spaces, enabling transformations and reducible representation. **Tensor representation** is defined as $(\rho_1 \otimes \rho_2)(g) \equiv \rho_1(g) \otimes \rho_2(g) \in \mathcal{L}(V_1 \otimes V_2)$. The tensor representation provides a huge analysis of equivalent representations of known groups that can be studied from (Jeevanjee, 2011).

Reducible representation ρ if each matrix $\rho(x)$ has the block structure: $\rho(x) = \begin{bmatrix} A(x) & B(x) \\ 0 & C(x) \end{bmatrix}$, then there is always a similarity transformation $\rho \rightarrow T^{-1}\rho T$ that reduces ρ to a direct sum: $T^{-1}\rho(x)T = \begin{bmatrix} \rho_1(x) & 0 \\ 0 & \rho_2(x) \end{bmatrix}, \forall x \in G$ of smaller representations, $\rho_1(x), \rho_2(x)$. This decomposition is unique, up to equivalence of representations and changing the order of the terms in the direct sum. The different ρ_i's are not necessarily distinct.

Identifying the inequivalent representations of a given group or Lie algebra is important. This is difficult but can be simplified using the fact that for each group or algebra, there exists a denumerable set of inequivalent representations (known as the "irreducible" representations), out of which all other representations can be built by a kind of summation.

Irreducible representation ρ is when there is no invertible square matrix T that can simultaneously block diagonalise all $\rho(x)$ matrices in the above way. According to Wedderburn's or Maschke's theorem of complete reducibility, the blocks ρ_i used in the decomposition above are called irreducible blocks.
A complete set of inequivalent irreducible representations of G, denoted as $\mathcal{R}_G$ or $\mathcal{R}$ finding is essential for decomposition. Any ρ ∈ $\mathcal{R}$ can be replaced by an equivalent representation $\rho^1(x) = T^{-1}\rho(x)T$. When, $\rho(x^{-1}) = (\rho(x))^{-1}\ \forall x \in G$, then these are **unitary** irreducible representations. Some essential properties are as follows:

- If G is finite, then $\mathcal{R}$ is a finite set.
- If G is compact but not finite, then $\mathcal{R}$ is a countable set.

An **irreducible character** is assigned an irreducible representation $\chi: G \rightarrow C$, such that it is the trace of the irreducible representation matrices, $\chi(x) = tr(\rho(x))$.
A complete set of irreducible characters form an orthogonal basis for the space of class functions, and with conjugacy classes, both can unambiguously label the irreducible representations of a finite group such that $\tilde{\rho}(x) = \rho(x),\ if\ x \in H$; otherwise, it is equal to zero.
The dual space $\hat{G}$ of group G is the space of characters. The Abelian groups' corresponding characters form a group under the operation $(\chi_1\chi_2)(x) = \chi_1(x)\chi_2(x)$. Pontryagin theorem states that the double dual $\hat{\hat{G}}$ is isomorphic to G, and the isomorphism is canonical in the sense that there is a unique $\xi \in \hat{\hat{G}}$ satisfying $\xi(\chi) = \chi(x)$ for any $\chi \in \hat{G}$. **Harmonic analysis** is founded on this theorem on Locally Compact Abelian (LCA) groups.
G-Module V used in φ: G → GL(V), which is equivalent to ρ: G → GL(V), identifies an **equivalence class** of equivalent representations ρ that are equivalent to mapping φ. V is defined with the basis $e_1, e_2, \dots, e_{d_\rho}$, from which the matrix entries of the representation matrix ρ can be recovered as $[\rho(x)]_{i,j} = [\rho(x)e_j]_i$.
The permutation representation GS **naturally constructs group representations** of group G associated with set S, forming a G-module with basis vectors labelled by elements of S on which G acts by $g(e_s) = e_g(s)$.
The restricted representation $\rho \downarrow^G_H, \rho \downarrow_H$ is defined as given group G, its representation ρ, and a subgroup H of G, then $\rho \downarrow^G_H = \rho(x), \forall x \in H$, which is just a subset of the matrices of the representation of G.
The induced representation $\rho \uparrow^G_H, \rho \uparrow^G$ is defined as given a subgroup $H, t_1, t_2, \dots, t_l$ be a transversal for the left cosets of H in G; we can induce a representation ρ of G, by the block diagonal matrix:

$$\rho \uparrow^G_H = \begin{bmatrix} \tilde{\rho}(t_1^{-1}xt_1) & \cdots & \tilde{\rho}(t_1^{-1}xt_l) \\ \vdots & \ddots & \vdots \\ \tilde{\rho}(t_l^{-1}xt_1) & \cdots & \tilde{\rho}(t_l^{-1}xt_l) \end{bmatrix}$$

, where $\tilde{\rho}(x) = \rho(x)$ if $x \in H$ and otherwise, it is zero.
For Symmetric group $\mathbb{S}_n$ **the conjugacy classes** correspond exactly to the collection of elements of a given cycle type as defined earlier. Hence, the irreducible representations of $\mathbb{S}_n$ can be labelled by the integer partitions $\lambda \vdash n$.
The conjugacy class of transpositions is defined as the permutations of the form (i, j). A cycle $(s_1, s_2, \dots, s_k)$ can be written as the product $(s_1, s_2) \cdot (s_2, s_3) \cdot \dots \cdot (s_{k-1}, s_k)$, the set of transpositions generates the entire symmetric group.
The sign of σ, denoted $sgn(\sigma) \equiv (-1)^m$, defines the **even permutations** for which sgn(σ) = 1, and the **odd permutations** for which sgn(σ) = -1. This creates an **alternating representation** of $\mathbb{S}_n$ of degree n, denoted A_n. Alternating groups and symmetric groups form a family of non-Abelian finite groups. **The trivial representation** ρ(σ) = 1 and the alternating representation ρ(σ) = sgn(σ) are both irreducible representations and the only two one-dimensional ones.
The defining representation describes $\mathbb{S}_n$ in terms of its action on (1, 2, ..., n) with the n-dimensional representation $[\rho_{def}(\sigma)]_{i,j} = \begin{cases} 1, & if\ \sigma(i) = j \\ 0, & otherwise \end{cases}$, such that the $\rho_{def}(\sigma)$ matrices are often called permutation matrices. The defining representation is reducible by the direct sum of trivial representations and some n-1 dimensional representation.

A Ferres diagram is a graphical representation of integer partitions consisting of simply laying down $\lambda_1, \lambda_2, \dots, \lambda_k$ empty boxes in k consecutive rows, such as the (3, 2) shape for the partition of 5: $\begin{array}{|c|c|c|}\hline \ & \ & \ \\ \hline \ & \ \\ \cline{1-2}\end{array}$

A Young tableau is a Ferres diagram bijectively populated by the numbers 1, 2, . . . , n, such as: $t = \begin{array}{|c|c|c|}\hline 3 & 2 & 5 \\ \hline 1 & 4 \\ \cline{1-2}\end{array}$

A tabloid is an equivalence class of tableau under permutations of the numerals in each row. For example, the set of tableaux of shape (3, 2), denoted as: $\{t\} = \dfrac{\overline{\ 3\ \ 2\ \ 5\ }}{\underline{\ 1\ \ 4\ }} =$

$$\left\{ \begin{array}{|c|c|c|}\hline 3 & 2 & 5 \\ \hline 1 & 4 \\ \cline{1-2}\end{array}, \begin{array}{|c|c|c|}\hline 3 & 5 & 2 \\ \hline 1 & 4 \\ \cline{1-2}\end{array}, \begin{array}{|c|c|c|}\hline 2 & 3 & 5 \\ \hline 1 & 4 \\ \cline{1-2}\end{array}, \begin{array}{|c|c|c|}\hline 2 & 5 & 3 \\ \hline 1 & 4 \\ \cline{1-2}\end{array}, \begin{array}{|c|c|c|}\hline 5 & 2 & 3 \\ \hline 1 & 4 \\ \cline{1-2}\end{array}, \begin{array}{|c|c|c|}\hline 5 & 3 & 2 \\ \hline 1 & 4 \\ \cline{1-2}\end{array}, \right.$$

$$\left. \begin{array}{|c|c|c|}\hline 3 & 2 & 5 \\ \hline 4 & 1 \\ \cline{1-2}\end{array}, \begin{array}{|c|c|c|}\hline 3 & 5 & 2 \\ \hline 4 & 1 \\ \cline{1-2}\end{array}, \begin{array}{|c|c|c|}\hline 2 & 3 & 5 \\ \hline 4 & 1 \\ \cline{1-2}\end{array}, \begin{array}{|c|c|c|}\hline 2 & 5 & 3 \\ \hline 4 & 1 \\ \cline{1-2}\end{array}, \begin{array}{|c|c|c|}\hline 5 & 2 & 3 \\ \hline 4 & 1 \\ \cline{1-2}\end{array}, \begin{array}{|c|c|c|}\hline 5 & 3 & 2 \\ \hline 4 & 1 \\ \cline{1-2}\end{array} \right\}$$

The permutation representation is a real-valued representation of shape λ that is defined such that if t and t′ are two members of some tabloid {t}, then their images σ(t) and σ(t′) for some $\sigma \in \mathbb{S}_n$ will also be members of a common tabloid σ ({t}). The set of tabloids of shape λ form **a homogeneous space of the symmetric group $\mathbb{S}_n$**.
The row stabiliser R_t of a tableau t of shape λ is defined as the subgroup of $\mathbb{S}_n$ which leaves the rows of t invariant, i.e., only permutes numerals within each row. **The column stabiliser** C_t is analogous to the row stabiliser.
The permutation module denoted M^λ is the submodule of $\mathbb{C}[\mathbb{S}_n]$, formed from the elements corresponding to tabloids of shape λ. Permutation modules M^λ are reducible, and they are used to construct irreducible representations of $\mathbb{S}_n$.
The Specht module S^λ is an irreducible submodule of each permutation module M^λ.
A complete set of irreducible representations is formed from the G-modules of G from the collection of Specht modules $\{S^\lambda\}^\lambda$.
A polytabloid is a linear combination of tabloids that is antisymmetric with respect to this subgroup: $e_t = \sum_{\pi \in Ct} sgn(\pi)\pi(\{t\})$. For example, the polytabloid corresponding to the previous example is:

$$e_t = \frac{3\ \ 2\ \ 5}{\underline{1\ \ 4\quad}} - \frac{1\ \ 2\ \ 5}{\underline{3\ \ 4\quad}} - \frac{3\ \ 4\ \ 5}{\underline{1\ \ 2\quad}} + \frac{1\ \ 2\ \ 5}{\underline{3\ \ 4\quad}}$$

Some examples are: for shape λ = n, $M^{(n)}$ corresponds to the trivial one-dimensional representation and is irreducible such that $M^{(n)} = S^{(n)}$. for shape λ = n-1, $M^{(n-1,1)}$ contains a copy of trivial Specht module $S^{(n)}$, such that $M^{(n-1,1)} = S^{(n)} \oplus S^{(n-1,1)}$. This continues until the opposite case of $M^{(1,1,\dots,1)}$ as the regular representation decomposes into the direct sum of S^λs where λ runs over all partitions of n.
Standard tableaux is defined such that numbers in each row and each column are increasing. **The standard irreducible representation** of $\mathbb{S}_n$ is defined from the linearly independent polytabloids corresponding to the standard tableaux of a given shape.
Young's orthogonal representation (YOR) for $\mathbb{S}_n$ is simpler than the standard irreducible representation, such that the rows of its representation matrices are orthogonal. It is based on labelling the dimensions of ρ_λ by standard tableaux of shape λ, without invoking polytabloids or the group algebra. It is restricted to the adjacent transpositions $\{\tau_1, \tau_2, \dots, \tau_{n-1}\}$, we can specify the matrix entries of $\rho_\lambda(\tau_k)$ explicitly. These matrices were proven to be very sparse such that the only non-zero entries in any row, indexed by the standard tableau t, are the diagonal entry $[\rho_\lambda(\tau_k)]_{t,t} = \frac{1}{d_t(k,k+1)}$, $d_t(k, k+1)$ is a special signed distance defined on Young tableaux.

The irreducible representations of GL_n are labeled by partitions λ, similar to $\mathbb{S}_n$. **Young symmetrizer** acts on basis vectors to form equivalence classes corresponding to the analogues of polytabloids. This yields the **Weyl module,** which is considered the irreducible GL_n-module. It has the following structure that shows a subgroup of GL_n to be isomorphic to GL_{n-1} as a form of embedding:

$$M = \begin{bmatrix} m_{1,1} & \cdots & m_{1,n-1} & 0 \\ \vdots & \ddots & \vdots & 0 \\ m_{n-1,1} & \cdots & m_{n-1,n-1} & 0 \\ 0 & \cdots & 0 & 1 \end{bmatrix}$$

The irreducible representation of GL_n takes the form D_λ can be constructed by a Gelfand-Tsetlin basis adapted to the tower of subgroups: $GL_n > GL_{n-1} \times \mathbb{C}^* > GL_{n-2} \times (\mathbb{C}^*)^2 > \cdots > (\mathbb{C}^*)^n$.

To illustrate representation theory, let's focus on group representations. A group representation is a homomorphism that maps elements of a group to invertible linear transformations on a vector space. This allows us to analyze the group through its action on vector spaces.

Mathematical Example:
Let's consider the symmetric group S_3, which consists of all permutations of three elements. We can represent this group using 3x3 permutation matrices.

Step 1: Define the group: $S_3 = \{(1), (12), (23), (13), (123), (132)\}$

Step 2: Choose a vector space: Let's work with $\mathbb{R}^3$, the three-dimensional real vector space.

Step 3: Construct the representation: We define a homomorphism ϕ: $S_3 \to GL(\mathbb{R}^3)$ that maps each group element to a 3x3 invertible matrix.

$\phi((1)) = I_3$ (identity matrix)
$\phi((12)) = P_1$ (permutation matrix swapping elements 1 and 2)
$\phi((23)) = P_2$ (permutation matrix swapping elements 2 and 3)
$\phi((13)) = P_3$ (permutation matrix swapping elements 1 and 3)
$\phi((123)) = R_1$ (rotation matrix)
$\phi((132)) = R_2$ (rotation matrix)

Step 4: Explore the representation: Now we can analyze how the group elements act on vectors in $\mathbb{R}^3$. For example, let's consider the vector $v = (1, 0, 0)^T$.

Applying $\phi((12))$ to v, we get $\phi((12))(v) = P_1 * v = (0, 1, 0)^T$. This corresponds to swapping the first and second coordinates of v.

Similarly, applying $\phi((123))$ to v, we get $\phi((123))(v) = R_1 * v = (0.5, 0.866, 0)^T$. This corresponds to rotating the vector v by 120 degrees in the xy-plane.

Source Code Example:
Let's provide a Python code snippet to demonstrate representation theory using the NumPy library for matrix operations:

```
import numpy as np

# Define the group elements
group_elements = [(1), (12), (23), (13), (123), (132)]

# Define the vector space
vector_space = np.array([1, 0, 0])

# Define the representation matrices
identity = np.eye(3)
P1 = np.array([[0, 1, 0], [1, 0, 0], [0, 0, 1]])
P2 = np.array([[1, 0, 0], [0, 0, 1], [0, 1, 0]])
P3 = np.array([[0, 0, 1], [0, 1, 0], [1, 0, 0]])
R1 = np.array([[0.5, -0.866, 0], [0.866, 0.5, 0], [0, 0, 1]])
R2 = np.array([[0.5, 0.866, 0], [-0.866, 0.5, 0], [0, 0, 1]])

# Define the representation mapping
representation = {
    (1): identity,
    (12): P1,
     (23): P2,
     (13): P3,
     (123): R1,
     (132): R2,
    }
```

Apply the representation to the vector

```
for element in group_elements:
    result = np.dot(representation[element], vector_space)
    print(f"{element}: {result}")
```

Please note that this is just a simplified example, and in practice, representation theory encompasses much broader concepts and applications.

5.2 Harmonic analysis

Intuitively, Harmonic Analysis is the study of symmetry originally introduced from music theory. According to the Nöether theorem, behind every conservation principle in physics, from conservation of energy to linear and angular momentum, lies a symmetry problem. Mahadevan's book (Mahadevan, 2008) explains how machine learning algorithms perform representation discovery using harmonic analysis utilizing the Fourier Transforms and wavelet analysis. The harmonic analysis maps a phenomenon that occurs over space or time into a frequency-oriented coordinate system, using a change of basis, or coordinate systems, as discussed previously. Representation discovery is enabled by learning from the data a (very small) orthogonal basis functions Φ that span a set of invariant subspaces that can uniquely generate/reconstruct all the data. These basis functions extract regularities from data and summarise them by projecting them into invariant subspaces.

An example of an invariant subspace is the one-dimensional space spanned by an eigenvector associated with a specific eigenvalue of a matrix. The choice of the right representative basis affects the efficiency of the machine

learning, optimization, or search algorithms in terms of accuracy and storage requirements. The Fourier analysis provides one form of a small set of bases in the frequency domain. The spectral analysis provided by the Laplacian operator analyses data in terms of its projection to orthogonal subspaces to identify structures and clusters. The wavelet analysis provides another multiscale basis discovery suitable to functions on data with discontinuities. In the context of data on groups, the natural choice of subspaces is called the isotypals, which are the irreducible subalgebras in the corresponding decomposition, as explained earlier in this chapter. Approximation methods can scale basis construction to large graphs, including exploiting symmetries in graphs matrix sparsification, low-rank approximation, graph partitioning, and Kronecker product approximation.
The group theoretic definition of Harmonic Analysis is that it is a projection of functions on an orthonormal basis. The convolution theorem, in particular, tells us that a mapping or function F is special because it corresponds to a decomposition of L(G), the class of all complex-valued functions on G into a sum of spaces closed under convolution (Risi Kondor, 2008).
A dataset in the form of a signal can be of various types. The following are some examples:

- Audio (sound waves that are generated from the vocal tract, musical instruments, or another audio recording and sensed by the ear),
- Video (continuous stream of images that are electromagnetic radiation that the eye can sense),
- Physical or mechanical interaction can be viewed as processes where a quantity: air pressure, electromagnetic field, physical bodies, or their positions are changing as a function of time, in which the harmonic analysis tests the response of these structures to loads that vary sinusoidally with time to predict if resonance would occur.
- Time-series, or any structures that experience vibrations or cyclic loadings, such as bridges, engines, and traffic flow problems.

Starting from the number systems, a number representation such as 3 (decimal), III (Roman), and 011 (Binary) all represent the same object. The decimal representation uses the place-value notation uses basis functions of 1, 10, 100, ... and so on. So, number 232 is expanded/**analysed** as $2*(10)^2+3*(10)^1+2*(10)^0 = 232$. Each coefficient is calculated/**synthesized** by dividing by the basis function relevant to its place/position, such as $232/(10)^2=2$ for the third position number. This analysis/synthesis is what learning the correct basis can do to a dataset by summarising it and identifying symmetries such that storage requirements can be reduced. For example, as we studied in chapter one, all vectors are synthesized from their coordinate basis e_i. Another example, a vector v describing an object such as a function on a graph, is synthesized from basis functions $\Phi = \{\phi_1, \dots\}$, as a linear expansion $v = \sum_i \alpha_i \phi_i$, where each coefficient α_i can be viewed as a "measurement" of the object. This makes v **analysed** as linear functionals $v = \{\langle v, \phi_1 \rangle, \dots, \langle v, \phi_n \rangle\}: V \times V \rightarrow \mathbb{R}$. This is expressed as linear functions of inner product form: $\alpha_i = \langle v, \psi_i \rangle$, where ψ_i are the synthesis features, which are the dual basis to ϕ_i. This makes the object **synthesized** as $\hat{v} = \sum_i c_i \psi_i = \sum_i \langle v, \phi_i \rangle \psi_i$, where c_i are the coefficients of the measurements in the dual space. This equation is defined as a vector's abstract Fourier series expansion. It is a full reconstruction when all synthesis coefficients are used in the finite dimension. If fewer c_is are selected, then this is an approximate reconstruction that can be applied using various constraints such as orthogonality, compactness, sparsity, and complexity, and these may be in conflict. One basis selection strategy is to use the bases with the largest inner product. Another approach is the usual iterative approach to minimise the error ϵ in reconstruction such that the choice of bases in the summation index i will produce a reconstruction $\hat{v} = \sum_i c_i \psi_i$, with $\|v - \sum_i c_i \psi_i\| \leq \epsilon$.
Fourier transform performs a change of basis to global basis from the space or time domains to the frequency domain. Due to its inability to handle smooth functions with local discontinuities and cannot reveal multi-scale regularities, wavelet analysis transforms the data from space or time to combined multi-scale space-frequency or time-frequency scales using a graph-based approach called diffusion wavelets. Fourier and wavelet analysis can be generalised from Euclidean spaces to non-Euclidean spaces defined by graphs, groups, and manifolds, enabling new basis discovery techniques to be developed in discrete data and search spaces. Abstract harmonic analysis

on finite Abelian and non-Abelian groups and its applications are further studied in (Mahadevan, 2008) and (Stanković, Moraga and Astola, 2005).

5.2.1 Fourier transforms

Fourier transforms real-valued functions and decomposes them as linear combinations of highly symmetric trigonometric functions. The change of basis of space or time in x (based on the nature of the dataset) to the frequency domain k using sines and cosines as basis functions is defined as the mapping $\mathcal{F}: f \rightarrow \hat{f}$. For example, a function f in the space or time domain is considered to be composed by summing several sinusoids of different frequencies, as shown in Figure 69 for two sine waves. This means any periodicity/symmetries in the data are captured as frequency amplitude, and the period is the frequency width, providing a compressed representation from which the original space or time data can be reconstructed by inverse transform. Example applications are the PCA, SVD, as explained in chapter two, and time-series and image-compression using Fast Fourier Transform (FFT), manifold, and graph-based methods such as diffusion maps, ISOMAP, LLE, and Laplacian eigenmaps (Spectral embedding), among many more in various disciplines. Chapter two, accompanying source code, showed a number of algorithms in the 2-way matrix form that belong to this class. Ch5.ipynb shows more examples using an audio dataset, applying harmonic analysis features extraction methods such as STFT (short-time Fourier transform) and Continous and Discrete Wavelet transform and their reconstruction errors and their effects on classification models learning time and accuracy.

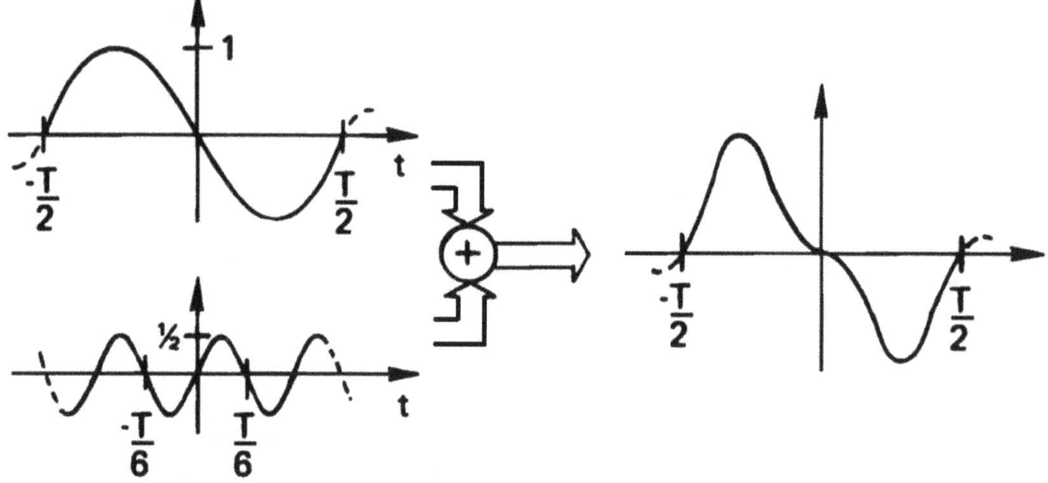

Figure 69: Two sine waves on the right-hand side are summed together to form a function in the time domain on the left-hand side adapted from (Brigham, 1988)

The Fourier transform is defined as:

$$\hat{f}(k) = \int e^{-i2\pi kx} f(x)dx$$

The Fourier series is a special case of FT, calculated as follows:

$$\hat{f}(k) = \frac{1}{2\pi}\int_0^{2\pi} e^{ikx} f(x)dx$$

The inverse FT is defined as the inverse mapping $\mathcal{F}^{-1}: \hat{f} \rightarrow f$ as follows:

$$f(x) = \sum_{k=-\infty}^{\infty} \hat{f}(k)e^{ikx} = \int e^{2\pi ikx} \hat{f}(k)dk$$

This requires that the input function f(x) has some integrability properties for the forward transform and continuity properties for the inverse. Working in the new frequency domain is equivalent but more compact than in the measurements domain; this includes the inner product norm, translation property, and convolution property. Parseval's theorem or Plancherel's theorem proves that the inner products to measure similarities between two functions before and after the transform are unitary, such that $\langle f.g\rangle = \langle \hat{f}.\hat{g}\rangle$. The translation property means if f translates by t, $f^t(x) = f([x-t]_{2\pi})$, where $[.]_z$ means modulo z, then $\hat{f}^t(k) = e^{2\pi itkx}\hat{f}(k)$. A shift by α in the space or time domain is multiplication by $\exp(-i\alpha k)$ in the frequency domain $f(x-\alpha) = \hat{f}(k)e^{-i\alpha k}$. A scaling by α in the space or time domain is scaling by the reciprocal of α in the frequency domain $f(\alpha x) = \frac{1}{|\alpha|}\hat{f}\left(\frac{k}{\alpha}\right)$. This is extended to the convolution theorem such that the convolution of f(x) by g(x) in the space or time domain is just a multiplication of their frequency domain transforms: $\mathcal{F}(f * g)(k) = \hat{f}(k)\cdot\hat{g}(k)$. Also, the derivative of a function in the time domain is equivalent to multiplying the frequency domain transform by the frequency value raised to the power of the order of the derivative: $\left(\frac{d}{dx}\right)^m f(x) \Rightarrow (ik)^m\hat{f}(k)$.
The FT is essential to the study of partial differential equations because when the underlying space has a natural differential structure, the FT relates to that in a canonical way: on the unit circle (parametrised by angle), we have $\widehat{\partial f}(k) = ik\ \hat{f}(k)$, while on the real line $\widehat{\partial f}(k) = 2\pi ik\ \hat{f}(k)$.
The group theoretic FT is based on the fact that the domain of f is a group G, such that $\mathbb{T} = \mathbb{R}/\mathbb{Z}, \mathbb{R}$ and $\mathbb{Z}_n$, these factors are the irreducible characters of G. This redefines FT as: $\hat{f}(\chi) = \mathcal{F}(f)(\chi) = \int_G \chi(x)f(x)d\mu(x)$, where χ ranges over the characters of G, and μ is the Haar measure on G. Since the irreducible characters of an LCA group form a dual group $\hat{G}$, the inverse transform is given by a similar integral over the dual group: $f(\chi) = \mathcal{F}^{-1}(\hat{f})(\chi) = \int_{\hat{G}} \chi(x^{-1})\hat{f}(x)d\hat{\mu}(x)$. This extends the harmonic analysis to LCA groups while maintaining all its properties by taking advantage of the fact that the irreducible characters of an Abelian group form an orthonormal basis for the group algebra. Using group and representation theory properties, a representation of f(x) can be restricted to $\rho(x)$ such that the FT can be defined as $\hat{f}(\rho) = \sum_{x\in G} f(x)\rho(x), \rho \in \mathcal{R}$, and the inverse is $f(x) = \frac{1}{|G|}\sum_{\rho\in\mathcal{R}} d_\rho tr[\hat{f}(\rho)\rho(x^{-1})]$.The derivation is provided in (Risi Kondor, 2008). The convolution of a group is defined as $(f * g)(x) = \sum_{y\in G} f(xy^{-1})g(y)$, satisfying the convolution theorem $\widehat{f * g}(\rho) = \hat{f}(\rho)\hat{g}(\rho)$, and consequently also the left- and right-translation properties $\hat{f}^t(\rho) = \rho(t)\hat{f}(\rho)$ and $\hat{f}^{(t)}(\rho) = \hat{f}(\rho)\rho(t)$.

An example application of Fourier analysis on groups is defined as studying the effect of sunlight(s), weed killer(w) and fertilizer(r) on the yield of wheat measured by $f(s,w,r)$. These three variables are assumed binary (high/low) or (+,-) for simplification and to reduce to a 2^k factorial design class of problems. For three variables, there are 2^3 possible permutations f_{+++}, f_{++-}, f_{+-+}, ... etc. The different linear combinations of these variables contain the zeroth order that computes the mean wheat yield independent of the effects of the variables, producing a grand mean as:

$$\mu = \frac{1}{8}(f_{+++} + f_{++-} + f_{+-+} + f_{+--} + f_{-++} + f_{-+-} + f_{--+} + f_{---})$$

First-order effects consider each factor in isolation and compute its mean yield. For example, the mean for the first factor (sunlight/s) is defined as:

$$\mu_s = \frac{1}{4}(f_{+++} + f_{++-} + f_{+-+} + f_{+--}) - \frac{1}{4}(f_{-++} + f_{-+-} + f_{--+} + f_{---})$$

Similar first-order effects are computed for the other two variables. A second-order effects measure the different combination of two variables' impact on the wheat yield producing a mean relative to the two variables specified. For example, the mean for the combined effect of the first and second variables is defined as follows:

$$\mu_{sw} = \frac{1}{2}\left(f_{+++} + f_{++-}) - \frac{1}{2}(f_{+-+} + f_{+--}\right) - \frac{1}{2}(f_{-++} + f_{-+-}) + \frac{1}{2}(f_{--+} + f_{---})$$

Notice that we add the partial means when both variables are positive or negative and subtract when they are different. The remaining two combinations of 2 variables can be computed similarly. The final third-order measures the effects of all variables combined on the wheat yield, producing the mean:

$$\mu_{swr} = \frac{1}{8}(f_{+++} - f_{++-} + f_{+--} - f_{+-+} + f_{-+-} - f_{-++} + f_{--+} - f_{---})$$

Notice the rearrangement of the (+/-)combinations and subtractions when two variables are negatives (low). These three orders of effects and their variable combinations give a complete representation of the data from which the original data can be reconstructed from them. This representation can be defined in a transform matrix form denoted $\mathbb{Z}_2^3$ as follows:

$$\begin{bmatrix} \mu \\ \mu_s \\ \mu_w \\ \mu_r \\ \mu_{sw} \\ \mu_{sr} \\ \mu_{wr} \\ \mu_{swr} \end{bmatrix} = \begin{bmatrix} 1 & 1 & 1 & 1 & 1 & 1 & 1 & 1 \\ 1 & 1 & 1 & 1 & -1 & -1 & -1 & -1 \\ 1 & 1 & -1 & -1 & 1 & 1 & -1 & -1 \\ 1 & -1 & 1 & -1 & 1 & -1 & 1 & -1 \\ 1 & 1 & -1 & -1 & -1 & -1 & 1 & 1 \\ 1 & -1 & 1 & -1 & -1 & 1 & -1 & 1 \\ 1 & -1 & -1 & 1 & 1 & -1 & -1 & 1 \\ 1 & -1 & -1 & 1 & -1 & 1 & 1 & -1 \end{bmatrix} \begin{bmatrix} f_{+++} \\ f_{++-} \\ f_{+-+} \\ f_{+--} \\ f_{-++} \\ f_{-+-} \\ f_{--+} \\ f_{---} \end{bmatrix}$$

The vector of μ's is the Fourier transform of f over this group. The specific subindices can be transformed to index k as follows: $\mu_k = \sum_{x \in \mathbb{Z}_2^3} \chi_k(x) f(x)$, such that the order of k establishes an isomorphism $x \to \chi_k$ from $\mathbb{Z}_2^3$ to its dual, with the identity being (+,+,+), the norm on $\mathbb{Z}_2^3$ is the count of negative components mapped to the dual. The zeroth-order effect will have norm 0; the first-order effects will have norm 1, ..., etc. This is similar to analyzing functions on $\mathbb{R}^n$ in terms of a hierarchy of Fourier components of increasing frequency. Check another Symmetric group example in (Risi Kondor, 2008).

Fourier Transform connects continuous mathematics, such as linear differential equations, to concepts in discrete mathematics, such as linear algebra and matrix theory, using the principle of diagonalisation. Diagonalising continuous spaces using a discrete version of the "Laplacian" operator yields a discrete FT. This operator is commonly called the graph Laplacian and is explained below.

Other FT algorithms are defined for various applications and for computational efficiencies, such as the Fast Fourier Transform (FFT), which reduces the computation from $O(n^2)$ to $O(n \log_2 n)$, where n is the number of data samples in f(x). A C++ implementation of FFT on the symmetric group using the Clausen FFT algorithm is provided by the author of (Risi Kondor, 2008) and is available at https://people.cs.uchicago.edu/~risi/SnOB/.

5.2.2 Laplace on functions and graphs

The Laplace operator is another tool for identifying symmetries. A Riemannian manifold is represented using an undirected graph of the points in the manifold. The graph Laplacian (as defined below) is of interest in several areas, including dimensionality reduction, Markov processes, spectral graph theory, and web page ranking.

In chapter three, the continuous Laplace operator was provided using the divergence operator of the gradient of a function and the trace of the Hessian matrix of the function, which is for a function of two variables is $\frac{\delta^2 f}{\delta x^2} + \frac{\delta^2 f}{\delta y^2} = tr(H(f))$, which is invariant to coordinate/basis change and measures function curvature. For a given graph G = (V, E, W), where |V| = n nodes, E is the edges list, an edge between nodes (u, v) ∈ E, edges' weights are given in the W matrix. Another form is to merge E & W and use adjacency matrix A, which includes either 1 or 0 in unweighted graphs or the weight value in the case of weighted graphs. Also, for directed graphs, the weight or the adjacency can be non-symmetric as the existence of (u, v) edge does not imply the existence of a (v, u) edge. For u ~ v, meaning an (undirected) edge between u and v, the degree of u is defined to be $d(u) = \sum_{u \sim v} w(u, v)$. D will denote the diagonal matrix defined by D_{uu} = d(u) as the row sums of W or A. Whether the graph is defined with an adjacency list or adjacent matrix, the discrete version of the Laplace operator can be defined as L = D-W or L = D-A. The normalized Laplacian $\mathcal{L} = D^{-1/2}(D - W)D^{-1/2}$. The Laplacian is an operator on the space of functions $F: V \to \mathbb{R}$ on a graph, such that $Lf(u) = \sum_{u \sim v}(f(u) - f(v))\ w(u, v)$, replacing the continuous derivatives with finite differences.

The fundamental property of the graph Laplacian is that projections of functions on the eigenspace of the Laplacian produce the smoothest global approximation respecting the underlying graph topology. This constructs the basis functions that best capture the graphs' structure due to the close Laplacian connection with classical Fourier analysis, the continuous Laplacian on manifolds, and random walks. Whether the normalised Laplacian is used or not, both have non-negative eigenvalues, with corresponding eigenfunctions that can be used as an orthonormal basis of smooth global functions to approximate any function on a graph. The projection of a function f on the smallest set S of the indices to produce the smallest acceptable error onto the top k eigenvectors corresponding to the smallest eigenvalues of the Laplacian is the smoothest approximation to f. The second eigenvector is the Fiedler eigenvector, which is the eigenvector associated with the smallest nonzero eigenvalue of the Laplacian matrix and is generally used to partition the graph. It characterises the sensitivity or a bottleneck in a graph that can be used in clustering or partitioning the graph. The basis functions are then computed by diagonalizing a Laplacian/ diffusion operator on the space of functions on the graph.
The Laplace operator can be calculated from the Fourier analysis by taking the Laplacian and finding its eigenvectors. It can also be calculated by doing a multi-scale wavelet analysis, which takes the powers of the random walk Laplacian and builds multi-scale representations at different spatial and temporal levels. Computing the Laplacian on a group, we turn the group into an undirected graph and define the neighbourhood of x~y, denoting the fact that x, y ∈ G are neighbours, and letting d_x denote the number of edges incident on x, then the graph Laplacian as the |G|×|G| matrix:

$$\Delta_{x,y} = \begin{cases} 1, & if\ x \sim y \\ -dx, & if\ x = y \\ 0, & otherwise \end{cases}$$

The diffusion kernels generalise the Gaussian kernels induced by captured local similarities by the Laplacian while regularising the function. The diffusion kernel of the above Laplacian is:

$$k(x,y) = \left[e^{\beta\Delta}\right]_{x,y} = \left[\lim_{n\to\infty}\left(1+\frac{\beta\Delta}{n}\right)^n\right]_{x,y}.$$

The Laplacian on functions on G is defined by $(\Delta f)(x) = \sum_{y\in G} \Delta_{x,y} f(y)$, the kernel is defined as: $\langle f, \Delta f \rangle = -\frac{1}{2}\sum_{x\sim y}(f(x) - f(y))^1$, such that $-\Delta$ measures how f violates the graph structure. Computing the Laplacian eigenvalues $\lambda_1, \dots, \lambda_{|G|}$ and eigenvectors $v_1, \dots, v_{|G|}$, we can express the kernel as:

$$K = \sum_{i=1}^{|G|} e^{\beta\lambda_i} v_1 v_i^T$$

And the discrete regularisation operator as:

$$\Upsilon = \sum_{i=1}^{|G|} e^{\beta\lambda_i/2} v_1 v_i^T$$

This diffusion kernel penalizes functions according to how much energy they have in the "high frequency" modes on the graph, i.e., the ones that violate many edges. For more examples and discussion of various applications, check (Risi Kondor, 2008).

The Hodge theorem states that the eigenfunctions of the Laplacian on a manifold provide a complete discrete basis for all square-integrable functions on a continuous manifold. The key problem in extending eigenfunctions to continuous spaces is how to extend sample values to new unobserved values: out-of-sample extension. Nyström interpolation provides a solution to the out-of-sample extension.
Spectral data embedding, as shown in chapter two's source code examples (Maniflods.ipynb), clustering, and edge detections, are general applications of the Laplacian. Scipy python implements the graph laplacian in their compressed sparse graph routines package, such as "scipy.sparse.csgraph.laplacian" function. OpenCV also implements the function. Both examples are demonstrated in ch5.ipynb accompanying source code examples.

5.2.3 Wavelet Analysis

Fourier Analysis use global basis functions of sines and cosines. Hence, they can transform stationary signals only. Stationary signals' amplitude and frequency do not change over time. Short-Time Fourier Transform (STFT) divides the time series into windows and applies FT on each window to identify its frequency amplitude. This produces uncertainties regarding the overlapping window sizes and variable frequencies within. Consequently, they can not adequately handle local discontinuous functions and multi-scale regularities. Instead of mapping space-time x to the frequency domain k, the wavelet analysis combines time or space into multi-scale/multi-resolution time-frequency or space-frequency of varying granularities.

Furthermore, the literature proposes variable basis functions called wavelets instead of using trigonometry basis functions. Also, a concept of dilation equations using a diffusion operator on the graph is used instead of diagonalisation and differential equations used in FT. The random walk method is used to construct the basis elements at multiple levels of spatial and temporal abstractions by constructing each level by dilating/scaling the ones at the previous level. This constructs a hierarchy of vector spaces and two sets of basis functions called scaling functions representing coarser views and wavelets representing the finer detailed view. The computation cost is reduced using matrix compression, sampling, and domain knowledge concepts.

In convolution, a filter (matrix) is multiplied by a region in a larger data matrix to identify the presence of the object of the filter content in this region, then slides over the remaining temporal or spatial regions to provide translation invariance. Similarly, different scales of the different wavelets are convoluted over the time or space data series to identify the location of the wavelet presence is found. Then all are summed up to identify the multi-scale/multi-resolution combined frequency-time or frequency-space domain.

The Haar basis is the earliest, simplest, and most adopted example of a wavelet basis. For a one-dimensional x variable, a decimal value of 7 can be decomposed using the Haar basis for 1D as:

$$7 = 4\phi(x) + 3\psi(x)$$

Such that $\phi(x) = \begin{cases} 1, & for\ 0 \le x < 1/2 \\ -1, & for\ 1/2 \le x < 1 \\ 0, & otherwise \end{cases}$, $\psi(x) = \begin{cases} 1, & 0 \le x < 1 \\ 0, & otherwise \end{cases}$, are the mother scale function and mother wavelet function, respectively. Other basis functions could be derived by scaling and translating them. The process is to repeat this average & difference process to obtain one scale coefficient and N-1 detail coefficients for N signals.

We can do this using the linear mapping transformation matrix from Vector space V to vector space W, as explained in chapter one $T: V \to W$, also called operator. To make the mapping apply basis changes from $B_1 = \{u_1, \dots, u_n\}$to $B_2 = \{v_1, \dots v_n\}$, it is denoted $[T]_{B_1}^{B_2}$. Given a vector, a in V expressed as $a = a_1u_1 + \dots + a_nu_n$, a transformation to vector b in W would include the basis transformation as $b = b_1T(u_1) + \dots + b_nT(u_n)$, such that $T(u_i) = u_i'$, and $u_i' = \sum_{i=1}^{m} \alpha_1 v_1$ is the direct sum of vectors, in case the dimensionality of the input space n is different from the dimensionality of the output space m, α_i are the transformation coefficients. For example, Haar basis for $\mathbb{R}^4$ is defined as:

$$e_{h_1} = \begin{bmatrix} 1 \\ 1 \\ 1 \\ 1 \end{bmatrix}, e_{h_2} = \begin{bmatrix} 1 \\ 1 \\ -1 \\ -1 \end{bmatrix}, e_{h_3} = \begin{bmatrix} 1 \\ -1 \\ 0 \\ 0 \end{bmatrix}, e_{h_4} = \begin{bmatrix} 0 \\ 0 \\ 1 \\ -1 \end{bmatrix}$$

The transformation matrix from the Haar unit basis H to the identity unit basis U in $\mathbb{R}^4$,

$$[I]_H^U \begin{bmatrix} 1 & 1 & 1 & 0 \\ 1 & 1 & -1 & 0 \\ 1 & -1 & 0 & 1 \\ 1 & -1 & 0 & -1 \end{bmatrix} \text{ and the inverse } ([I]_H^U)^{-1} = [I]_U^H = \begin{bmatrix} 0.25 & 0.25 & 0.25 & 0.25 \\ 0.25 & 0.25 & -0.25 & -0.25 \\ 0.5 & -0.5 & 0 & 0 \\ 0 & 0 & 0.5 & -0.5 \end{bmatrix}$$

The rows of the Haar basis change matrix's inverse are the Haar basis's dual basis, which are the scaled (÷0.25) original Haar basis because they are orthogonal. These bases are more efficient than the unit vector basis. For example, given a vector v in $\mathbb{R}^4$ as $[5, 4.5, -4, -5]$, can be represented using a linear combination of the Haar basis as:

$$v_H = ([I]_H^U)^{-1} v_U \begin{bmatrix} 0.25 & 0.25 & 0.25 & 0.25 \\ 0.25 & 0.25 & -0.25 & -0.25 \\ 0.5 & -0.5 & 0 & 0 \\ 0 & 0 & 0.5 & -0.5 \end{bmatrix} [5 \quad 4.5 \quad -4 \quad -5] = \begin{bmatrix} 0.125 \\ 4.625 \\ 0.25 \\ 0.5 \end{bmatrix}$$

One basis vector, the second of 4.625, dominates the rest, and we can construct a reasonable approximation of this vector to get the approximation $v = \begin{bmatrix} 5 \\ 4.5 \\ -4 \\ -5 \end{bmatrix} \cong 4.625 \begin{bmatrix} 1 \\ 1 \\ -1 \\ -1 \end{bmatrix} = \begin{bmatrix} 4.625 \\ 4.625 \\ -4.625 \\ -4.625 \end{bmatrix}$, where the error in approximation is around 0.8. Also, this basis transformation allows decomposition into the product of smaller matrices, and its inverse is its transpose because it is orthogonal (Mahadevan, 2008).

Other wavelet basis functions are introduced in the literature to choose from, such as db4, db16, coif1, sym4, sym8, bior1.3, and bior3.1. Scipy.signal Python package has continuous wave transform (cwt) using wavelets Morlet and Ricker. PyWavelets is another Python package that implements more wavelets as rbio, dmey, gaus, mexh, morl, cgau, shan, fbsp, cmor. Also, diffusion wavelet bases are adapted to the geometry of a graph and can be learned adaptively from sampling a data set or a state space. A reader can research how each one is designed and what useful properties they offer to be suitable for a particular application. Ch5.ipynb accompanying source code examples include some of these wavelet functions to compare to stft feature representation method and their effects on reconstruction error, classification learning time, and accuracy. The models presented are very simple to introduce the idea, but each model can be enhanced in many other ways to achieve higher accuracy and less convergence time.

5.3 Learning on groups

As explained in chapter one, estimating a mapping function $f: \chi \rightarrow \Upsilon$ between the input space χ, and the output space Υ is the aim of machine learning (ML) algorithms. Chapter two introduced various input vector space mapping $f: \chi \rightarrow \tilde{\chi}$ learning to estimate the transformation matrix between both spaces aiming at reducing the dimensionality. ML algorithms generalise the mapping from input to output for prediction, regression, and other objectives. Most ML algorithms are based on a probabilistic framework assuming a single probability distribution D on $\chi \times \Upsilon$ in which both training and testing examples are drawn, each sample entity being statistically independent of the others. In predictive models such as the frequentist probability methods and supervised machine learning, the distribution is not important to be understood. The Bayesian methods, on the other hand, expect the distribution to be pre-defined and parameterised to the algorithm, to build a generative model that estimates the spaces of $\chi \times \Upsilon$. In both cases, an ML algorithm would learn a mapping function $f: \chi \rightarrow \Upsilon$ to predict a y for a given test x from a set of functions known as a hypothesis set. The training phase, given a loss function L defined over the space: $L: \Upsilon \times \Upsilon \rightarrow \mathbb{R}$, aims to minimise the expected value over the distribution D of the input and output spaces $\min E_{(x,y) \sim D}[L(\mathrm{f}(x)), \mathrm{y}]$. The various machine learning algorithms parametrise the loss function to use, the distribution of the input and output spaces if required by the algorithm, and other detailed requirements to accommodate different classes of problems.

If the model overfits the coefficients of the mapping function, then a regularisation parameter λ will attempt to reduce the values of the coefficients, and the regularizer $\Omega[f]$ measures the smoothness of the function. On the other side, Kernel methods are based on reproducing kernel Hilbert spaces. This class of algorithms belong to the set $\Omega[f] = \langle f, f \rangle$ for some appropriately defined inner product between hypotheses, and trade-offs for the smoothness of the function and performance of the model.

5.3.1 Hilbert space learning algorithms

Chapter two introduced the kernel methods for SVM and stated that the data need to be mapped to the Hilbert space of infinite dimensions such that a non-linearly separable dataset can become linearly separable in the higher dimension. An exhaustive search on the best higher dimension would grow to the largest dimensional space is $\mathbb{R}^{|\chi|}$, where $|\chi|$is the cardinality of input space χ. This can be further reduced to $\mathbb{R}^{|w|}$, where $|w|$ is the cardinality of the parameters to learn w, for a reduced hypothesis set. Kernel functions even reduce this space using inner products between input space samples.

The previous definition is good enough to use these methods properly. Since this book deep dives, to an extent, into the new layer of abstract algebra and how it has advanced computer science algorithms in the past three decades, this section will explain further how to define an inner product on Hilbert spaces.
Remember from chapter one that a scalar product on $\mathbb{R}^n$ is defined as $(v|w) = \sum_{i=1}^{n} v^i w^i$. A Hermitian scalar product on a function such as $L^2([-a,a])$ on $\mathbb{C}^n$, extends the definition of the scalar product on $\mathbb{R}^n$, to be defined as $(v|w) = \sum_{i=1}^{n} \bar{v}^i w^i$, where the bar on v denotes complex conjugation (Hermiticity). $L^2([-a,a])$ is a square-integrable complex-valued function on an interval [-a, a] with expansion $f = \sum_{n=-\infty}^{\infty} c_n e^{i\frac{n\pi x}{a}}$. This is known as the Fourier series of f, and c_n, are the Fourier coefficients, which are the components of the vector f in the basis $\left\{e^{i\frac{n\pi x}{a}}\right\}_{n\in\mathbb{Z}}$. $L^2([-a,a])$ structure is an infinite-dimensional Hilbert space because the basis allows for infinite linear combinations.
Given f, g $\in L^2([-a,a])$, $(f\,|g) \equiv \frac{1}{2a}\int_{-a}^{a} \bar{f} g dx$, where a bar on f denotes hermiticity again, defines the inner product (.|.) on $L^2([-a,a])$. This inner product turns $L^2([-a,a])$ to a Hilbert space. A Hilbert space H has the set $\{e_i\}\subset H$ as orthonormal basis if $(e_i|f)=0, \forall i \Rightarrow f = 0$, such as $\left\{e^{i\frac{n\pi x}{a}}\right\}_{n\in\mathbb{Z}}$. $L^2([-a,a])$ is the set of all expressions of the expansion form defined above, and when the following condition is satisfied:

$$\frac{1}{2a}\int_{-a}^{a} |f|^2 dx = \sum_{n=-\infty}^{\infty} |c_n|^2 < \infty$$

$L^2([-a,a])$ then defines the infinite-dimensional Hilbert spaces. A basis for a Hilbert space is an infinite set whose infinite linear combinations, together with some suitable convergence condition, form the entire vector space. Dealing with spatial degrees of freedom, as opposed to 'internal' degrees of freedom like spin, Hilbert spaces like $L^2([-a,a])$ and $L^2(\mathbb{R})$ are often encountered, which are most conveniently described by 'basis' vectors which are eigenvectors of either the position operator $\hat{x}$ or the momentum operator $\hat{p}$.
There is an oft-unwritten rule that one should take the tensor product of the corresponding Hilbert spaces to add degrees of freedom. For example, by adding an additional translational degree of freedom for a spinless particle constrained to move in one x dimension; the quantum mechanical Hilbert space for this system is $L^2(\mathbb{R})$ with basis $\{|x\rangle\}_{x\in\mathbb{R}}$ (this is the ket notation explained in chapter one, which means x is a vector in vector space X) adding a second y dimension with its own Hilbert space $L^2(\mathbb{R})$ with basis $\{|y\}_{y\in\mathbb{R}}$, then the particle can move in these two dimensions in a Hilbert space defined by the dot product of each individual Hilbert space, $L^2(\mathbb{R}) \otimes L^2(\mathbb{R})$ with basis $\{|x\rangle \otimes |y\rangle\}_{x,y\in\mathbb{R}}$ and so forth for higher dimensions. Adding spinning requires adding basis in the $\mathbb{C}^3$ space (Jeevanjee, 2011).

Hilbert space is formally defined as a complete linear inner product space. Starting from the inner product on a vector space V over $\mathbb{R}$, it is defined as a function $V \times V \to \mathbb{R}$, denoted $\langle v, w\rangle$, satisfying:
$\langle u + v, w\rangle = \langle u, w\rangle + \langle v, w\rangle$,
$\langle \alpha u, v\rangle \ = \ \alpha\langle u, v\rangle$,
$\langle u, v\rangle \ = \ \langle v, u\rangle$,

$\langle u,u\rangle \geq 0$ with equality only when $u = 0_V$, for all $u,v,w \in V$ and $\alpha \in \mathbb{F}$. Such an inner product gives rise to the norm $\|u\| = \sqrt{\langle u,u\rangle}$, and this provides V with a topology and a distance metric $d(x,x') = \|x - x'\|$.
A sequence $a_1, a_2, \ldots$ in a metric space is said to **converge** to $a \in M$ if $\lim_{i\to\infty} d(a_i, a) = 0$ and is called a Cauchy sequence if $\lim_{\min(I,j)\to\infty} d(a_i, a_j) = 0$. The space M is said to be a complete metric space if every Cauchy sequence in M converges to some $a \in M$.
A Hilbert space is a vector space $\mathcal{H}$ that is a complete metric space because of the inner product-induced norm. The Hilbert space formalises the presence of three different but closely related structures: the vector space, the inner product, and the topology. A Hilbert space is defined over any field, not only $\mathbb{R}$, and can be finite or infinite dimensional. Any finite Hilbert space is isomorphic to the Euclidean space $\mathbb{R}^n$. In the infinite-dimensional, we can define a basis for $\mathcal{H}$, and if we label the basis vectors with elements of some countably or uncountably infinite set S, we can expand any $v \in \mathcal{H}$ as:

$$v = \sum_{s\in S} \alpha_s e_s \, , \alpha_s \in \mathbb{R}$$

This makes the Hilbert space defines a space of functions $v(s) = \alpha_s$, in which all linear algebra carries over to the infinite dimension. The Kernel functions defined on them are computationally efficient. As defined in chapter two, a kernel function is $k(x,x') = \Phi(x).\Phi(x')$. In chapter three, a pull-back is defined as moving a differential form from one manifold to another manifold. This is clearly what the kernel function k is doing, moving the metric from the Hilbert space inner product to the χ space. This makes the kernel function $k: \chi \times \chi \to \mathbb{R}$ symmetric, $k(x,x') = k(x',x)$, with any linear combination $f = \sum_{i=1}^{m} \alpha_i \Phi(x_i), \alpha_1, \ldots, \alpha_m \in \mathbb{R}, x_1, \ldots, x_m \in \chi$, must satisfy $\langle f,f\rangle = \sum_{i=1}^{m}\sum_{j=1}^{m} \alpha_i\alpha_j \langle \Phi(x_i), \Phi(x_j)\rangle \geq 0$, equivalent to $\sum_{i=1}^{m}\sum_{j=1}^{m} \alpha_i\alpha_j \langle x_i, x_j\rangle \geq 0$.
This adds the definition of positive as well as semi-definite because of accepting equal or greater than. Adding also the condition $\sum_{i=1}^{n} \alpha_i = 0$, makes this a symmetric conditionally positive semi-definite. These conditions are sufficient to have a Hilbert space corresponding to the kernel function k used to characterise the input space.
The steps below do the construction of **reproducing kernel Hilbert space (RKHS)** to characterise the function space corresponding to a given k as stated in (Risi Kondor, 2008):

1. Define the functions $k_x(\cdot) = k(x,\cdot)$, and form a vector space V with basis labelled by $\{k_x\}_{x\in\chi}$.
2. Define an inner product between basis vectors by $\langle k_x, k_{x'}\rangle = k(x,x')$ and extend this by linearity to the rest of V. This set of functions taken as basis will span the linear combinations of $k_x's$.
3. Finally, complete V to $\mathcal{H}$ by adjoining to it the limits of all Cauchy sequences and extending the inner product by continuity. Remember, a Cauchy sequence is an infinite sequence in which successive terms tend to get closer together and converge to a limit. This can reach the largest dimension $\mathbb{R}^{|\chi|}$ but on a linearly independent set.

The representer theorem of Kimeldorf and Wahba (1971) states that given χ be an input space, Υ an output space, $T = \{(x_i, y_i)\}_{i=1}^{m}$ a training set, $L: \Upsilon \times \Upsilon \to \mathbb{R}$ a loss function, and $\mathcal{H}$ a reproducing kernel Hilbert space induced by some positive definite kernel $k: \chi \times \chi \to \mathbb{R}$. Then the minimizer f_T of any regularized empirical risk (loss of the training data) functional of the form $R_{reg}[f] = \frac{1}{m}\sum_{i=1}^{m} L(f(x_i), y_i) + \lambda \|f\|^2$.
The regularizer $[f] = \langle f,f\rangle$, identifies $\Omega[f]$ with the squared Hilbert space norm $\|f\|^2 = \langle f,f\rangle$. The regularisation parameter λ>0 is expressible as a linear combination $f_T(x) = \sum_{i=1}^{m} \alpha_i k_{x_i}(x), \alpha_i \in \mathbb{R}$. Some machine learning algorithms raise $\|f\|$ to a different power than 2, but 2 is sufficient according to the representer theorem.

This theorem reduces searching the large space $\mathcal{H}$ to just finding the optimal values of the m coefficients $\alpha_1, \ldots, \alpha_m$. This is a non-parametric model because it does not attempt to fit a fixed model with a finite number of pre-defined parameters. The literature has various kernel functions, and continuous research will present more in the future. A number of them are introduced in chapter two, and more are discussed in (Risi Kondor, 2008).

Each one of them applies a different regularisation scheme. The most popular kernel on $\mathbb{R}^n$, the Gaussian (RBF) kernel discussed in chapter two, contains a length scale parameter (or variance parameter) σ. Letting $\hat{f}$ denote the Fourier transform of f and $\hat{\Upsilon}$ the frequency space regularization operator $\hat{\Upsilon}\hat{f} = \widehat{\Upsilon f}$, which was shown that $(\hat{\Upsilon}\hat{f})(\omega) = e^{|\omega|^2\sigma^2}\hat{f}(\omega)$ penalises high-frequency components in f by a factor exponential in $|\omega|^2$, providing natural regularisation. An alternative description of Υ in terms of derivatives of f is $\|\Upsilon f\|_F^2 = \int_\chi \sum_{i=0}^{\infty} \frac{\sigma^{2i}}{i!2^n} \left\|(\mathcal{O}^i f)(x)\right\|_{L_2}^2 dx$, where for i even $\mathcal{O}^i = \Delta^{\frac{i}{2}}$, and for i odd $\mathcal{O}^i = \nabla\Delta^{\frac{i-1}{2}}$, and Δ is the Laplacian operator explained previously. This again penalises functions which have a large amount of energy in their high-order derivatives, i.e. they are not smooth. For more discussions on how the choice of kernels and loss function define various machine learning algorithms such as Gaussian Processes, SVM, and Kernels for different learning problems, such as learning symmetries in data and translation invariance as in convolution neural networks (CNN) expressed using group theory, and learning permutations check (Risi Kondor, 2008).

These kernel machines, aka neural networks, build up the hypothesis set by going through the dataset in iterations to minimise the empirical loss. Their ability to generalise to unseen data as well is justified by the kernel function choice.

5.4 Invariance

In machine learning, data, for example, images must be represented individually in translation- rotation- and scale-invariant forms. Learning the representation invariant subspace requires a change of bases from the measurement basis to the transformation invariant basis. A vector is covariant if its components change proportional to the change in the basis. It is a contravariant vector when its components change inversely proportional to the change in the basis. Representation discovery is the process of identifying an invariant subspace under some mapping operator T. A subspace V is invariant under T, when every vector v in V, when the operator is applied on it yields a vector w, it $Tv \rightarrow w$, such that w also is in V. Invariant subspaces are useful since they enable irreducible representations of linear mappings. As explained in the wavelet section, a transformation operator T in a given subspace χ is denoted $[T]_\chi = T|_\chi$. In previous chapters, we studied matrix and tensor decompositions that reduce a matrix/tensor into a linear sum of simpler rank-one matrices/tensors, which are essentially just the outer product of these simpler structures. For example, combining the Haar basis with its dual basis, construct a set of invariant subspaces that results in a direct sum decomposition of the original vector space V. Given the same vector used before $[v]_U = [5, 4.5, -4, -5]^T$, we can decompose this vector as the sum of four vectors, each produced from the outer product of the Haar basis vectors with their corresponding dual basis vectors multiplied by the invariant rank-one Haar representation $[v]_H$:

$$[v]_U = \begin{bmatrix} 5 \\ 4.5 \\ -4 \\ -5 \end{bmatrix} = \begin{bmatrix} 0.125 \\ 0.125 \\ 0.125 \\ 0.125 \end{bmatrix} + \begin{bmatrix} 4.625 \\ 4.625 \\ -4.625 \\ -4.625 \end{bmatrix} + \begin{bmatrix} 0.25 \\ -0.25 \\ 0 \\ 0 \end{bmatrix} + \begin{bmatrix} 0 \\ 0 \\ 0.5 \\ -0.5 \end{bmatrix}$$

There are many methods to construct invariant subspaces, such as eigenspace decomposition in which the space spanned by the eigenvector is an invariant space to the input matrix, QR Decomposition, and Gram–Schmidt Orthogonalization, and SVD. The mapping to the Hilbert space, using the inner product norm, is a transformation to a coordinate-free or infinite dimensional invariant space. The abstract Fourier expansion $\hat{v} == \sum_i \langle v, \phi_i \rangle \psi_i$, where ϕ_i represents the analysis basis space and ψ_i represents the synthesis basis space, generalises and projects to general Hilbert space, and constructs unknown vectors in the invariant space from known measurements in the input space. The Reproducing Kernel Hilbert Space (RKHS) is also a special class of the Hilbert space that uses a reproducing kernel function. The Gram matrices for any $m \times n$ matrix A, is A^TA and is always symmetric. The kernels induce Gram symmetric matrices G on a given set of samples,

$$G(\phi_1,\ldots,\phi_n) = \begin{bmatrix} \langle\phi_1,\phi_1\rangle & \cdots & \langle\phi_n,\phi_1\rangle \\ \vdots & \ddots & \vdots \\ \langle\phi_1,\phi_n\rangle & \cdots & \langle\phi_n,\phi_n\rangle \end{bmatrix}$$

The Gram matrices enable extending basis functions computed on a set of samples in α basis to new points β basis, such as: $G(\phi_1,\ldots,\phi_n)\,\alpha = \beta$(Mahadevan, 2008).

As discussed earlier in this chapter, invariance can be captured in groups since group captures symmetries. The translation property of the Fourier Transform is explained earlier on groups and their representations as the left- and right-translation properties: $\hat{f}^t(\rho) = \rho(t)\hat{f}(\rho)$ and $\hat{f}^{(t)}(\rho) = \hat{f}(\rho)\rho(t)$ respectively, and was extended to convolution invariant as $\widehat{f * g}(\rho) = \hat{f}(\rho)\hat{g}(\rho)$. To generalise, data represented as a group G acting transitively on a set χ, we may find invariants of functions $f: \chi \rightarrow \mathbb{C}$ with respect to the induced (translation or other) action $f \rightarrow f^g$ defined $f^g(x) = f(g^{-1}(x)), g \in G$. The simplest example is $G = \chi$ acting on itself by left-multiplication, in which case f^g is the left-translate of f.

This leads to defining any matrix-valued functional $s: L(G) \rightarrow \mathbb{C}^{d_\rho \times d_\rho}$, which obeys ρ-covariant, $s(f^t) = \rho(t)s(f)$, while ρ-contravariant functionals are defined to transform according to $s'(f^t) = s'(f)\rho(t)^\dagger$. For example, a ρ-contravariant function is $s': f \rightarrow \hat{f}(\rho)^\dagger$.

The power spectrum of f is defined as a system of translation invariant matrices; Given unitary irreducible representations $\rho \in \mathcal{R}$, the product of a ρ-contravariant and a ρ-covariant function is invariant to translation: $s'(f^t)s(f^t) = s'(f)\rho(t)^\dagger\rho(t)s(f) = s'(f)\,s(f)$. This defines the power spectrum of f as $\hat{a}f(\rho) = \hat{f}(\rho)^\dagger\hat{f}(\rho), \rho \in R$. For more details on the invariance on groups in different settings, read (Risi Kondor, 2008) and (Stanković, Moraga and Astola, 2005).

5.5 Applications

The thesis in (Risi Kondor, 2008) presented two learning applications in groups. We will review one application that uses the invariant features required for representing images. Any image is better transformed from the spatial x-y grid pixel values to the spectral/Fourier terms/frequency domains. This achieves the desirable properties of this transformation, such as scale, shift, translate, rotation invariance, and compression for applications such as edge or motion energy detection, filtering, directional derivative, textural signature, statistical structure identification such as objects, and Optical character recognition. An image is represented by a linear combination of basis functions: $f(x,y) = \sum_k a_k \Psi_k(x,y)$, as a 2D Fourier analysis, $\Psi_k(x,y) = \exp(i(u_k x + v_k y))$, where $\exp(i\theta) = \cos(\theta) + i\sin(\theta)$.
The transform finds a set of complex coefficients a_k for every spatial frequency and orientation in the 2D Fourier domain spanned by the 2D frequency variables (u_k, v_k). a_k are computed as the orthonormal projection of the function f(x) onto one complex exponential $\exp(-i(u_k x + v_k y))$. The Fourier Transform may compute these coefficients: $a_k = \int_X \int_Y \exp(-i(u_k x + v_k y))\, f(x,y)dxdy$, and $\hat{f}(u,v) = \int_X \int_Y \exp(-i(u_k x + v_k y))\, f(x,y)dxdy$, such that each $\hat{f}(u,v)$ is a complex coefficient that defines the magnitude and phase of a sinusoid basis function/coordinates called vector spatial frequencies. An array of them must span the (u,v) Fourier plane in a uniform Cartesian lattice. OpenCV Python package has a discrete FT function "dft" and its inverse "idft", and "numpy.fft" module contains discrete FT functions for 1D, 2D, ND arrays and their inverses.
These computed Fourier coefficients a_k are complex-valued. If the function f(x) is real-valued, then its frequency domain representation has two-fold redundancy. The real parts of the a_k have even-symmetry: $a_k = a_{-k}$, and their imaginary parts have odd symmetry: $a_k = -a_{-k}$. Given this "Hermitian" symmetry, all coefficients are obtained by computing only half of them.

Complex exponentials $\exp(i\theta)$, with the real part as a cosine wave, and the imaginary part as a sine wave, are the Eigenfunctions of linear systems $\exp(iu_k t) \rightarrow h(t) \rightarrow A\exp(iu_k t)$. Therefore, the Fourier transform becomes a linear operation: $\mathcal{F}\big(\alpha f(x) + \beta g(x)\big) =: \alpha\mathcal{F}(f(x)) + \beta\mathcal{F}(g(x))$. The Euler relation $e^{i\pi} + 1 = 0$, connects the five most important mathematical constants and harmonic analysis of four branches of mathematics: 1) {0, 1} represents arithmetic, 2) π≈ 3.14 represents geometry, 3) $i = \sqrt{-1}$ represents algebra, and 4) e≈2.718 represents the analysis. FT can then be computed by taking the limit of $\left(1 + \frac{1}{n}\right)^n$ as $n \rightarrow \infty$, that can be computed using the power-series definitions for the transcendental functions: $exp\ (\theta) = 1 + \frac{\theta}{1!} + \frac{\theta^2}{2!} + \frac{\theta^3}{3!} + \cdots$, $cos\ (\theta) = 1 - \frac{\theta^2}{2!} + \frac{\theta^4}{4!} - \frac{\theta^6}{6!} + \cdots$, $sin\ (\theta) = 0 - \frac{\theta^3}{3!} + \frac{\theta^5}{5!} - \frac{\theta^7}{7!} + \cdots$ ('Euler's formula', 2023).
The properties identified earlier for 1D FT are extended to 2D FT as follows:

- A shift by α, β in the spatial domain is multiplication by $\exp(-i(\alpha u + \beta v))$ in the frequency domain $f(x - \alpha, y - \beta) = \hat{f}(u,v)e^{-i(\alpha u + \beta v)}$,
- A scaling by α, β in the spatial domain is scaling by the reciprocal of α, β in the frequency domain $f(\alpha x, \beta y) = \frac{1}{|\alpha\beta|}\hat{f}\left(\frac{u}{\alpha}, \frac{v}{\beta}\right)$.
- A convolution of f(x,y) by g(x,y) in the spatial domain is just a multiplication of their frequency domain transforms: $\mathcal{F}(f * g)(u,v) = \hat{f}(u,v) \cdot \hat{g}(u,v)$.
- The derivative of a function in the spatial domain is equivalent to multiplying the frequency domain transform by the frequency value raised to the power of the order of the derivative: $\left(\frac{d}{dx}\right)^m \left(\frac{d}{dy}\right)^n f(x,y) \Rightarrow (iu)^m (iv)^n \hat{f}(u,v)$. This enables the filtering of an image using different filter kernels g(x, y). This leads to isotropic differentiation, which treats all directions equally (for which the lowest possible order of differentiation is the 2nd-order, which is defined earlier as the Laplacian operator Δ^2) is equivalent simply to multiplying the 2DFT of the image by a paraboloid: $\Delta^2 f(x,y) = \left(\frac{d^2}{d^2x} + \frac{d^2}{d^2y}\right) f(x,y) = -(u^2 + v^2)\hat{f}(u,v)$.
- Also, in 2D, a rotation by angle θ in the spatial domain is a rotation by the same angle in the frequency domain: $f(x\cos(\theta) + y\sin(\theta), -x\sin(\theta) + y\cos(\theta)) = \hat{f}(u\cos(\theta) + v\sin(\theta), -u\sin(\theta) + v\cos(\theta))$.
- A change to the log-polar coordinates (r, θ), where $r = \log(\sqrt{(u^2+v^2)}$, and $\theta = \tan^{-1}(\frac{v}{u})$, enables dilation/size change in the original pattern to become simply a translation along the r-coordinate, and any rotation of the original pattern becomes simply a translation along the orthogonal θ-coordinate. This adds size and orientation invariance in the Fourier domain.
- The power spectrum of an image is its 2DFT multiplied by its conjugate complex: $\hat{f}(u,v)\hat{f}^*(u,v)$. The conjugate complex is computed by reversing the sign of i in the imaginary part of the 2DFT: $\hat{f}^*(u,v) = \int_X \int_Y \exp(i(u_k x + v_k y))\ f(x,y)dxdy$. The translation by α, β is invariant in the power spectrum as: $\hat{f}(u,v)\hat{f}^*(u,v) = e^{-i(\alpha u + \beta v)}\hat{f}(u,v)\ e^{i(\alpha u + \beta v)}\hat{f}^*(u,v)$.

An energy signal (almost all non-periodic signals) has finite energy and no power, such as the pulse signal has finite energy, though power is zero. A power signal (almost all periodic signals) has infinite and finite energy, such as the sinusoid signal. The power spectrum of a signal in the Fourier domain enables translation- size- and orientation-invariant pattern representations. In computer vision, this enables patterns' representation in a manner that is independent of the patterns' position in the image, their orientation, and their size (i.e., the Poincaré group of transformations). The power spectrum is the Fourier transform of the autocorrelation, which is the convolution of the signal with itself (not flipped), where delay/lag is the parameter that identifies how much a signal overlaps with itself over different lag values over time. In the classical cases $\hat{f}(u,v)$, we have the energy

in each frequency mode and its phase information. The translation-invariant power spectrum loses the overall phase of the signal, while the relative phases of the different components contain important information.
Bispectrum addresses the lost phase problem of the power spectrum while maintaining the translation-invariance property. It is defined over triple correlation by coupling different Fourier components. It has the form $\hat{a}_{3,f}(\mathrm{k}_1, \mathrm{k}_2) = \hat{f}(\mathrm{k}_1) * \hat{f}(\mathrm{k}_2) * \hat{f}(\mathrm{k}_1 + \mathrm{k}_2)$, taking two arguments and is a highly redundant representation of f. It is the Fourier Transform of the triple correlation: $a_{3,f}(\mathrm{x}_1, \mathrm{x}_2) = \sum_{i=0}^{n-1} f(i - \mathrm{x}_1) * f(i - \mathrm{x}_2) * f(i)$, showing that it is shift-invariant, and translation invariant by t is proven by $\hat{a}_{3,f^t} = (e^{-i2\pi \mathrm{k}_1 x} \hat{f}(\mathrm{k}_1)) * (e^{-i2\pi \mathrm{k}_2 x} \hat{f}(\mathrm{k}_2)) * (e^{-i2\pi(\mathrm{k}_1+\mathrm{k}_2)x} \hat{f}(\mathrm{k}_1 + \mathrm{k}_2) = \hat{a}_{3,f}$. $|\hat{f}(k)| > 0$ for all k, i.e., it is complete and uniquely determines f, up to translation. It is computed by recurrence from base cases: $\hat{f}(0) = (\hat{a}_{3,f}(0,0))^{1/3}$, $\hat{f}(1) = (\hat{a}_{3,f}(0,1)/\hat{f}(0))^{1/2}$ or $\hat{f}(1) = e^{i\varphi}(\hat{a}_{3,f}(0,1)/\hat{f}(0))^{1/2}$ for any phase factor $\varphi \in [0, 2\pi)$. Then the recurrence is $\hat{f}(k) = \frac{\hat{a}_{3,f}(1,\mathrm{k}-1)}{\left(\hat{f}(k-1)\right)^2}$.
Because of possible dividing by zero and hard-to-compute higher dimensional generalisations using tensors, other methods are proposed, such as the skew spectrum on compact groups reducing computation steps using the inherent symmetries. For complete formulation using group and tensor decomposition and applications to homogenous space, refer to (Risi Kondor, 2008).
The bispectrum serves as a complete source of invariants for homogeneous spaces of compact groups, including such important domains as the sphere S^2, which is helpful for computer vision by providing a compact set of rotation invariants that improves discrimination and detects bilateral reflection symmetry.
To apply the bispectrum on images to be translate- and rotation-invariant, $ISO^+(2)$ need to be compactified by exploiting a local isomorphism between the action of $ISO^+(2)$ of rigid body motions R^2 and the action of SO(3) on the two-sphere S^2. The author derived the bispectrum on the SO(3) and showed that representing the MNIST digits images dataset using bispectral representation outperforms the baseline representation of the images. This was confirmed by using linear and Gaussian RBF SVMs as 2-class SVMs for all ten class combinations. The preprocessing included rotations by a random angle between 0 and 2π, clipping, and embedding at a random position in a 30 × 30 patch for each of the 1000 original images of 28 × 28 pixels in size, but most of them only occupy a fraction of the image patch. The Broyden–Fletcher–Goldfarb–Shanno (BFGS) algorithm is used as the iterative method for solving unconstrained nonlinear optimization problems to find the bispectrum images closest to a given bispectrum because the bispectrum consists of a collection of cubic polynomials, and inverting the mapping (Risi Kondor, 2008).
Another application to representation learning is in the Transformer DNN model. The Transformer Deep Learning model was first proposed in NLP applications as an embedding learning approach that implements a unique encoding function that connects a word to its predecessor and successor words in the complete sentence. It was soon applied to various non-textual datasets, such as images. It was concisely introduced in chapter four and will be discussed in chapter six. Here, the context of this chapter requires a mention of data representation learning applications of the Transformer model as introduced in (Merrill and Althoff, 2021) and (Zhang *et al.*, 2022). The Spatial Transformer Network (T-net) is a layer that can be added to CNN models (that has translation invariance by design) to learn a representation that is translation-, scale-, and rotation-invariant (Jaderberg *et al.*, 2016). Their code is published at https://github.com/kevinzakka/spatial-transformer-network.
Furthermore, Point clouds are a set of points identified by their 3D coordinate based on the image acquisition method and might belong to multiple objects based on the view characteristics, such as the view angle, occlusion, light condition, and source. Point Cloud analysis is the process of aligning the point and registering it, or in CAD models, using it in surface reconstruction. Four popular DNNs for point cloud analysis are PointNet, PointNet++, SpiderCNN, and Dynamic Graph CNN (DGCNN). Various tensor decomposition methods have been applied to this problem, such as Tucker (Li, Zhang and Tran, 2019), Tensor block-wise singular value decomposition (Tamilmathi and Chithra, 2022), and Tensor regression (Yan, Paynabar and Pacella, 2019).
The 3D-Rotation-Equivariant Quaternion Neural Networks (REQNN) proposed in (Shen *et al.*, 2020) identified the conditions in which using quaternion learns a permutation-invariant and rotation-equivariant representations of 3D point cloud analysis. Their code is published at https://github.com/ada-shen/REQNN.

The Rotation Transformation Network (RTN) proposed in (Deng *et al.*, 2021) utilizes an Euler-angle-based rotation discretization manner to learn the pose of input 3D objects and then transforms them into a view-invariant pose by reducing their Rotation Degree of Freedom (RDF) to zero. The authors used the Princeton ModelNet dataset, a collection of 3D CAD models of objects used for object classification. Objects are also identified as belonging to SO(0) with zero RDF, i.e., their pose does not change in 3D space, SO(1) with one RDF, i.e., they are on a plane in the 3D space, or SO(3) with three RDF, i.e., they have an arbitrary pose in a centralized 3D space. The authors noticed that T-net performance degrades with increasing RDF. They proposed the RTN layers added to the existing architectures and identified that RTN+DGCNN has the highest instance and average per-class accuracy. Their code is published at https://github.com/ds0529/RTN.

In the book (Mahadevan, 2008), the author applied representation discovery to a stochastic state-space planning problem, such as Markov Decision Processes (MDP), using the Reinforcement Learning (RL) framework. Sequential decisions approximate a utility function that is often approximated using pre-defined basis functions. Harmonic analysis was used to synthesise basis functions that were shown to outperform the best manually pre-defined basis. The unknown environment and utility functions were modelled by an agent using the random walk to build a graph with nodes identifying states, and the adjacency is built based on the succession of states temporally or based on achieved rewards in the exploratory phase. Then, the method applies the Laplacian operator on the graph, diagonalizing it, and finding the smoothest eigenvectors corresponding to the smallest eigenvalues to approximate a policy representation capturing the underlying manifold of the samples collected. This means the manifold's topology representing a particular control task's state (action) space non-parametrically constructs the new representation basis dynamically using the most concise (non-uniform local density regions). The identified smooth eigenvectors form the columns of the basis function |S| × k matrix φ. These Laplacian basis functions can be used in conjunction with a standard "black box" parameter estimation method, such as Q-learning or least-squares policy iteration (LSPI), to learn the optimal policy that maximises the action-value function; the encoding $\varphi(s): S \rightarrow \mathbb{R}^k$ of a state s is computed as the value of the k proto-value functions on that state. Then this learned policy can be added to a list of policies, and the process can be repeated iteratively to learn more policies. More details on the algorithm, its application in various control tasks, and a comparison to pre-defined representation bases are presented (Mahadevan, 2008).

Another application of representation learning presented in (Mahadevan, 2008) was in 3D object compression. The classic 2D image compression approach JPEG relies on the discrete cosine transform, a type of Fourier analysis on 2D arrays, and JPEG-2000 relies on the wavelet transform. Both approaches do not scale well to 3D object compression, which relies on identifying the 3D vertices in an object and defining their topology graph. Hundreds of megabytes of vertices can be defined in the input unit bases. A highly sparse representation basis can be identified in run-time using harmonic analysis methods presented in this chapter, whether by Fourier analysis or Wavelet analysis. More details about the performance of each approach as compared to the classic approaches are presented in the book. The third application in information extraction and retrieval (IR) from text datasets was presented in the book. The classical approach of latent semantic indexing (LSI) uses SVD, which is a form of Fourier analysis, to construct the term-document matrix. The author showed that employing diffusion wavelets instead reveals multiscale regularities across documents.

The work of (Armenta and Jodoin, 2021) explains how the quiver representation as a directed graph that allows multiple arrows and loops is used in various concepts of neural networks such as fully-connected layers, convolution operations, residual connections, batch normalisation, pooling operations, and even randomly wired neural networks. Data are also represented as quiver representation and mapped to a geometrical space called the moduli space.

In chapter four, two applications of tensor factorisation were discussed. The work of (Yang and Hospedales, 2017) presents a multi-task learning (MTL) representation learning using tensor factorisation (Tucker and TT) as a generalisation of the matrix factorisation (such as PCA) to share knowledge across tasks in fully connected and convolutional DNN layers. They compare their method to Single Task Learning (STL) vs MTL, using user-defined representation vs the learned representation on shallow and deep layer networks. The increased accuracy of learning the representation using tensor factorisation on deep layers is due to the end-to-end training of both the

classifier and feature extractor. They published their code at https://github.com/wOOL/DMTRL/blob/master/demo.ipynb.
There is a wealth of contributions in representation learning algorithms. For example, given a network, the representation can be learned using various methods, as surveyed by (Zhang *et al.*, 2018). OpenNE is a Python package that implements many network embedding (NE) and network representation learning (NRL), such as DeepWalk, LINE, node2vec, GraRep, TADW, and GCN. Their published code is at https://github.com/thunlp/OpenNE. Similarly, given a graph structure, various methods exist to learn their representation (Chen *et al.*, 2020). The authors contributed GRLL (Graph Representation Learning Library) as a python package that implements many of these algorithms and evaluates their performance. Their code is published at https://github.com/yunchengwang/graph-representation-learning.
For the latest papers and code on this topic, the Paper-with-code task https://paperswithcode.com/task/representation-learning keeps benchmarks, datasets, and papers contributing to the field.

Chapter 6: Tensor Computation Applications

This chapter presents higher-level application domains for the various methods discussed in the previous chapters to identify trends and challenges. Tensor computing and analysis have been successful across multiple application domains, such as social network analysis, brain data analysis, web mining, information retrieval, healthcare analytics, signal processing, machine learning, and predominantly psychometrics and computational chemistry. In this chapter, we will select several applications to investigate how the various tensor analytics models have been applied, identifying some preprocessing steps, details of application methods and programming environment used, results' analysis and performance evaluation compared with matrix methods.
It is impossible to be comprehensive or select the best representative research outcome. An attempt to diversify the application domains and methods applied was made. Most models are 3-way models. In chapter four, we discussed a 3-way model of MicroRNA-Disease Associations, a 4-way model of a video application, and a higher-order model of the BSS application. Chapter five discussed various applications of representation learning and feature extraction methods, followed by one application using tensorial methods in Multi-Task Learning. The applications in this chapter will span scientific computation applications, data science using various dataset types and requirements, and deep learning models. We will summarise in an attempt to create a general framework for tensorial methods in machine learning applications.

6.1 Scientific Computing Applications

Since Tensor computing was initially exploited in the psycho- and chemo-metrics communities and was founded by the quantum mechanics & physics community, we will start with one application from each of these three domains. We already covered a bioinformatics application in chapter four, covering the popular areas of scientific computing. We will then move on to data science and machine learning up to deep learning models.

Pieter Kroonenberg is one of the founders of multi-way analysis algorithms, from data preprocessing, model selection, and application problems in psychometrics, and social and behavioural sciences to agriculture, environmental sciences, and chemistry, to results interpretation and their validation and visualisation. His book (Kroonenberg, 2008) offers a rich, easy-to-read explanation of the methods with reduced mathematical notation. The methods covered vary from Tucker and CP tensor decomposition, dataset preprocessing and handling of missing data to core factors interpretation to achieve multi-way PCA, multi-way correspondence analysis, multi-way factor analysis, and multi-way clustering. Then, model improvements were discussed by scaling and rotation, and finally, results' validation and analysis of residuals. His website at https://three-mode.leidenuniv.nl/, published the implemented algorithms, their applications, and the datasets. He has the software "3WayPack" that can be downloaded in Windows XP to execute the applications discussed in the book. The datasets are also available on the website to download and experiment with other recent development methods such as Matlab, R, Python, and others. We will review the Happiness dataset and rebuild the model he explained in the book using Python. The survey dataset has a predictor in the first mode as the number of school years a subject finished (4 ordered categories), a second predictor in the second mode as the number of siblings (5 ordered categories), and their dependent variable is the happiness score in the third mode (3 ordered classes). The analysis is a correspondence analysis to identify the interactions between the variables. Data preprocessing included analysis of correlation and analysis of variance. The book evaluated five models, from 1x1x1 tensor to 2x2x2 tensor evaluating the Tucker3 to identify the Residual Sum of Squares SS as SS(Total of Mode A) = SS(Fit of Mode A) + SS(Residual of Mode A), and similarly for the other two modes. Thus, $SS(Residual)_i$ / $SS(Total)_i$ is the proportional or relative lack of fit of the ith level of mode A. This showed that the 2x2x2 model is the best model with a Proportional SS(Fit) of 86% as opposed to smaller models down to 0.69% for the 1x1x1 model. The results were validated using X^2 (chi-square) statistic scores for expected different pair-wise interactions between each predictor and the dependent variable, then the combined interactions of both predictors on the target variable. The extended statistical investigation is interesting to follow to validate the end-to-end results of some AI output. This problem was reproduced in Python in the motivating problem of section 3.1 in chapter three accompanying source code "multi-wayExamples.ipynb".

For the chemo-metric application, we will review a chromatography application using a tensor decomposition example that is recently published. In computational chemistry, chromatography separates a compound into its individual components for separation or identification objectives. Traditionally it can be solved by ICA methods such as in the BSS problem introduced in chapter two. The dataset used in the analysis is multi-way by nature—for example, different chemicals, solvents and stationary phases. A two-dimensional gas chromatography (GC×GC) is usually accompanied by a time-of-flight mass spectrometer (GC×GC-TOFMS) and has applications in food/drug/environmental contaminants/petrochemicals or other compounds safety and quality analysis. The lab process is to inject a solvent of a specific type into a tube containing a compound to separate its molecules. Then measure the Time Of Flight (TOF) of sample molecules on a detector such as an ion mirror/reflector on which ions with higher energy penetrate more deeply inside, extending the time when they are reflected. The detector performs regular measurements at regular intervals. Since the flight times of the separated ions are proportional to the square root of respective mass-to-charge ratio (m/z values), identifying the different molecules' types.

An excised region is a vector of length I, where I is the number of acquisitions in the region of interest of a single chromatogram. A multivariate detector spans the second mode of J variables or channels. This is usually performed over several runs. The challenge is that chemical components are free to shift independently along the first and second chromatographic modes between runs and employ different chromatographic modes. (Armstrong et al., 2022) proposed using a fourth-order tensor $X^{I \times J \times K \times L}$ of I mass spectral acquisitions, J mass-to-charge ratios (mass channels), K modulations, and L samples as multiple samples from the same region of the chromatogram or entire chromatograms.

The authors applied PARAFAC to decompose X as $X = F_2(D_l \odot F_1 \odot A)^T$, such that F_2 is as I × R matrix, A is a J × R matrix, F_1 is a K × R matrix, and D_l is an L × R matrix. They employed a tensor unfolding in the first two modes to produce the third order $X_l^{I*J \times K \times L}$ avoiding the problem of drift in two modes by artificially reducing the problem to drift along one combined retention mode. Another approach is to form tensors of similar orders by stacking second-dimension retention profiles for an $X_{kl}^{I \times J \times K*L}$, and first-dimension retention times' $X_{il}^{K \times J \times I*L}$. Each model has useful properties, and using both models simultaneously to minimise (using ALS), the 4-way tensor reconstruction from the 3-way tensors arrives at optimal convergence at a retention mode at which the highest resolution between closely co-eluting (extraction) chemical factors is achieved. The approach is called the PARAFAC2×2 algorithm and is shown to achieve good results in synthetic and real data from a metabolomics study and is extensible to higher-order chromatographic separations. They published their Matlab code at https://github.com/mdarmstr/parafac2x2. Earlier simpler Parafac on three-way tensor decomposition method compared to PCA for chromatography are explained in chapter ten in (Smilde et al., 2004). A sample three-way chromatography dataset can be downloaded from https://three-mode.leidenuniv.nl/data/chromatographyinfo.htm.

The physics community and the mathematicians found everything about tensors, groups, representation and transformation. It is worth including some physical applications to tensor computing methods, besides the recurring example of Inertia matrix and SO(3) matrices and their applications in computer graphics and robotic motion control. Later in the neural networks section of this chapter, an application of quantum mechanics will be reviewed. In chapter four, some applications of the TT decomposition method were discussed, including the density matrix renormalisation group (DMRG) algorithm optimising tensors with variable directions that have applications in solid-state physics for solving eigenvalue problems. Another TT application is the iterative alternating minimal energy (AME) algorithm that has applications in approximating solutions of higher dimension and multi-dimension systems of linear equations Ax=b, on which the Gaussian Elimination method would be intractable. Matrix factorisations have been used to speed up the computation when $n \times n$ matrix A is of a large n dimension, such as LU decomposition keeping the computation in $O(n^3)$. Also, Iterative methods such as the generalized minimal residual (GMRES) algorithm based on Krylov subspaces are in $O(n^2)$ complexity class but have

problems of orthogonality for dense high dimensional matrices. The authors in (Lantsov, 2021) discuss converting the linear equations matrix to a tensor and applying tensor decomposition methods to reduce the memory requirements and speed up the calculations. Modern radio-frequency (RF) circuits and simulation of electronic circuits in CAD systems are high dimensional. For example, in CAD, electronic circuit design tools require analysis of different types such as static mode analysis (direct currents analysis, DC), small-signal analysis (linear analysis), transient analysis (time domain analysis), non-linear distortion analysis (based on Volterra series), harmonic balance analysis, and several others as identified by the authors. The authors represented the equations high dimensional $n \times n$ matrix A with n^2 elements as a low-rank tensor of n-order, using the TT decomposition as a tensor B with 2^{2D} elements, where D = $\log_2$ n.
Similarly, matrix b was converted to the TT format. The conversion used a binary decomposition algorithm that they implemented in Matlab. Solving for x, the authors applied the DMRG algorithm, which was not as reliable as the AME algorithm, but both are computationally more efficient than the GMRES algorithm. DMRG and AME algorithms are implemented in TT Matlab Toolbox and other programming languages, including in Python in https://www.tensors.net/p-dmrg and explained in http://tensornetwork.org/mps/algorithms/dmrg/.

6.2 Data Mining Applications

We will consider any machine learning application, whether working on a text dataset, image or video dataset, semantic web or knowledge graphs, or any other format, as a data mining application. The first few applications are working on text datasets. However, no semantic encoding of the words is applied. Other NLP applications are reviewed while reviewing neural network applications.
The first application of tensors in data mining to review is contributed by Acar et al. (Acar et al. 2005), (Acar et al., 2006), who applied different tensor decompositions to the problem of discussion disentanglement in online public chatrooms on the Internet Relay Chat (IRC), and how social networks evolve. The authors implemented their own bot to collect their dataset and simulated some, containing the text messages with timestamps, nicknames of identities, and timestamps of nicknames quit/leave or kick. The nicknames could belong to the same person, pretending to be of any age and gender. The topics' keywords were semantically analysed, and data distributions were estimated. A similar dataset without the nicknames is found at https://www.tensorflow.org/datasets/catalog/irc_disentanglement. The dataset is multidimensional and noisy.
The authors constructed a tensor T of order three, capturing users, keywords, and time in each mode, respectively, such that where T_{ijk} is user i, sent several of keyword j during time slot k. Then Tucker1 and Tucker3 were applied to identify user groups, which are set of users sharing a maximal keyword set in a given time period. This is achieved by an indeterministic c-means clustering algorithm running 100 times, which returns multiple memberships for each data point. The authors added different levels of Gaussian noise. Methods such as SVD as a 2-way dimensionality reduction method were applied in this paper on a matrix of users and keywords (UK) and another matrix of users and time stamps (UT). SVD clustered user groups with common keywords independently and another cluster using the second matrix of users chatting at the same period. By tracing the resulting groups from all experiments at three different noise ratios, the multi-way structure connecting the three modes was more accurately captured by the multi-way tensor decomposition methods (Tucker1 and Tucker3) than by the SVD on UT method, while it failed by SVD on UK method. Then they defined a 4-way Tensor to add the IRC server as the fourth mode to identify the computational efficiencies of tensor higher-order representations and decomposition methods compared to the corresponding pair-wise approaches.
The main lesson to learn from the previous paper is the data collection for tensor decomposition. Most datasets available in the public domain, such as Kaggle, Google Datasets, and UCI, are in matrix form. Data reformatting from matrix to tensor forms as presented in the "tensorisation.ipynb" and "multi-wayExamples.ipynb" or other creative methods need to be planned for every experiment.
In text analysis applications, (Bader et al., 2008) used CP for automatic conversation detection in the Enron Email dataset over time using an m term x n author x q month 3-way tensor $X^{m,n,q}$. This dataset is available at

https://www.cs.cmu.edu/~enron/. Based on previous literature on the analysis of this dataset, the authors selected an interesting subset of this dataset that makes a tensor $X^{69157,\ 197,\ 12}$ with 1,042,202 non-zeros entries scaled to their weighted frequency. The authors used a non-negative tensor to avoid subtractive basis vectors and encoding interactions that are found in PCA-like methods. They applied Parafac decomposition using ALS such that $\|X - \sum_{l-1}^{r} A_l \circ B_l \circ C_l\,\|^2$. The decomposed tensor factors were $A^{m\times r}$ containing the highest scores for terms/topics, $B^{n\times r}$ containing the highest scores for authors, and $C^{q\times r}$, containing the highest scores for these topics over time; they chose a 12-month duration. The rank r was chosen to retrieve a specific number of topics in the data, setting it to 25. Eight topics out of the 25 were interpretable in the context of other events happening in the same time duration, as compared to the two-way (term-author) NMF method that could not extract these discussions. The decomposition predicted discussion threads and produced charts of previous focused discussions over time.

6.2.1 Knowledge Graphs

Probabilistic graphical models like Bayesian and Markov networks are classical approaches to learning from network and graph data. However, they require defining priors and data distributions and are compute-intensive for high-dimensional datasets (Schlüter, 2014). Tensor decomposition approaches are more accurate in the collective learning of network data and the prediction of new relations in knowledge graphs, with a trade-off between expressivity and computational efficiency than non-tensorial methods. They were first used with probabilistic graphical models, such as the Bayesian Clustered Tensor Factorization (BCTF) as proposed by (Sutskever et al., n.d.), in which CP tensor decomposition was used to analyse network traffic and bibliographic data. The authors of (Nickel et al., 2011) proposed a relational learning approach RESCAL based on the DEDICOM tensor decomposition method with relaxed constraints. They exploited a three-way tensors $X^{n,n,m}$, n entities x n entities x m relationships such that when $X_{ijk} = 1$, this means that entity i has a relationship of type k with entity j. Entities. Domain data is given in the form of Resource Description Framework (RDF) triplets. A tensor decomposition of the form Xas $X_k = AR_kA^T$, where A is a n×r matrix containing the latent-component representation of the repeated entities in two modes from the domain and R_k is an asymmetric r×r matrix that models the interactions of the entities in the k-th predicate. This is very close to a relaxed DEDICOM or, equivalently, an asymmetric extension of the Individual Differences in Orientation Scaling (IDIOSCAL) tensor decomposition method. RESCAL is an efficient minimisation algorithm with a regularisation term based on the ASALSAN (Alternating Simultaneous Approximation, Least Squares, and Newton") variant of the ALS approach. The computed low-rank representation of the domain data is used in the prediction of a link as $\hat{X}_{ijk} > \theta$, for some threshold θ. The collective classification can be performed by slicing the low-rank reconstructed tensor for a given class relationship or actually reconstructing the relevant slice only. Also, Link-based clustering of entities can be performed using a similarity measure between entities based on their similarity across multiple relations. The authors compared the performance of RESCAL compared to standard tensor factorizations such as CP and DEDICOM, and relational learning algorithms such as statistical unit node set (SUNS) and the aggregated SUNs+AG. The conducted various experiments on various datasets such as Cora dataset (https://relational.fit.cvut.cz/dataset/CORA), Kinships in Australian Tribes, Nations (clusters of countries, clusters of interactions between countries, and clusters of country features) and UMLS (Unified Medical Language System) that can be found at (https://github.com/ZhenfengLei/KGDatasets). They showed that the results of RESCAL and DEDICOM outperform both CP and SUNS on all datasets.

The authors repeated the experiment (Nickel et al., 2012) using the noisy, large and high-dimensional Semantic Web's Linked Open Data (LOD) cloud that contains millions of entities, hundreds of relations and billions of known facts, found at https://lod-cloud.net/ and explained at https://www.ontotext.com/knowledgehub/fundamentals/linked-data-linked-open-data/. When writing this paper, it connected 300 datasets; now, it connects 1,255 datasets with 16,174 links. They employed the YAGO 2 ontology (that can be found at https://yago-knowledge.org/) that at the time contained $4.3\text{x}10^{14}$ possible triplets

to improve the learning by factorising a large knowledge base using an extended RESCAL tensor factorisation method to include in the factorisation the attributes of the entities, i.e. the literal values in LOD. Due to the large dataset content, the authors used a map-reduce parallel programming paradigm to employ distributed computing nodes to speed up the processing. RDFs are based on ontologies that contain the T-Box (terminological component), while the instance data are contained in A-Box (assertion component). The formed tensor $X^{n,n,m}$ represent both T-Box and A-Box simultaneously, making ontology a soft constraint, and the model is data-centric and ontology-driven. The model was tested for ranking and unknown triplets prediction and retrieval of similar entities using the latent factors in the decomposed core matrix A.
Another application is the proposal of new ontologies' terms from the data to knowledge database engineers as decision support systems to evolve an ontology by grouping/clustering instances. Out of 87 predicates relation in YAGO 2 at the time, 38 were used to form a sparse tensor $X^{3000417,3000417,38}$ with 41 million entries and a sparse attribute matrix $D^{3000417,1138407}$ with 35.4 million entries. Of the 4.3x1014 possible triplets in YAGO 2, only 4x107 non-zero entries were available. The authors compared the RESCAL to other tensor factorisation and classical relational learning methods, showing that RESCAL is more efficient in predicting RDF triplets and other machine learning tasks.
The authors of (Padia et al., 2016) further extended the RESCAL tensor decomposition method to RESCAL+ approach by adding a similarity matrix to the minimisation algorithm to force slices of the relational tensor to decrease their differences between one another to achieve unequal contribution of the slices. They tested using the DBpedia-Person dataset found at https://www.dbpedia.org/. They compared their link prediction performance against the original RESCAL method and its non-negative variant NN-RES and showed that their method achieves higher AUC scores and diagonal confusion matrix scores. The RESCAL method is implemented in Python at https://github.com/mnick/rescal.py and in the scikit-tensor library along with CP, Tucker, DEDICOM, and INDSCAL found at scikit-tensor library.
The authors of (Lacroix et al., 2020) applied CP decomposition to predict dynamic knowledge graph links. They created a 4-mode tensor of subject, predicate, object, and time. They proposed a new dataset for temporal knowledge graphs parsing Wikipedia. They compared their model to other models on their proposed dataset and other datasets to show that their results are promising. They published their code at https://github.com/facebookresearch/tkbc.
A generative model using Bayesian Tucker decomposition is proposed by (Castellana and Bacciu, 2019) that is suitable for tree-structured data. The Markov model is an expressive model that grows in size and becomes intractable for practical problems. Tensor factorisation enables the model to be a non-parametric Bayesian model as well.

6.2.2 Computer Vision

Eigenfaces is an algorithm for face recognition. It models several images for the same person as an unfolded vector of each image that is stacked in a matrix. Then, Eigen decomposition using principal component analysis (PCA) is applied to reduce the dimensionality of the images to use only the uncorrelated variables. The result is the eigenface with the smallest Euclidian distance to which the person resembles the most (Turk and Pentland, 1991). Their code is implemented at https://github.com/svetlana-topalova/eigenfaces. The spatial image content is represented in XY matrices for P people, so each matrix represents only one person. Capturing pair-wise variance build models that work best when only a single factor varies; in eigenfaces, it is the person's identity but loses efficiency when compound factors vary, such as poses, viewpoint, and others. The authors of (M. Alex O. Vasilescu and Terzopoulos, 2002) pioneered the use of Tucker decompositions in computer vision to disentangle the multiple factors an image is composed of, such as scene structure, different facial geometries (people), expressions, head poses, lighting conditions, and imaging. They contributed TensorFaces, representing the tensor decompositions' cores as a set of facial components. They applied a HOSVD on facial images (512 × 352 decimated by a factor of 3 and cropped, yielding 7943 pixels) dataset of 28 people x 5 poses x 3 illumination conditions x 3

facial expressions x 7943 pixels. This created a 5-mode tensor $D^{28,5,3,3,7943}$, that is decomposed by HOSVD to: $D = Z \times_1 U_{people} \times_2 U_{views} \times_3 U_{illumnation} \times_4 U_{expression} \times_5 U_{pixels}$, such that $U_{people} \in R^{28\times28}$spans the space of people's image parameters, $U_{views} \in R^{5\times5}$spans the space of viewpoint parameters and so forth for the remaining factor matrices. Each Factor matrix is computed as $U_n = D_{(n)} V_n \Sigma^+$, where $D_{(n)}$is mode n flattening of D, and computing SVD on $D_{(n)}$ to have the right matrix V and the singular values in the diagonal matrix Σ, considering U_n to be the left matrix of the SVD. This method generalises the eigenfaces method as factor matrix U_{pixels} is the eigenimage. Solving for the core matrix Z calculates the interactions of all modes considered in this experiment, as explained in the Tucker Decomposition in chapter four.
PCA is a change of basis mapping, such as in eigenfaces. Each person will be represented parsimoniously using the different PCA coordinates. Similarly, Z and all U_n for all the modes considered, can be thought of as a change of basis/coordinates mapping functions to retrieve slices of the Tensor D that abstract a person as poses change, or as illumination changes, or as expression changes. This is achieved by reducing the intra-class or intra-person interactions so as not to confuse people together by maximising the inter-class or inter-person interactions of the changing conditions considered. You can refer to the original paper to view the images independently abstracting the variation of illumination, poses and expressions.
A sample Tensorfaces implementation using only 3-mode tensors using the Tensorly Python package can be found at https://github.com/tensorly/Proceedings_IEEE_companion_notebooks/blob/master/tensorfaces.ipynb. They formed a 3-way tensor $X^{38,50,2900}$ of 38 people x 50 illuminations condition x and 2900 pixels from the Yale Face Database found at http://vision.ucsd.edu/~leekc/ExtYaleDatabase/ExtYaleB.html.
Additional modes such as camera angle and more can also be incorporated using the tensors machinery. The authors compared TensorFaces to eigenFaces and PCA approaches to facial recognition and found the accuracy of TensorFaces is significantly more accurate than standard PCA techniques and can separate each factor's interactions while considering compound interactions as well (M.A.O. Vasilescu and Terzopoulos, 2002). They also worked on reducing the dimensionality (working on subspaces) of every core matrix to achieve compression and remove irrelevant effects, such as illumination, shadows and highlights were removed, while retaining key facial features (Vasilescu and Terzopoulos, 2003).
The authors of (Lehky et al., 2020) expanded the analysis of the TensorFaces representations to measure the reconstruction errors at different complexities levels (ranks). They used synthesized faces generated by FaceGen software (https://facegen.com/), which they modelled in a 4-mode tensor, keeping the spatial image width and height as the first two modes (Tensorfaces was vectorising the image as 1D in one mode), a colour dimension, and the different individuals' dimension. The training dataset contained 128 faces, and the test set contained 40 faces, all equally from males/females and from four different races at the same rotation, pose and camera angle. Their aim was to attempt a reconstruction of these faces at different levels of complexity and measure the reconstruction error to decide the best level of complexity. They experimented with various measures of complexity and errors using TensorFaces, and other pair-wise methods such as PCA and ICA. They showed that low-complexity representations are better for novel faces (not seen in the training dataset) than high-complexity representations. This means that tensorial methods achieve regularization as well as multi-way interactions.
Vasilescu in (Vasilescu, 2002) has also applied the Tucker decomposition to human motion as a composite of multiple actions. The author had multiple aims, to extract a human movement signature as a subset of actions (analysis), to resynthesize new motions from the learned ones (synthesis), and recognise a specific person or action (recognition). The author defined a tensor $D^{N,M,T}$, where N is the number of people, M is the number of action classes, and T is the number of joint angle time samples. The author applied the same N-mode SVD applied in TensorFaces, $D = Z \times_1 P \times_2 A \times_3 J$. The people core matrix P has N person-specific rows containing the human motion signatures. The action core matrix A has M action-specific rows encoding action invariances across people. The last joint angle matrix J has T joint angles rows, the eigenmotions typically computed by PCA. The analysis is achieved by a change of basis to capture a person-associated motion by $C = Z \times_1 P \times_3 J$, and the change of basis to capture an action-associated motion is achieved by $B = Z \times_2 A \times_3 J$. The synthesis is achieved by the knowledge of the core tensor Z capturing all multi-way interactions, core matrix A generalising the actions, and core matrix J generalising the joint angles. To synthesize an action of a new person not seen before is a Tensor

completion or a regression problem to predict $D_{p,a}$ of a new person p doing action a, as $D_{p,a} = B_a \times_1 p^T$, where $B_a = Z \times_2 a_a^T \times_3 J$ for the specific action a. If the aim is to synthesize a motion for a new individual, then $p^T = d_a^T B_a^{-1}$, where d_a^T is the flattened tensor in the people mode, and choosing the specific action Transpose, and the complete set of motions for the new individual is $D_p = B \times_1 p^T$. If the aim is to synthesize a new action for a known person whom we have other actions recorded for, the new action $a^T = d_p^T C_p^{-1}$, then synthesizing this action for all people in the database is $D_a = C \times_2 a^T$. This makes this tensor decomposition a generative model. In machine learning, discriminative models, like most classification models, learn from a prelabelled dataset how to discriminate the different classes. While a generative model, specifically the Bayesian probabilistic model, understands how samples are generated and can create new data instances from the known ones. Also, the recognition task is achieved in this tensor decomposition by identifying a person from action parameters as the projection $p = B_a^{-T} d$. Similarly, identifying a person's specific action is the projection $a = C_p^{-T} d$. In both cases, the nearest neighbour algorithm returns the nearest person or action in the learned motion data d.
The author experimented using a Human limb motion dataset collected using a VICON system that employs four video cameras detecting the 3D position of 18 infrared markers placed on each person's legs. Six persons moved in different actions across a 12-meter walkway, so two cameras could observe each marker during the three different motions (walking, ascending/descending stairs). A similar dataset is collected by (Wang et al., 2021), and others are found at https://www.handcorpus.org/?tag=humanmotiondata. Vasilescu validated the ability of the tensor decomposition model to synthesize new motions for people and identify people from motion or actions from recorded motions.

6.3 Deep Neural Networks Compression

All previous applications in this chapter and other chapters required hand-tailored feature engineering to define a suitable feature extraction of best representation based on some criteria. The criteria can be to achieve dimensionality reduction, model compression, model regularisation, or data representation invariance to some transformations such as translation, rotation, scale and others. DNN, since 2006 have been evolving to solve many problems using linear algebra concepts hierarchically to model non-linear relationships without hand-crafting the representation of the features or the model parameters. Neural Networks are considered function-approximators, starting from the simplest regression model using one input layer and one output layer. Adding more layers learns more complex data representation and functions. Traditional Machine learning approaches use feature engineering that are known to enhance their performance. Features transformations include Fourier Transforms and their variants, such as STFT, MFCC, or wavelets transform and their variants, and others, such as SOFT, HOD for image, audio and video datasets, BoW and TF-IDF for text datasets.
While neural networks implicitly learn the representation, they achieve compression and regularisation by approximations that are achieved through the layers by neglecting irrelevant contents, such as the pooling layers in CNNs applying different pooling functions. This process studies the structural data interactions, forming an embedding representing the data that can be used for the given machine learning task at the output layer. The depth of the neural networks adds more parameters to estimate, causing the curse of dimensionality in big data analytics. It was observed that the weights within a layer in CNN can be estimated by a 5% subset of its parameters, indicating the DL models are over-parameterised (Denil et al., 2014).
The increase in parameters from the increased number of layers created the need for tensor structures and algorithms to reduce the computational complexity without losing multi-way interactions by the overly-simplistic pair-wise interactions. A direction of improvements for DNN performance was labelled compressive DNN, which aims to reduce hardware requirements and enable running in embedded devices such as phones and IoT (Wu et al., 2020).
The simplest method to compress a NN is to add the famous pooling layer that primarily applies the max (to keep only the highest values as the bright colours of an image only) or average or other functions based on the application requirements, on the weights specifying how much spatial reduction in size is required. This is a blind

compression method. Another blind compression is the famous dropout layer that randomly sets some neurons to zero; this approach is called pruning. This is useful for regularisation to prevent the network from overfitting. Other methods work to learn which neurons to drop out in a structured approach, such as (Fan et al., 2019) and (Knodt, 2022).
Other compression approaches, such as Vector quantisation methods, were applied to the CNN parameters and storage requirements. These methods include binarization (1-bit quantization) by turning off neurons with negative values. Another Quantisation method uses lower precision, such as converting floating point types to integer types compressing the network four times and speeding it up 2:4 times. Moreover, scalar quantisation uses k-means to cluster the weights and use representative neurons of each cluster. Also, Product quantisation divides the weights vector space into many disjoint subspaces and quantises them by raising them to different powers and applying k-means on all and storing their cluster indices only. Finally, the residual quantisation performs clustering by k-means and then identifies the residuals to reapply the clustering on them (Gong et al., 2014).
Another NN compression approach is HashedNets (Chen et al., 2015), which uses a hash function to group connection weights in hash buckets. A single parameter for each hash bucket is stored for the connections sharing the bucket. The traditional matrix factorisation methods (low-rank matrices), such as SVD on the weights matrix and only storing the highest singular values corresponding weights. Layer Fusion (Graph Optimization) is another compression approach that minimises computation, memory storage, and bandwidth by combining successive computational graph nodes into a single node for kernel execution.
Also, various tensor factorisation algorithms have been applied to achieve NN compression. This approach requires tensorizing and decomposing the weight matrices into a series of low-rank tensors to reduce redundant weights by using sparse representations. Due to the DL enhancements, both applications of computer vision and NLP applications research advanced through the years. We will start with these two application domains. Then, deep generative models, multi-modal applications and graph neural network (GNN) models will be discussed.

6.3.1 Computer Vision

The first application advances were facilitated by using CNN with deeper layers than ever due to the hardware advances of multi-core, GPU, and other technologies. Although the transform to the Fourier Domain was observed to speed up the convolution performance by 200% to achieve higher accuracies in capturing more complex interactions in a dataset, deeper layers have always been the solution, increasing the number of parameters and leading to the need for NN compression. Although, research trends are still mixing up explicit representation encoding by adding more layers, such as (Nair et al., 2020) propose using Fourier Transform Layer in CNN to optimise object detection. The need for model compression is needed in all network models.
The authors of (Novikov et al., 2015) replaced fully connected layers in CNN with a Tensor Train (TT-Layer) that they called TensorNet, which is compatible with the same training algorithm. As explained in the previous chapters, all tensor decomposition approaches capture more multi-way structural interactions in the dataset, making them more expressive than pair-wise matrix factorisation or compression approaches. TT Format is more immune to dimensionality curse and simpler for basic operations (addition and multiplication by a constant, summation and entry-wise tensor products, the sum of all elements and Frobenius norm) than Tucker and Hierarchical Tucker tensor decompositions. They proposed a mapping function between the weights metric and the TT-format and introduced the NN layer with weights stored in TT-format to be a TT-layer, which, when used in any NN, makes it TensorNet. A fully connected layer computes $y = Wx + b$, while a TT-layer converts all to tensors in TT-format $Y(i_1, \dots, i_d) = G_1(i_1, j_1) \dots G_d(i_d, j_d) X(j_1, \dots, j_d) + B(i_1, \dots, i_d)$, where G_i are the d core tensors of the TT-format of the original weights matrix, and Y, X and B are the d-dimensional tensors formed from the corresponding vectors y (dependent/target/outcome variable), x (independent/predictor/feature variable(s)), and b (bias), respectively. The paper details how the loss function can be performed in the TT-Format. They experimented with MNIST, and CIFAR-10 datasets, comparing a baseline two-layer fully connected network

with the two-TT-Layer TensorNet using different ranks (compression factors) to show that they achieved 200,000 times fewer parameters and compressing the size of the whole network by a factor of 7, without compromising the accuracy on TT-ranks all equal to 8. They tested the ImageNet dataset using a different arrangement of layers of TT with various ranks, FC, and MR (matrix rank restricted) on the VGG-16 and VGG-19 networks. All experiments show TensorNet to be the most compressed, most accurate and faster both on CPU and GPU and has the potential to improve the performance of wide (more neurons) and shallow (fewer layers) networks that were known for overfitting. More details about their experimental setup details can be found in their paper, and their Matlab code is published at https://github.com/Bihaqo/TensorNet. The Python Tensorly package implemented TT-layer at https://github.com/tensorly/Proceedings_IEEE_companion_notebooks/blob/master/tt-compression.ipynb/.
The previous application employed TT tensor decomposition on the single layers of the network to efficiently store the dense weight matrices of the fully-connected layers of a VGG network. Conversely, (Calvi et al., 2020) introduced the Tucker Tensor Layer (TTL) as an alternative to the dense weight matrices of neural networks. They also showed how the number of parameters in the neural layer is reduced while deriving a Forward and back-propagation on tensors algorithm that preserves the physical interpretability of Tucker decomposition and provides an insight into the learning process of the layer. Using various compression factors, they also tested using the MNIST, Fashion-MNIST, and CIFAR-10 datasets using the VGG-16 network. For example, they achieved a 66.63% compression with 82.3% accuracy compared to the 86.3% accuracy of the uncompressed model.
The Hierarchical Tucker (HT) tensor decomposition method performs better in compressing the weight matrices in Fully Convolutional layers because HT prefers the tensor with balanced dimensions lengths, as shown in (Gabor and Zdunek, 2022). The authors experimented with medium-scale CNNs on the CIFAR-10 dataset and large-scale CNNs, such as VGG-16 and ResNet-50, on the ImageNet dataset. They compared HT-2 to other tensor factorisation and other NN compression approaches to show its competitiveness in the achieved compression without much drop in accuracy. Their code is published at https://github.com/mateuszgabor/ht2.
A hybrid tensor decomposition combining TT and HT is proposed by (Wu et al., 2020). The authors tensorized the input X and the weight matrices W, applied the tensor decomposition on the weights tensor and updated the forward pass WX multiplications for fully connected layers, RNNs and LSTMs. They also tensorized the kernels in CNNs and then explained the tensorized gradient calculations in the back-propagation step. They compared HT formats to TT-LSTM (Yang et al., 2017) and TR-LSTM (Pan et al., 2018) models on the UCF11 and UCF50 video classification datasets. Then they compared kernel compression in CNNs on the CIFAR-10 dataset and adopted 3D-CNNs to recognize videos on UCF11 and CVRR-HANDS 3D datasets. They show that RNNs/LSTMs in the HT format have higher compression than those in the TT format when compressing weight matrices but with worse accuracy than regular uncompressed RNNs. They also showed that the TT format is more suitable for CNNs, achieving higher accuracy but similar compression to the HT format. Comparing the proposed hybrid tensor decomposition method on CNN models, it has both higher accuracy and higher compression than the TT format and outperforms the uncompressed models in the CVRR dataset.

6.3.2 NLP Application

Bag of words (BoW) and other frequency-based methods such as Term Frequency – Inverse Document Frequency (TF-IDF) of encoding text data were used to capture some semantic context for the data. These methods failed to capture the different meanings one word could have when placed in different sentences with other words or even in a different order in a sentence with the same words. Initially, semantic understanding of text depended on rule-based creation, such as building ontologies and semantic web tools such as Resource Description Framework (RDF). This provided trinary relationships in which many words' meanings and contexts can be captured. These methods can be easily built using a graph database.
(Socher et al., 2013) proposed Recursive Neural Tensor Network (RNTN) that uses a high-order neural network for structured data that leverages a full 3-way tensor for aggregating children's information in binary parse trees within a natural language processing application. Their method built the Stanford Sentiment Treebank dataset

that is available at http://nlp.stanford.edu/sentiment. They built a tree for the word vectors in the embedding matrix $L \in R^{d \times |V|}$, where d is d-dimentional word vector, and |V| is the number of words. This binary tree has leaves of the ordered words in the corpus and learns the parent p_i as hidden vectors that are functions (such as tanh) of the two children that, at the first level, are two given words. The recursive neural networks (RNN) models generally learn these hidden vectors in a bottom-up fashion to learn a classification using weights matrix W, such that the classification into C sentiment classes becomes the posterior probability of the classes computed as $y^a = softmax(W_s a)$, where $W_s \in R^{C \times d}$ is the sentiment matrix, multiplied by a word vector a. The word vector a is computed as a tri-gram as a parent with two children in a binary tree. It can be at any level in the tree or at the leaves of the hidden computed parents. This allows the word vectors to interact through a non-linear function. Another model is Matrix-Vector RNN (MV-RNN) which represents words as vectors and longer phrases as trees, such as each n-gram are represented as a list of (vector, matrix) pairs and a parse tree. This enables the interaction between words in phrases but increases the number of parameters to estimate. RNTN uses a tensor composition function for all nodes such that each slice of the tensor captures a specific type of composition on words' multiplicative interactions. The authors explained the back-propagation algorithm for tensors and used AdaGrad for this non-convex optimisation.

RNTN achieved the highest performance for shorter sentences compared with standard RNN, MV-RNNs, and baselines such as neural networks that use a bag of words ignoring word order and a bag of words' features with Naive Bayes and SVMs, as well as Naive Bayes with a bag of bigram features. The bag of words method works well with longer sentences. The authors experimented with the different n-gram lengths to show all models' performance. They also experimented with the complexity of sentences, such as negation, using "but" to identify the most positive and the most negative sentences. This application uses a neural network model that could have benefitted from more deep layers to capture more complex interactions, reducing hand-crafting of the semantic representation.

As evident from the previous application, semantic tree approaches are domain-specific and sometimes require vast numbers of human experts to define the required relationships manually. The following application falls in between this category (building ternary relationships) and learning an embedding. After reviewing this, we will resume other methods based on learning an embedding from a given text corpus.

The authors in (Weber et al., 2017) presented a natural language understanding application where tensors are used to capture multiplicative interactions combining predicate, object and subject, generating aggregated representations for event prediction tasks. The RNN models are sequential in events, while additive models create a compound effect of the variables using additive functions. A generalised additive model can be defined as $y = \beta + f_1(x_1) + f_2(x_2) + \cdots + f_n(x_n) = \sum_{i=1}^{n} f_i(x_i)$, or even $y = \beta + \sum_{i=1}^{n} f_i(x_i) + \sum_{i \neq j} f_{i,j}(x_i, x_j)$ as defined in (Hastie and Tibshirani, 1999). Multiplicative models are more sensitive to small changes in the arguments interactions. Tensor-based provides multiplicative models that were utilised in the Weber et al. paper to learn tensors P of the predicate, subject, and object to predict an event e computed as tensor contraction P(s, o), such that the event vector e_i, is learned as $e_i = \sum_{ijk} P_{i,j,k} s_j o_k$, from the s and o as subject and object vectors, respectively. The authors used a predefined word embedding to create the tensor $W^{d,d,d}$, where d is the dimension of the input embedding, and each row is a word. The predicate tensor P is learned as $P_{ijk} = W_{ijk} \sum_a p_a U_{ajk}$, where $U^{d,d,d}$ is a tensor capturing the linear functions for each one-dimensional row of W, determining how the predicate embedding p should scale that dimension. This makes Tensor-based Event Composition (as the first model) that predicts an event $e_i = \sum_{a,ijk} p_a s_j o_k W_{ijk} U_{ajk}$. The authors used training data from the New York Times Gigaword Corpus, extracting the event triplets using the Open Information Extraction system Ollie. They initialized the word embedding layer with 100-dimensional pre-trained GloVe vectors. A second model is proposed as the Role Factored Tensor model, such that $e = W_s v_s + W_0 v_s$, such that $v_s = T(s, p)$, and $v_o = T(o, p)$, where $T^{h \times d \times d}$ with h as the size of the output and d as the dimensionality of the embedding, is a tensor composed of factored composition strategy that captures interactions between the predicate and its arguments separately to combine these interactions into the final embedding. They trained a baseline as a two-layer compositional neural network model $e = W \times tanh\ (H[s; p; o])$, where W and H are the model parameters to estimate using the Adagrad learning algorithm with a 0.01 learning rate and minibatch size

of 128. The second baseline is a multiplicative two-layer NN concatenating the elementwise multiplications between the verb and its subject/object such that $e = W \times tanh\,(H[s; p; o; p\odot s; p\odot o])$, where $\odot$ is the element-wise multiplication. They created another variant to predict the next word, not just the next event. They evaluated the model using the Coherent Multiple Choice Narrative Cloze dataset (CMCNC), which is used to estimate which event has been held out from a document from a small set of randomly drawn events, found at https://paperswithcode.com/dataset/cmcnc. They used another automatic variant to this benchmark (MCNC) and showed that the accuracy of the Role Factor Tensor approach is higher in predicting events and words than the Predicate Tensor and the other two NN baselines using Spearman's correlation. The Predicate Tensor approach was better in one case predicting words (which was always more accurate than predicting events), using Hard similarity scores as a percentage of cases where the similar pair had higher cosine similarity than the dissimilar pair. The authors also used their learned tensor to draw an event schema starting from a seed event and connect all possible events that could occur next using the nearest neighbour algorithm. Their code is published at https://github.com/stonybrooknlp/event-tensors.
The NLP application advances were achieved by using word encoding that captures the multiplicative interactions and considers word order efficiently, and also by using deeper NN layers. NLP advancements grew throughout stages from manually crafting the words' embeddings, algorithms capturing word semantics relations such as Word2Vec, to algorithms capturing cooccurrences between words like GloVe, to adding a layer that learns this embedding from a given dataset in RNN or LSTM models. This led to transfer learning to use pre-trained models and fine-tune to specific applications. The RNN model learns sequential dependence of the input over temporal or spatial dependence, making it useful in word order semantics required in NLP applications. RNNs were used in sequence-to-sequence models such as encoder-decoder NN and for applications such as language translation (input as a sequence of words of the source language and output as a sequence of words of the destination language of variable lengths). The last hidden state of the encoder is the source language embedding, which is used by the decoder to generate the equivalent sentence in the destination language. LSTM uses more complex gates, in which some states are remembered for longer than others, adding another level of sophistication in learning the word order complexities and solving the vanishing gradient problem of RNNs on the cost of longer computation of at least four times the computational cost of RNN cells.

Then, the attention mechanism evolved to expose all encoder layers to the decoder to prevent the final hidden layer production bottleneck while focusing on relevant parts (by assigning different weights) of the input sequence when making predictions. This requires exposing all states by assigning weights to decide which state to use. These weights are learned from the training dataset. Common scoring functions include dot product, additive, and multiplicative attention.

Then comes the Transformer encoder/decoder model. The Transformer encoder has two sublayers, a self-attention layer and a Feed Forward NN layer, instead of the RNN (sequential naturally) or LSTM cells. Transformers use positional encoding to compensate for the missing sequencing due to the elimination of RNNs and LSTMs. Then the decoder component uses the abstract vector representation of the input sequences to generate one word at a time, attending to previously generated words using a similar mechanism to the encoder but adding a third sub-layer to perform multi-head attention over the output of the encoder stack, allowing the model to focus on different positions or sub-spaces.

The self-attention is implemented in many ways to capture interactions between all words within the same sequence or sentence. The original Google proposal was called the scaled dot-product attention that used three matrices, query Q (representing the current word), key K (representing labels for all the words in the segment to score against to identify relevance to the query) and value V (actual word representations), such that the n token embedding is multiplied by them. Q, K, and V are linear projections of the original input embeddings. Similarity scores S nxn matrix is calculated from the scaled dot-product of Q and K vectors, identifying similar ones with large values. The attention weight W nxn matrix is calculated by normalising the similarity scores S using the softmax function. Then the self-attention layer output is produced by multiplying the weights with the value V vector. Instead of one embedding, three embeddings are created for Q, K, and V independently, and then each one of them is projected through multiple linear projections creating multiple heads for the attention layer. These scores identify the relevance of focusing attention on what to remember rather than what to forget in LSTM models. The positional encoding of words in sentences is one of the characteristics of the Transformer model, and it can be absolute positional, relative positional, or rotary positional (Vaswani et al., 2017).

Transformers are considered the most advanced NLP approach with applications beyond NLP in computer vision (Dosovitskiy et al., 2021), automatic speech recognition, time series modelling and other machine learning applications. While capturing the input interactions in forward and backward dependence, the Transformer design is also parallelised because of recurrence sequential processing elimination and the use of multi-heads and multilinear mappings. Many Transformer based models have been proposed in the literature; some build on the encoder only, the decoder only, or the encoder/decoder model—some examples include BERT, RoBERTa, GPT, and DistilBERT, which combine self-attention and transfer learning. The HuggingFace platform (https://huggingface.co/) provides various architectures using a unified codebase for various ML tasks and datasets. For a tutorial style on the Transformer using Python, read the book (Tunstall et al., 2022).
The Transformers estimate a large number of parameters and can benefit from compression techniques such as parameter sharing across layers and low-rank approximations. These can be achieved by tensor decompositions methods such as Block-Term Tensor Decomposition (BTD), which is proposed by the authors of (Ma et al., 2019). BTD combines both CP decomposition and Tucker decomposition, such that a tensor is decomposed into P Tucker decomposition, each with its core tensor and d factor matrices, such that P is the CP rank. The authors first used Single-block attention based on the Tucker decomposition to use a linear function of a set of vectors. Then they built the multi-head attention using the BTD, enabling parameter sharing across multiple blocks, higher compression (8 times fewer parameters), and lower complexity. They tested using PTB, WikiText-103 and One-billion language modelling tasks, and English-German neural machine translation WMT-2016 to show that their method is more compressed and more accurate than Transformer, Transformer XL, TT-format tensor factorised Transformer model, and other models using RNN, LSTM, and others. Their code is published at https://github.com/szhangtju/The-compression-of-Transformer.

6.3.3 Generative DNN Model

As the previous section shows, an uncompressed deep neural network (DNN) can be reconstructed using the corresponding compressed tensor network representation. Using tensor decomposition approaches, the DNN model can be simplified to achieve the desired trade-off between parameterisation and predictive accuracy. Finally, the compressed tensor network is mapped back into the corresponding uncompressed DNN. This is not limited to computer vision or NLP applications but to any NN or DNN architecture solving any particular ML task. Another generative DNN architecture model is the Restricted Boltzmann Machines (RBM) which estimates the probability distribution of various datasets. Mapping an RBM to the Tensor Networks States (TNS) has been successfully applied by (Chen et al., 2018). TNS has been applied to various problems in quantum-many-body physics. The physics communities refer to Tensor Chain (TC) decomposition as the Matrix Product State (MPS), which is a special case of the Hierarchical Tucker (HT) decomposition and the simplest TNS. MPS is equivalent to the TT format. The authors applied concepts from the quantum information theory, which has developed at a faster pace in the past decades, to define the necessary and sufficient conditions to transform a TNS into an RBM representing quantum states. For example, they map the RBM weights to terms in tensors to form the TNS and then represent the TNS as MPS. They further use the RBM undirected probabilistic graphical model structure and employ the conditional independence property to provide an optimal MPS model. They discussed other TNS models, adding more deep layers, and how the number of parameters does not increase while the model performance increases. Their code is published at https://github.com/yzcj105/rbm2mps.

For Python examples applying these concepts, many are contributed as open source in the public domain. For example, Tensorly Python package authors compressed an FC layer using TT format at https://github.com/tensorly/Proceedings_IEEE_companion_notebooks/blob/master/tt-compression.ipynb.
They also have a Tensor Regression Layer (TRL) https://github.com/tensorly/Proceedings_IEEE_companion_notebooks/blob/master/tensor_regression_layer.ipynb
A Tensorial RNN can be found at https://github.com/Tuyki/TT_RNN that includes FC, Simple RNN, LSTM and GRU in their Tutorials using PyTorch. Many python packages implement the TT decomposition, such as scikit_tt (https://github.com/PGelss/scikit_tt/).
The Fully Connected layer tensorization and the CNN layer tensorization are implemented in Python and published at https://github.com/timgaripov/TensorNet-TF/tree/master/experiments/cifar-10/FC-Tensorizing-Neural-Networks, and https://github.com/timgaripov/TensorNet-TF/tree/master/experiments/cifar-10/conv-Ultimate-Tensorization.

6.3.4 Multi-modal Neural Networks & Data Fusion Techniques

Multi-modal problems rely on two or more datasets, each coming from its domain and representation requirements. A data fusion step is required to create a unimodal projection out of the multi-modal different spaces representation, capturing the multi-way interactions between all modalities. A simple approach is concatenating the vectors or applying an element-wise sum or product between the different modalities. This will not capture complex interactions between the different modalities. Outer-Product methods are used to capture bilinear interactions between all elements of two vectors, such as an outer product q⊗v between visual v and textual q embeddings. This approach will generate a massive number of parameters to learn. For example, for two modalities with dimensions, $n_1 = n_2 = 2048$ and the dimension of the weights matrix linearised is z =3000, the number of parameters is 12.5 billion. Multi-modal Compact Bilinear pooling (MCB) uses FFT to compress further the outer product (Fukui et al., 2016). More compression, expressive, and interpretable fusion are required for fusing more than two modalities. The tensor multi-way analysis is an intuitive solution to these applications.

The authors in (Ben-younes et al., 2017) address the Visual Question Answering (VQA) task by using tensors to fuse visual and textual representations. They proposed a multi-modal tensor-based Tucker decomposition to capture the interactions between images and textual modalities with fewer parameters (compression) than other bilinear models. The images' internal representation v is learned using a CNN architecture; the textual representation q is learned using GRU sequential architecture. Then a Tucker representation $T = [T_c; W_q, W_v, W_o]$ with a core tensor T_c, text matrix W_q, image matrix W_v and the output matrix W_o. The output vector $y = \left(\left(T_c \times_1 (q^T W_q)\right) \times_2 (v^T W_v)\right) \times_3 W_o$ produces an answer. They tested the model using the VQA dataset that can be downloaded from https://visualqa.org/. They compared the performance with other state-of-the-art models to show performance improvements. Their code is published at https://github.com/Cadene/vqa.pytorch.

For a modalities' fusion example, the work in (Li et al., 2020) created a multi-modal sentiment analysis (MSA) using the MOSI/CMU-MOSI dataset of the form (A, V, L), where $A = \{A_1, \ldots, A_T\}$, $V = \{V_1, \ldots, V_T\}$ and $L = \{L_1, \ldots, L_T\}$, denote the time series of the length T w.r.t. the acoustic, visual and language data, respectively. The dataset is published at https://paperswithcode.com/dataset/multimodal-opinionlevel-sentiment-intensity and https://github.com/A2Zadeh/CMU-MultimodalSDK. The aim is to learn the composite function $\hat{y} = f(\varphi_a(A), \varphi_v(V), \varphi_l(L))$where $\varphi_i(X)$ is the sub-mapping from the raw data to the features. This function includes the fusion phase and is learned by an LSTM model using a preprocessed features representation that keeps the uni-modal representation and concatenated data from the different modalities for each time step, then across k-time steps. They proposed Time Product Fusion Network (TPFN) that builds on the temporal tensor fusion network (T2FN). TPFN applies implicit outer product methods across sliding time windows to capture the model interaction across modalities in the data fusion phase. CP is the method for low-rank decomposition, and regularisation on the low-rank representation handles incomplete datasets. Their code is published at https://qibinzhao.github.io/publications/ECCV2020_LiChao/TPFN.zip.

In (Hou et al., 2019), the authors addressed the Multi-modal sentiment analysis (MSA) problem by proposing a High-order polynomial tensor pooling (PTP). PTP concatenated features form a Tensor by tensor product operation of order P to represent all possible polynomial expansions up to order P. As P increases, so does the number of parameters to learn, but the higher polynomial interactions between tensors can be captured. Using CP decomposition, the weights tensor is compressed. Then Hierarchical polynomial fusion network (HPFN) is formed assuming 2D feature map time series. HPFN recursively learn the local temporal modalities pattern by arranging PTP in multiple layers. This borrows many features from CNN, including receptive fields, sharing parameters, scanning window, and PTP 'fusion filters'. Their code is published at https://qibinzhao.github.io/publications/NeurIPS_2019_HouMing/HPFN.zip.

Tensorising Activation functions:

In the first building block of a neural network design, the choice of activation function is typically achieved by a weighted sum of the inputs for vectorial data using the inner product between the weight vector and the input vector. In tensorizing the neural network, the tensors can be used to modify input aggregation functions to be suitable for input in tree-structured data, such that a specific node in the tree, the neuron, recursively computes its activation by a weighted sum of the activations of its children, with appropriate weight sharing assumptions. Such an aggregation function can be easily tensorized. Working with tree data structures usually requires recursion and graph data structures, which will be discussed in the following section.

6.3.5 GNN applications

This chapter reviewed the advances in Deep Neural Networks (DNN) and how tensor decompositions have been applied to them. The literature provides many applications of Graph Neural Networks (GNN) and how graph data structures have been applied in DNN and using Tensor decomposition approaches using graph and network data structures. NN build the computational graph as a multipartite graph; however, using graph input data structures to train a deep neural network enables various graph theory and network analytics algorithms to benefit from the depth and non-linearity of the network.

The authors of (Kwon and Chung, 2022) proposed a recursive tensor decomposition method that is based on the CP decomposition by choosing orthogonal vectors in the SVD step creating a decomposition tree. They experimented on MNIST, CIFAR-10, and ILSVRC 2012 datasets to achieve a 154× reduction in weight parameters with only a 1% accuracy drop compared to the original baselines for these datasets. This method is more suitable for the neuromorphic systems that will be reviewed in the next chapter.

The work in (Hamdi and Angryk, 2019) presents tensor decomposition-based node embedding algorithms that learn node features from arbitrary types of graphs: undirected, directed, and/or weighted, without relying on computationally expensive eigendecomposition or requiring tuning of the word embedding-based hyperparameters as a result of representing the graph as a node sequence similar to the sentences in a document.

The work in (Jermyn, 2017) presents tensor trees as efficient tensor computer representations based on both optimal brute force and greedy algorithm heuristic that performs well for higher-rank tensors tree decompositions.

Based on these advances, I find the advances in Graph Neural Networks (GNN) to be complementing tensor decomposition and their applications in DNN. GNN is another active research topic and almost reaching maturity, as presented in (Liu and Zhou, 2020). The book explains how various architectures of DNN (CNN, LSTM, Attention, Residual and Hetregenous) are constructed from graph and network analysis algorithms. The GNN builds NN from

graph structures with node and edge attributes and can use different representations, such as real-valued vectors and tensors. The introduction to GNN presented in (Bacciu et al., 2020) identifies Graph Neural networks as recursive neural units with cycles between the node states to capture the mutual dependence, while the term Neural Network for Graphs defines the architecture that captures the mutual dependence through layers and passing on representations while eliminating recursion. The authors provide a tutorial on Deep Graph Networks (DGN) and variants such as Bayesian and Generative.
The advantages of GNN are closely related to the compressive DNN tensor decomposition methods, such as using traditional spectral graph theory to reduce the computational cost of shared weights on one side. On the other side, the hierarchical patterns that capture features of different sizes can be represented with multi-layer graph structures. For graph transformation, graph-tensors proposed in (Malik et al., 2019) learn embeddings of time-varying graphs based on a tensor framework. There are also matrix networks proposed in (Sun et al., 2018) and graph tensor neural networks (Liu and Zhu, 2021). Spektral is a framework of different GNN models that are developed at https://graphneural.network/. The Deep Graph Library (DGL) is a framework for different GNN models that scale to large graphs using GPUs and distributed architectures. Their codebase and examples are published at https://www.dgl.ai/. PyTorch geometric is another GNN framework hosted at https://www.pyg.org/. Nvidia offer platforms to parallelise the training of DGLs and PyG GNNs on GPUs using Memgraph, cuGraph, and graph-as-a-service, as illustrated in https://developer.nvidia.com/gnn-frameworks.

6.4 General Framework

Tensor Computing is far from being an established field, and a general framework might not be precisely defined at this stage. However, broad steps to organise the process of building a multi-way analysis model or compressing an existing model can be proposed, subject to many possibilities at every step, and open for creativity and research outcome proposals. Below is an attempt to define sample steps to tensorize ML and DL tasks:

- Make sure Data is in Tensor format or can be reformatted.
    - Choose already formatted multi-way data, such as
        - http://www.models.life.ku.dk/nwaydata,
        - https://three-mode.leidenuniv.nl/.
        - https://github.com/zhaoxile/reproducible-tensor-completion-state-of-the-art.
    - Create a script to collect the data in the required format. fMRI, EEG and similar data, signal processing data, and multiset data in which at least one of the modes consists of different entities at each level are all types of data that can be used to create a tensor format.
    - Extract data using a network/graph dataset that is already multi-way.
        - For NLP data, ontologies, RDFs or platforms such as https://github.com/knowitall/ollie can be used.
    - Apply a tensorisation step such as Binarisation, Segmentation, decimation, folding, reshaping, Hankelization, multi-way Toeplitz Löwner and higher-order statistics (Debals, 2017).
        - Sometimes the data contains enough information to connect all modes of tensorisation; for example, the time mode is naturally related to the spatial modes in videos. Other datasets might require adding an extra variable to connect the modes, for example, adding a time mode of an experiment to tensorise a set of experiments each in matrix form, or an extra variable such as illumination/poses in tensor faces to connect the Eigenfaces matrices.
    - Make sure the created tensor properties are suitable to the original data properties, tensor decomposition readiness and to the required analysis to be done.
- Standardise all data to centre the mean around zero and rescale to a standard deviation of one. Some tensorisation steps will benefit from standardisation on the original dataset eliminating redundancy.

- Handling large datasets whose tensors can not be created in memory:
    - Choose random samples to create the tensor from or block sampling.
    - Use incomplete tensors.
    - Apply some dimensionality reduction method on the original dataset, as explained in chapter two, or representation learning method, as explained in chapter five, to transform the data into a compact form better than randomization.
    - Attempt identifying the components of the tensor decomposition that you can multiply together to resume with a reconstructed tensor from those components, such as the method implemented in the Tensorfaces paper. This is called implicit tensorization, which combines tensorization with tensor decompositions without the explicit construction of a tensor. Tensor recognition as well is the process of identifying an implicit tensor and the ability to construct it from a given dataset (tensor representing multi-way dataset) or a problem definition (tensor representing multi linear function and polynomials). Tensor recognition is a skill that can be gained through exposure to various tensorised problems and approaches (Debals, 2017).
    - Tensor networks can be diagrammatically drawn, and the tensor contraction code is generated, as shown in the tool published at https://www.tensortrace.com/.
- Turn into the tensor form using examples from the Python code in "tensorisation.ipynb" and "multi-wayExamples.ipynb".
- To achieve dimensionality reduction, use a tensor decomposition approach.
- Choose the machine learning model to apply. Pass only the core decomposed tensors for the data and compute the metrics to evaluate.
- For DNN models, choose where to apply the tensorization steps discussed earlier and experiment with the performance evaluation to identify the most suitable for a given problem and dataset.
- Using transparent, simpler code built from scratch for NN and DNN enables complete control over all computation and having code that can survive the many waves of the existing DNN platforms' evolution and broken compatibility. For example, the following are simpler models: https://github.com/Sentdex/NNfSiX , https://github.com/ahmedfgad/NumPyANN, https://github.com/ahmedfgad/NumPyCNN, https://github.com/revsic/numpy-rnn, https://github.com/pangolulu/rnn-from-scratch, https://github.com/CaptainE/RNN-LSTM-in-numpy, https://github.com/3outeille/GANumpy, https://github.com/gmontamat/poor-mans-transformers, and many more. Otherwise, keep a virtual machine with all dependencies and do not update any module independently.

Chapter 7: Parallelisation, Challenges and Future Trends

This chapter discusses parallel and distributed features inherent in tensor modelling, their current implementations in C/C++, and how to use them in Python packages. Then the book is summarised with a discussion of challenges and future trends in tensor decomposition applications.

7.1 Tensor Computing Parallelisation

Since machine learning, particularly deep learning, is compute-intensive and memory-intensive because of the ever-increasing size and dimensionality of the available models, datasets, and compute iterations, parallelisation is essential, whether on the software or hardware level. What is known as Moore's law is the observation made by Gordon Moore in 1965 that the number of transistors in a dense integrated circuit (IC) doubles every 18 months, increasing processing speed. This observation held true from the 1950s up until around the 2010s. Adding more transistors and ever-decreasing ICs size reached their physical limits causing heat dissipation that can not be solved using the same miniaturisation approach. New approaches continue feeding the increasing need for faster processing of the many sectors dependent on it. Various technologies competed to provide speed-ups, such as multi-CPU, multi-core, 3D CPU transistors, GP-GPU, TPUs, ASICs, microcontrollers, SoC, SiP, and distributed processing over clusters of computing nodes such as instances in the cloud, supercomputers, IoT devices connecting various sensors, BioChips, and many other passive components. Most machine learning and deep learning packages are designed on a massive stack of optimised algorithms that run on the detected hardware from CPUs and GPUs. You might need to set the library to use these technologies at the higher stack level. You can learn the logic, syntax, and semantics of using these libraries while programming your own algorithms.
The serial programming approach solves the problem logic using a sequence of instructions that are executed sequentially, one after another, in one processor. On the other hand, the parallel programming approach divides the solution steps into discrete independent parts that can be solved concurrently on several cores and computing nodes using any of the Parallel Computer Architectures. Speed-ups are achieved by carefully planning the division of independent partitions of the logical sequence or managing the dependencies without losing the speed-ups gained by communication latency.
Computer architectures with a single CPU or multiple processors/cores have shared memory and enable multiple threads. When a network connects an arbitrary number of such computing elements, this architecture will have distributed memory and need message passing. A computer with a GPU card will require moving the processing between CPU device memory and GPU device memory. Python packages to implement parallel programs include threading for multiple threads, mpi4py for message passing, and Numba for GPU processing. These are mainly C or C++ packages for faster processing with Python wrappers. Each of these packages has its online documentation and tutorials from which mastering them first-hand from the developers is easy. Numpy is the Python package for working with optimised arrays with vectorisation, which is the process of computing in parallel all the elements of an array, unlike the built-in sequential arrays of Python.
Building a parallel algorithm requires taking care of various implementation details such as shared memory synchronised access using mutexes or similar structures, distributed processing synchronised sending and receiving, and creating barriers and waves of computation. The edX course of Linear Algebra For Frontiers is managed by the authors of a package, "Flame for Matrix Partitioning," that implements matrices without manual index manipulations. This is based on a predecessor package, "PLAPACK", with a methodology that can derive parallel algorithms (Geijn and Quintana-Ort´, 2008). A detailed Python parallel and distributed programming experience can be gained from (Zaccone, 2015). Also, the work in the PhD thesis for Tensor Partitioning on a cluster of computing nodes provides an example of wavefront processing of N-D arrays applied to the Multiple

Sequence Alignment problem (Helal *et al.*, 2008) (Helal *et al.*, 2009). In this thesis, ND arrays are also expressed dynamically using a data structure accepting N, shape, and data as parameters and creating a linear array in memory. The N-dimensional index is then parameterised to access a specific location in the array or update it. This is very important not to fix the array dimensionality and shape the way Numpy, MatLab, Mathematica and others do, limiting the ability to dynamically create these arrays, particularily in the tensoriation step as shown in the tensorisation notebook.
Google TensorFlow, Facebook PyTorch, Apache MXNet, Microsoft CNTK, and the many DL Frameworks are built over a stack of optimised algorithms that run in parallel in various hardware architectures that they can be compiled to during installation. Table 5 summarises the features of some of the available DL frameworks in terms of hardware readiness and the type of computational graph built. The Open Neural Network Exchange (ONNX) has been proposed to provide interoperability between frameworks. It accepts a model in one of the supported frameworks as input, identifies the common operators, and generates a file for a lower-level compiler optimised for a particular hardware platform.

Table 5: DL Framework comparison

	Static Graph	**Dynamic Graph**	**Both**
General Purpose HW: CPU/GPU	TensorFlow/ TensorRT / Caffe/ CNTK	PyTorch	MXNet
Embedded: ARM/IoT	TensorFlow Lite	PyTorch Mobile	Gluon
High-Level API	Keras	FastAI	Gluon

The numerical recipes optimising solving equations and various Linear Algebra computations are standardised in the Basic Linear Algebra Subprograms (BLAS) libraries. DL computations have been standardised in similar libraries such as MKL-DNN and cuDNN. Nvidia TensorRT accepts models from all DL frameworks and uses optimisation accelerators on supported hardware platforms. It supports graph optimisation (e.g., layer fusion) and low-bit quantisation with an extensive collection of highly optimised Nvidia GPU kernels. TensorRT also enables Kernel-Auto Tuning by choosing the best data layer and parallel algorithms for the target hardware platform. It also has Dynamic Tensor Memory (Memory optimisation) feature that reduces memory footprint and improves memory re-use by allocating memory for each Tensor only for the duration of its usage, and a Multi-Stream Execution feature that scales to multiple input streams by processing them in parallel using the same model and weights. For example, a PyTorch 1.4.0 model is accelerated by quantisation from FP32 to FP16 using TensorRT to Cuda 10.1 Titan V, i7-7800X achieved almost double speed-up than the original model. ***Research Project:*** BLAS was introduced in 1969 with vector operations, updated in the 70s for matrix-vector operations and in the 80s for matrix-matrix operations. Tensor-tensor operations BLAS for the fourth order tensors were implemented in (Liu and Wang, 2017), including tensor (Kronecker) product, KhatriRao product, Hadamard product, tensor contraction, t-product, or L-product. There is a need for a similar highly optimised Tensor Decomposition for a variable (n) order tensors mathematical library that is efficient in computational tractability and interoperable between the different DL frameworks and hardware.
Please note that Tensor in TensorFlow, TensorRT, and many other DL current frameworks are limited to predefined ordered two- or three- or four-dimensional arrays and are still working on the traditional vectorised pair-wise models or spatial matrices for convolutions layers. The first dimension is usually the Batch number (learning occurs through epochs of applying input batches to the input layer), the second or last dimension is usually a timestep/or channel, and the data is in vector form in the remaining dimension for Fully connected layers. For 2D convolution, two dimensions are used for the spatial dimensions, such as image width and height. The video dataset has three spatial dimensions; the extra dimension is for the time or frames. Therefore, the data is in vector form, fixed 2D, or fixed 3D ordered dimensions, while the framework's name has Tensor in it, implying that it can grow as a multi-way for any multi-way dataset. Graph Neural Networks (GNN) are currently well-

developed to accept data as adjacency matrices of graph data structures. The various NN tensorisation projects reviewed in chapter six did not create a framework yet. I will mention Tensor Decomposition models to mean the ability to accept input in N-D arrays as implemented in Numpy and Tensorly with the ability to define the modes in any order based on the problem requirements. ***Research Project:*** Tensorised NN Frameworks can be built with all Tensorised Layer types implemented, tensorised activation functions, and tensorised forward and backward propagation algorithms such as the SGD with DMRG algorithms, AutoDiff (Paszke *et al.*, 2017) and DDSP (differentiable digital signal processing) (Engel *et al.*, 2020).
The chips/processors that were designed for AI are called XPU. These include GPUs, FPGAs, and Application Specific Integrated Circuits (ASICs), such as neural processing units (NPUs).
Matrix operations specialised/dedicated hardware has been built to optimise DL performance, such as Google Tensor Processing Unit (TPU), Hisilicon NPU, Apple Bonic, tensor cores in NVIDIA Volta/Turing Architecture, Intel Nervana neural network processors (NNP), Tensor Computing Processor BM1684, Amazon Inferentia with NeuroCores, Hanguang Alibaba Ali-NPU, Knupath Hermosa, Baidu XPU, Qualcomm Cloud AI 100, Cambricon MLU270, Graphcore GC2, AVX512 vector units and tensor core, and FPGA DL ready components.
The TPU is 15 to 30 times faster than current GPUs and CPUs. A TPU uses a matrix as a primitive instead of a vector or scalar in CPUs and GPUs, which means ND-Arrays still need to be matricised. It includes Matrix Multiplier Unit (MXU), Unified Buffer (UB), and Activation Unit (AU), which is driven with CISC instructions by the host processor. The MXU is power and area optimised and is composed of a systolic array to perform matrix multiplications. The TPU architecture has bottlenecks that are identified in (Wang et al., 2019). Their study proposed a new parameterised deep learning benchmark suite (ParaDNN) to evaluate the performance of six DNN models on Google TPU, Nvidia V100 GPU, and Intel Skylake CPU platforms.

The neuromorphic systems are inspired by biological brain science, such as IBM's TrueNorth and Intel's Loihi. TrueNorth employs high connectivity between artificial neurons to simulate the brain tissues. The pulse-time-dependent synaptic plasticity model (STDP) mechanism is employed by Loihi, simulating the brain's regulation of the synaptic strength by the relative time of pre-synaptic and post-synaptic pulses. These systems are still in their infancy and more suitable for long-term learning than large-scale modelling. For example, (Sharifshazileh *et al.*, 2021) designed a neuromorphic system with a neural recording head-stage with a spiking neural network (SNN) processing core for processing intracranial Electroencephalography-EEG (iEEG) for the detection of High-Frequency Oscillations (HFO) from Brain Tissues. These systems have low power and latency compared to CPUs and GPUs and read the analogue signal directly from the head stage.

DL compilers have been proposed that compile a model in a given framework to a given hardware architecture, such as TVM (Tensor Virtual Machine), Tensor Comprehension (TC), Glow, nGraph, XLA, and FPGA-specific DL code generators such as DNN Weaver, AngelEye, ALAMO, FP-DNN, SysArrayAccel, fpgaConvNet, DeepBurning, Haddoc2, and AutoCodeGen. The survey in (Li *et al.*, 2021) provides anatomical design steps for building a DL compiler, such as the Front-end dealing with the input framework and creating a NN Intermediate Representation (IR) that is passed on to the back-end that uses mature compiler toolchains targetting specific hardware such as LLVM. The back end turns the high-level IR into a lower-level IR and uses third-party toolchain optimisation and code generation, including multiple compilation passes, memory allocation, and HW parallelisation, along with other possible features. The survey evaluates these compilers by creating 19 sample NN models (ResNet, DenseNet, VGG series, and lightweight models: MobileNet and MNASNet series) on Torchvison, and the GluonCV, then used ONNX-specific relays such as tvm.relay. front-end.from_onnx for TVM, and the other corresponding relays of the other compilers. They evaluate the compilers' features' presence and the generated output model speed of execution on CPUs and GPUs on coarse-grained level (end-to-end) and fine-grained level (per-layer) performance metrics. They identified the successful compilation per Model type, compiler, and architecture and the lack of compatibility of some models with some compilers. They conclude that TVM is among the best performance in several experiments. ***Research Project:*** I assume none of these is suitable for tensorised DL applications, but an extensive study should experiment with their readiness or what it needs to achieve similar compilers for Tensor decomposition and tensorised NN models

Production servers also enable better use of available CPU, GPU and hardware resources by launching multiple instances of one or more ML models as required, using a scheduler and static or dynamic batching of inference requests to reduce response latency and increase throughput. NVIDIA Triton Inference, IBM Watson Studio, MS Azure Machine Learning, Kubeflow, and others offer different services to utilise in deploying ML models for inference. Various performance metrics can be collected to help optimise an ML model configuration with profiling.

Figure 70 illustrates the technologies below Tensor structures from lower levels, highly optimised libraries, to hardware. It also shows the algorithms up to the applications and compilers that can benefit from tensor computation methods. Further investigations are still an active research area with potential innovation at every level.

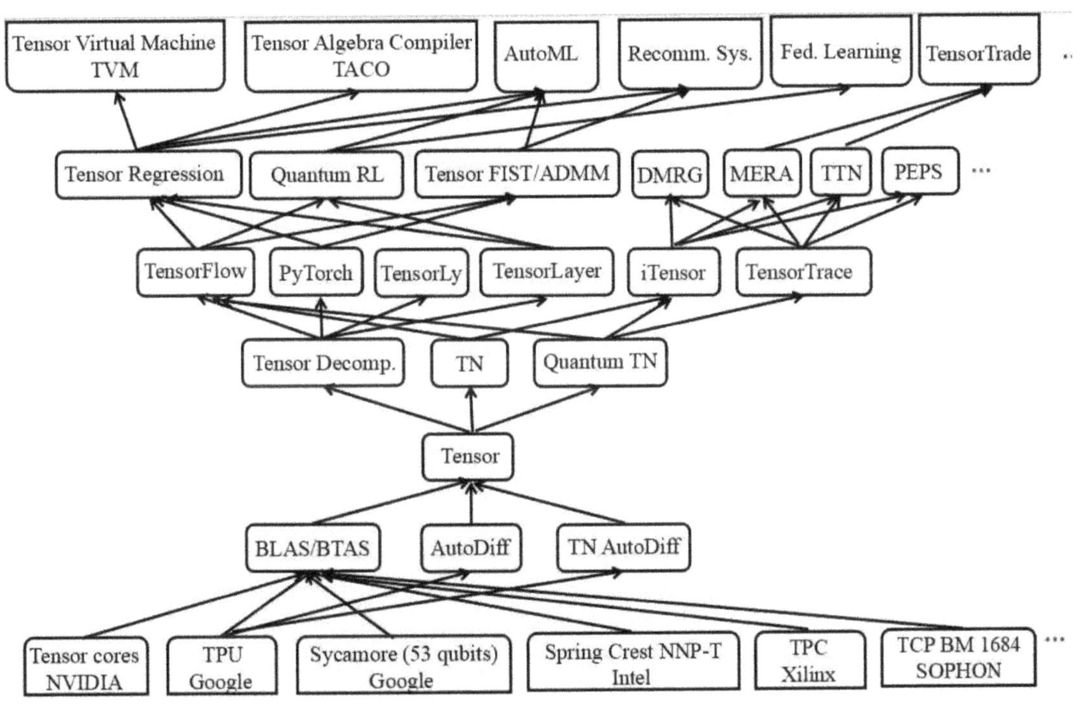

Figure 70: Tensor and Tensor Network Hourglass architecture described by (Liu, Zhao and Walid, 2021), showing the hardware at the bottom, the applications on top, and how tensors and tensors networks are in the middle layer central to all future developments and calling for standardisation.

7.2 Challenges and Future Trends

This section summarises state-of-the-art with discussions of existing challenges and expected future trends. As discussed in chapter six, tensorizing NN takes place at the various building blocks of building the network. The number of blocks at which the tensorisation occurs, the type of tensorisation, and the collective performance evaluation is still active area of research. We have seen examples of tensorisation at one NN layer, multiple layers, or Tensor Networks models expressing the whole network. There are tensorisation approaches at the forward phase of neural models (i.e. computing of the neural activation), at the backward phase (i.e. learning), and both. Also, the activation function choice using recursive tree inputs has been attempted. ***Research Project:*** The type of tensor decomposition used, such as CP, Tucker, HT, TT, or others, needs to be further studied to evaluate the enhancement of the trade-off between compression and performance and the interpretability of different models and the different applications. Preferably, building benchmarks with clear metrics can enhance comparing future proposals. Multimodal DL models as well will benefit from tensorisation. Currently, large-scale trained models are merged on deployment, such as in Nvidia Deepstream https://developer.nvidia.com/deepstream-sdk. Merging the representation during training will reduce the model size, training time, and deployment cost and achieve better representation and regularisation due to multi-way structure capturing. Investigating through the theory, the empirical results, and the deployment technologies can be pursued.

Chapter six briefly reviewed some work on multi-relational data analysis on single networks, on collections of structured tree samples, Graph NN and DGN, showing that the interpretation of the representation achieved better performance of the various tensorised models than the untensorized models. ***Research Projects:*** Generalising these to handle datasets of graph samples with unconstrained topology also needs to be evaluated. For example, hypergraphs connect a node to a subset of the graph rather than to other nodes only, creating hierarchical models. Systematic evaluation of the expressiveness achieved after tensorisation due to the enhanced representation would clarify the performance evaluation of the newly proposed models (Errica, Bacciu and Micheli, 2020). Also, time-evolving graphs/temporal-spatial learning graphs or online learning rather than batch learning using tensorised models on graphs would be an exciting direction to enhance and evaluate. Tensorising graphs would also be an ideal research direction for compression, expressiveness, and accuracy trade-off evaluations.

As identified in the parallelisation section earlier in this chapter and from the Python code online examples mentioned in the previous chapters, it is clear that many software libraries in various programming languages, not only Python, implement different tensor methods. Merging all efforts to create a framework using similar conventions to scikit-learn and other DL models, such as TensorFlow or Keras, with some embedded systems-ready packages will promote the wide adoption of these methods and enhance their performance. A current list of implementation are as follows:

- scikit-tensor integrates some consolidated tensor decomposition (Tucker, CP and the like) into the scikit-learn universe https://github.com/mnick/scikit-tensor .
- TensorD provides a Python tensor library built on Tensorflow with basic tensor operations and decompositions supporting parallel computation (e.g. GPU). Their code and examples are published at https://github.com/Large-Scale-Tensor-Decomposition/tensorD (Hao *et al.*, 2018).
- TensorLy is a Python library implementing a wide range of methods for tensor learning, allowing it to leverage different computation back-ends, including NumPy, MXNet, PyTorch, TensorFlow, and CuPy.

Tensorly implements CP, Tucker and TT decompositions. Their documentation is found at http://tensorly.org/stable/user_guide/tensor_decomposition.html . They also implemented Tensor Regression, and their documentation is at http://tensorly.org/stable/user_guide/tensor_regression.html. (Kossaifi *et al.*, 2019)

- HOTTBOX is a recent standalone Python toolbox for tensor decompositions, statistical analysis, visualisation, feature extraction, regression and non-linear classification of multi-dimensional data. Their code is published with examples at https://hottbox.github.io/stable/index.html (Kisil *et al.*, 2021).
- "scikit_tt" (https://github.com/PGelss/scikit_tt/)
- ttrecipes by (Cichocki *et al.*, 2016, p. 1) and published at https://github.com/rballester/ttrecipes.
- "tednet" implements various neural network layer types compressed using different tensor decompositions, such as compressing an RNN layer using TR decomposition (TR_RNN). They support ResNet Layers, LSTM Layers, CNN, and Linear Layers, among others (Pan, Wang and Xu, 2022), https://github.com/tnbar/tednet.
- "tensortools" implements time-shifted CP decomposition (Williams *et al.*, 2018). Their code is published at https://github.com/neurostatslab/tensortools.
- "T3F" is built on top of Tensorflow, providing Tensor Train decomposition for neural networks with Riemannian optimisation (Novikov *et al.*, 2020). Their code is published at https://t3f.readthedocs.io/.
- Other essential websites keeping track of tensors decomposition algorithms developments include https://www.tensors.net/, http://tensornetwork.org/software/, and https://qibinzhao.github.io/.

Research Project: Continue expanding the application domain of tensorisation approaches to problems such as graph analysis such as graph clustering, and signal processing for telecommunications and biomedical sciences, such as medical imaging and signals of various modes such as MRI, EEG, ECG, hyperspectral imaging, chemical shift brain imaging, and others, scientific computing problems such as excitation-emission spectroscopy, chromatography, and many more.

In chapter four, Tensortrace tool hard-codes the graphical user input into the Python code. Another possible Master's or PhD thesis project (based on the level of investigation) is to write the code for dynamically creating these tensor shapes with their indices and networks, then the contraction dynamically for datasets. This could be an extension to the game maker studio application or in Python only with or without graphical interfaces. It could be to load a dataset file, identify the tensorisation requirements based on some user input from the examples in previous chapters, repeat for all required datasets, build the tensor network, and contract it into one tensor. Tensorisation so far has been tailored to particular applications in this book. Parametrising the tensorisation requirements from the dataset shape and analysis requirements to provide some automation and representation learning is an exciting project. Then test the dynamic tensor, indices, networks, and contraction to some real datasets and some quantum many-body Physical experiments such as the dataset and the benchmark in http://quantum-machine.org/datasets/.

Research Project: A constant review of the physics and math communities' advances and how to benefit from them in developing ML and DL applications is required. Other scientific computation communities are active contributors to the advancement of ML and DL approaches, such as the chemometrics and psychometric communities and others. All these communities produce their own software that is usually specified to a given problem. Computer science professionals/researchers are trained in generalising and creating frameworks using software engineering approaches that maintain backward compatibility while continuously evolving to new or enhanced features or components. A joint effort can contribute to the understanding and wide adoption of methods from one research community to another.

A pronounced research direction comes from chapter five, discussing representation theory, abstract algebra and group theoretic frameworks. Many group theory implementations, such as GAP, are not ready for higher-scale calls and wrappers from other programming languages to build further machine learning and deep learning models on top of them.

References

Altmann, S.L. (1986) Rotations, quaternions, and double groups. Oxford [Oxfordshire] : New York: Clarendon Press ; Oxford University Press (Oxford science publications).

Armenta, M.A. and Jodoin, P.-M. (2021) 'The Representation Theory of Neural Networks'. arXiv. Available at: http://arxiv.org/abs/2007.12213 (Accessed: 25 July 2022).

Ashburner, J. and Friston, K.J. (1997) 'Spatial Transformation of Images', in Human Brain Function. First Edition. Academic Press USA, p. 36. Available at: http://www.fil.ion.ucl.ac.uk/spm/doc/books/hbf1/.

Bacciu, D. and Mandic, D.P. (2020) 'Tensor Decompositions in Deep Learning'. arXiv. Available at: http://arxiv.org/abs/2002.11835 (Accessed: 28 June 2022).

Bader, B., Harshman, R.A. and Kolda, T.G. (2007) 'Temporal Analysis of Semantic Graphs Using ASALSAN', in Seventh IEEE International Conference on Data Mining (ICDM 2007). Seventh IEEE International Conference on Data Mining (ICDM 2007), Omaha, NE, USA: IEEE, pp. 33–42. Available at: https://doi.org/10.1109/ICDM.2007.54.

Banner, A.D. (2007) The calculus lifesaver: all the tools you need to excel at calculus. Princeton, NJ: Princeton University Press (A Princeton lifesaver study guide).

Belton, A. et al. (2019) 'x', in, pp. 117–165. Available at: https://doi.org/10.1007/978-3-030-14640-5_5.

Bishop, C.M. (2006) Pattern recognition and machine learning. New York: Springer (Information science and statistics).

Borg, I., Groenen, P.J.F. and Mair, P. (2013) Applied multidimensional scaling. Berlin London: Springer (SpringerBriefs in statistics).

Böttcher, A. et al. (2018) 'Trace your sources in large-scale data: one ring to find them all'. arXiv. Available at: http://arxiv.org/abs/1803.08882 (Accessed: 11 August 2022).

Brigham, E.O. (1988) The fast Fourier transform and its applications. Englewood Cliffs, N.J: Prentice Hall (Prentice-Hall signal processing series).

Brown, T.A. (2006) Confirmatory factor analysis for applied research. New York: Guilford Press (Methodology in the social sciences).

Burges, C.J.C. (1998) 'A Tutorial on Support Vector Machines for Pattern Recognition', SUPPORT VECTOR MACHINES, 2, pp. 121–167.

Burges, C.J.C. (2009) 'Dimension Reduction: A Guided Tour', Foundations and Trends® in Machine Learning, 2(4), pp. 275–364. Available at: https://doi.org/10.1561/2200000002.

Cairns, H. (2016) 'A short proof of Perron's theorem.' Lecture Notes in Probability Theory II Course, Cornell University. Available at: https://pi.math.cornell.edu/~web6720/Perron-Frobenius_Hannah%20Cairns.pdf.

Carter, T.A. (1995) Linear Algebra, An Introduction to Linear Algebra for Pre-Calculus Students. Rice University.

Chahal, J.S. (2018) Fundamentals of Linear Algebra: With Applications in Computer Science, Economics, Engineering, Mathematics, and Physics. Boca Raton: CRC Press, Taylor and Francis Group.

Charles Van Loan et al. (2009) Future Directions in Tensor-Based Computation and Modeling. Arlington, Virginia at the National Science Foundation,. Available at: http://www.cs.cornell.edu/cv/TenWork/Home.htm.

Chen, F. et al. (2020) 'Graph Representation Learning: A Survey', APSIPA Transactions on Signal and Information Processing, 9(1). Available at: https://doi.org/10.1017/ATSIP.2020.13.

Cichocki, A. et al. (2016) 'Low-Rank Tensor Networks for Dimensionality Reduction and Large-Scale Optimization Problems: Perspectives and Challenges PART 1', Foundations and Trends® in Machine Learning, 9(4–5), pp. 249–429. Available at: https://doi.org/10.1561/2200000059.

Cichocki, A. et al. (2017) 'Tensor Networks for Dimensionality Reduction and Large-Scale Optimizations. Part 2 Applications and Future Perspectives', Foundations and Trends® in Machine Learning, 9(6), pp. 249–429. Available at: https://doi.org/10.1561/2200000067.

Corke, P. (2017) Robotics, Vision and Control. Cham: Springer International Publishing (Springer Tracts in Advanced Robotics). Available at: https://doi.org/10.1007/978-3-319-54413-7.

Debals, O. (2017) Tensorization and Applications in Blind Source Separation. Available at: https://lirias.kuleuven.be/retrieve/464228 (Accessed: 27 August 2022).

Deisenroth, M.P., Faisal, A.A. and Ong, C.S. (2019) Mathematics for Machine Learning. Cambridge University Press.

Deng, S. et al. (2021) 'Rotation Transformation Network: Learning View-Invariant Point Cloud for Classification and Segmentation', in 2021 IEEE International Conference on Multimedia and Expo (ICME), pp. 1–6. Available at: https://doi.org/10.1109/ICME51207.2021.9428265.

Dixon, G.M. (2002) Division algebras: octonions, quaternions, complex numbers and the algebraic design of physics. 2. print. Dordrecht: Kluwer Academic (Mathematics and its applications <Dordrecht>, 290).

Downey, A. (2013) Think Bayes. First edition. Sebastopol, CA: O'Reilly.

Dym, H. (2007) Linear algebra in action. Providence, R.I: American Mathematical Society (Graduate studies in mathematics, v. 78).

Eade, E. and Drummond, T. (2013) 'Lie Groups for 2D and 3D Transformations in Computer Graphics and Vision', Foundations and Trends® in Computer Graphics and Vision, 8(2–3), pp. 155–270.

Ekman, M. (2021) Learning deep learning: theory and practice of neural networks, computer vision, nlp, and transformers using tensorflow. First edition. Boston: Addison-Wesley.

Engel, J. et al. (2020) 'DDSP: Differentiable Digital Signal Processing', in. International Conference on Learning Representations, arXiv. Available at: http://arxiv.org/abs/2001.04643 (Accessed: 13 September 2022).

Errica, F., Bacciu, D. and Micheli, A. (2020) 'Theoretically Expressive and Edge-aware Graph Learning'. arXiv. Available at: http://arxiv.org/abs/2001.09005 (Accessed: 25 August 2022).

'Euler's formula' (2023) Wikipedia. Available at: https://en.wikipedia.org/w/index.php?title=Euler%27s_formula&oldid=1133385369 (Accessed: 18 January 2023).

Farrell, P. (2020) The statistics and calculus workshop a comprehensive introduction to mathematics in Python for artificial intelligence applications. Available at: http://www.vlebooks.com/vleweb/product/openreader?id=none&isbn=9781800208360 (Accessed: 25 October 2021).

Fortney, J.P. (2018) A Visual Introduction to Differential Forms and Calculus on Manifolds. Cham: Springer International Publishing. Available at: https://doi.org/10.1007/978-3-319-96992-3.

GAP4 (2022) 'The GAP Group, GAP -- Groups, Algorithms, and Programming'. Available at: https://www.gap-system.org.

Geijn, R. van de (2012) ULAFF: Linear Algebra: Foundations to Frontiers. Available at: http://www.ulaff.net/ (Accessed: 6 March 2021).

Geijn, R.A. van de and Quintana-Ort´, E.S. (2008) The Science of Programming Matrix Computations. www.lulu.com. Available at: http://z.cs.utexas.edu/wiki/LA.wiki/books/TSoPMC/.

Gelß, P. (2017) The Tensor-Train Format and Its Applications. PhD Dissertation. Universität Berlin Institut für Mathematik.

Ghojogh, B. et al. (2020) 'Locally Linear Embedding and its Variants: Tutorial and Survey'. arXiv. Available at: http://arxiv.org/abs/2011.10925 (Accessed: 6 September 2022).

Ghosal, S. and Vaart, A.W. van der (2017) Fundamentals of nonparametric Bayesian inference. Cambridge ; New York: Cambridge University Press (Cambridge series in statistical and probabilistic mathematics, 44).

Gilmore, R. (2005) Lie groups, Lie algebras, and some of their applications. Mineola, N.Y: Dover Publications.

Glazer, A.M. (2021) A journey into reciprocal space: a crystallographer's perspective. Second edition, Version: 20210701. Bristol, UK: IOP Publishing (IOP ebooks). Available at: https://doi.org/10.1088/978-0-7503-3875-2.

Glen., S. (2015) 'Multidimensional Scaling: Definition, Overview, Examples', StatisticsHowTo.com: Elementary Statistics for the rest of us! Available at: https://www.statisticshowto.com/multidimensional-scaling/.

Haarmann, J. et al. (2014) 'Homotopy equivalence of finite digital images'. Available at: https://doi.org/10.1007/s10851-015-0578-8.

Hao, L. et al. (2018) 'TensorD: A tensor decomposition library in TensorFlow', Neurocomputing, 318, pp. 196–200. Available at: https://doi.org/10.1016/j.neucom.2018.08.055.

Harshman, R.A. (1970) 'Foundations of the PARAFAC procedure: Models and conditions for an explanatory multi-modal factor analysis', UCLA Working Papers in Phonetics, 16, pp. 1–84.

Haykin, S.S. (2009) Neural networks and learning machines. 3rd ed. New York: Prentice Hall.

Helal, M. et al. (2008) 'Parallelizing Optimal Multiple Sequence Alignment by Dynamic Programming', in. IEEE, pp. 669–674. Available at: https://doi.org/10.1109/ISPA.2008.93.

Helal, M. et al. (2009) 'Search Space Reduction Technique for Distributed Multiple Sequence Alignment', in. IEEE, pp. 219–226. Available at: https://doi.org/10.1109/NPC.2009.43.

Hou, M. (2017) Tensor-based Regression Models and Applications. PhD Dissertation. Universite Laval.

Huang, F. et al. (2021) 'Tensor decomposition with relational constraints for predicting multiple types of microRNA-disease associations', Briefings in Bioinformatics, 22(3), p. bbaa140. Available at: https://doi.org/10.1093/bib/bbaa140.

Jaderberg, M. et al. (2016) 'Spatial Transformer Networks'. arXiv. Available at: http://arxiv.org/abs/1506.02025 (Accessed: 10 August 2022).

Jeevanjee, N. (2011) An introduction to tensors and group theory for physicists. New York: Birkhäuser.

Jeremiah (2012) 'Understanding Quaternions', 3D Game Engine Programming, 25 June. Available at: https://www.3dgep.com/understanding-quaternions/ (Accessed: 8 August 2022).

Ji, Y. et al. (2019) 'A Survey on Tensor Techniques and Applications in Machine Learning', IEEE Access, 7, pp. 162950–162990. Available at: https://doi.org/10.1109/ACCESS.2019.2949814.

Jolliffe, I.T. (2010) Principal component analysis. 2. ed. New York: Springer (Springer series in statistics).

Kiers, H.A.L. and Mechelen, I.V. (2001) 'Three-way component analysis: Principles and illustrative application.', Psychological Methods, 6(1), pp. 84–110. Available at: https://doi.org/10.1037/1082-989X.6.1.84.

Kisil, I. et al. (2021) 'HOTTBOX: Higher Order Tensor ToolBOX'. arXiv. Available at: http://arxiv.org/abs/2111.15662 (Accessed: 25 August 2022).

Kolda, T.G. and Bader, B.W. (2009) 'Tensor Decompositions and Applications', SIAM Review, 51(3), pp. 455–500. Available at: https://doi.org/10.1137/07070111X.

Kossaifi, J. et al. (2019) 'TensorLy: Tensor Learning in Python', Journal of Machine Learning Research, 20(26), pp. 1–6.

Kruskal, J.B. (1964) 'Nonmetric multidimensional scaling : a numerical method.', 29(b), pp. 115–130.

Larhmam (2018) Maximum-margin hyperplane and margin for an SVM trained on two classes. Samples on margins are called support vectors. Available at: https://commons.wikimedia.org/wiki/File:SVM_margin.png#metadata (Accessed: 2 November 2021).

Leskovec, J., Rajaraman, A. and Ullman, J.D. (2014) Mining of Massive Datasets. Second edition. Cambridge: Cambridge University Press.

Li, J., Zhang, X.-P. and Tran, T. (2019) 'Point Cloud Denoising Based on Tensor Tucker Decomposition', in 2019 IEEE International Conference on Image Processing (ICIP). 2019 IEEE International Conference on Image Processing (ICIP), Taipei, Taiwan: IEEE, pp. 4375–4379. Available at: https://doi.org/10.1109/ICIP.2019.8803602.

Li, M. et al. (2021) 'The Deep Learning Compiler: A Comprehensive Survey', IEEE Transactions on Parallel and Distributed Systems, 32(3), pp. 708–727. Available at: https://doi.org/10.1109/TPDS.2020.3030548.

Li, X., Zhou, H. and Li, L. (2013) 'Tucker Tensor Regression and Neuroimaging Analysis'. arXiv. Available at: https://doi.org/10.48550/arXiv.1304.5637.

Liu, X.-Y. and Wang, X. (2017) 'Fourth-order Tensors with Multidimensional Discrete Transforms'. arXiv. Available at: http://arxiv.org/abs/1705.01576 (Accessed: 13 September 2022).

Liu, X.-Y., Zhao, Q. and Walid, A. (2021) 'Tensor and Tensor Networks for Machine Learning: An Hourglass Architecture', in. International Workshop on Tensor Network Representations in Machine Learning, Japan, p. 7.

Lu, H., Plataniotis, K.N. and Venetsanopoulos, A.N. (2011) 'A survey of multilinear subspace learning for tensor data', Pattern Recognition, 44(7), pp. 1540–1551. Available at: https://doi.org/10.1016/j.patcog.2011.01.004.

Lu, H., Plataniotis, K.N. and Venetsanopoulos, A.N. (2014) Multilinear subspace learning: dimensionality reduction of multidimensional data. Boca Raton, Florida: CRC Press/Taylor & Francis Group (Chapman & Hall/CRC machine learning & pattern recognition series).

Mahadevan, S. (2008) Representation discovery using harmonic analysis. 1. ed. San Rafael, Calif.: Morgan & Claypool (Synthesis lectures on artificial intelligence and machine learning, 4).

Mangan, T.C. (2008) 'A Gentle Introduction to Tensors', p. 12.

Margalit, D. and Rabinoff, J. (2019) Interactive Linear Algebra. Georgia Institute of Technology. Available at: https://textbooks.math.gatech.edu/ila/index.html (Accessed: 10 November 2022).

Marmin, A., Castella, M. and Pesquet, J.-C. (2020) 'Globally optimizing owing to tensor decomposition', in EUSIPCO 2020 - 28th European Signal Processing Conference. Amsterdam, Netherlands, pp. 990–994. Available at: https://doi.org/10.23919/Eusipco47968.2020.9287511.

Merrill, M.A. and Althoff, T. (2021) 'Transformer-Based Behavioral Representation Learning Enables Transfer Learning for Mobile Sensing in Small Datasets'. arXiv. Available at: http://arxiv.org/abs/2107.06097 (Accessed: 10 August 2022).

Milne, J.S. (2021) Group Theory. Available at www.jmilne.org/math/. Available at: https://www.jmilne.org/math/CourseNotes/GT.pdf.

Miwakeichi, F. et al. (2004) 'Decomposing EEG data into space–time–frequency components using Parallel Factor Analysis', NeuroImage, 22(3), pp. 1035–1045. Available at: https://doi.org/10.1016/j.neuroimage.2004.03.039.

Novikov, A. et al. (2015) 'Tensorizing Neural Networks', arXiv:1509.06569 [cs], 28. Available at: http://arxiv.org/abs/1509.06569 (Accessed: 24 February 2021).

Novikov, A. et al. (2020) 'Tensor Train Decomposition on TensorFlow (T3F)', Journal of Machine Learning Research, 21(30), pp. 1–7.

Olguín Díaz, E. (2018) 3D Motion of Rigid Bodies. New York, NY: Springer Berlin Heidelberg (Studies in Systems, Decision and Control, (SSDC), 13304).

Oseledets, I.V. (2011) 'Tensor-Train Decomposition', SIAM Journal on Scientific Computing, 33(5), pp. 2295–2317. Available at: https://doi.org/10.1137/090752286.

Pan, Y., Wang, M. and Xu, Z. (2022) 'TedNet: A Pytorch Toolkit for Tensor Decomposition Networks', Neurocomputing, 469, pp. 234–238. Available at: https://doi.org/10.1016/j.neucom.2021.10.064.

Paszke, A. et al. (2017) 'Automatic differentiation in PyTorch', in. 31st Conference on Neural Information Processing Systems, CA, USA, p. 4.

Pfeifer, R.N.C. et al. (2015) 'NCON: A tensor network contractor for MATLAB'. arXiv. Available at: http://arxiv.org/abs/1402.0939 (Accessed: 10 September 2022).

Qu, T. and Cai, Z. (2017) 'An improved Isomap method for manifold learning', International Journal of Intelligent Computing and Cybernetics, 10(1), pp. 30–40. Available at: https://doi.org/10.1108/IJICC-03-2016-0014.

Risi Kondor (2008) Group theoretical methods in machine learning. Ph.D. thesis. COLUMBIA UNIVERSITY.

Sharifshazileh, M. et al. (2021) 'An electronic neuromorphic system for real-time detection of high frequency oscillations (HFO) in intracranial EEG', Nature Communications, 12(1), p. 3095. Available at: https://doi.org/10.1038/s41467-021-23342-2.

Shen, W. et al. (2020) '3D-Rotation-Equivariant Quaternion Neural Networks'. arXiv. Available at: http://arxiv.org/abs/1911.09040 (Accessed: 10 August 2022).

Singh, S.P. and Alistarh, D. (2020) 'WoodFisher: Efficient Second-Order Approximation for Neural Network Compression'. arXiv. Available at: http://arxiv.org/abs/2004.14340 (Accessed: 19 September 2022).

Sivia, D.S. and Skilling, J. (2006) Data analysis: a Bayesian tutorial. 2nd ed. Oxford ; New York: Oxford University Press (Oxford science publications).

Smilde, A., Bro, R. and Geladi, P. (2004) Multi-Way Analysis with Applications in the Chemical Sciences. Chichester, UK: John Wiley & Sons, Ltd. Available at: https://doi.org/10.1002/0470012110.

'Spin representation' (2022) Wikipedia. Available at: https://en.wikipedia.org/w/index.php?title=Spin_representation&oldid=1099865063 (Accessed: 17 January 2023).

Stanković, R.S., Moraga, C. and Astola, J. (2005) Fourier analysis on finite groups with applications in signal processing and system design. Piscataway, NJ : Hoboken, N.J: IEEE Press ; Wiley-Interscience.

Stegeman, A. (2007) 'Comparing Independent Component Analysis and the Parafac model for artificial multi-subject fMRI data', p. 38.

Stillwell, J. (2008) Naive lie theory. New York ; London: Springer (Undergraduate texts in mathematics).

Sun, L.-H., Huang, Xin-Wei, Alqawba, Mohammed S. and Kim, J.-M., Emura, Takeshi (2020) Copula-Based Markov Models for Time Series: Parametric Inference and Process Control. Singapore: Springer Singapore : Imprint: Springer.

Suykens, J.A.K. et al. (eds) (2014) Regularization, optimization, kernels, and support vector machines. ROKS, Boca Raton London New York: CRC Press, a Chapman & Hall book (Chapman & Hall/CRC machine learning & pattern recognition series).

Tamilmathi, A.C. and Chithra, P.L. (2022) 'Tensor block-wise singular value decomposition for 3D point cloud compression', Multimedia Tools and Applications [Preprint]. Available at: https://doi.org/10.1007/s11042-021-11738-7.

The Tensor Network (no date) Tensor Network. Available at: https://www.tensornetwork.org (Accessed: 10 September 2022).

Vasilescu, M.A.O. and Terzopoulos, D. (2002) 'Multilinear Analysis of Image Ensembles: TensorFaces', in A. Heyden et al. (eds) Computer Vision — ECCV 2002. Berlin, Heidelberg: Springer Berlin Heidelberg (Lecture Notes in Computer Science), pp. 447–460. Available at: https://doi.org/10.1007/3-540-47969-4_30.

Vince, J. (2021) Quaternions for computer graphics. Second edition. London: Springer.

VON HILGERS, P. and LANGVILLE†, A.N. (no date) 'THE FIVE GREATEST APPLICATIONS OF MARKOV CHAINS'. Available at: http://langvillea.people.cofc.edu/MCapps7.pdf.

Watts, S. (2016) 'The Gaussian Copula and the Financial Crisis: A Recipe for Disaster or Cooking the Books?', p. 25.

Williams, A.H. et al. (2018) 'Unsupervised Discovery of Demixed, Low-Dimensional Neural Dynamics across Multiple Timescales through Tensor Component Analysis', Neuron, 98(6), pp. 1099-1115.e8. Available at: https://doi.org/10.1016/j.neuron.2018.05.015.

Yan, H., Paynabar, K. and Pacella, M. (2019) 'Structured Point Cloud Data Analysis Via Regularized Tensor Regression for Process Modeling and Optimization', Technometrics, 61(3), pp. 385–395. Available at: https://doi.org/10.1080/00401706.2018.1529628.

Yang, Y. and Hospedales, T. (2017) 'Deep Multi-task Representation Learning: A Tensor Factorisation Approach', in. International Conference on Learning Representations (ICLR), arXiv. Available at: http://arxiv.org/abs/1605.06391 (Accessed: 25 July 2022).

Zaccone, G. (2015) Python parallel programming cookbook: master efficient parallel programming to build powerful applications using Python. 1. publ. Birmingham Mumbai: Packt Publ (Quick answers to common problems).

Zhang, D. et al. (2018) 'Network Representation Learning: A Survey'. arXiv. Available at: http://arxiv.org/abs/1801.05852 (Accessed: 9 August 2022).

Zhang, J., Li, S.Z. and Wang, J. (2005) 'Manifold Learning and Applications in Recognition', in Y.-P. Tan, K.H. Yap, and L. Wang (eds) Intelligent Multimedia Processing with Soft Computing. Springer Berlin Heidelberg (Studies in Fuzziness and Soft Computing), pp. 281–300. Available at: https://doi.org/10.1007/3-540-32367-8_13.

Zhang, L. et al. (2022) 'Visual Representation Learning with Transformer: A Sequence-to-Sequence Perspective'. arXiv. Available at: http://arxiv.org/abs/2207.09339 (Accessed: 10 August 2022).

Zhao, Q. et al. (2016) 'Tensor Ring Decomposition'. arXiv. Available at: http://arxiv.org/abs/1606.05535 (Accessed: 23 June 2022).

www.ingramcontent.com/pod-product-compliance
Ingram Content Group UK Ltd.
Pitfield, Milton Keynes, MK11 3LW, UK
UKHW050145280726
14058UKWH00006B/837

9 781916 626331